# THE RESISTANCE

Also by Matthew Cobb

THE EGG AND SPERM RACE

# THE RESISTANCE

## The French fight against the Nazis

### MATTHEW COBB

SIMON &
SCHUSTER

London · New York · Sydney · Toronto

A CBS COMPANY

First published in Great Britain in 2009 by Simon & Schuster UK Ltd
A CBS COMPANY

3 5 7 9 10 8 6 4 2

Simon & Schuster UK Ltd
1st Floor
222 Gray's Inn Road
London
WC1X 8HB


www.simonandschuster.co.uk


Simon & Schuster Australia
Sydney

The publisher would like to thank the following for permission to
reproduce material: *Notre Guerre* © by Agnes Humbert, 1946, English
translation, *Résistance*, © by Barbara Mellor, 2008 published by
Bloomsbury Publishing PLC

A CIP catalogue for this book is available
from the British Library.

ISBN: 978-1-84737-123-2

PICTURE CREDITS

Rue des Archives: 1, 2, 3, 6, 7, 8, 9, 10, 11, 12, 13, 14, 15, 16, 17, 18, 19,
20, 21, 22, 26, 29, 30, 31, 32
Author's collection: 4, 23
Musée de l'Ordre de la Libération, Paris: 5
Collection Marc Chantran: 24
Roger Viollet: 25, 27, 28

Typeset in Baskerville by M Rules
Printed in the UK by CPI Mackays, Chatham ME5 8TD

For Remi Malfroy, Dave Hughes, Jonas Nesic,
Bruce Groves and Bill Ford.
I wish you were all here to argue with me about this.

Nothing is ever completely wasted. The apparently futile events of history ... such as the Paris Commune, or the Spanish Civil War, or the French Resistance, are not failed experiments. The good seeds will grow – later, no doubt, much later – but first they must be sown.

Jean Cassou

A word to young historians – when we read your studies about our underground world, they appear a bit cold. Without wishing to be pretentious, you should not be afraid of dipping your pens in blood: behind each set of initials you describe with such academic precision, there are comrades who died.

Pascal Copeau

# Contents

The division of France after June 1940. The northern regions of the Occupied Zone were under the direct military control of the Nazis. From 1941 the Atlantic coastal regions became a 'forbidden zone', which non-residents could visit only with a special pass. From November 1942 to autumn 1943 the Italians occupied the south-eastern corner of France

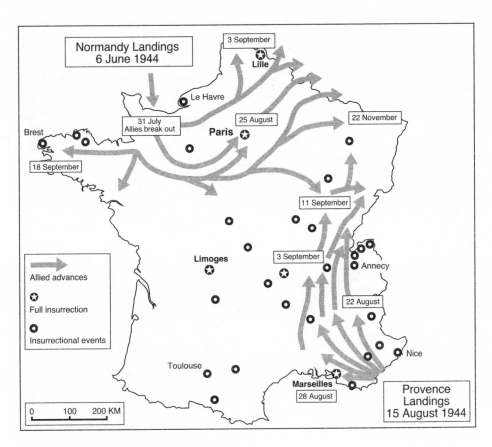

The liberation of France June–November 1944, showing towns that were liberated by insurrections (data from Buton, 1993).

# Introduction

The next time you visit Paris, imagine the public buildings draped with swastika flags, the streets crowded with the grey-green uniforms of the German army, the humiliation of Jews wearing yellow stars on their clothes, threatened with deportation and death. That was the reality of the Occupation of France during the Second World War.

Then look at the walls. Look at the bullet-holes spattered over the Préfecture de Police opposite Notre-Dame cathedral, or on the École des Mines on the Boulevard Saint-Michel. Look at the plaques on anonymous buildings, commemorating the forgotten men and women who died during the Occupation. Look at the names of the Métro stations – 'Guy Moquet', 'Jacques Bonsergent', 'Corentin Cariou' or 'Charles Michel' – which pay homage to victims of Nazi repression. These are all traces of the Resistance, of the price paid to drive the Nazis out of France.

Similar signs can be seen throughout the country. Many towns have their own Resistance museum, telling the story of how the region was liberated, of the people who fought and died to free their country. There are memorials at the side of country roads, marking the location of secret landing strips for tiny aircraft flying in from Britain. There are families who still tell stories of how parents and grandparents made their contribution to the Resistance, and who still mourn loved ones crushed by the fascist juggernaut. This book is full of the personal stories of some of those hundreds of thousands of men and women who risked everything to fight the Nazis.

In the 1960s, when I grew up, the Resistance was everywhere – from schoolboy comics to television series, from true-life accounts to films. It saturated British culture, a constant reference in a world that was still dominated by the war, which had finished only twenty years earlier. Not only did we accept without question the heroism and self-sacrifice of the men and women of the Resistance and of those Britons who helped them, we were awed by their bravery, even slightly jealous of the fact that these people knew how they would behave under terrible pressure.

Times have changed. In France and elsewhere, the heroic view of the Resistance has faded. Few people know exactly what the Resistance did, beyond a general sense that they blew up trains and shot Nazis, although in reality these were relatively rare events. Even in France, where the Resistance remains an ever-present theme in popular culture, most ordinary people no longer know the detail of this story. The number of surviving *résistants* has inevitably dwindled (virtually none of those mentioned in this book are still alive), while the two main political forces that claimed the heritage of the Resistance – Gaullism and Communism – have been transformed utterly, largely losing their connection with this decisive period in French history. The names of most of the Resistance leaders have long since slipped from public awareness. There are no more French postage stamps showing the portraits of Resistance heroes.

These changes are not only due to the passage of time, but also to a general shift in attitudes. We are less deferential than in the past, age and experience command less respect, while tales of bravery and self-sacrifice are more likely to provoke a cynical smile than awed regard. Popular views of the war years in France have also been affected by the widespread suspicion that the true reality of the Occupation was not the heroic acts of the Resistance, but rather the behaviour of a population that apparently accepted the orders of the new fascist masters.

There are some good reasons for this feeling. Following the crushing defeat at the hands of the Nazis in June 1940, the French military, supported by the political and business leaders, sought to work with the Nazis. A new government was set up with the task of negotiating an Armistice that would accept the Occupation. Based in the small spa town of Vichy, the new government initially enjoyed widespread support, and many people believed that its leader, Marshal Pétain, was secretly preparing to turn the tables on the Nazis. Nothing could be further from the truth. It was Pétain himself who coined the term that came to symbolize the politics of Vichy: collaboration. Although Vichy technically ruled over the whole country, the Germans occupied the north – and, after November 1942, the whole country. In the regions where the Nazis had troops, they had control. From the outset, Vichy's independence was severely limited, and after the Nazi invasion of the south nearly two-and-a-half years later it was non-existent. Pétain and his Vichy colleagues endorsed every important Nazi decision relating to France, from the systematic exploitation and pillaging of the country, through the arbitrary conscription of hundreds of thousands of young men to work in Germany, to the deportation of tens of thousands of Jews, the vast majority of whom would never return.

After an initial 'honeymoon' period, important sections of the French population began to realize that although Pétain had provided peace, in the sense that no pitched battles were being fought on French soil, a terrible price had been paid. This price had many facets: plummeting living standards (malnutrition began to spread, infantile mortality soared, mass unemployment and low wages became rife); the loss of the most elementary democratic rights (letters and phone calls were systematically intercepted and their contents transmitted to the paranoid state apparatus); the misery and distress produced by the division of the country and the brutal Nazi-inspired laws. But above all, the price paid by Vichy was moral and political. Vichy was a willing accomplice in the Holocaust, enthusiastically applying laws that slowly transformed the country into an anti-Semitic police state, viciously persecuting all those who opposed it.

Nevertheless, for most of the war, the vast majority of the French did little or nothing to oppose Vichy and the Occupation. They may have hated the division and exploitation of their country, they may have been shocked and appalled by the deportation of the Jews, they may have looked with approval on the acts of the Resistance, but in general all this had little practical consequence. Less than two per cent of the population – at most 500,000 people – were involved in the Resistance in one way or another. Up to 100,000 *résistants* are thought to have died during the war – executed, killed in combat or dying in the camps – an indication of the dangers that were faced by this determined minority.

Many historians now rightly argue that resistance took a wide variety of forms. As well as direct action against the Nazis and their Vichy allies, people wore red, white and blue (the colours of the French flag), listened to the BBC (which was illegal), or offered aid and succour to the persecuted Jewish population. However, at the time 'resistance' was used above all to describe organized actions against the Nazis and Vichy. And until the final days of the Occupation, most of the French population watched and waited. Only a tiny minority felt they had to oppose the Occupation and, as many of them put it, 'do something'. Even before the Armistice had been signed, the first signs of resistance were seen. A few individuals made heroic but ultimately futile gestures of physical opposition to the Nazis, often risking imprisonment or even death. Others chose a more literary approach – in Brive, south of Limoges, Edmond Michelet produced a leaflet consisting merely of six quotations from the French writer and philosopher Charles Péguy, calling for the fighting to continue. It did not have the desired effect. After the Occupation began, and Pétain's regime started its sinister rule in the south, a series of small Resistance organizations sprang up, producing amateurish publications. In most cases they were smashed by the Nazis in a matter of months. Not one of the scores of Resistance organizations was created by the man who came to represent them – General Charles de Gaulle. Indeed, de Gaulle appeared to have little time for the Resistance, which in turn was profoundly suspicious of the French general, while recognizing his importance as a symbol of opposition to Vichy and the Nazis.

The reason for this clash between the Resistance and what became known as the 'Free French' around de Gaulle was that the two groups had fundamentally different objectives. A tiny fraction of the French army leadership – basically, de Gaulle and a handful of others – together with a rag-bag of adventurers and right-wing patriots, had travelled to Britain to continue the struggle. Their intention was to create an exile army that would participate in the Allied war effort to drive out the Nazis, thereby preserving the honour of France, and setting up an alternative government and state apparatus that could take over from the discredited Vichy regime and regain control of the French Empire.

The outlook of the Resistance was rather different. It also wanted to drive the Nazis out of France, but it was never a disciplined and coherent single organization. Composed of disparate groups, it encompassed a wide range of political views, from the far right to the far left.

Eventually, even some of its more right-wing leaders changed their opinions, and began to see the Resistance as a revolutionary army that could transform French society in a socialist direction. This inevitably led to more conflicts with de Gaulle, who sought to control all armed action in France, and appeared dismissive of the strength and sacrifice of the Resistance.

Created in France, the Resistance grew in stature partly as a result of its links with the Free French and also with the British secret services, in particular the Special Operations Executive (SOE). Military supplies and money were parachuted into France, providing a vital lifeline for the Resistance. Nevertheless, throughout the war the Allies remained ambivalent about both the Resistance and the Free French. London and Washington were uncertain about the true influence of the Resistance, although they accepted that it could be useful in providing intelligence and military support after D-Day. These suspicions and doubts were even greater with regard to the Free French. President Roosevelt loathed de Gaulle; he rightly felt that the French leader's prickly independence would threaten Allied plans to occupy France and dismember her Empire after the war was over. Although Churchill was more sympathetic to de Gaulle, he followed the US President's lead. As a result of these tensions, the story of the Resistance – a tale of heroism and sacrifice against terrible odds – was played out against a backdrop of conflict and mutual suspicion. Underlying all these disputes was the fundamental question of what kind of France would emerge from the Occupation.

This book deals primarily with the Resistance, but de Gaulle looms large, simply because within a few weeks of the fall of France, he was transformed from an unknown, low-ranking General, into the most notable representative of all those who opposed the Occupation. That transformation came about through the power of radio. De Gaulle's regular BBC broadcasts from London – which were occasionally suspended during some of his bitterest spats with the Allies – provided ordinary French people with a sign that all was not lost, and gave the bolder among them the confidence to stand against the Nazi tide. The scattered forces of the Resistance eventually rallied to de Gaulle precisely because of his renown within France, and because of his links with the British. This in turn reinforced his power and influence.

The frictions between the Allies, the Free French and the Resistance became stronger in the run-up to D-Day. London and Washington considered that liberation was the task of the Allied troops, who would then occupy France under the authority of an Allied Military Government that would run the country for as long as necessary. Important sections of the Resistance, on the other hand, wanted a mass uprising of the French population to help drive out the Nazis and produce major changes in French society – a revolution. De Gaulle, meanwhile, sought to use the action of both the Allies and the Resistance to consolidate his own influence and to realize his vision of a re-born France under his command. It is one of history's sharper ironies that in this triangular tension it was de Gaulle who eventually triumphed, even though he owed virtually everything to the two rival forces. But this was not an inevitable outcome – history could have written a different ending. This book also explores what might have happened, and the path the Resistance could have forged for France.

The use of strongly patriotic language makes many of the declarations of the Resistance and of the Free French seem hopelessly anachronistic. Chauvinist appeals to 'the glory of eternal France' are unlikely to strike many chords today. This is partly due to the political and sociological changes that have occurred over the last sixty-five years, which have weakened the power of patriotism, in particular among young Europeans. It is also because, to put it simply, there is no war. At the time the war and the Occupation changed everything. In wars, ordinary people are allowed to kill other people – indeed, they are expected to do so. As de Gaulle put it with characteristic bluntness in a broadcast in 1942:

> It is completely normal and completely justified that Germans should be killed by Frenchmen and women. If the Germans did not wish to be killed by our hands, they should have stayed at home and not waged war on us. Sooner or later, they are all destined to be killed, either by us or by our allies.

The starting point of the Resistance, and of de Gaulle, was that all French people, irrespective of their class or status, had a common national interest in driving the Nazis out of the country. In the 1914–18 war, both sides used appeals to the 'national interest' to justify a horrendous slaughter which was the result of conflicting commercial and political interests, none of which had any real significance for the vast majority of those caught up in the war. The situation after June 1940 was different. France had been invaded, carved up and exploited; a country that had its own globe-spanning Empire was in its turn being transformed into a colony. Those now in charge were Nazis who destroyed all democratic rights (with the help of the Vichy government), and proceeded to first repress and then exterminate those they considered to be sub-humans – Jews, Communists, homosexuals, gypsies and others – and all those who opposed the Occupation. Everyone in France who was not a supporter of the Vichy regime did indeed have a common interest in driving out the Nazis. Their very survival was at stake. For hundreds of thousands of ordinary people, standing by was not an option. They had to do something. They had to resist. This book is theirs.

So why did I have to write it? Telling the powerful personal stories of the *résistants*, describing their successes and failures, focusing on their courage and sacrifice, feels like a duty. By keeping their stories alive, the *résistants* themselves can be brought back to life in our memories. I have wanted to write this book since the mid-1980s, when I was living in Paris. One evening, I was watching TV and bumped into a documentary about the Occupation. It was like getting an electric shock: there was my adopted home city, draped in Nazi swastikas. Instantly, my vague knowledge of what happened during the war turned into something much more visceral: I felt a glimmer of the outrage, the fury and the desire to fight back that motivated so many during the war years. After the documentary was over, there was a debate between various historians and old *résistants*. At one point, Jacques Chaban-Delmas, a *résistant* who had subsequently been a right-wing Prime Minister from 1969–1972, and was not at all on my political wave length – turned to the camera and said: 'I want to say to all the young people watching, who do not know what it was like to be in the Resistance: it was one of the greatest times to be alive.'

That phrase, and my shock at the image of Occupied Paris, have remained with me over the years. In the pages that follow I have tried to transmit the emotions that were experienced by the members of the Resistance – the moments of joy and the times of terrible depression; the euphoria of victory, the bitterness of betrayal and the sorrow of sacrifice. There are moments that inspire, others that make you think long and hard, and there are points at which I had to stop to wipe away the tears. That is why this book had to be written, and why it has to be read.

*Manchester, January 2009*

# 1

# *France Falls*

June 1940. In six short weeks, the French army – widely considered to be the most professional and powerful force in the world – had been swept aside by a lightning German offensive. France was crushed under Hitler's iron heel. Its territory was occupied, its population was humiliated, its mood was cynical and introspective. Dramatically, and against all expectations, France had fallen.[1]

The war had begun in September 1939, with the Nazi invasion of Poland. Without great enthusiasm, Britain and France declared war on Germany. But so little happened over the first seven months that it was called the 'phoney war'. For young René Balbaud, a French-Canadian soldier with a wife and baby daughter, the beginning of the war was almost like a holiday. Shortly after the call-up, he was skinny-dipping with ninety comrades in the river Moselle, splashing and joking. Once they had dried off, they collected ripe yellow plums from the nearby orchards.[2] As the autumn wore on, Balbaud spent his time decorating a local village hall for a marriage, rustling geese for the regimental pot and complaining to his diary that only two shells had been aimed at him in the space of three weeks.[3] Although the winter was particularly hard and morale suffered accordingly, by the time spring came things were starting to look up again, and Balbaud was able to make the most of his leave in Paris, flirting with a young woman at the Gare de l'Est. Within a few weeks, however, Balbaud's world, and that of the whole French population, changed in ways that no one expected.[4]

Throughout the 1930s the French had been preparing for the war. At a cost of 7 billion francs, they had built the Maginot Line – a vast array of armed fortresses, linked by an underground railway, and housing tens of thousands of soldiers – along the north-eastern border with Germany. The Maginot Line discouraged any offensive and defended the vital Lorraine coalfields and steel-producing regions. The French were certain that, as in 1914, the Germans would attack through Belgium, so they positioned their crack regiments on the northern border, ready to meet the worst that the Nazis could throw at them.

On 10 May Hitler finally launched his long-expected attack on Belgium and Holland. Nazi tank battalions surged westwards, backed by wave after wave of bomber support. Despite the vigour and the ferocity of the offensive, the French generals were confident; the Germans were doing exactly what had been predicted. But the German attack had another aspect, which the French command initially paid little attention to. In the hilly and heavily wooded Ardennes region, at the point where the Maginot Line ended, the Germans launched a massive tank attack, sending 134,000 men and 1,222 tanks weaving along the winding country roads, then crashing through the undefended countryside. In 1938 the French had carried out an exercise based on this possibility; they had calculated that it would take the Germans sixty hours to get through the mountains, and the invaders would then have to deal with the problem of crossing the river Meuse. This, thought the French, would provide enough time for them to reinforce the troops defending the crossing points around Sedan.

The French strategists were not entirely wrong. It did indeed take the Germans sixty hours to get to the Meuse. But the French high command completely underestimated the size and density of the armoured attack through the Ardennes, and the impact of German air support. After the Allies had got wind of the Germans' original battle plans at the beginning of the year, the Nazis had completely changed their strategy. Hitler had been swayed by the vision of General Heinz Guderian, a fifty-two-year-old Prussian who in the 1930s had argued for the large-scale use of tanks backed up by air power. Under Guderian's plan, the attack on the Netherlands and northern Belgium was merely a feint, designed to draw the French away from the central Nazi thrust, which would take place where the French least expected it – through the Ardennes and across the Meuse.

In terms of men and equipment, the two sides seemed evenly matched. They had around the same number of men on the Western Front (144 Allied divisions, as against 141 German divisions), and each was armed with about 2,900 tanks. But the forces were deployed in completely different ways. The Germans grouped their tanks into 10 divisions of around 270 each, while most French tanks were scattered along the line – only 960 were grouped in armoured divisions, each of around 160 tanks. This meant that when the Germans attacked, they had far more machines on the battlefield than the French. Furthermore, the German tanks were linked by two-way radios, giving them a flexibility that far outstripped the French vehicles, many of which lacked any kind of communications.

It was in the air, however, that the Germans had a decisive advantage. Although France had as many serviceable planes as the Germans when the invasion began, these were scattered all over the empire, many of them far from the front line. As for the British, their bases were far away; to be fully operational, planes had to refuel at French or Belgian aerodromes. When it came to putting planes into the sky over north-eastern France and Belgium, the Nazis had the upper hand, with around twice as many aircraft.[5] This air superiority was used by the Germans to back their armoured offensive, with the aim of weakening and demoralizing enemy ground forces even when the number of casualties inflicted from the air was relatively small. It was devastatingly effective. On 16 May René Balbaud found himself on the Belgian border, the terrified victim of an attack by Stuka dive-bombers. These two-seater, single-engine planes had first been used to support Franco's fascists in the Spanish Civil War. With their strikingly arched wings, they looked particularly predatory, adding to their psychological impact. During an attack, the Stukas came hurtling out of the sky, the sirens under their wings screaming, terrifying people on the ground, then released their deadly payload of bombs.

At noon on the 16th, Balbaud heard the deep roar of aeroplane engines and dived for cover. He wrote in his diary:

> One hundred and fifty planes! It's staggering. The noise of the motors is already overwhelming . . . and then there is this terrible whistling

that sets your nerves jangling . . . And then suddenly it's raining
bombs. Trees fall and burn, the earth bucks, stones fly, smoke and
dust form a blinding cloud, while there is a choking stench of gun-
powder . . . And it goes on and on! . . . Not a single French plane, not
a single British plane, not a single round of anti-aircraft fire . . . Finally,
they leave. We look at each other. Our uniforms are red with the red
soil, damp. Few of us are injured, but our faces are drawn, exhaustion
rings our eyes. Our morale is shattered.[6]

The troops that were subjected to this relentless, terrifying attack at
Sedan – it involved a thousand planes and lasted around eight hours –
were some of the weakest and most poorly equipped of the whole
French army. Composed almost entirely of reservists, they had been
called up in September and were not young – the average age was thirty-
one. Above all, they were not equipped with anti-aircraft or anti-tank
weapons, nor had they been given any decent training during the
phoney war. Despite valiant actions by the doomed French reservists,
the Germans were able to cross the Meuse with relative ease; Rommel,
commanding troops to the north, was also able to penetrate deep into
French territory, even without the scale of air support that had been
used near Sedan.

As soon as the Germans broke through, the French collapse began.
Rumours of German tanks being sighted miles behind French lines
spread panic among the untrained and poorly armed men. This panic
was fuelled by a series of major tactical mistakes by the leadership on the
ground, coupled with a catastrophic lack of communication, so that
neither the head nor the body of the army knew what was happening.
For example, faced with the collapse of his 71st Infantry Division and a
corresponding German advance, General Poncelet moved his command post away from the purpose-built, heavily defended bunker near
Sedan with its dedicated telephone line. Taking his staff officers with
him, he retreated to a house in the forest, which had no communication
system at all.[7] As a result, Poncelet had no idea what was happening at
the front – or even where the front was. And when the men at the front
tried to obtain orders by telephone, they got no reply. The phone rang
unanswered in Poncelet's deserted bunker. This further undermined

morale: if the leaders had apparently deserted the fight, why should the rank and file stay?

Elsewhere, resistance was more substantial. On the morning of 12 May a massive tank battle began near Hannut in central Belgium. Far from being a walkover for the Nazis, the battle showed that French armour could effectively take on the Germans. On that beautiful May morning, the 35th Panzer Regiment suddenly encountered the French along the banks of the river Petite Gette. Tank commander Ernst von Jungenfeld wrote: '. . . enemy tanks popped up at every corner . . . the situation grew hot, and on occasion the enemy grew so strong that he took the offensive.' Von Jungenfeld summed up the first day's fighting as 'hard and bloody, many a brave *Panzermann* had to lay down his life for the Fatherland, many were wounded, and a large number of tanks was lost'.[8]

Modern tank warfare was also accompanied by bloody episodes of close combat. As the Germans renewed their westward drive, French Lieutenant Le Bel's tiny Hotchkiss tank, riddled with bullets and anti-tank rounds, was retreating. As it drove past a Panzer tank, apparently abandoned by the side of the road, a German soldier leaped up onto the front of the Hotchkiss, waving a hammer and took a swipe at the driver. Unable to hold on, the German fell to the ground and disappeared. Le Bel ordered the tank to stop, then clambered down. To his horror, the left track was covered with bloody human remains and tattered bits of uniform. The Hotchkiss had simply crushed the desperate and foolhardy German to a pulp.[9]

The war in the air was far more dispersed, with death delivered at a distance in vast volumes of space. As reconnaissance pilot Antoine de Saint-Exupéry put it: 'The density of aerial warfare? Specks of dust in a cathedral.'[10] Nonetheless, in the cathedral of air that hung over northern France, men died every day. Saint-Exupéry's unit contained twenty-three of the French air force's fifty reconnaissance crews. 'In three weeks,' he wrote, 'seventeen of the twenty-three had vanished. Our group had melted like a lump of wax.'[11] On 10 May, when the Germans launched their offensive, the RAF had 135 bombers in France. Two days later, only seventy-two were still in service. On 14 May, when the French launched a counter-attack against the invaders, the RAF sent out seventy-one bombers to destroy bridges and disrupt the German supply lines. Only forty-one returned – one of the highest operational loss rates ever experienced by the RAF.

In less than a week the German bridgehead in France had become ninety-five kilometres wide, representing a huge problem for the Allied armies. Nevertheless, the French strategists were not downhearted. They were convinced that the Nazis would now turn sharply south and east and attack the Maginot Line with its thousands of well-armed men. At the same time, crack French forces could be brought down from Belgium to catch the Germans from the rear. But that was not what the Nazis had in mind. Guderian's bold plan was simply to ignore the Maginot Line, leaving its troops stuck inside their eastern bunkers, far away from the fighting. Instead he would cut France in two by continuing westwards and racing his tanks to the Channel. This would isolate the Allied forces in Belgium from their supply lines, surrounding them from the south with the Panzer forces that had come storming through the Ardennes and from the north with the divisions that had crashed through the Netherlands.

By the time the French general staff realized what was happening, it was too late. Indeed, Guderian's progress towards the sea was so rapid that the Germans became suspicious, and on 17 May Guderian was ordered to stop his advance. Furious, he threatened to resign unless he was allowed to continue, and his commanders relented the following day. Two days later the Germans reached the Channel at the mouth of the Somme. The French armies and troops of the British Expeditionary Force (BEF) were trapped. Arthur Koestler, watching in horror from Paris, described the German advance as 'a narrow wedge of steel which pierced right through the body of France until it came out the other side, twisting round in the wound, enlarging the hole, crushing the country's flesh'.[12]

By 25 May the British realized that there was no possibility of breaking through the encircling German forces; nor did the French have the strength to weaken the Nazi stranglehold by counter-attacking from the south. With London's agreement, General Gort, the commander of the 200,000-strong BEF, headed for Dunkirk, the last major Channel port not under German control. Ironically, he was able to do this only because, on 24 May, Hitler once again hesitated and halted the German advance. This three-day pause imposed by Berlin allowed the British to save an important part of their armed forces.[13]

French troops were not immediately given the order to evacuate – this finally came through on 29 May. At this point, although 120,000 troops had been transported to Britain, only 6,000 of them were French. This apparent discrimination reinforced traditional anti-British sentiment among the French, even though it was a consequence of the decision by the French military leadership to keep their men on French soil.[14] In the final phase of the evacuation, which ended on 4 June when the Germans broke through the French lines, thousands of British sailors and airmen died, while French soldiers sacrificed themselves in a rearguard action. As a result, a further 140,000 French and Belgian soldiers escaped to safety through Dunkirk.

One of those French soldiers was René Balbaud. In the two weeks of fighting, his unit had been completely destroyed. The last straw came on 28 May. After retreating 250 kilometres along the Belgian frontier, the group was finally encircled by Nazi tanks, repeatedly bombed and strafed from the air. The men were hungry, tired, terrified. The commanding officer of Balbaud's unit received the order not to hinder anyone who wanted to get to the coast. Most chose to stay and surrendered to the advancing Nazis. Balbaud and a friend decided to take their chance and trudged towards the coast, hiding from the Germans. Eventually they bumped into a group of British soldiers and were told to head for Dunkirk. After wading through miles of flooded fields, surrounded by distressed livestock, they saw, far off, endless clouds of black smoke piling high into the air. The sky above the port was swarming with German bombers, and the town was in flames.

At the same moment another French soldier, Lieutenant Barlone, was also retreating towards Dunkirk, struggling through the thousands of French civilians fleeing the fighting. When he finally arrived at the port he saw a vision from hell:

The westerly wind beats down the immense columns of grim, black smoke from the flaming oil tanks. Truly this is the suffocating breath of the last judgement. Long sheaves of bright flames shoot up from the huge burning buildings. Broken bricks and mortar, windows, paving stones dislodged by shells strew the ground. Immense open spaces stretch farther than the eye can see with only a fragment of wall standing here and there, and the carcasses of the monster cranes in the docks despairingly hold up their great black arms towards a ghastly sky, rent unceasingly by the explosions of whining shells. Squadrons of planes circle above us, dropping sticks of bombs in quick succession. The men flatten out on the ground, making use of stacks of coal or trucks, or anything, for protection.[15]

Even then the ordeal was not over. Evacuated soldiers waded out into the sea and scrambled on to vessels of all sizes, many of them commandeered or captained by volunteers. They then had to run the gauntlet of Nazi bombardment and aerial attack, defended only by the incessant buzzing of British fighters. When the Nazis finally took Dunkirk, on 4 June, the beach was strewn with abandoned guns, uniforms and equipment. Overall, 350,000 Allied soldiers escaped, including Balbaud and Barlone.

*

Dunkirk was not the end of the Battle of France, but it demonstrated that the Nazis had the upper hand and that the Allies would have to show bold military and political initiative if the Germans were to be beaten back. Neither Britain nor France was in ideal shape for such a turnaround. In the weeks before the German attack, both countries had been in political turmoil – Winston Churchill replaced Neville Chamberlain at the head of the British government on the day Hitler attacked, while Paul Reynaud took over as French Prime Minister from Édouard Daladier. Neither of the new leaders had a particularly secure position. Churchill's fellow Conservatives were deeply suspicious of him: Chamberlain's Parliamentary Private Secretary wrote that the 'kind of people surrounding Winston are the scum'.[16] For the French (and for many in Britain), Churchill was a reckless adventurer.[17] As for Reynaud, he presided over the seventeenth French government in seven years. Most of his predecessors had simply reshuffled the same tired political cards in the increasingly forlorn hope of finding a winning hand. There was little reason to believe that Reynaud would be any different, and his slogan – 'We will win, because we are the strongest' – rang hollow when the German offensive began.

After Dunkirk fell on 4 June, the Nazis turned their gaze southwards and saw a French military leadership that was convinced it had lost the war. Two weeks earlier, Reynaud had sacked the French Supreme Commander of Land Forces, General Maurice Gamelin, who had been responsible for the defence strategy that had proved so useless. Reynaud had a problem, however, as there was no suitable replacement – all of the leading French generals were either directly tainted by the disaster or were out of action (one had a mental breakdown; another was killed in a car accident). His only choice was the seventy-three-year-old Maxime Weygand, who had been brought out of retirement the previous year. This career officer was stoutly anti-German, but he had somehow managed to get through over half a century of soldiering without ever once coming under fire – hardly the man to inspire French troops faced with the Nazi onslaught.[18]

But if Weygand was a poor choice, Reynaud's second appointment was calamitous. In an attempt to strengthen the government's influence among both the population and the armed forces, Reynaud named eighty-four-year-old Marshal Philippe Pétain as Deputy Prime Minister. Although Pétain had a reputation as an inspiring commander in the First World War, he was now widely reputed to be semi-senile (he slept through many Cabinet meetings). Neither Weygand nor Pétain thought the Germans could be repulsed, and both were soon leading figures in a growing capitulationist wing within the Cabinet and the army. Far from uniting the government, the arrival of Pétain and Weygand prepared its collapse, which duly took place within a month.

In glorious June weather – forty-four-year-old art historian Agnès Humbert noted in her diary 'Never has Paris looked more beautiful, never has it been such a mass of flowers'[19] – the German advance towards Paris continued. Despite brave defensive actions, key French positions fell like dominoes. The roads south were crowded with fleeing civilians. In the second half of April ninety per cent of the 200,000 population of Lille had left their homes, together with eighty-five per cent of the 82,000 population of Turcoing. Now the fighting began to catch up with them, so they had to move further south. An astonishing 8 million people – nearly a fifth of the total French population – are thought to have become refugees during this period, known in France as 'the Exodus'. Antoine de Saint-Exupéry talked to some of them:

> 'Where are you bound?'
> 'Nobody knows.'
> They never knew. Nobody knew anything. They were evacuating. There was no way to house them. Every road was blocked. And still they were evacuating. Somewhere in the north of France a boot had scattered an anthill, and the ants were on the march.[20]

On 3 June 300 German aircraft bombed the Citroën and Renault factories on the south-western edge of Paris, killing 254 people, including 195 civilians. On 6 June Nazi ground troops breached the French lines on their southward thrust; on the same day, at a meeting of the War Committee in Paris, Weygand sharply reproached the RAF for their lack of support in May, shouting shrilly at the British representatives. For one of the British officers present, Weygand's attitude gave 'the clear indication that, before the fate of the present battle was cast, it was considered lost by the Commander-in-Chief and his excuse for this was British duplicity'.[21] Two days later distant artillery fire could be heard in the capital; on 9 June the Nazis took Rouen with ease. The historian Marc Bloch, who at the time was an ordinary soldier, later wrote: 'The Germans took no account of roads. They were everywhere . . . They relied on action and on improvisation. We, on the other hand, believed in doing nothing and in behaving as we always had behaved.'[22] Meanwhile, the government began to totter.

As Paris baked in the June heat, a kind of resigned panic began to seize the capital. Eerily, on Saturday 8 June trains heading south from the Gare d'Austerlitz had no announced destination – they were simply leaving, going somewhere, anywhere. Over the next few days the stations were in continual chaos as people sought to escape the inevitable occupation, storming trains, crowding at the ticket offices, desperate for a way out. Soon the roads were equally full. But not everyone fled. Many of the cars leaving on the evening of Sunday 9 June met the traditional traffic jam on the other lane, as people returned from a day in the countryside, oblivious to the advancing danger from the north. Although the richer, western sections of Paris gradually emptied, most of the working-class inhabitants of the eastern side of the city stayed where they were. The poor had nowhere to go, and no means of getting there.[23] Even the rich had difficulties – petrol shortages meant that cars were often useless, the volume of traffic made the shortest journey take hours, and when the refugees did arrive somewhere, what would they eat? One refugee wrote:

> All these human beings in movement were marked by lack of sleep and lack of food. We slept however we could, wherever we could. A few hours later, we were on the move again. It was impossible to feed such a column of people in towns that were already overpopulated. Could we demand more milk, more meat, than the region contained?[24]

On Monday 10 June the government officially left Paris, heading south for the Loire Valley, where the various ministries were scattered around a series of châteaux commandeered for the purpose. Despite British urging, there was no question of using Paris as an obstacle, a way of tying up the Germans in a long and bloody fight, street by street. Pétain dismissed the idea out of hand: 'To make Paris into a city of ruins will not affect the issue,' he said.[25] The French government preferred to leave, but where it was going, and why, was never clear. Reynaud had instructed Weygand to prepare plans for holding Brittany against the Nazis, retaining sea and air links with Britain. But despite British support, this plan came to nothing. Weygand thought it was pointless, while Reynaud simply forgot about it, caught up in a series of mood swings that punctuated his slow downfall. In his more excitable moments, Reynaud talked of the government leaving for French North Africa, or for French territories in the Americas, but no real plans were ever made.

On the afternoon of 11 June Churchill and a small British delegation flew to meet the French government at Briaire in the Loire Valley. Escorted by twelve Hurricane fighters, the small twin-engine de Havilland Flamingo landed late in the afternoon, and the visitors were taken to the Château du Muguet, 'a hideous house . . . expanded by successful business in groceries or indifferent champagne into a large monstrosity of red lobster-coloured brick, and stone the hue of unripe Camembert'.[26] The château had only one telephone (accessed via a toilet), which worked only when the village operator was on duty – she finished work at 6 p.m. and took a two-hour lunch-break.[27] As a result, the meeting was effectively isolated from the outside world and from the terrible events taking place where the Germans were advancing.

Desperate to rally his allies, Churchill cranked up the rhetoric, urging the French to fight in the capital, conjuring up 'the lurid glow of burning cities, some as beautiful as Paris, collapsing on garrisons who refused to accept defeat'.[28] The French were unmoved. Weygand's response was that the battle of Paris had already been lost and that every other French city would also fall unless the British intervened decisively. Over and again, the two governments looked at things from completely different points of view, each expressing their own national interest. For the French, the British would soon collapse under the inevitable Nazi onslaught, so they might as well throw everything they had into the Battle of France. For the British, the Battle of France was a mere prelude to the Battle of Britain and, above all, they felt that both sides should try to hold out until the USA could be persuaded to enter the war.

This difference in outlook was strikingly expressed when Weygand again demanded that the RAF immediately put every one of its planes into the sky over France, leaving no reserve to defend Britain, proclaiming: 'Here is the decisive point . . . this is the decisive moment.' Churchill replied, equally forcefully: 'This is not the decisive point, this is not the decisive moment.'[29] More of the same followed when Churchill argued that a campaign of guerrilla warfare in France would delay, and could even halt, the German advance. Pétain awoke from his sleep to reject the idea out of hand: 'It would mean the destruction of the country,' he grunted.[30]

It became clear that the French were going to sue for peace, and on 12 June Churchill returned to London armed only with a French promise to consult the British government before they came to a final decision. But within a day Churchill was summoned back to France for a meeting at which the French leader Reynaud asked whether France could be released from the three-month-old treaty which stated that neither country would enter into a separate peace.[31] Churchill rejected the request, asking perceptively: 'What is the alternative? The alternative is the destruction of France, more certain than if she fights on, for Hitler will abide by no pledges.'[32] Once again, Churchill urged the French to hold out until President Roosevelt could persuade the Senate and the US public, both of which were strongly anti-interventionist, that the USA should enter the war against Hitler.

Later that day one of the most absurd events in a series of tragicomic governmental antics took place. At a French Cabinet meeting in Cangé, near Tours, Weygand announced that the Communists had seized power in Paris, that the mob had disarmed the police and that all telephone communications with the capital had been cut. Mandel, the Minister of the Interior, calmly phoned the Prefect of Paris, and got Weygand to come and hear that his story was utter nonsense.[33] Despite this public humiliation, Weygand continued unabashed and proceeded to argue that the government should have remained in Paris in order to negotiate with the Nazis, before calling for the arrest of the most junior member of the government – General Charles de Gaulle, who had been made Under-Secretary of State for National Defence and War merely a week before – for having begun to send men and material to North Africa without consultation. Like many of Weygand's rants, this one went unchallenged and unacted on – for the moment.

Meanwhile, Paris awaited the arrival of the Nazis. The government had declared the capital an open city – that is, a city that was 'open' to the invader, and which would not be defended. To add to the apocalyptic atmosphere, the sky was blotted out for hours on end, as thick black smoke from the burning oil depots at Rouen settled over the capital. As the streets emptied, the Paris-based Swiss journalist Edmond Dubois walked through one of the smartest parts of Paris and stumbled on a surreal scene:

Wednesday 12 June, at 6 p.m., a herd of cows . . . wanders unhindered through the Place de l'Alma. Nobody is with them. The animals are hungry and their lowing resounds sadly along the deserted riverside roads. The odd passer-by barely bothers to glance at this surprising spectacle.[34]

The same day, Sergeant Guy Bohn, a lawyer, was ordered to blow up the Eiffel Tower to prevent the radio transmitter from falling into enemy hands. Bohn, who had absolutely no explosives training, was horrified and had no idea how to proceed. He eventually managed to persuade his superiors that the project was doomed to failure, and he was instead sent off to the fort at Issy-les-Moulineaux, where despite his inexperience he successfully destroyed a more reasonable target – a small military transmitter.[35]

Christian Pineau, who was working at the Ministry of Information, helped evacuate the ministry on 11 June, and then left with a convoy carrying personnel and key papers. But when they reached Moulins, 230 kilometres south of Paris, they realized that they had left behind them files containing names that would greatly interest the Gestapo. Together with three other volunteers, Pineau clambered into an old Citroën and drove all the way back to Paris against the flow of refugees. Having burned the papers late into the evening of 13 June, Pineau then crossed the Seine to spend the night at his empty apartment. The following morning, as the Nazis were about to enter the city, Pineau returned to the car. Only two of the three helpers turned up. The third had disappeared with the contents of the Ministry's ample wine cellar.[36]

A few days earlier, two decisive but highly secret events had taken place. First, a convoy of a dozen vehicles had left Paris for Vincennes, carrying replicas of a German Enigma coding machine. The fact that the Allies could read Nazi messages encoded by the Enigma machine was one of the biggest secrets of the war. The Poles had first cracked the Enigma code in 1933 and had given two replica machines to the French in 1939, one of which was then handed on to the British and was used at Bletchley Park to help decode Nazi messages.[37] Had the Nazis captured the French machine, they would have realized that their communication system was not secure, and the shape of the war – and even its outcome – could have been very different. As it was, this machine stayed hidden in the south of France throughout the war. At around the same time, the French physicist Frédéric Joliot-Curie left Paris with France's entire supply of 'heavy water' (deuterium oxide) sloshing around in jerrycans strapped to the bottom of his car. The Nazis were using heavy water as part of their nuclear weapons programme and would have been delighted to get their hands on the material that Joliot-Curie managed to get to the UK within a week.

On 15 June the *Manchester Guardian* published the following report:

> The main German forces entered the city at noon yesterday. They came from the north-west and by the Aubervilliers Gate from the north-east. From the north-western suburbs they marched through the west end down the Champs-Elysées – tanks, armoured reconnaissance cars, anti-tank units, and motorized infantry. Machine-gun posts were set up at important points, and the wireless stations were seized. The people left in Paris watched the entry in silence, reports the Associated Press correspondent. Small groups of people still sat along the terraces and boulevards and in the cafés. Shops were boarded up. In the Place de l'Opéra stood a solitary motor-car with a big 'for sale' sign. The Paris police still patrolled the streets. Occasionally could be heard the drone of an unmolested plane.[38]

What the newspapers did not report is that around a dozen suicides took place on 14 June.[39] For some, the fall of Paris was the end of everything.

\*

As the Nazis draped Paris with swastika flags, the French government left its ramshackle and dispersed headquarters among the châteaux of the Loire and headed for Bordeaux, desperate to keep a reasonable distance between itself and the advancing German troops. The final, brief scene in the rather pathetic French governmental drama lasted only a few days, as the capitulationist wing in the army and the government gradually came to dominate.

In a final attempt to galvanize Reynaud and those who wanted to continue the fight, and desperate to keep the powerful French fleet out of the Nazis' hands, the British proposed an immediate 'indissoluble union of our two people and our two empires'.[40] The proposal was dictated over the phone by de Gaulle, who was in London pressing the British to send more troops and aircraft. It briefly made Reynaud perk up, but the defeatists scornfully dismissed the idea as a British attempt to grab the French Empire. Pétain showed what he thought of Britain's chances against the Germans when he asked why anyone would want to 'fuse with a corpse'. His fellow defeatist Ybarnegaray – a pre-war fascist – was even clearer: 'Better to be a Nazi province. At least we know what that means.'[41] Reynaud abandoned the idea without even putting it to a vote. With Roosevelt not only refusing to come to the aid of France, but even forbidding the French government from making public his telegrams of support (the US President was campaigning for re-election), a crushed Reynaud resigned during the evening of 16 June. Pétain became Prime Minister and immediately contacted the Nazis to discover what the peace terms would be.

At the same time, Weygand began to move against those who wished to carry on fighting. He had already been bugging Reynaud's phone and had been mobilizing young recruits in the Bordeaux area in preparation for a military coup, should the government prove intransigent. His final target was de Gaulle, who had returned from London only to see the government disintegrate. De Gaulle was concerned that he might be arrested by Weygand, and was determined that the struggle against the Nazis should continue even if the government collapsed. He therefore insisted to Major-General Edward Spears, Churchill's personal envoy, that he had to return to London. On the morning of 17 June Spears and de Gaulle left Bordeaux airport, bound for London.[42] De Gaulle's personal luggage contained only a spare pair of trousers, four clean shirts and a family photo.[43]

At midday Pétain went on French radio. In his thin, metallic voice (Arthur Koestler wrote in his diary that it 'sounded like a skeleton with a chill'[44]) Pétain announced: 'It is with a heavy heart that I tell you today we must cease hostilities. The fighting must stop.' Although no armistice had been signed, and French soldiers were still engaging German troops, the clear implication was that the French armed forces should lay down their arms. That was the conclusion drawn by the drunken soldiers encountered by André Dewavrin, a naval officer who had recently arrived back in Brest: '"The war is over – Pétain said so!" they shouted. "Why should we go and get killed, if the war is over? We might as well go home!"'[45] Dewavrin, like many others, initially thought the broadcast was a Nazi ruse. He soon had to accept that Pétain, and the whole military establishment, had thrown in the towel. A few hours later the broadcast was repeated, with the key sentence changed to 'we must try to cease hostilities', but the damage was done.[46] Within four days the armistice was signed – in the same railway carriage as the 1918 armistice, but with victor and vanquished reversed and with the terms imposed by the Nazis.

The overwhelming response by French soldiers to the armistice was one of relief and acceptance. Captain Henri Frenay reported:

> I saw our men, who had fought so well right up to the last minute, throw down their arms, abandon their field packs and organize folk dances on the road and in forest clearings.[47]

Jean-Pierre Levy, a reserve artillery lieutenant who fought up until the bitter end, wrote:

> It's sad to say, but, alas, it's the truth: around me there was widespread relief at the announcement of the news. Soldiers and officers were in favour of ceasing hostilities and did not hide it. Everything happened in a virtually unanimous consensus.[48]

Some soldiers were less enthusiastic. Lieutenant Barlone, who had returned to France following his evacuation from Dunkirk, wrote in his diary:

> We learn by wireless that Pétain and Weygand have asked for an armistice. Several officers weep bitterly. Others remain indifferent as if struck dumb by the disaster.[49]

The full implication of the fall of France was still unclear to many. On 18 June Arthur Koestler passed groups of refugees on the road to Périgueux in the Dordogne, seemingly unaware of what was to come. As he caustically remarked in his diary:

> All the way saw families camping by the roadside with cars parked off the road, on the spot where the last drop of petrol gave out. It is a sort of general stay put. All wait for armistice to be signed and 'everything

to become normal again'. They really believe life will be as it was before. Meanwhile, they eat and drink in the sunny meadows and play *belotte*. The apocalypse as a family picnic.[50]

Under the terms of the armistice, the country was divided into two zones: an Occupied Zone in the north and a Non-Occupied Zone (or 'Free Zone') in the south. A 'demarcation line' – a frontier in all but name – snaked across the country, allowing the Nazis to control traffic between the two zones. France was carved up like a carcass. First pickings went direct to Germany: the coal-rich regions of the north were put under Nazi command, while the coal- and steel-producing areas of Alsace-Lorraine in the east, which were not mentioned in the armistice agreement, were simply annexed by Germany (speaking French was forbidden, Jews were banned from the area and all men were subject to Nazi conscription). Italy – which had opportunistically declared war on France on 10 June – got a small area around Menton, in south-eastern France.

Hitler wanted to turn France into a colony, and Pétain was his stooge. By agreeing to do the Nazis' work for them, Pétain and the Vichy regime made a total German occupation unnecessary. Crippling reparations were imposed – the astronomic sum of 20 million Reichsmarks per day – as the Nazis set about bleeding their victim dry. Over the next few years all major production was integrated into the German war machine. The fact that the industrial and raw material-producing areas in the north and the east were under German control made this easier. Thousands of trainloads of food and industrial products travelled to Germany, while the French population was subject to severe rationing. Furthermore, 1.8 million French prisoners of war were held as hostages and potential slave workers in prison camps in the heart of the Nazi machine in Germany. The huge number of prisoners, together with the dead and seriously injured – numbering perhaps up to 300,000 – meant that France was missing about ten per cent of its male population.

Once the ceasefire came into effect on 25 June, the defeatist clique around Pétain set about creating a new state. The seat of government was moved to the sleepy spa town of Vichy in the Non-Occupied Zone, and on 10 July the National Assembly, convened by Pétain, voted for its own dissolution, by giving all power to the aged Marshal and allowing him to draw up a new constitution. To their credit, a small minority of French parliamentarians refused to go along with the new constitution – eighty deputies, virtually all of them Socialists (the Communist deputies had been banned since September), voted 'Non'. This protest was simply ignored. Encouraged by Pierre Laval, a newspaper magnate turned far-right politician, Pétain abolished the Third Republic and replaced it by the 'French State'. The revolutionary motto *Liberté, Egalité, Fraternité* was scrapped in favour of the crushing conservatism of *Travail, Famille, Patrie* ('Work, Family, Fatherland'). The programme of the French State was simple: a 'national revolution' designed to root out the Freemasons, Communists and Jews who were deemed to be the root of France's woes. To accompany this reactionary recipe, Pétain added a quasi-religious flavour, declaring to the French public that he would make 'a gift of my person' to the country. This promise helped reinforce Pétain's undoubted popularity on both sides of the demarcation line.

Neither the major political parties, nor the leading industrialists and bankers, nor the armed forces showed any inclination to back de Gaulle and continue the fight. Instead, they apparently considered that it was best to be 'realistic' and to go along with the Occupation. This not only involved a morally fatal compromise with the new Nazi masters, it also meant accepting the introduction of a paranoid state surveillance apparatus. In both zones, counter-intelligence services were deployed against those who opposed the new regime, informers and police spies were encouraged to betray their neighbours, while the police and the gendarmerie spent a substantial part of their time opening private letters and reporting on changes in public opinion. In August 1940, Arthur Koestler correctly predicted what happened in the months that followed: 'France will go fascist without noticing it', he wrote.[51]

The Vichy government found itself in an ambiguous position. It was nominally an independent state, in that its laws governed the whole of France, yet it had no decisive control over more than half the country. The presence of Nazi troops in the northern zone meant that the Germans had effective power in these areas, even though Vichy was the civil authority for the whole country. In the south, the formal independence of the government occasionally allowed for some surprising events – sections of the armed forces and police apparatus sometimes took action against Nazi spies in the south, or helped protect Resistance forces. Up until the total occupation of the country (November 1942), there was little the Germans could do to stop this. The word that soon came to symbolize Vichy – 'collaboration' – initially meant just that: active cooperation and support, not simple subservience. But as the months went by, Vichy gradually became nothing more than a puppet regime, increasingly populated by enthusiastic Nazi stooges and fanatical anti-Semites.[52]

For the next four years the division of the country shaped all aspects of life. For those in the Non-Occupied Zone, there was the illusion of freedom, while for those in the north there was the brutal reality of Occupation. The demarcation line cut through the country, dividing families, making once routine visits to friends and relatives impossible. Nazi bureaucracy, enthusiastically applied by the Vichy administration, soon became a regular part of life. Even in the Non-Occupied Zone, everyday life repeatedly reminded the French that they were a subjugated people, beaten in a lightning war by their powerful neighbours, reduced to the role of observers in the cataclysmic events that were shaking the planet.

\*

While Pétain, Weygand and the other leaders had been carefully paving the way to defeat, most of the French armed forces had been fighting valiantly. As Saint-Exupéry put it 'there were clusters of infantrymen still giving up their lives in undefendable farmhouses. There were aviation crews still melting like wax flung into a fire.'[53] Around the Maginot Line, where Levy's and Frenay's units were based, fierce fighting continued right up until the armistice. According to German reports, their troops were 'pinned down with heavy losses' as the French felled trees to block the roads, then used the cover to attack with artillery, snipers and machine guns.[54] Overall, German casualty rates actually increased after the fall of Dunkirk, with an average of 750 deaths per day, as against around 550 in the three weeks after the invasion began.[55] Even in the air, where the Germans enjoyed undoubted superiority, the Battle of France inflicted significant damage on the Nazi war machine. By mid-June the Luftwaffe had lost around forty per cent of its aircraft. Overall, British and French losses were greater (1,921 Allied aircraft were destroyed, as against 1,469 German planes[56] – RAF losses were higher in the Battle of France than in the Battle of Britain),[57] but the loss of German pilots and machines proved to be decisive, weakening the Luftwaffe just as it was ordered to turn its attention to Britain.

Many civilians also showed honour and bravery in the face of the Nazi offensive. After the German troops swept through and around Paris, they came to Chartres, a small town about fifty miles south of the capital, home to a beautiful medieval cathedral. The Prefect of Chartres, Jean Moulin, was one of the republic's high-flyers – once the youngest prefect in the country, and one-time senior civil servant in the Air Ministry. As German troops swept into his deserted and looted city on 17 June, Moulin remained at his post to organize an orderly transfer of power. But when the Nazis tried to make him sign a false declaration that a series of war crimes in the region had been carried out by French African troops, Moulin refused and was promptly arrested, beaten and abused. Still he refused to sign. Early in the morning of 18 June, crushed by the power of the Nazis, unable to see any way out of the dishonour created by the Germans' total victory, Moulin tried to commit suicide by slitting his throat with a piece of broken glass. But the suicide bid, like so much in the warm summer of 1940, was a failure. Moulin survived, although for the remaining three years of his life he would wear a scarf around his neck to hide the scar.[58]

Despite these signs of bravery and determination, overall the Nazis won an easy victory in France. Paradoxically, this success ultimately proved an advantage for the Allies, reinforcing Hitler's fantasies of world domination, and making him overconfident in the effectiveness of the blitzkrieg.[59] The Führer was so impressed with the outcome of the French campaign that on 31 July, even before the Battle of Britain had begun, he instructed the military to prepare the invasion of the USSR – his fundamental political, economic and ideological enemy. From the outset, this had been his main objective. As Hitler put it in August 1939:

> Everything that I undertake is directed against Russia. If those in the
> West are too stupid and too blind to understand this, then I shall be

forced to come to an understanding with the Russians to beat the West, and then, after its defeat, turn with all my concerted force against the Soviet Union.[60]

For many in France, the cause of the defeat was the legacy of the pre-war left-wing Popular Front government, which won the election of spring 1936 and was greeted by a huge general strike, leaving the French right wing obsessed with the threat of Communism.[61] On his return to Britain, Spears scornfully reported that Weygand was 'far more concerned about the danger of revolution in France than about the consequences of capitulation to the Nazis'.[62] In early May a leading right-wing parliamentary deputy argued that 'whereas victory would mean revolution, defeat would save France, for it would, at the cost of a certain loss of territory and prestige, preserve the social order'.[63] Taken together with Ybarnegaray's comment that it would be better for France to be a Nazi province than to unite with Britain, it is clear that many of France's leaders had little stomach for a fight with fascism. This was obvious to many ordinary French people. In mid-June Victor Serge asked soldiers in Paris why the battle was being lost. Their answer was straightforward:

> . . . we've been sold out, betrayed, by Jove! By the officers who legged it sharpish with their bits of skirt, by the high-ups, by the *cagoulards* [pre-war fascists] who wanted their revenge over the Popular Front.[64]

Traditional anti-Communism among army generals – and the leaders of many of the political parties, including the Socialists – had been reinforced in August 1939, when Stalin suddenly announced that he had signed a non-aggression pact with Nazi Germany. Previously, the French Communists had been enthusiastically pro-war and anti-German – a consequence of the Franco-Soviet mutual defence pact, which had been signed in 1935. Now, loyalty to Moscow obliged the Party to oppose the war against their master's new ally. Understandably, the vast majority of Communist Party members were distraught. Tens of thousands ripped up their Party cards in disgust – the 7,000 PCF members in the Calais region plummeted to 250 within a month.[65] The French government banned the Party, arrested its deputies and suspended its local councils.

By the end of May 1940 around 5,500 Communist militants had been arrested, under suspicion of forming part of a supposed Nazi 'Fifth Column' of saboteurs and agitators.[66] This was the context that fuelled Weygand's excited claim about the Communists having seized power in Paris, and led US Ambassador Bullitt to send a coded telegram to Washington labelled 'Personal and Secret for the President':

> Will you please have put on the next Clipper twelve Thompson sub-machine guns with ammunition, addressed to me for the use of this Embassy. I am fully prepared to pay for them myself. There is every reason to expect that if the French Government should be forced to leave Paris, its place would be taken by a communist mob.[67]

The machine guns duly arrived. The Communist mob did not.

In truth, the PCF could barely organize itself, never mind a mob. Its influence was severely weakened, its leadership was either in jail, in hiding or in exile, its policies were not understood by any but the most loyal members. Its working-class constituency, still scarred by the experience of 1914–18, had reluctantly gone along with the war and had then been battered, bombed, misled and finally abandoned. Despite the nightmares of Weygand, Bullitt and their like, the workers were in no mood for revolution. Arthur Koestler neatly punctured the fevered imaginings of the right, roving through 150 years of French history to explain why the government had rushed into the arms of defeat:

> Both in 1792 and in 1870 the French ruling caste had betrayed the nation and preferred the Prussians to revolution. In 1940 there was no danger of a revolution; the proletariat was tired and apathetic; while the bourgeoisie had found its symbolic expression in a living mummy. It was an unreal drama of shadows: the ghost of the French ruling class committing suicide, scared by the spectre of revolution.[68]

Ultimately, however, the fall of France was not simply a French defeat. It was an Allied defeat. In a matter of weeks the Belgians capitulated, the Dutch government fled to London. Unable to resist their own demons, the French leadership sued for peace, while the British could not convince their allies to fight on. The single factor that enabled all these events to take place was the absence of the USA from the war. Without the power of the American military machine, the Europeans had no chance against the aggressive expansionism of the German ruling class and their fascist leader, driven not only by economic aims but also by the stinging desire to burn away twenty years of humiliation at the hands of the Great Powers following defeat in the First World War. The French and the British desperately pleaded with Roosevelt to go beyond his private pledges of support and his piecemeal public deliveries of weapons, but to no avail. It took a direct attack on the USA eighteen months later for it to enter the war.

*

As France was crushed under the Nazi heel, two speeches were made within hours of each other in London. In the afternoon of 18 June Churchill rose to his feet in the House of Commons. History could have made what he said next appear ridiculous, foolhardy and full of bravado. Instead, because of the way events turned out, it seems to have been invested with immense foresight. With his customary growling rhetoric, Churchill outlined the 'disastrous military events' that had taken place in the previous fortnight, simultaneously apportioning blame and arguing that the reckoning would have to be drawn up by future historians. After surveying the state of Britain's armed forces, Churchill concluded with words that have become famous, but which at the time were more an expression of his personal will than the conviction of the country:

> What General Weygand called the Battle of France is over. I expect that the Battle of Britain is about to begin. Upon this battle depends the survival of Christian civilization. Upon it depends our own British life, and the long continuity of our institutions and our Empire. The whole fury and might of the enemy must very soon be turned on us. Hitler knows that he will have to break us in this Island or lose the war. If we can stand up to him, all Europe may be free and the life of the world may move forward into broad, sunlit uplands. But if we fail,

then the whole world, including the United States, including all that we have known and cared for, will sink into the abyss of a new Dark Age made more sinister, and perhaps more protracted, by the lights of perverted science. Let us therefore brace ourselves to our duties, and so bear ourselves that, if the British Empire and its Commonwealth last for a thousand years, men will still say: 'This was their finest hour.'[69]

Shortly after Churchill sat down in the Commons, General Charles de Gaulle made his way to Broadcasting House and was taken down into studio B2. The day before, he had left France without any clear idea of what he was going to do. De Gaulle was the most junior general in the army – only a few weeks earlier he had been a mere colonel. He had no army, no troops, no supporters. He was virtually unknown in France, with little influence and few contacts. Yet on 17 June de Gaulle decided he should broadcast an appeal, directed primarily at French soldiers, sailors and civilians in Britain, calling on them to rally to him and continue the fight. De Gaulle wanted to oversee the reconstitution of the French armed forces, and in particular hoped to win over the powerful French navy, which he naively supposed might come over to the Allied cause. The next day, when he asked for permission to use the BBC to broadcast to France, the War Cabinet, with Chamberlain in the chair (Churchill was absent), turned down the request. They were still not convinced that Pétain would sign the armistice and wanted to leave all their options open. Spears, who had witnessed the slow decomposition of the Reynaud government with a growing mixture of fury and nausea, rushed to see his old friend Churchill and argued that the Cabinet decision had to be reversed. It was.[70]

De Gaulle's short broadcast went out on the BBC French service in the early evening.[71] Nobody in London thought to record it. Speaking in his singsong voice, de Gaulle, like Churchill earlier in the day, gave a brief summary of his view of the fall of France, pointing the finger at the inability of the French high command to cope with German tactics. He then reminded his listeners that the outcome of the war would be decided on a planetary scale, that the French Empire had yet to be defeated and that joint naval action with the British could repulse the

Germans. Finally, he closed with an appeal which has since gone down in French history:

> I, General de Gaulle, now in London, call upon the French officers and soldiers who are or who may find themselves on British soil, with or without their weapons, I call upon the engineers and the skilled workers in the armaments industry who are or who may find themselves on British soil, to join me.
>
> Whatever happens, the flame of French resistance must not and shall not die.
>
> Tomorrow, as today, I shall speak on the radio from London.[72]

Although few people heard de Gaulle's speech, it was widely reproduced in the French press in the days that followed. Agnès Humbert, who had fled from Paris to Limoges, ran through the garden 'like a lunatic' to tell a military friend the news. The officer was unimpressed: 'It's all a lot of nonsense . . . he's a crackpot, that de Gaulle, you mark my words,' he said. But Humbert wrote in her diary: 'It is thanks to that "crackpot" that this evening I decided not to put an end to everything . . . He has given me hope, and nothing in the world can extinguish that hope now.'[73]

But Humbert's response was unusual. In the main, de Gaulle's declaration fell on deaf ears. The French population was bitter, depressed, cynical. Calls to arms from a nobody had little purchase on people who no longer trusted their military leaders. One of the few accounts of popular reactions to de Gaulle's speech comes from Georges Sadoul, who heard the broadcast with a group of his fellow soldiers. Their responses were forthright: 'Go fight yourself, you bastard. You've got your arse in an armchair and you want other people to go on getting themselves killed.'[74]

Within a few months that attitude began to evaporate. People realized that they could resist, that they should resist. But de Gaulle's role in awakening the fightback would be minimal. The Resistance was born in France, not London.

# 2

# *A Glimmer of Light*

France was stunned. Pétain enjoyed the numb support of much of the population, simply because he had ended the horror of the war. It took some time for most people to realize the moral, political and economic price that would be paid for such a peace. While France had apparently stepped out of the conflict, the country was split into two. The Vichy regime was unique in the whole of Occupied Europe: it was the only government to agree willingly to the occupation and division of its country. The proud possessor of an Empire had been reduced to the status of a defeated, occupied state. On an international scale the Nazis appeared to be unstoppable: in the middle of July Hitler launched his long-awaited air attack against the British Isles – the Battle of Britain had begun. Thousands of German aircraft leaped into the skies above the Channel, the first step in Hitler's plan to subdue his last enemy in Europe. It seemed as though the Nazi wave would roll over the whole continent.

Something like normal life resumed in the Non-Occupied Zone, where Vichy pretended to reign supreme. All over the country, the millions who had taken to the roads during 'the Exodus' gradually returned home. But the reality of fuel rationing soon changed the face of France – the Occupation gave the Nazis access to a stock of petrol that was larger than Germany's annual production, and they diverted a huge proportion of that fuel to their war effort, leaving the French with virtually nothing.[1] Private cars vanished, bicycle rickshaws replaced taxis and lorries were commandeered by the army. Paris streets looked like pictures from a weird parallel universe – all deliveries were horse-drawn, road-signs were written in German gothic script, while the twelve bus routes that remained were operated by strange hybrid vehicles: single-decker buses with a huge container on the roof to carry the gas that now powered them.[2]

All over the country, modern road transport disappeared. Charles d'Aragon remembered life in Vichy France: 'The big cities, which yesterday were so close, became distant once more. Villages that were neighbours ceased to be so. The kilometre regained the value it had in the previous century. Distances were measured in paces – of man or horse.'[3] Things were not quite so bucolic in the northern Occupied Zone. Paris was covered in German road signs, the buildings were festooned with swastikas and Nazi soldiers crowded on to public transport and into bars, restaurants and cinemas. The capital became a Nazi town. Elsewhere, the Germans poured troops into the western coastal regions, setting up garrisons and taking over French naval and air force infrastructure. It was here, in the towns and villages along the Atlantic coast, that the first signs of friction between the French population and the occupying army appeared.

Some of the first people to defy the Nazis were women. Six weeks after the armistice was signed, a laundrywoman from Rennes was sentenced to three months in prison 'for publicly insulting the German army', while two seamstresses were each sentenced to one week in prison for the same offence. Some of these protests were organized. In Toulouse, twenty-one-year-old Hélène Cazalbou slapped a German officer in the street, while her accomplices threw leaflets, which read 'You are here and in Paris, but soon we will be in Berlin'.[4] Cazalbou was lucky – she got away with a one-year suspended prison sentence. For others, confrontation with Nazi troops meant death. In Bordeaux a Polish Jew named Israel Karp threw himself at a group of German soldiers who were hoisting the Nazi flag in one of the city's main squares; convicted of 'acts of violence against members of the German army', Karp was executed.[5]

Nazi 'justice' was not only harsh; it was indiscriminate. All over the Atlantic coastal region the Germans laid down dedicated phone lines, creating a Nazi communications web. In July cables in Brittany, near Rennes, Fougères and Angers, were repeatedly cut. In August and September two cables near Nantes were cut twice. Each time, the Germans responded by fining the town they deemed to be 'responsible' – for example, following the sabotage of one of the cables near Nantes, the city was fined 2 million francs. For the saboteurs, the punishment was savage: on 19 June – before the armistice – an agricultural worker named Étienne Achavanne cut the telephone lines linking the German command in Rouen with a Luftwaffe airbase. Achavanne was captured and on 7 July was shot by a German firing squad. The official end of the Franco-German war did not make Nazi 'justice' any less vicious: later in the summer, Marcel Brossier, a thirty-one-year-old mechanic, was found guilty of cutting telephone cables and was executed at Rennes. A few days earlier, Pierre Roche, a teenager from La Rochelle, was executed for cutting the cable to Royan.

Roche's sabotage prompted the Nazi commandant of the region to requisition French civilians to protect the cable by patrolling it through the night. Christian Pineau was one of those assigned this tedious task. Pineau, who had been burning official papers from his Ministry shortly before the Nazis arrived in Paris, had fled with millions of other refugees during 'the Exodus' and had finally ended up in the Charente-Maritime, near La Rochelle. Like dozens of local men, he had no choice but to follow the Nazis' orders and make the best of a bad job:

> Each farmer had to devote on average six hours to the stupid task of wandering up and down next to a wire. In fact, the job was not too unpleasant because the nights were warm; we took provisions to pass the time, emptied bottles of wine, sang our hearts out or played cards . . . By the time the guard was changed, some of us were completely drunk.[6]

This kind of mute rejection of the Occupation was typical of the early weeks following the military debacle. In August a fifty-one-year-old socialist civil servant and journalist, Jean Texcier, gave voice to this sentiment, in the form of '33 Conseils à l'occupé' ('33 Hints to the Occupied'), a brief text composed of thirty-three short paragraphs, which he published anonymously – and illegally – in Paris.[7] This gently ironic pamphlet outlined how the population should passively resist the Nazis because, as Texcier put it, 'THEY ARE NOT TOURISTS. They are conquerors.' Texcier's proposals were hardly radical – polite aloofness if a German soldier tried to strike up a conversation, pretending not to understand German, refusing to attend public concerts given by German troops, and so on – but he struck a chord when he suggested that the time would come for a settling of accounts: 'On the outside, pretend you do not care; on the inside, stoke up your anger. It will serve you well.'

Texcier's low-key document had an immediate impact. As well as the original printed version, the text was re-copied by hand or by typewriter, and was slipped into letter boxes and left lying on Métro seats. Agnès Humbert was one of the many who came across Texcier's pamphlet. She had returned to Paris at the beginning of August, after fleeing to Limoges. On 18 August she wrote with undisguised joy in her diary:

> Will the people who produced the *33 Conseils à l'occupé* ('33 Hints to the Occupied') ever know what they have done for us, and probably for thousands of others? A glimmer of light in the darkness . . . Now we know for certain that we are not alone. There are other people who think like us, who are suffering, and organizing the struggle.[8]

For most people, the 'struggle' consisted simply of listening to the BBC. Every evening, thirty minutes of news and sketches were broadcast in French, including a five-minute slot for de Gaulle's 'Free French'. This daily dose of propaganda helped make de Gaulle's name synonymous with opposition to Vichy. A new word entered the language to describe hostility to the Occupation and the division of the country: 'Gaullism'. There was no other public figure who adopted such a clear stance, and the French began to look to the exiled General as the figurehead of opposition to the Nazis.

The wit and quality of the entertainment on the BBC, plus its slightly puckish humour, endeared it to a huge part of the French population. A joke that went the rounds in autumn 1940 shows the popularity of the BBC, and the subversive way in which it was viewed:

> – Do you know what happened recently? At 9.20 p.m. a Jew killed a German soldier, cut him open and ate his heart.
> – Impossible. For three reasons. A German has no heart. A Jew eats no pork. And at 9.20 p.m. everyone is listening to the BBC.[9]

Along with comical songs and long-running sketches, there were pastiches of commercial jingles, each of which had a clear message. Probably the most famous was directed against the BBC's main rival, the Nazi-controlled Radio Paris.[10] To the catchy tune of 'La Cucuracha', a voice would softly sing '*Radio Paris ment, Radio Paris ment, Radio Paris est allemand*' ('Radio Paris tells lies, Radio Paris tells lies, Radio Paris is German').

The BBC programmes made no secret of their highly partisan attitude. The overall title – *Les Français parlent aux Français* ('The French speak to the French') – neatly implied that neither Radio Paris nor Radio Vichy truly represented the voice of the French people. And every evening the programme would open with a reminder of how long the Occupation and division of France had lasted. On 22 September – the day the Battle of Britain was won – the opening declaration was: 'This is the ninetieth day of resistance by the French people against oppression.' This sombre statement was updated every day until the end of the war.

Listening to the BBC was neither simple nor safe. The Nazis beamed out powerful jamming signals, and listening became an offence punishable by six months in prison.[11] Paris and Vichy adopted such extreme measures because they were alarmed at the success of the BBC's programmes. Although there were around 5 million radio sets in France, plenty of households – especially in the south – did not have access to one. In many parts of the country listening to the BBC became a social activity – over a dozen people regularly gathered around a radio in an apartment in Montpellier, most of the inhabitants of a small village near Clermont-Ferrand would assemble to listen together, while a bar owner in Marseilles would listen in the back room – with the sound turned up so loud that all the customers could hear.[12]

The widespread enthusiasm for the BBC was all the more surprising, given the wave of Anglophobia that swept the country in the summer. On 3 July the Royal Navy bombarded the French fleet, at anchor in the North African port of Mers-el-Kebir, to keep it out of German hands. For ten hellish minutes, artillery shells rained down on the unsuspecting French vessels. Then it was over. The battleship *Bretagne* had capsized, and 1,297 French sailors had been killed – more than the number of German sailors the British had killed since the outbreak of the war. Sinking an immobile, unprepared target was hardly the Royal Navy's finest hour, and it was exploited by Vichy, who argued that it revealed the true nature of 'perfidious Albion'.

For the British, the attack was the dreadful result of Vichy's refusal to put the fleet – the most powerful in the Mediterranean – out of the reach of the Nazis by sailing the ships to British ports or to the West Indies, or by scuttling them.[13] In keeping with widespread French revulsion, de Gaulle called the attack a 'deplorable and detestable' occurrence, but he bravely justified it: 'There cannot be the slightest doubt,' he said on the BBC, 'that, on principle and of necessity, the enemy would have used them against Britain or against our own Empire. I therefore have no hesitation in saying that they are better destroyed.'[14] Tragic and deplorable Mers-el-Kebir may have been, but there was a war going on, and Vichy and its supporters had placed themselves firmly on the side of the Nazis.[15]

On 21 October, after the Nazis' failure to win the Battle of Britain, and as the London Blitz began, Churchill broadcast in the BBC's evening slot, speaking French with a thick English accent. In a slow, grandfatherly tone, he encouraged the French to keep faith with the British, held out the prospect of American intervention and made one of his typically bold statements:

> Here in London, which Herr Hitler says he will reduce to ashes, and which his aeroplanes are now bombarding, our people are bearing up unflinchingly. Our air force has more than held its own. We are waiting for the long-promised invasion. So are the fishes.[16]

Churchill's broadcast made a huge impact. A teacher of English in a Versailles lycée instructed his pupils to take down as much as they could make out through the interference, and the following day the speech was reconstructed, in its entirety, in the classroom. In Marseilles a typist took down the speech in shorthand, then typed it up and circulated it around her office for those who had missed it. On a more personal level, the response of Simone Martin-Chauffier's family, huddled around the radio in Paris, was typical. They laughed at Churchill's joke about the fishes, and young Claudie said: 'It was marvellous, wasn't it, Mummy? And he spoke French! I love the English accent.'[17]

At around the same time as Churchill made his speech, Jean Texcier was overjoyed to hear the BBC broadcast extracts from his 'Hints to the Occupied', a copy of which had made its way across the Channel. One of the key bits of Texcier's advice – that people should stoke up their anger, rather than express it immediately – had been echoed by Churchill. Much to Simone Martin-Chauffier's irritation, Churchill had suggested that those in the Occupied Zone should wait for a lead from the Free Zone – where conditions were easier – before they took action. But within a month Churchill and Texcier would learn that young Parisians were not prepared either to wait for Vichy or to simply contain their anger.

\*

Four months after fighting ceased on French soil, the reality of the Occupation began to sink in. The war was turning into a long-drawn-out conflict, and the Nazis were not going to be leaving soon. Worse, they were sucking the country dry. No sooner had the portraits of Hitler been hung on office walls than the Nazi bureaucracy set about meticulously cataloguing French economic and military resources – in both Zones – in order to pillage them. For example, they found 363,000 tons of non-ferrous metals; within seven months, over half was shipped to Germany. Ten thousand of France's most advanced machine tools were dispatched to help the Nazi war effort – 'No available machines that are necessary to Germany must remain in France' went the order. Production in France was increasingly focused on German military needs. Any commercial order to a French company that related to supplies for the German armed forces had priority over all other orders. And the Nazis were good customers – in the first three months of the Occupation, they placed over 12 billion francs' worth of orders, forging strong ties with French industry.[18]

As a result of this reorientation of the French economy, and the effects of the sea war, rationing was imposed at the end of September. From the outset, the nominal amounts available for each person per week were low – 100 grammes of butter, 50 grammes of cheese and 2.5 kilogrammes of bread.[19] As the war continued, these amounts were gradually reduced – within three months the bread ration had been cut by fifteen per cent. Coffee soon disappeared completely, to be replaced by a vile brown concoction made from chicory and called 'national coffee'; on the other hand, Coca-Cola was still available in Parisian bars.[20]

Having a ration ticket was one thing, finding a shop with food was another. At the beginning of 1941 teacher Jean Guéhenno noted, 'Life in Paris is very difficult. We have ration tickets, but we can't buy anything with them. The shops are empty. At home, we have survived the last two weeks thanks to the gifts of friends,'[21] while twenty-year-old Liliane Jameson complained in her diary: 'It's virtually impossible to find butter, cheese or meat. Don't even mention fish. There are no fruit or vegetables.'[22] A week later Jameson was indulging in a food fantasy: 'Oh, to be able to eat an enormous plate of scrambled eggs with loads of butter, a pork chop and rind with lentils, and a chocolate mousse with bananas,' she wailed.[23] More seriously, the cumulative effects of malnutrition over the war years were devastating – mortality rates in the cities shot up, by twenty-four per cent in Paris, and fifty-seven per cent in Marseilles; children grew slowly, and puberty was delayed.[24] People took it in good heart, though: 'Let England win, we'll eat later,' wrote one correspondent to the BBC.[25]

By the beginning of November the politics of Pétain had a name, which the ageing Marshal proudly pronounced when he shook Hitler's hand at a widely publicized meeting at Montoire, about eighty miles south-west of Paris, on 24 October. Designed to seal the agreement between the two men, the meeting helped seal the Marshal's fate in history. 'It is in the spirit of honour, and to maintain the unity of France,' proclaimed Pétain, '. . . that I enter today upon the path of collaboration.' Collaboration. A new, insidious and shameful meaning had been given to the word. France began to divide into those who collaborated with the Nazis and those who would not. The country's future was being forged around two words: the one Pétain used – collaboration – and another, which was being spoken more and more often: resistance.

For many people on both sides of the demarcation line, the handshake at Montoire brought home the reality of Vichy's role in the Occupation and division of France. Many of those who had nurtured the hope that Pétain was simply biding his time, preparing to turn the tables on the Nazis, began to admit what had been obvious to the most clear-sighted. Pétain was Hitler's willing ally. With Pétain now openly siding with the Nazis, and all the political parties either hopelessly split or compromised by their support for him (or, in the case of the Communists, their support for the Stalin–Hitler pact), the implication was plain: if anything was to be done, then ordinary people were going to have to do it on their own.

The first indication of this profound mood change appeared in the run-up to Armistice Day – 11 November. Since 1919 this had been a public holiday marked by solemn commemorations of the terrible impact of the First World War. Nearly 1.7 million French people lost their lives in the 1914–18 conflict, including 300,000 civilians, while 3.5 million soldiers were wounded – over a million men lost a limb. In Paris the Tomb of the Unknown Soldier in the Place de l'Étoile, underneath the Arc de Triomphe, was the traditional focus of the commemorations. In 1940, with Nazi troops goose-stepping in the streets of the capital, the event threatened to become a focus for anti-German feeling. Four days after the Pétain–Hitler handshake at Montoire, the head of the Paris police wrote a confidential report in which he warned of difficult times ahead: 'There is talk of demonstrating on 11 November . . . Montoire has already had an effect: it has stimulated Gaullist propaganda amongst the students.'[26]

The military commander of Paris grew increasingly concerned, and on 9 November he decided to ban any commemoration. The 11th of November was to be an ordinary day, with work and school as usual. Predictably, this decision merely inflamed matters. In the week before 11 November school students in the Paris lycées (high schools) had circulated handwritten leaflets and stickers, calling on their comrades to boycott classes that day, and to go to the Place de l'Étoile at 5.30 p.m. On the evening of 10 November the BBC called on people to join the demonstration. Fourteen-year-old Micheline Bood heard about the plans, and, with the insouciance of youth, wrote in her diary: 'That'll be fun! If it all kicks off, we'll go to jail! No more homework, no more teachers, no more detention! That'd be great.'[27] As it turned out, the demonstration was even more important than Micheline's girlish excitement suggested: it represented the first collective stirring of resistance to the Nazi Occupation.

In the day before 11 November meetings were held in the lycées to mobilize for the demonstration, and students were sent to neighbouring schools and to the university, calling on their comrades to join the movement. Already, students close to the Communist Party had been calling for a demonstration as part of their campaign to free Professor Paul Langevin, a world-renowned physicist at the Sorbonne, who had been arrested on 31 October. But when Armistice Day finally came around, it was the Paris lycées that provided most of the participants. This was a day for teenagers.

The events unfolded in three phases. First, throughout the day well-behaved mourners paid their respects at the Tomb of the Unknown Soldier underneath the Arc de Triomphe, and at the statue of Clemenceau, halfway up the Champs-Elysées. Clemenceau had been Prime Minister at the end of the First World War, and for many was a symbol of France's victory over Germany. According to the French police, around 20,000 people laid over 1,800 bouquets and around 60 wreaths during these ceremonies, which were tolerated by both the French and German authorities.

Then, in mid-afternoon, several hundred lycéens from schools near the Place de l'Étoile disobeyed their headmasters and simply walked out of their schools. An impromptu march towards the Arc de Triomphe was headed by a group of students from the Lycée Janson de Sailly, singing the 'Marseillaise' as they marched along the boulevard. Sensing the potential for trouble, shopkeepers hastily pulled down their shutters. These students were led by two lads carrying a floral Lorraine cross – the double-barred cross that was the symbol of de Gaulle's Free French, and which the florist had gone to great pains to colour red, white and blue, the colours of the French tricolour. As they arrived at the Arc de Triomphe, the two young men were caught in a pincer movement with French police on one side and German troops on the other. Before dashing off, they managed to lay the floral cross on the Tomb, then skipped away from the truncheons of the French police. The Nazi troops removed the cross immediately.

As night fell and the November air thickened with damp before turning to rain, matters became more serious. Up to 3,000 youngsters, mainly school students, gradually gathered near the statue of Clemenceau. In a shambling, disorganized way, they drifted on to the Champs-Elysées and began marching towards the Arc de Triomphe. As they marched, they shouted 'Vive la France', 'Vive l'Angleterre', 'Down with the Hun'. There was still a festive atmosphere – one joker carried two fishing rods, which he waved above his head, shouting 'Vive!' This was a schoolboy pun – a word for fishing rod is 'gaule', so the young lad was effectively saying, 'Long live de Gaulle!'[28]

As they neared the Place de l'Étoile the crowd passed a brasserie called Le Tyrol, which acted as the headquarters for Jeune Front ('Youth Front'), a fascist youth organization. There was shouting and about a hundred demonstrators surged into the bar, ripping down German posters and chasing after the young fascists. More yelling, whistling and gesticulating followed as scuffles broke out with the police, who piled in after the demonstrators. Then, shortly after 6 p.m., right next to the Place de l'Étoile, the German soldiers moved in. Troop cars and lorries were driven into the crowd, sending people running away, pinning some against the railings. Covered lorries parked in the surrounding streets suddenly spewed out grey-uniformed soldiers, who spread out across the boulevards, while the gates to the Métro station slammed shut. The protesters were trapped. Micheline Bood got her wish: it all 'kicked off'.

The troops charged with fixed bayonets, and shots were fired into the air.[29] The crowd shivered and squirmed away, like a shoal of fish escaping from a predator. Stun grenades were fired, dazing some students and wounding others as shrapnel flew through the rain. Pierre Lefranc was hit in the leg and bolted down the road like a rabbit, while his comrade, Jean Colson, was chased into a doorway and then coldly shot in the thigh by a German NCO. Édouard Martin was brought to the ground, beaten with rifle butts, and then stabbed. Eighteen-year-old Michel Tagrine, a student at the music conservatoire, had foolishly turned up with his violin; he was more concerned about keeping it safe than he was about protecting himself.

Edwige de Saint-Wexel, seventeen years old at the time, recalled the fear that streaked through the crowd like an electric shock:

A fusillade of shots rang out, mostly, I think, over our heads. But someone off to the left of me fell down. We panicked and began to run in all directions, squirming through the army and police lines. I saw an opening into the Avenue Kléber and scurried through like a mouse into a hole in the wall. I ran down the avenue, dodged into the side streets as though demons were after me. I've never been so frightened.[30]

Some of the youngsters stood their ground and fought back. Micheline Bood described the scenes in her diary:

Some Huns had been wounded in the fighting and ambulances were called. The French were elated, the Huns were miserable. And then we bumped into a group of people who were playing with a German officer like he was a punching-ball. They were hitting him over and over again, swearing at him with each blow . . . Yvette and I were jubilant . . . tough on him, but he's a Hun.[31]

Overall, however, the Nazis had the upper hand and were able to snuff out the first signs of a riot, smashing heads, breaking noses, clubbing necks. When Pierre-André Dufetel grabbed a soldier's rifle and started tussling with him, or when René Chuzeville hurled himself at an officer who was slapping a young girl, overwhelming numbers of Nazi reinforcements soon put an abrupt and violent end to attempts to fight back.

By 7 p.m. the streets were clear. A hundred and forty-three people had been arrested, the vast majority of them school students. Taken to a military prison, they were beaten, slapped, dragged by their hair and made to stand in a courtyard all night in the pouring rain, with their hands on their heads. Some were lined up against a wall by a group of soldiers pretending to be a firing squad. This macabre piece of intimidation was halted by a German general, who stared, amazed, at the scene and exclaimed: 'But they are just children!'

The youngest demonstrators were released that night, but around a third of those arrested had to wait until the beginning of December, while others were held until Christmas. Even after the demonstration, the arrests continued. The university was closed, and all the students in Paris had to report to the police each day. Edwige de Saint-Wexel was questioned as to her whereabouts on 11 November. She lied, saying she was at the library. The police discovered this was untrue, then searched her apartment, where they found leaflets and her diary, 'filled with anti-German sentiments'. Two SS men beat her, stubbed out lighted cigarettes on her chest and temples, scarring her for life, then threw her into a cell:

> They kept me there in that cellar from November through February 1941. It was three months, but I had no concept of time. I lived like an animal, unwashed, famished, lapping up my own soup, no one to talk to, no idea what was happening, nor orientation beyond my cell. It was like living in a cold, black hell. I was less than human.[32]

Inevitably, some who had nothing to do with the demonstration were caught up in the wave of repression. In evening of 10 November a twenty-eight-year-old engineer, Jacques Bonsergent, was on his way back from a wedding party, together with a group of friends. Leaving the Gare Saint-Lazare in the dark of the blackout, they bumped into a group of German soldiers. An accidental collision turned into a mini brawl, and a soldier was punched. In the confusion, Bonsergent's friends managed to get away, but he was arrested, beaten and thrown in prison when he refused to give the Nazis the names of his friends. After being held incognito for nineteen days, he was taken to court, tried in a single day and sentenced to death 'for an act of violence against a member of the German army'. Despite hopes that his sentence would be commuted, Bonsergent was executed on 23 December.[33] Various explanations have been put forward to explain the severity of the sentence – a warning to the population after the events of 11 November, a squabble between the Gestapo and the German army over who was in charge of repression in Paris, or Nazi fury with Vichy, where Hitler's favourite, Pierre Laval, was first kicked out of the government, then arrested before being released under pressure from Berlin. Whatever the case, the message was clear: the Nazis were determined to crush all opposition.

Despite the viciousness of the Nazi reprisals, the demonstration of 11 November was a watershed. It showed everyone – the Nazis, Vichy, the

British, the Americans, de Gaulle and, most important, the French themselves – that resistance was possible, and that the French would not simply accept the Occupation and division of their country. Micheline Bood, high on rebellion, sensed the importance of the event when she scribbled euphorically in her diary as soon as she got home:

> Right now, it's seven o'clock. They are fighting on the Avenue d'Alma, with grenades and rifles. Ah, my friends! There will be some terrible reprisals! But I can say 'I WAS THERE!'[34]

*

As the first mourners turned up at Clemenceau's statue on the morning of 11 November, they were amazed to see, propped up against the base, a metre-long visiting card, in the name of General de Gaulle. It was quickly whisked away by the French police, although not soon enough to stop word of its magical presence spreading through the city. That stunt was the work of far-left lawyer André Weil-Curiel and of Léon-Maurice Nordmann, who was a member of an underground group called Avocats Socialistes (Socialist Lawyers). But Weil-Curiel was not simply a pro-Gaullist socialist prankster; he had been sent to France as a Gaullist agent – a spy.

When de Gaulle arrived in London in June 1940, he was virtually alone. With few exceptions, the generals, admirals and ministers stayed firmly at Pétain's side while the company directors and the heads of the banks knew there was money to be made in France, not London. As a result, de Gaulle was the undisputed military and political figurehead of what was first called 'La France Libre' ('The Free French') and then, from 1942, 'La France Combattante' ('The Fighting French' – for simplicity's sake, the term 'Free French' will be used throughout this book). These official English terms reveal the gulf that separated de Gaulle's conception of what he was doing from that of his British allies. In each case the accurate translation should have been 'France', not 'French' ('Free France' and 'Fighting France'). De Gaulle considered, quite simply, that he and his supporters *were* France, and he did not have the slightest complex about saying so in public: 'We are France!' he would declare, leaving the listener to decide whether he was a visionary or merely delusional, and whether the 'we' was the royal plural or not.[35]

When de Gaulle began to set up his headquarters in London, he had so little in the way of material support that when the first French man asked to join, on June 19, de Gaulle had to ask him for a piece of paper to write down his name.[36] Even more than office space and paper, de Gaulle needed people. One of the first to join him was André Dewavrin, the twenty-nine-year-old naval officer who had returned to Brest at the moment of the fall of France. Dewavrin made his way to England and, at the end of June, met de Gaulle. He later recalled that at the end of their brief interview de Gaulle said:

> 'You will be head of military intelligence-gathering and operations. Goodbye. We will meet again soon.' The conversation was over. I saluted and left. The encounter was glacial and the only contact I felt with the General was his grey, piercing gaze.[37]

As Dewavrin freely admitted, he had not the slightest idea what being in charge of intelligence actually involved. He was a teacher at the military training school at Saint-Cyr, not a spy. But Dewavrin was a quick learner – his steely mind, his taste for manipulation and his absolute self-confidence all helped. He adopted a pseudonym, Passy (after a Paris Métro station) and, before the summer was out, enlisted the help of MI6 to send his first agents into France, on simple intelligence-gathering missions. Within a few months both men were able to return with valuable information about German coastal fortifications in the north-west, and with contacts that laid the basis for future intelligence operations.

Passy was on the far right of French politics – not a fascist, but not far off. His robust views, coupled with his taste for the shadow-play and deceit that were part and parcel of the world of espionage, meant that he was subsequently viewed with great suspicion by many in the Resistance. This distrust (which Passy positively revelled in) was reinforced by the clique conflicts and jealousies that split the small group of French exiles in London. As a result of this infighting and squabbling, one section of the Free French often did not know what another was doing. Weil-Curiel's mission was an example of this kind of secret within a secret.

Weil-Curiel's orders came from de Gaulle's chief assistant, Claude Hettier de Boislambert. He was to gauge the public mood, and to persuade writers, intellectuals and trade unionists – the kind of people he knew from before the war – to come to London.[38] For reasons that remain obscure, this mission was kept hidden from both Passy and British Intelligence. Weil-Curiel adopted the cover of a repatriated soldier and joined the thousands of French troops in Britain who eventually returned home. By the middle of August he was back in Paris, and within a few weeks he had come into contact with some of the first Resistance organizations.[39]

A member of one of those groups remembered how it all began:

> It was on a beautiful evening in July '40, on the Boulevard Montparnasse, that three friends discovered their mutual disgust at Pétainist cowardice and decided they had to prepare the fightback.[40]

Those three friends were left-wing intellectuals – Jean Cassou, Claude Aveline and Marcel Abraham. Barely a week after that discussion on the Boulevard Montparnasse, Cassou received a visit from his friend Agnès Humbert, who had just returned from Limoges. Humbert – 'an outgoing woman, impetuous and courageous,' said Cassou[41] – catalysed his vague sentiments into a concrete plan. As Humbert wrote in her diary that evening:

> Suddenly, I blurt out why I have come to see him, telling him that I feel I will go mad, literally, if I don't do something, if I don't react somehow . . . The only remedy is for us to act together, to form a group of ten like-minded comrades, no more. To meet on agreed days to exchange news, to write and distribute pamphlets and tracts, and to share summaries of French radio broadcasts from London. I don't harbour many illusions about the practical effects of our actions, but simply keeping our sanity will be success of a kind.[42]

At one level the Resistance really was that simple – ordinary people, who were angry, humiliated or ashamed, or all three at the same time, decided to change things, despite the fact that they had neither the experience nor the means to make things happen. They had the will, and that was enough. Jean Cassou later wrote: 'A moral revolt, a moral fact, was the key starting point for all *résistants*, the essence of the Resistance.' In the years that followed, the same scene – the same moral revolt, the same decision to act – took place over and over again, all over France.

Like all Resistance organizations, the small group set up by Cassou and Humbert grew through a series of friendships and chance meetings.[43] Cassou's friend, Paul Rivet, the director of the Musée de l'Homme in Paris, allowed the group to use the Musée's duplicator, and on 25 September 1940 they produced their first leaflet. The group soon expanded to include an anthropologist at the Musée, Germaine Tillion. She was already involved in resistance work through retired Colonel Paul Hauet, who ran a charity that helped French prisoners of war. When Tillion volunteered to help him, Hauet explained that they would also be organizing an escape network for French POWs. Over the next year their group in the east of France helped around 5,000 men return home.[44]

Tillion in turn recruited the Musée's librarian, Yvonne Oddon, and her fiancé, the Russian exile Anatole Lewitsky, who studied shamanism.[45] They then drew in one of the most dazzling, mercurial and tragic figures of the Resistance, the Russian anthropologist Boris Vildé. Tall, blond and well built, Vildé was born in St Petersburg in 1908, moving first to Estonia, then to Berlin, where he was jailed for anti-fascist activities. He arrived in Paris in 1932, where he married the daughter of a professor of history, and eventually worked at the Musée de l'Homme, studying Arctic peoples. Vildé made a striking impression on everyone he met – Agnès Humbert described his 'cool and luminous intelligence and his remarkable character',[46] while Simone Martin-Chauffier seems to have been in awe of him: 'He was there, so present and, at the same time, as absent as a god, a thinker, a lost child.'[47] It was Vildé's idea to produce a newspaper that would carry material from the international press, analyses of the political and military situation, and above all calls to action. That active orientation was reflected in the title they adopted: *Résistance*. Paul Rivet put his finger on the source of some of Vildé's ideas: 'Vildé is a son of the Revolution,' he said; 'he carries the Revolution within him, he understands how revolutions work.'[48] Whatever the case, Vildé soon became the leader of the group, and his ideas shaped its brief life.

The first issue of *Résistance* appeared on 15 December. It was only four pages long, and most of the articles dealt with the Nazi exploitation of France, the growth of anti-Semitism or the politics of the USA. What set *Résistance* apart from the rest of the early underground press was the rousing tone of the front-page editorial:

> Your immediate task is to get organized so that, when you receive the order, you can resume the struggle. Carefully recruit determined men, and give them the best leaders. Support and convince those who doubt or who have lost all hope. Seek out and keep watch on those who have disavowed the Nation and those that betray it . . . In accepting to be your leaders, we have sworn to sacrifice everything to this task, to be hard and pitiless. Yesterday we did not know each other; none of us were involved in the old party squabbles that took place in government or in the Assembly; we are independent, simply French, chosen for the action which we promise to carry out. We have only one ambition, one passion, one desire: to recreate France, pure and free.[49]

*Résistance* claimed to be the 'Bulletin officiel du Comité national de salut public' ('Official Bulletin of the National Committee of Public Safety'). This was a reference to the revolutionary committee created in 1793, but there was no highly organized group behind *Résistance*. The reality was far more prosaic. As Agnès Humbert imprudently wrote in her diary:

> We met in Louis Martin-Chauffier's office, where a minuscule fire was burning. How wonderful it felt not to be frozen: all four of us were thrilled by this touch of luxury. Simone Martin-Chauffier brought us a tray of tea – proper tea – with bread and butter. The atmosphere was snug and cosy. The men wrote and talked, while I typed up their articles.[50]

The tone adopted by Vildé in the editorial was a calculated gamble. A small minority of French people wanted to resist, to be given a plan of action – to be led. *Résistance* hoped to attract them, simply by claiming to be that leadership. Vildé adopted the same attitude with his own comrades, when he told them that they already had more than 12,000 armed men in Paris.[51] This was simply not true. Despite this boastful exaggeration, he had made an astonishing number of contacts in a very short time – even now, the full extent of his work is not known.[52]

In a matter of weeks Vildé made links with an escape network around Béthune in the north of France, which was run by a garage owner called Sylvette Leleu, together with a nun, Sister Marie-Laurence, and Madeleine de Gaulle, niece of the General. Leleu also introduced Vildé to her young trainee accountant, René Sénéchal. Sénéchal, also known as 'Le Môme' ('The Kid'), soon became Vildé's right-hand man, transporting documents and people across the demarcation line, making contacts in Toulouse, Marseilles, Bordeaux, Lyons and Perpignan. At around the same time, Vildé also recruited Albert Gaveau, an unemployed mechanic from Béthune who would soon be involved in much of the group's activity.

Through his father-in-law, Vildé met Robert Fawtier, Professor of Medieval History at the Sorbonne, who had established an intelligence circuit that included railway workers who provided information about troop movements. He also recruited society fashion photographer Pierre Walter, a good-looking man in his thirties, who shared an apartment with a pilot, Georges Ithier, in a flea-ridden Parisian hotel that doubled up as a knocking shop for prostitutes servicing the Nazi army. While the troops were getting their kicks on the second floor, Ithier and Walter organized the duplication of *Résistance* and helped Vildé set up a series of safe houses and an escape route across the Pyrenees.

This bewildering array of contacts reinforced Vildé's charismatic reputation and made even his closest comrades wonder about how extensive the group was. Simone Martin-Chauffier wrote:

Sometimes I wondered how many of us there might be – Dozens? Hundreds? Thousands? And how many groups like ours were there? Did anyone know? Did we all depend on some leader, who was pulling the strings from afar?[53]

Agnès Humbert was certain there was something going on, but she was unsure exactly what it was:

> Vildé is in contact with an organization of major influence. The Intelligence Service? The Deuxième Bureau [Vichy Intelligence], or perhaps another French group born out of present circumstances? We have no idea, and we all know that we mustn't ask questions. We have put our trust in Vildé and we must be guided by him.[54]

Germaine Tillion was slightly less enthusiastic:

> I personally felt I had to consider the English as allies, and act accordingly – which did not stop me from feeling a certain disgust at the idea of seeing our resistance activities coordinated from London by the Intelligence Service.[55]

The exact details of Vildé's connections with British Intelligence – if any – are not known (all MI6 archives are permanently closed).[56] But by whatever route, information collected by the Musée de l'Homme network found its way back to London. Some of this intelligence turned out to be extremely important. A sociologist at the Musée de l'Homme, René Creston, had friends in Brittany who gave him drawings of the German submarine pens at Saint-Nazaire, and of the immense dry dock – the biggest on the Atlantic coast. These drawings were sent to London and used as part of the planning for Operation CHARIOT, which took place in March 1942 when a British destroyer loaded with explosives was rammed into the dock gates. The charges were on timers to enable the crew to escape; the ship eventually exploded as she was being inspected by German officers who thought that the attack had failed.[57] In the hours before the explosion, intense fighting left 169 British troops dead, along with 16 French civilians. Two young boys, Henry Thibaud and Michel Savary, recalled what happened:

> Around four in the morning we heard artillery fire. From the window we could see cars in the street – we quickly got dressed. My father opened the front door, but two Huns said 'Get back in!' Everyone in the build-

ing came down into the hall. An Algerian who lived on the first floor said, 'The British have landed with a small boat and a big boat full of explosives. It has broken down the dock gates.' My father went out on his bike. But he was arrested. The Huns came and searched our house. They asked everyone for their papers, then they left. The next morning when we went outside, there was blood all over the streets. The Germans were armed with rifles, grenades and machine guns. Suddenly a lorry went past in the Rue de Méan, and I saw it was full of British prisoners. They made a 'V' sign with their fingers, which meant victory.[58]

The captured soldiers were right: the dry dock had been put out of action for the rest of the war. As a result, the largest German battleship – the *Bismarck* – could not be used in the Atlantic sea war, and U-boat activity in the North Atlantic was severely affected.

Producing an underground newspaper merely endangered those brave or foolhardy enough to be involved. But intelligence work could lead to the loss of innocent lives. Agnès Humbert struggled with this moral dilemma as she trudged her way through the slush-filled Parisian streets at the end of 1940. She had the possibility of getting information about a German airstrip to the north of Paris, but realized the potential implications. As she wrote in her diary:

> Because of my meddling, there will be widows, inconsolable mothers, fatherless children . . . As a direct result of my meddling, people – French people, living peaceful lives – will be killed and wounded, children maimed. Where are all my lofty humanitarian ideals now?[59]

But then, as she walked past the Gare de l'Est, Humbert saw two German officers striding towards the station, and the full reality of the Occupation struck home:

> Trudging in front of them are three porters weighed down with packages: bolts of cloth with I don't know how many shoeboxes tied on to them with string. Suddenly I am reminded of one of those old colonial newsreels – *Afrique vous parle* ('Voice of Africa') or some such – with those long processions of 'native bearers' carrying the baggage of

two or three white explorers, or exploiters. A pitiful sight, it always made my heart contract with pain. And now, as I stand in the slush outside the station watching this same spectacle unfold, the same but even more sordid, I am rooted to the spot. We simply have to stop them, we can't allow them to colonize us, to carry off all our goods on the backs of our men while they stroll along, arms swinging, faces wreathed in smiles, boots and belts polished and gleaming. We can't let it happen. And to stop it happening we have to kill. Kill like wild beasts, kill to survive. Kill by stealth, kill by treachery, kill with premeditation, kill the innocent. It has to be done, and I will do it.[60]

*

The activity of the people around Vildé began to attract the attention of the Nazis. The first sign came when Weil-Curiel had to return to England. Vildé knew Weil-Curiel through Nordmann, who distributed *Résistance*; at the end of December Vildé persuaded a Breton fisherman to take the Free French agent back across the Channel, and sent Gaveau along to see that all went well. But the Germans raided the boat, arresting the fisherman. Luckily, the two *résistants* managed to escape – Weil-Curiel to the Mediterranean, Gaveau to Paris.[61] Then in February the police raided the site where the second issue of *Résistance* was being duplicated, discovering a list with the names of the people to whom it was to be delivered. At the top of the list was Nordmann. A couple of days later he was arrested as he travelled with Gaveau, who again managed to escape. As the Resistance became more experienced and more professional, Gaveau's repeated 'luck' would be seen as suspect, but Vildé's group was extremely naive.

Worried that the noose was tightening around the group, Yvonne Oddon and Anatole Lewitsky persuaded Vildé to leave Paris for the Non-Occupied Zone. They should have heeded their own advice: a couple of weeks later they were arrested by the Gestapo in a night raid on their apartment. Earlier that evening the Nazis had ransacked the Musée de l'Homme, having been tipped off about the Saint-Nazaire plans. They were closing in. From the other side of the demarcation line, Vildé got a message through to Claude Aveline, ordering him to leave Paris;

Cassou was also on the point of leaving. The editorial board of *Résistance* was falling apart, but there was no question of stopping work. Agnès Humbert asked Pierre Brossolette, a talented young left-wing journalist who had stopped writing at the beginning of the Occupation, to break his self-imposed silence and join the group. Brossolette eventually agreed, making a decision that would change his life.

One evening in March Agnès Humbert was producing the next issue of *Résistance*, written entirely by Brossolette. They no longer had access to a duplicator, so Humbert had to type as many copies as she could. There was a knock at the door, and there was Vildé, grinning broadly. 'You're mad,' she said. 'I had to come back,' he replied. Things had gone badly in the south – The Kid and Ithier had been arrested – and Vildé felt he had to return to reorganize the group. This was another mistake. On 26 March Vildé had lunch with Walter and Gaveau, and then left to see Simone Martin-Chauffier, who was going to get him some false papers. He never arrived: the Gestapo arrested him on the way. Three weeks later Humbert was arrested at her house as she typed a leaflet. Shortly afterwards, Walter and his girlfriend were eating with Albert Gaveau; Gaveau complained of feeling ill and left. A few minutes later the Gestapo arrested Walter and his girlfriend. *Résistance* was dead.

For nine months the Nazis prepared the trial of what later became known as the Musée de l'Homme group.[62] They had been betrayed by Gaveau, who had been working for the Nazis from the moment he had been recruited by Vildé.[63] But the Nazis were not able to penetrate any further into the nebulous network of groups in which Vildé and his comrades were involved. They got *Résistance* and the Béthune escape network, but not Abraham, Aveline, Brossolette, Cassou, Fawtier, Hauet, Simone Martin-Chauffier or Germaine Tillion. As the Nazi judge, Ernst Roskothen, complained: 'We knew everything that Gaveau knew and absolutely nothing else.'[64]

The trial, which began in Fresnes prison in January 1942, was a strange affair. Although the prosecutor was a caricature of a sneering, anti-Semitic Nazi second-rater, happy to lie and to bully, the rest of the Germans maintained a quiet dignity. Roskothen, by all accounts an honest man doing a dishonest job, was determined to follow the book, and a mutual respect between the judge and the nineteen accused soon set in. The members of the network were overjoyed to see each other again, and a kind of festive atmosphere developed at certain points. Many of the prisoners felt an odd pleasure at the number of people who had been charged – it showed that they had been involved in something substantial. As Agnès Humbert put it: 'There are so many of us! Many people I don't know at all.'[65]

At the end of the trial, five of the accused were acquitted, three received prison sentences and Agnès Humbert was sentenced to deportation. The remainder, including three women, were sentenced to death. The last to be sentenced was Vildé. After the sentence was passed, he pleaded that Sénéchal, The Kid, should be spared.[66] Then, remarkably, Vildé asked to shake hands with the judge. Roskothen was so moved by this request for reconciliation from a man he had just condemned to death that he had to hurry from the room to vomit. The prisoners, meanwhile, seemed to enter another world. They hugged each other, joked about the future and were philosophical about their fate. 'We can't complain, we gambled, we knew the risks, and we lost. Tough on us – but there will be others who will continue our work,' said Nordmann.[67] The clerk of the court – a German soldier – went up to Vildé and said he hoped he would be spared. Vildé laughed, took the German's hands and swung their arms back and forth, making both men giggle. But despite the bonhomie of the courtroom, the Nazi death machine was relentless. Although the three women had their sentences commuted to deportation, on a cold afternoon on 22 February 1942 the seven men were taken up to Mont Valerien, an army hill fort to the west of Paris, where they were executed. At his own request, Vildé was the last to be shot.

During his long months in prison, Vildé had written in a notebook, trying to make sense of what was happening to him. His thoughts give an insight into his motivations, and those of many other *résistants*:

I love France. I love this beautiful country. Yes, I know it can be small-minded, selfish, politically rotten and a victim of its old glory, but with all these faults it remains enormously human and will not sacrifice its stature and its human sentiment . . . For the true France to be reborn one day, sacrifices will be needed. Believe me, there are no useless sacrifices . . . We must know how to wear our destiny like a crown.[68]

\*

In September 1944 Vildé's comrade Claude Aveline returned to liberated Paris and wrote an article about the Musée de l'Homme group, entitled 'Souvenirs des Ténèbres' ('Memories of Shadows'). It concluded:

I write these notes by candle-light, deep in an immense silence, in the room where, nearly four years ago, by a wood fire . . . the three founding friends, helped by a faithful accomplice and her typewriter, produced *Résistance* . . . Here it is, once again, on my table, four duplicated pages that we saw born with such satisfaction and pleasure! Vildé came round in the early afternoon, bringing raw material – English, American and Swiss newspapers. We worked joyfully until evening. Then he would come back, or would send round gentle Lewitsky, his colleague from the Musée de l'Homme and his lieutenant. They took our manuscripts to unknown destinations and unknown duplicators. Some of these mysteries have since been revealed, but not all . . .

But then the arrests began . . . I can't bring myself to tell the rest of the story. Vildé's unreal arrest, the endless run-up to the trial – a whole year – the ten death sentences, Fresnes prison, Mont Valerien, Vildé asking to die last. I can see him now, solid, sure of himself, sitting square in the plush-covered armchair he liked so much; X . . ., of whom we have had no news for so many months; Cassou, who has just been wounded in Toulouse; our secretary, our friend, whom the Gestapo sent to the depths of Germany – is she still alive? One man alone has returned to this first battlefield. Alone, with this duplicated sheet, this tiny candle-flame, and this heart – full of joy, broken by sadness.[69]

# 3

# *Lighting the Fuse*

In the middle of July 1940, in the heat of the Côte d'Azur, a man who looked like a cross between Clark Gable and Peter Cushing lounged on a bed in a Cannes hotel room, smoking opium. He was a gadfly socialist journalist and ex-naval lieutenant named Emmanuel d'Astier de la Vigerie. In the room with him were his brother and a friend. The two men listened intently as the drug-addled d'Astier outlined a plan to set up a group that would oppose the Nazi Occupation. His friend was embarrassed:

> I completely agreed with him; I desperately wanted to join an organization. But although his ideas were remarkably brilliant and logical, he was presenting them while lying down smoking opium! It seemed so absurd to throw my lot in with a *résistant* who had such a weakness that I refused.[1]

About three weeks later, and not far away, Captain Henri Frenay was snug in his mother's house at Sainte-Maxime near Saint-Tropez, having escaped from the Germans at the beginning of the month. Bitter at the scale of the defeat, but convinced that Pétain was preparing to attack the Germans, Frenay sat in his bedroom, listening to the cicadas chirping in the trees and writing a manifesto for the future of France. Before the war, Frenay's views had appeared unusually radical for a career officer – due mainly to the influence of his lover, feminist socialite Berty Albrecht. But stunned by the incredible shock of the fall of France, the infantry captain reverted to type. His manifesto proclaimed that

France's enemies were Germans, Bolsheviks, Freemasons and Jewish capitalists, affirmed a 'passionate attachment' to the work of Marshal Pétain and closed by hoping that 'Marshal Pétain lives long enough to support us with his great authority and his incomparable prestige'.[2]

These inauspicious beginnings – the dreams of an opium addict and the far-right ravings of an elitist officer – led directly to the creation of the two main resistance groups in the south, Libération and Combat. Over the next four years, d'Astier and Frenay, so different in their origins and outlooks, repeatedly clashed over the orientation and actions of the Resistance. Their first task, however, was to face reality and actually start resisting.

Most Resistance movements followed the same pattern – a handful of friends got together, decided they had to 'do something' and then eventually found a way of producing stickers, leaflets or a newspaper. The exact number of such groups is unknown and unknowable, but over 1,100 different publications have been recorded, the vast majority with tragically brief existences.[3] Frenay's group was different – after writing his ill-considered manifesto, he did not worry about publicizing it but instead drew up a structure for his organization, with all the precision of a military commander. According to this schema, the group would be divided into three sections: Recruitment, Propaganda and Action. Frenay's first task was therefore to recruit fellow thinkers, which he did in the most guileless and melodramatic fashion:

> Whenever I met someone, I would start the same conversation. I would sound out his feelings about England and Hitler's Germany. I would acquaint him with my personal conviction that Germany would lose the war . . . I would then pause to get my interlocutor's reaction. If it seemed sympathetic, I would go still further. 'Men are already gathering in the shadows. Will you join them?'[4]

With this bold approach, Frenay was able to recruit a handful of comrades in both Zones. They first produced a typewritten *Bulletin*, containing news items from the BBC and the foreign press, then in spring 1941 they came into contact with a group in the Nord-Pas-de-Calais which produced a paper called *Les Petites Ailes de France* ('The

Little Wings of France'), in reference to an underground newspaper produced during the German occupation of 1914–18. Frenay took over this title in the first of a confusing series of name changes: in what remained of the year, he changed the paper's title three more times – first to *Vérité* ('Truth'), then to *Vérités* ('Truths') before eventually settling on its final title, *Combat*.

During this period d'Astier, shocked by the brush-off from his friend after the meeting in Cannes, kicked his opium habit. By November he had convinced one other person to set up a group called La Dernière Colonne (The Last Column).[5] At the beginning of December d'Astier was sitting in a café in Clermont-Ferrand, indiscreetly discussing how to fight the Nazis, when two philosophy teachers sitting at the next table chipped in. They were Lucie Samuel (later known as Lucie Aubrac) and Jean Cavaillès, and they soon joined d'Astier's group. By the end of the year, d'Astier had assembled a strange collection that included his niece, a journalist, a wealthy businessman who was allegedly in contact with British Intelligence, a film actor and a physician.

Despite this range of talents, the group had little idea about what it should actually do beyond scrawling slogans on walls and in public urinals. At one point they carried out a minor sabotage action that would have cost them dear had they been discovered. As Lucie Aubrac recalled:

> . . . we learned that a sugar train was coming in from Spain, headed for Germany. We found out from friends in the marshalling yards where the Spanish freight was being parked. Then, at night, armed with oilcans, we crawled up like Indians and surrounded the sugar train, broke open the freight doors, and began injecting oil into the sacks of sugar. I suppose it was infantile, but it made us feel good to be taking direct action and it showed us what we were capable eventually of doing.[6]

The height of La Dernière Colonne's activity came at the end of February 1941, when they decided to put up 10,000 anti-collaboration stickers in six towns on the same night. All went well, except in Nîmes, where the police arrested four glue-covered students. Within a couple of days d'Astier's niece, Bertrande, was arrested and eventually sentenced to thirteen months in jail. As a result, d'Astier arrived at the same conclusion as Frenay, and decided that a more security-conscious internal structure was needed, with cells of three or four members and little contact between them. The group also realized that they needed a public face – Cavaillès, who by this time had moved to Paris, had come into contact with a newspaper called *Libération* and was very impressed. D'Astier and his comrades decided to adopt the same name for their publication, which first appeared in July 1941.

The northern *Libération* was created by Christian Pineau and a group of trade unionists. The first issue, which appeared on 1 December 1940, was typed up using carbon paper and had a print-run of seven (one of which was carefully stored in a bottle, for the sake of posterity). Through a great deal of effort and discipline, Pineau's group was able to produce the paper every week until the end of the Occupation. They eventually got access to a duplicator, and by the end of 1941 the circulation of *Libération* had increased to a hundred, with small groups distributing the paper in Paris, Normandy and Brittany.[7] The newspaper was sent anonymously to potential contacts, and Pineau was delighted when he eventually received a copy himself.

The publication that most reflected the material difficulties faced by the Resistance was *Valmy*,[8] a little newspaper that was produced using a toy printing set. The small group of friends who published *Valmy* had assembled around 2,000 tiny rubber characters, which they had to set painstakingly in a small block. Each night, 'Paul Simon' (real name Paulin Bertrand) would compose four lines and print them on to each sheet, in an infuriatingly slow process that will be familiar to anyone who played with one of these toys as a child. In 1942 Simon complained: 'You try looking on a dark floor for a thin piece of rubber that has sprung out of your tweezers and has bounced some distance from where it fell.'[9] The first issue – really more of a leaflet than a newspaper – had a print-run of fifty copies and took a month to produce. Although *Valmy* was extremely amateurish, with corrections handwritten on each copy,[10] in some ways this only made its hostility to the Nazi Occupation more moving. In December 1941 Simon left for London as the police closed in; *Valmy* continued to appear without him until the beginning of 1943.

On both sides of the demarcation line, one figure dominated the outlook of the early Resistance: Pétain. Initially, most people shared Frenay's view that the Marshal was carrying out some kind of ruse and was preparing to turn on Hitler. The most graphic, but secret, expression of these illusions occurred within what remained of the French army in Vichy France. A handful of army officers stashed arms in the hills, ready for the day when Pétain would turn against the Germans. For these people, de Gaulle was a criminal and Pétain was their true leader. Because of this widely held belief in the Marshal, Resistance publications went to great pains not to alienate their readers by attacks on him. But by spring 1941 the growing evidence of the meaning of collaboration led to a slow change in public opinion, and *Libération* felt able to write:

Until recently, the people of France could still be favourably inclined to believe in the value and good will of the Marshal; now there can be no hesitation: the head of state supports his Prime Minister's treason . . . Through greed or senility, Marshal Pétain is betraying France.[11]

These illusions in Pétain, now so difficult to understand, were shared by British and American diplomats. Well into 1941, the Foreign Office continued to try to come to a secret agreement with Pétain, while Washington was certain that Pétain was fundamentally hostile to Hitler. In April 1941 US Secretary of State Cordell Hull claimed it was 'entirely necessary to hold the hands of the Pétain branch of the French Government at Vichy; . . . we have been struggling almost daily since the French Government left Paris to uphold that element in the French Government which opposed Hitlerism and Hitler'.[12]

The Americans were right to argue that the Vichy government was not at first a solid pro-Nazi block. Important sections of Pétain's first government – such as General Weygand – were anti-German and would not embrace the more extreme collaborationist positions. But the Americans were profoundly mistaken when they expected there would be a split in the Vichy regime, and were simply foolish when they imagined that Pétain would lead that split over to the Allied camp. Most of the

French military leaders were Anglophobic – this had been demonstrated in the weeks running up to the fall of France, and had been reinforced by the Royal Navy's attack at Mers-el-Kebir. Further evidence was provided in summer 1941, when General Groussard of the French army left Vichy to try to convince Churchill to come to an agreement with Pétain. When he returned from London, empty-handed, he was promptly arrested.[13] Vichy would have no truck with the British. Furthermore, from June 1940 onwards events repeatedly demonstrated that the real power within the 'French State' lay with the collaborationists, and that Pétain was at best a semi-senile dupe and at worst a willing figurehead. One of the most obvious signs was Vichy's attitude towards the Jews, which fused a specifically French anti-Semitic tradition with the ferocious anti-Semitism of the Nazis. In August 1940 Pétain abolished legislation against anti-Semitism, and in October the first Jewish Statute was adopted, which excluded Jews from most public offices, including teaching and running a newspaper. Nine months later a series of other forbidden professions was added to the list, including banking.[14] The implications of the handshake at Montoire were as clear as daylight, and even if they were not, Pétain's own declarations and actions should have sufficed.

However, although Vichy collaborated with the Nazis, it was formally an independent government. It even prosecuted Nazi spies – between January 1941 and June 1942, 698 suspected Nazi agents were arrested, and 30 were sentenced to death through the work of Vichy counter-intelligence.[15] This strange ambiguity was also reflected in the fact that sections of Vichy Intelligence (the 'Deuxième Bureau') and counter-Intelligence hedged their bets by maintaining contact with British Intelligence and even aided parts of the Resistance. Frenay worked for the Vichy Deuxième Bureau for about three months, before resigning in January 1941 when his position became intolerable. His contacts there gave him information, as well as access to a duplicator and even forged documents that enabled him to cross the demarcation line. But when they suggested they should control his group, he refused. Frenay rightly felt there should be a distinction between the untrustworthy shadow world of intelligence and the activities of a Resistance group.

None of the early Resistance movements had any particular confidence in de Gaulle. The attitude of *Libération-Nord* was typical. In February 1941 Pineau wrote:

General de Gaulle is currently one of the men who is fighting the Germans and we can only approve without hesitation his military action . . . Does that mean that we have a definite opinion about the political role General de Gaulle should or should not play after the British victory? Not in the slightest! . . . Let us not create any confusion in the minds of many French people by speaking of Gaullism or anti-Gaullism. We have only one party: France. We have only one enemy: Nazism. For the moment, everything else is secondary.[16]

At this stage, virtually the only Resistance publication to claim allegiance to de Gaulle was *Pantagruel*, which called on its readers to 'rally to General de Gaulle, who alone is maintaining the French traditions of heroism and of keeping your word'.[17] Like most early Resistance newspapers, *Pantagruel* merely wanted to inform its readers, not act as any kind of leadership. That was probably just as well, as the people behind *Pantagruel* seemed to have a slender grasp on reality. Pineau met them in 1941 and asked how many supporters they had. 'A million!' was their reply. As Pineau wearily recalled: 'in their enthusiasm, they expected the final moment, the great struggle, the general insurrection, for the summer. They wanted to act immediately, to get the equipment they needed, to draw up a battle plan.'[18]

Being a *résistant* was a risky business and required a huge amount of courage. But for those in the Occupied Zone, where the French police were aided by the Gestapo and the Wehrmacht, things were particularly difficult. Frenay, d'Astier and their comrades in the Non-Occupied Zone were subject only to the relatively less effective attentions of the Vichy police and counter-intelligence services. When Pineau made a journey south to Lyons, he was amazed at the conditions: 'The leaders of the Resistance walked around unhindered, had meetings in cafés or fine restaurants, not hiding in the slightest. It was almost as though they had visiting cards printed with their underground title.'[19] As a result, the *résistants* in the Occupied Zone were deeply suspicious of the potentially lethal amateurism of those from the south: for Pineau 'the most dangerous groups were those from the Free Zone – they ran fewer risks than us, and did not follow the prudent rules that we had adopted'.[20] This view was reinforced when Pineau eventually met Frenay in the middle of 1941:

> However attractive and brave he might be, he scared me because he wanted to know all about our activities – his approach was not appropriate to the situation in the Occupied Zone. His aide Robert had serious problems in Normandy, where a series of arrests had decimated the group he had built, all in a few days. By giving out arms too early, he had his comrades pointlessly shot.[21]

The lesson was clear: taking immediate action against the Nazis could have lethal consequences. Planning and disciplined organization would be the keys to success.

*

On both sides of the demarcation line, the French population was faced with the harsh effects of the Occupation. The responses of ordinary people to this reality – the way in which they struggled to survive despite the food and fuel shortages, their moral support for the Jews, or the help for single mothers whose husbands were held in Nazi prisoner of war camps – were all forms of Resistance. However, this is a recent view. At the time, 'Resistance' was generally seen in terms of action, either overt or clandestine. Inevitably, only a minority was involved in this classic form of Resistance: most ordinary people did not participate either because they did not know how to, or if they did know, their lives did not permit it.[22] However, protesting against the Occupation did not necessarily mean being involved in an underground organization. Towards the end of March 1941 Micheline Bood – still not fifteen years old – told her diary about a walk in Paris with her friend Yvette:

> The British radio has called on people to write V for victory everywhere, and they are all over the place, even on shop-fronts. They are also written on blackboards, on tables – everywhere. Even better,

there's a new badge: a V made with two crossed pins and worn on the lapel. Yvette and I counted seventy-five in five minutes! . . . On the Rue d'Astorg, I scribbled a V on a German car. I heard the sound of boots behind me, and moved off quickly. The Hun came up to us, looked at the mark on the car, turned towards Yvette and gave a huge grin. My God! We scribbled hundreds and hundreds of Vs! I would never have believed that it was so easy in broad daylight.[23]

Micheline's story is not as unlikely as it might sound. The German rank-and-file conscript soldiers were not all committed fascists – prior to Hitler's triumph in 1933, Germany had the largest Communist and Socialist Parties in the world. Some of those millions of left-minded workers were now in Paris, wearing the grey-green uniform of the Wehrmacht. Indeed, at the beginning of 1941 the Paris Gestapo reported: 'We can state with utter certainty that, among the soldiers of the Paris garrison and in the Paris region, there are many ex-Communists who, without any aid, are encouraging the work of demoralization.'[24]

Resistance Vs appeared all over the country,[25] while the BBC's adoption of the Morse code for V (ba-ba-ba-bom) as its signature provided an aural equivalent to the scrawled V. Teenager Marcel Gramme, riding home one evening on his bicycle, whistled 'ba-ba-ba-bom' as he went, and counted fourteen replies from open windows and passers-by.[26] The V campaign meant ordinary people could feel they were doing something, however symbolic, to protest against the Occupation.[27] The Nazi propagandists soon tried to turn this campaign to their own benefit and plastered the capital – including the side of the Eiffel Tower – with their own Vs, referring to Nazi victory.[28] But as Jean Guéhenno noted in his diary in mid-August:

German propaganda has vainly tried to take possession of the Vs. The battle continues, and there is no possible confusion. The German Vs are few in number, but are colossal; they sprawl over public buildings, on flags, on posters. The Vs of the Resistance, however, are tiny, but countless: Métro tickets folded into a V, matches broken into a V . . .[29]

Scrawling V, listening to the BBC or reading a Resistance publication was the closest most French men and women came to fighting the Nazis. People tried to lead ordinary lives, but the Occupation made that virtually impossible. Apart from the big issues – hundreds of thousands of Nazi troops occupying the north of the country, a nation split in two, nearly 2 million fathers and husbands locked up in Nazi prison camps – there was also the more immediate question of simply surviving. Hundreds of thousands of people had been made unemployed as war and the Occupation threw the country into a major economic crisis. At the beginning of the cold winter of 1940–41 there were 537,000 jobless in the Paris region alone. By the end of January there were 100,000 more. For those lucky enough to be in work, salaries were between twenty and forty per cent lower than 1939 levels.[30]

Low pay eventually led to one of the first signs of wide-scale opposition to the effects of the Nazi Occupation – a miners' strike that swept through the Nord-Pas-de-Calais in May to June 1941.[31] Before the war the region produced two-thirds of France's coal and twenty per cent of its electricity. When coal imports from Britain ceased after June 1940 – these had formed forty per cent of French annual consumption – coal from the Nord-Pas-de-Calais became even more important. The Nazis needed French industry to churn out food, supplies and equipment for the German armed forces. That in turn meant coal: to meet Berlin's targets, production had to increase by a quarter over 1938 levels. All that extra tonnage was to come from the huge coalfield that stretched in a 120-kilometre band between Lille and Arras. This whole region had been annexed by the Nazis and was under the direct control of their military headquarters in Brussels.

Today the mines are shut, and the spoil-heaps have been turned into ski slopes or secured and left like the pyramids of a dead civilization. But nearly sixty years ago the region was peppered with hundreds of pitheads, each surrounded by a pit village with a set of identical miners' cottages, dwarfed by the spoil-heaps. A spiderweb of railway lines spread across the flat land, taking the coal from pithead to coke plant and power station or off to coal-hungry industry. At the heart of this key part of the French economy were 140,000 miners with traditions of struggle that went far back into the nineteenth century.

The strike began when the mining companies tried to change the way in which miners' pay was calculated, junking over fifty years of wage agreements. The miners objected, adding to their grievances simple demands such as more soap and washing powder.[32] On Tuesday 27 May, at 11 a.m., workers 350 metres down in pit number 7 of the Dahomey colliery stopped work. Then the afternoon shift refused to get in the cage lifts. In less than a week the whole of the Nord-Pas-de-Calais coalfield was on strike. A hundred thousand miners were refusing to obey the managers and their Nazi masters. Coal supplies halted, and within ten days gas supplies to the Paris region were affected. All of French industrial production was threatened. Even more dangerously for the Nazis, local ceramic and engineering factories came out in solidarity, together with thousands of women textile workers and workers in the railway workshops.[33] What had begun as a minor economic issue was turning into a massive confrontation with the occupier.

When the Germans realized the scale of the movement, they brought in troops to protect the phone lines and electricity transformers. At the same time, intimidation was used across the region: troops occupied the pitheads; hundreds of random arrests terrorized the community; cafés, restaurants and cinemas were shut; and the sale of alcohol and tobacco was banned. Despite these measures, the strike was hugely popular. Calls for solidarity were spread by leaflets, word of mouth and above all by stickers – 'Live working or die fighting, that's also the slogan of the miners'. 'Arrests! The bosses who starve the workers should be arrested. For the workers, the right to strike is the right to life.'[34] There was nothing about the strike in the press, and even the BBC remained silent, although they knew about the movement. London apparently thought that this was a mere industrial conflict, with no implications for the war. They were wrong. Although the strike had begun over purely economic issues, with no political resonance and certainly no link to any Resistance group, everything about the movement – from its demands, through the way it was organized, to its implications – was shaped by the harsh reality of the Occupation and led implicitly to resistance against the Nazis who controlled the region.

Nazi repression caused the strike leaders to go into hiding. During a local strike earlier in the year, the miners' delegates had been arrested by Nazi troops when they tried to negotiate a settlement. To avoid this danger, the organizers of the May strike held secret meetings in the woods, communicated only through declarations signed in the name of miners who were no longer in the region, and above all did not appear in public. Since the men were threatened with arrest, miners' wives and daughters formed strike pickets at the pit gates and on the roads out of the miners' estates. The women intimidated strike-breakers in novel ways, trashing their gardens, or grabbing them and stripping them to their underwear. In response, the Nazis banned women from leaving their houses half an hour before and after each shift change. When the troops came to break up the pickets, they drove lorries into the crowds, shooting at the women demonstrators, wounding some. On other occasions they drenched the women with fire hoses, herded them into fields and made them stand under the baking summer sun for hours on end without food or water.[35] To help the Nazis break the strike, the mining companies used spies to record the names of women demonstrators; these lists were then handed to the Germans, who arrested the women and hauled them in front of emergency courts where many were sentenced to deportation. Conditions in the Nazi prison camps meant that this was often a death sentence.[36]

Despite the high levels of intimidation, the strike was so popular that the Nazi chain of control in the region began to break down. The French gendarmes became unreliable – for example, when a woman slapped a foreman at Mazingarbe, they stood by:

> Faced with the crowd of angry people who were present, we felt it was impossible to arrest this person . . . Given the agitation that continues to dominate the miners' estates, it seems unlikely that she will be arrested later. It is to be feared that the population would come and protest violently at the Commissariat.[37]

Local government leaders began to waver. Many refused to post Nazi declarations about the strike, and only one mayor in the whole region backed Vichy's call for a return to work. Although not strictly speaking an act of resistance, the strike not only undermined war production and united a community against the occupier, it also showed that the Nazis' grip on France could be weakened.

Unable to intimidate the miners back to work, the Nazis used the oldest strike-breaking technique: hunger. Special miners' rations were restricted to non-strikers, and pay for the second half of May was withheld. Whole villages began to suffer as shopkeepers, intimidated by the Nazis, refused credit to strikers. Having resisted the hundreds of arrests and deportations that destroyed families all over the coalfield, having even braved Luftwaffe planes swooping over the pit villages in threatening displays, the miners were eventually starved back to work.[38] By the night of 6 June the miners' leaders realized that the movement was crumbling and organized a mass return to work four days later. The Nazis refused any immediate concessions to the workers, while the mining companies were compensated by Vichy for their lost profits during the strike.[39] Eventually, food rations for the miners improved, and they also received extra soap and clothing. Finally, a week after the end of the strike, the Vichy government awarded a pay rise to all French workers, hoping to prevent any similar movements.

The mining community paid a terrible price for these meagre gains. Over 400 men and women had been arrested, of whom 270 were deported to Germany on the first of hundreds of trains that deported more than 150,000 French *résistants* and Jews to the concentration camps. Around half of the deported miners and their wives never returned. The strike showed that a profound change had taken place. A struggle over wages had revealed the grim reality of the Occupation. Throughout the strike the mining companies had worked hand in glove with the Nazis – they were more concerned with profits than with the German Occupation. Miners' leader Julien Hapiot wrote in an underground union paper: 'From now on, the Occupier knows that workers who suffer in misery will not always accept the yoke of national oppression.'[40] This view was shared by a Vichy civil servant who visited the region a month after the end of the strike and reported back glumly:

The day the tide turns against the government, a large number of weapons will appear in the hands of people who have been stocking them. The insurrection which would then take place would be both social and national.[41]

\*

Less than two weeks after the end of the miners' strike, there was a dramatic change in the war. Early in the morning of 22 June Hitler launched Operation BARBAROSSA, his long-planned attack against the Soviet Union which would lead to the deaths of around 20 million Soviet citizens and millions of Germans. Nearly seventy years later, the scale of the onslaught is still mind-boggling. The blitzkrieg against France was successful partly because of the audacity of the Nazi commanders and the concentration of mechanized power. The attack on the Soviet Union was to succeed by sheer weight of numbers. Over 3 million Axis soldiers attacked the USSR – over two-thirds of them from Nazi Germany – supported by 600,000 motor vehicles and around 625,000 horses.[42] The initial results were almost as spectacular as in France, but on a gargantuan scale. By the end of August 300,000 Soviet soldiers had been imprisoned after the fall of Minsk; a further 500,000 were killed or captured in mid-September following the fall of Kiev and the subsequent Nazi occupation of the Ukraine and the Donetz industrial basin. Things were going Hitler's way.

As Churchill instantly realized, Stalin was now the enemy of Britain's enemy, and was therefore her ally. An Anglo-Soviet treaty was duly signed on 12 July. Three days after the beginning of Operation BARBAROSSA, Roosevelt decreed that the Neutrality Act no longer applied to the USSR, enabling the US to begin arms sales. Ordinary people throughout Occupied Europe rejoiced, believing that Hitler, like Napoleon, would inevitably be defeated in Russia. Micheline Bood's diary entry was typical: 'From 5h05 this morning, Germany and Russia are at war. Isn't that fantastic? That's a mouthful it'll take the Huns a while to digest. Hope is reborn . . .'[43]

The thousands of French Communists were relieved they could finally oppose the Occupation openly.[44] Since the beginning of the war, many Communist Party members had been disorientated by the Stalin–Hitler pact. In June 1940, at Moscow's suggestion, their leaders had tried to get the Nazis to legalize the Party's newspaper, *L'Humanité*. Even the most loyal members were horrified. Young Communist Maroussia Naïtchenko was 'stupefied . . . stunned . . . nauseated'[45] when she heard about the discussions.[46] The terms 'Nazi' and 'fascist' were banished from Party publications in September 1939 (they began to reappear only at the beginning of 1941), while *L'Humanité* did not even mention the demonstrations of 11 November 1940.[47] As tensions grew between Stalin and Hitler in the first half of 1941, subtle shifts began to appear in the policies of the underground Communist Parties throughout Occupied Europe. By May *L'Humanité* was calling on the French people to fight for 'national liberation' and argued for the creation of 'a National Front for the independence of France'.[48] However, the Party remained completely hostile to de Gaulle, arguing he was a puppet of the British, with reactionary and colonialist aims.[49]

As the Nazis made deep advances into Soviet territory in the summer of 1941, Moscow encouraged the Communist Parties in Occupied Europe to do all they could to disrupt the Nazi war effort. As *L'Humanité* put it on 29 July:

> What is required to help the USSR and Britain crush Hitler? To hasten the liberation of France? Sabotage, again sabotage and once again sabotage. Sabotage in the factories, in the stations, in the countryside, sabotage to stop the enemy from taking anything from our country.[50]

For most French Communists, this was hard to swallow. There was a long anarchist tradition in France of sabotaging machines and killing policemen, which the Communists had always fiercely opposed. The key thing, they said, was the class struggle, not individual actions. Now the Party leadership was proposing exactly the tactics they had argued against, and at a time when the vast majority of the population would not understand such a policy. Faced with the Party faithful's refusal to cooperate, the leadership turned to a group it could be certain would respond enthusiastically to the new line: the Party's youth section, the Jeunesses Communistes. Untrained in Marxist traditions, eager to take action, a few dozen Paris teenagers would show the older members of the Party how to fight the Nazi Occupation. They would also represent an important change in the social composition of the embryonic Resistance. Not only were they young, but they were also predominantly poor and working class – very different from the officers, academics, journalists and teachers who made up most of the early Resistance groups.

In the hot summer of 1941 these young activists carried out a series of daring street actions, during which a handful of militants would throw leaflets in the air or march briefly along the street shouting slogans. Their first attempt, on 13 July, in the working-class district of Belleville on the hilly eastern side of Paris, was a complete failure. They barely had enough time to get their leaflets out before the police turned up and the dozen teenagers had to flee.[51] The next day was Bastille Day, and the Nazis had banned all the traditional patriotic demonstrations. Nevertheless, the youngsters met in small groups of two or three and made their way to the Place de la République, boys and girls both wearing red, white and blue clothes. One of the participants, Liliane Lévy-Osbert, twenty-three years old at the time, remembered:

> The experience of the previous day – still fresh – put us on our guard, making us suspicious and circumspect. And above all, worried.[52]

This time things went slightly better – they were able to run along the street for about a kilometre, shouting and throwing leaflets in the air. Eventually the police caught up and arrested a few demonstrators, who were extremely lucky to get away with only four months' imprisonment.

Over the next two weeks the Jeunesses Communistes carried out a number of these stunts, always in the working-class districts in the north and east of Paris. Each time the police got closer. Liliane Lévy-Osbert recalled the end of a demonstration on 27 July when the police nearly caught the youngsters:

> We ran in all directions, then regrouped and exchanged information. Phew! No damage done, but what a scare! I can still sense the bitter taste that filled my mouth, the nervous trembling that shook my

body, the sharp, shallow breaths that lifted my chest. My heart was beating so fast, my legs were jelly, I was shaking like I was freezing. Finally, I calmed down. I looked at my friends. My God! They were barely in a better state than me. Panting, pale-faced, hollow-eyed – we'd had a close shave.[53]

On 13 August the biggest demonstration yet took place: up to a hundred young militants were to march from the Saint-Lazare station, or was it to be the Boulevard Saint-Denis? – different messages suggested different starting points.[54] All afternoon, small bands of confused demonstrators wandered around the north of Paris, hoping to meet up and find out where the demonstration was starting from. Then it began:

> Suddenly, we set out into the Boulevard Saint-Denis, just like that, moving into the traffic. It was the same technique as before. The first group charged in, the rest followed. The contingent took shape. We had barely marched a few hundred metres when a convoy of German vehicles pulled up in front of us. Danger! And that was the end of the demo. They turned round and drove into us. The French police were there, too. The balance of forces had completely changed. Shots rang out. The Germans were firing at us. I remember we scattered. Some of us ran onto the pavement on the right and disappeared into the small roads going off the boulevard. The others ran onto the pavement on the left, and tried to hide in doorways. They were caught. I was so stunned I just stood still. In front of me, everything was confused. Everything happened so quickly.[55]

Six Jeunesses Communistes members were arrested, including Smulz 'Titi' Tizselman. Six days later Titi – 'a Communist Jew,' said the Nazis – was executed, together with his comrade, Henri Gautherot, under new laws that allowed the Nazis to respond with unrestrained violence to any illegal action.[56] The next day the Nazis used the events as a pretext to turn on the Jewish community in the eleventh arrondissement, which was also the district of Paris with the greatest number of anti-German leaflets and graffiti, launching the first large-scale round-up of Jews in France, helped by the Parisian police.[57] As a Nazi report put it:

Following a demonstration that was led by Jews, and to intimidate the whole Jewish community, around four thousand Jewish men aged between eighteen and fifty, irrespective of nationality, were arrested in a lightning action on 20 August, and were interned in the Drancy camp. The collaboration of the French police (around 2,500 officers) was good.[58]

Two days after the executions, on 21 August, Pierre Georges and Gilbert Brustlein waited on the platform of the Barbès-Rochechouart Métro station at 8 a.m. Although only twenty-one years old, Georges – better known by his pseudonym, Fabien – was an experienced Communist militant. At the age of seventeen Fabien had seen action in the Spanish Civil War, and had just been appointed military leader of a shadowy, tiny, underground Communist group, which, until very recently, many historians thought was a figment of Communist Party mythology – the Bataillons de la Jeunesse (Youth Battalions).[59] Their mission that morning had been decided by the highest echelons of the Party leadership. As the Métro rattled into the station, a group of German sailors prepared to get on board, accompanied by their officer, who wore a magnificent uniform.[60] Just as the doors began to close, Fabien pulled out a lady's revolver and shot the officer in the back.[61] Alfons Moser fell forward into the carriage and lay dead on the floor, his feet sticking out over the platform. Fabien and Brustlein escaped without difficulty. 'Titi is avenged,' said Fabien to his comrades.

*

Titi might have been avenged, but the Communists' campaign against the Nazi troops was just beginning. A few hours later, Fabien's group tried to kill an officer in the Bastille Métro station. There was even what now appears to have been a copycat action. On 27 August Paul Colette shot and wounded Hitler's chief Vichy ally, Pierre Laval, during a ceremony in Versailles.[62] Although the Nazis and Vichy blamed the Communists, Colette appears to have acted alone. However, this attack severely heightened the atmosphere of tension and repression that hung over the Occupied Zone in general and the Paris region in particular. Over the next few weeks Fabien's group carried out a series of largely ineffective sabotage attempts – of the sixteen attacks on the railways that took place up to the end of October, only six were even vaguely successful, and no serious damage was done. But above all they prepared for further attacks against German soldiers, with a near-complete disregard for security. On 6 September Bernard Laurent took a shot at a German soldier, a mere 150 metres from his own house. Even more dangerously, Brustlein bought three revolvers off a contact, André Hubert; another militant, Roger Hanlet, foolishly let Hubert's new girlfriend see the guns and boasted about how he had helped sabotage the railways. Alarmed to discover what her boyfriend was mixed up in, the girl confessed everything to her ex, Maurice Cocrelle.

In mid-October Brustlein and a group of Jeunesses Communistes members, including another veteran of the Spanish Civil War, Spartaco Guisco, were sent to Nantes. The idea was for the Communist Party to show that it could strike outside the capital, and to get the Nazis to turn their repression away from Paris for a while. The group – which was part of a double operation, the other militants being sent to Bordeaux – was to carry out some sabotage and then kill a German. Having attracted the attention of the local police by camping outside the house of a known Communist Party member, the Nantes group tried to blow up a German troop train but succeeded only in destroying a fifty-centimetre stretch of rail after the train had passed. Then, early in the morning of the next day, Monday 20 October (Guisco's thirtieth birthday), Guisco and Brustlein wandered the streets, looking for their victim:

> Spartaco elbowed me; there, in front of us, two superbly dressed officers were walking across the square. We quickly made towards them, and followed them to the pavement of the Rue du Roi-Albert. 'You take the one on the right, I'll take this one.' I took out my two 6.35-millimetre revolvers and Spartaco took out his 7.65. We were on the pavement, just behind them, half a metre away. We fired . . . [in fact Spartaco's gun jammed]. As he collapsed, the officer in front of me began to make inhuman, terrifying screams. The other officer turned his head slightly. I turned round and ran; Spartaco followed me. We ran down the street;

we reached a boulevard; a tram was passing – we waved our arms, the tram slowed down, the conductor reached out and hauled us aboard.[63]

The storm was about to break. Completely by chance, Brustlein had killed Lieutenant-Colonel Karl Hotz, the military commander of Nantes and probably the most important Nazi in the west of France.

The reaction in Nantes was overwhelmingly hostile. Hotz was a well-read Nazi whose sophisticated ways went down well with the Nantes middle class – his good manners apparently blinded them to his strict application of Nazi anti-Semitic policies.[64] Far more important, the assassination raised the immediate prospect of vicious Nazi reprisals against local hostages. From the very beginning of the Occupation, the Nazis had taken hostages – mainly local politicians and dignitaries – to ensure that the population was acquiescent. The worst that had ever happened to any of them was imprisonment. But new laws allowed the Nazis to make extreme responses: following Fabien's action at Barbès-Rochechouart in August, they had executed three hostages in Paris; a further twelve were shot on 20 September.[65] Hitler furiously criticized the Paris military commander, Otto von Stülpnagel, for his apparent lack of ruthlessness: 'If there is another assassination,' he ordered, 'there must immediately be at least 100 executions for each German killed.'[66]

Within three hours of Hotz's murder, Hitler was informed. He over-ruled von Stülpnagel and personally ordered the execution of fifty hostages, to be followed by a further fifty if the culprits were not captured within forty-eight hours. That evening the stakes were raised even higher, as the group of Bataillons members sent to Bordeaux killed German military adviser Hans Reimers.[67] The Parisian press announced a reward of 15 million francs for information leading to the arrest of the culprits. Jean Guéhenno noted acerbically that the sum was printed 'in huge capitals, as though it was a new prize in the Lottery'.[68] The Vichy Minister of the Interior, Pierre Pucheu, tried to convince the Nazis that the threat of mass executions was an overreaction – like von Stülpnagel, he feared it would make collaboration more difficult. When this failed, Pucheu suggested the Nazis should select hostages whom he considered to be particularly dangerous – Communists. He even went so far as to impose death sentences retrospectively, to provide the Nazi policy with the veneer of Vichy 'justice'. Pétain went on the radio, denouncing the murders and calling on those responsible to give themselves up. Even Brustlein's Communist mother, who knew nothing of her son's role in the affair, thought that the culprits should hand themselves in.[69]

On 22 October forty-eight hostages were executed in reprisal for the assassination of Hotz.[70] Twenty-seven men – including Communist and trade union leaders and two Trotskyists – were taken from the Chateaubriant internment camp, where around five hundred and eighty political prisoners were held, while a further twenty-one were executed in Nantes prison. Among all these deaths, the one that encapsulated the tragedy in the public imagination was that of Guy Moquet, only seventeen years old, son of a Communist deputy and a close friend of fellow Young Communist Maroussia Naïtchenko. Moquet had been arrested in November 1940 outside the Gare de l'Est in Paris for giving out Communist Party leaflets. In his last letter to his parents, he wrote:

> I am going to die! All I ask you, in particular my dear Mother, is to be brave. I am, and I want to be, as brave as those who have gone before me. Of course, I want to live. But what I want with my whole heart is that my death serves a purpose . . . seventeen and a half years! My life has been short! I have no regrets, apart from leaving you.[71]

His final words, which inspired generations of people during and after the war, were: 'Those of you who remain, be worthy of us.'

The next day Jean Guéhenno wrote in his diary:

> The list of forty-eight shot hostages . . . appears in the newspapers, hidden away on page three, through fear or shame. The forty-eight are of course called 'Communists'. In Belgrade, Sofia and in Brussels, there are similar mass executions. It is the new order. One cannot think of anything else. This morning the young people at school were utterly appalled.[72]

As Guéhenno wrote those lines, things were getting worse: another fifty hostages were shot in Bordeaux. The next day his response to the rapid descent into barbarism summed up many people's feelings: 'We are lost in the horror.'[73]

Stunned by the public hostility to the campaign of shootings and by the terrible consequences of their actions, which had led to the death of Party leaders and of young people like themselves, Brustlein and his comrades roamed the streets of Paris, foolishly hanging out in known Communist bars and apartments. The police soon got a lead from Maurice Cocrelle, the jealous ex-boyfriend of the girl who had seen the guns used to kill Hotz. They began a tailing operation and over the next two weeks arrested thirty people more or less involved in the actions of the Bataillons. Through a mixture of threats, promises and physical violence, they managed to get some detainees to talk, and finally arrested and executed everyone involved, apart from Fabien and Brustlein, both of whom escaped. Fabien continued to play an important role in the Communist Party's armed wing, while Brustlein made his way to the UK, returning to France after the war.

Despite the wave of repression and widespread public hostility, the Communist Party continued its activities. Although its attacks were concentrated in the Paris region, Charles Debarge, a twenty-nine-year-old miner who had played an important role in the June 1941 strike, had already begun a long campaign of sabotage and attacks in the Nord-Pas-de-Calais. On 29 July 1941 Debarge wrote in his diary that he had to be 'relentless in supporting as much as possible our Russian comrades on the battlefield, and to work harder for our liberation'.[74] The results of Debarge's actions – which led to his death in 1942 – were meagre: one sentry was killed in Lens in April 1942, and a number of machines, electricity cables and railway lines were sabotaged.[75] On the other hand, dozens of Debarge's comrades were arrested and either executed or deported. And as a direct consequence of his most spectacular action – the killing of the sentry at Lens – thirty-five hostages were killed the same day and several dozen were deported.[76]

The turn to armed struggle was so unpopular that the Communist Party never admitted its role in the assassination of Hotz in Nantes, although the Party leadership was secretly pleased at the death of such a high-ranking officer.[77] As far as Party members were concerned, it was not even certain that the assassination of Hotz was a political act:

*L'Humanité* initially claimed that he was killed as part of a sex scandal, while a local Breton Communist publication said that the whole thing had been staged by the Gestapo to discredit the Resistance.[78]

On 23 October, the day after the forty-eight hostages were executed, de Gaulle spoke from London. He sharply distanced himself from the tactics the Communists were using, trying both to ride on the widespread opposition to the assassinations and to set himself up as the leader of the Resistance:

> It is completely normal and completely justified that Germans should be killed by French men and women. If the Germans did not wish to be killed by our hands, they should have stayed at home and not waged war on us. Sooner or later, they are all destined to be killed, either by us or by our allies . . . But in war there are tactics. The war of the French must be carried out by those in charge, that is, by myself and by the National Committee. All combatants, those in the country and those outside, must observe precisely the advice I give for the occupied territory, which is not to kill Germans. This for a single, but very good reason, that is, at the moment it is too easy for the enemy to respond by massacring our troops, who are temporarily disarmed. On the other hand, once we are in a position to turn to the attack, you will receive the necessary orders.[79]

These criticisms, and the brazen attempt by de Gaulle to pose as the sole leader of the Resistance, only reinforced the Communists' conviction that the General in London could not be trusted. The Communists were even more galled by the fact that they were also criticized by their hated enemies, the Trotskyists. This small group pointed out that because of lack of public support, such a military campaign was not yet appropriate. Worse, they said, the Communists were actually weakening the chances of final victory by sacrificing their members in a largely futile campaign.[80] Communist militants realized that the bulk of the population was opposed to attacks against the Nazis – they heard what people said in cafés, and they found it difficult to convince their close contacts. As Liliane Lévy-Osbert recognized, they were virtually alone:

People disapproved of anti-German actions, they did not want to fight, they rejected any idea of rebellion. They were particularly influenced by the fear of reprisals. Fear, timidity and terror faced with the appalling example of so many death sentences terrorized the population. Worse, people turned their anger and their criticisms against the 'adventurers' who threatened the lives of ordinary people. Which was what the Germans wanted. However, I think that, deep down, there may have been some kind of compassion and understanding for those young twenty-year-olds who were sacrificing their future.[81]

That kind of comprehension did indeed exist. In his diary, Jean Guéhenno tried to explain the actions of these young men, and why the campaign of military action continued, despite the repression:

You need to understand the pact that links comrades, the commitments they have made to each other, the support they have given each other, despite the risk, living and dying for each other. The assassin could be in the place of the hostage, just as the hostage could be in the place of the assassin – it's a matter of chance. Everyone holds to this pact with an iron will, and does what he has to do. Yes, that is frightening, but it is also magnificent.[82]

While this was an astute attempt to appreciate the determination of Communist militants, Guéhenno understandably did not realize the situation of those involved. These were not hardened cadres but youngsters, with all the selflessness, enthusiasm and roller-coaster emotions that this implied. When Maroussia Naïtchenko and her boyfriend Georges Grünberger saw the name of Guy Moquet on the list of executed hostages in September 1941, the terrible consequences of their campaign were brought home to the two young lovers:

Georges was sitting on a seat of the Métro, on his way to work, reading the paper. Suddenly, he thrust it at me. I didn't understand what he wanted. He had gone red, his lips were turning purple. Even before looking at the paper, I was frightened by his face . . . The list of hostages was there, and the name of Guy Moquet was among them . . .

The shock produced by the news left us deeply distressed . . . We got out of the Métro and went to work, completely overcome.[83]

In spring 1942 the few remaining members of the Bataillons joined the Organisation Spéciale (OS), the Communist Party's newly-created armed wing. In turn, the OS eventually formed the basis of one of the main armed Resistance groups, the Franc-Tireurs et Partisans (FTP – Sharp-Shooters and Partisans). However, the balance sheet of the Communist Party's initial turn to armed struggle makes depressing reading. The effect on the Nazi war machine was not even that of a fleabite on an elephant. Figures from the Vichy police suggest there were around twenty actions every fortnight.[84] Given that most of these failed, and that at this time the battles of the Eastern Front were killing thousands of men each day, destroying military vehicles and equipment at a terrifying rate, the events in France were simply irrelevant from a strategic point of view, no matter how irritating they might have been to the Nazis. At this stage, armed struggle was limited to the Paris region, Normandy and the Nord-Pas-de-Calais, and involved fewer than a hundred militants. Despite subsequent Communist claims, fewer than fifteen German soldiers were assassinated in the first year of armed struggle. Sabotage, which was supposed to be at the heart of the campaign, was a near failure, with the notable exception of two derailments near Caen, in April 1942, which killed thirty-eight soldiers and injured thirty-nine.[85]

On the other hand, Nazi repression was extremely effective: 814 hostages were executed in the year following October 1941, further weakening public support for an armed struggle that most people found bewildering.[86] Waves of arrests, executions and deportations ripped the heart out of the Communist organization. For example, in the Non-Occupied Zone in the last six weeks of 1941 alone, 12,850 'Communists' were arrested. In the final three months of 1941, 193 hostages were executed, including leading Communist deputy Gabriel Péri. Throughout the spring of 1942, more union and political leaders were executed, along with scores of hostages, while three major show trials led to fifty-two executions.[87]

In 1942 the PCF leader responsible for maintaining contact with the Gaullists discussed the impact of the Nazi execution policy with his Free

French opposite number, and was candid about its effect: 'as soon as the news is given out that five or ten of our men have been shot, we get fifty or a hundred new recruits.'[88] While it is undoubtedly true that some young fighters were attracted to the Communist Party because of its 'martyrs', these figures are exaggerated. Until the middle of 1943 the armed wing of the Party was marked by an incredibly high turnover as the new recruits were killed. Because of lax security, overconfidence, foolhardy risk-taking and occasional bad luck, the young militants who were the first to be thrown into the fire had an incredibly short life expectancy. On average, a member of the Bataillons lived a mere seven months after taking up the armed struggle. Twenty of these brave young people survived three months or less.[89] They knew the sacrifice they were making – one friend warned Maroussia Naïtchenko: 'we have two months to live.'[90]

In 2003 Maroussia Naïtchenko, aged nearly eighty and one of the few survivors of the Bataillons de la Jeunesse, was shown the true balance sheet of the actions of her comrades. 'All dead for that?' was her aghast comment.[91] Indeed. But that does not make their deaths any less courageous, nor their motivations any less noble. No matter how reckless they may seem in retrospect, and irrespective of the fact that they were cynically manipulated by their Stalinist leaders, these young people were some of the first in France to take decisive action against the Nazis.

*

The Nazis' spiral of repression also claimed the life of an aristocratic naval lieutenant, Honoré d'Estienne d'Orves, a committed Catholic and royalist. After a brilliant career, d'Estienne was declared a deserter when, in July 1940, he left his ship along with 300 sailors and made his way to London, where he joined Free French Intelligence as part of Colonel Passy's BCRA (Bureau Central de Renseignement et d'Action – Central office of intelligence and action). On 21 December he was taken to France by a group of Free French fishermen, together with his hand-picked radio operator. In a matter of days he set up an intelligence circuit, code-named NIMROD, and made his way to Paris, where he met Christian Pineau, to whom he was presented as 'the official representative

of General de Gaulle in Paris'.[92] While d'Estienne was merely embarrassed by the title, Pineau was deeply disturbed by the ease with which
security had been breached and unimpressed by the amateurishness of
the operation. D'Estienne also met Germaine Tillion and planned to
link up with Vildé and the rest of the *Résistance* group. But before the
meeting could take place, d'Estienne was arrested on 21 January, after
merely a month in Occupied France. Gaessler, his radio operator, had
gone over to the Nazis a few days earlier. As well as winding up the
NIMROD circuit, the Nazis used Gaessler to feed London fake information – French Intelligence in London was so pleased with his apparent
work that he was promoted, and for six months they persistently ignored
suggestions from Swiss and British Intelligence that he had been turned
by the Nazis.

The two-week trial of d'Estienne and the other members of the
NIMROD circuit took place in May 1941. In the previous weeks d'Estienne
had been imprisoned in the Cherche-Midi prison, together with Agnès
Humbert of the Musée de l'Homme network. Relentlessly cheerful,
and buoyed up by his resurgent Catholic faith, d'Estienne accepted
entire responsibility for the activity of the circuit – much to the irritation of the judge. In delivering his verdict, the judge accepted that the
accused were 'men and women who proved themselves to be people
of merit, who had a great strength of character and who acted only
through the love of their country',[93] but emphasized that he had no
choice but to sentence them to death or life imprisonment with hard
labour. Yan Doornik, on hearing he was sentenced to death for spying
and to imprisonment for recruiting young people to the British cause,
asked: 'Do I have to carry out my prison sentence before or after my
execution?'[94] After the sentences were passed – d'Estienne was also
sentenced to death – the judge, deeply moved, shook hands with each
of the accused.

Over the next three months the Vichy state mobilized to save
d'Estienne, whom they apparently considered to be one of their own –
he was, after all, an officer and a fervent Catholic royalist. But the shot
fired by Fabien at Barbès-Rochechouart scuppered attempts to get
d'Estienne's sentence commuted. On 24 August, faced with the changing security situation in France, Hitler personally decided to reject

d'Estienne's plea for clemency, and the forty-year-old father of four was executed five days later. Through the bloody tide of executions, the death of d'Estienne d'Orves struck a chord which was amplified in 1943, when the Stalinist poet, Aragon, wrote an extremely influential poem, 'La rose et le reseda' ('The rose and the mignonette'), which showed the links between the execution of two very different Resistance martyrs – d'Estienne and Guy Moquet ('he who believed in heaven, and he who did not').

D'Estienne's enthusiastically amateurish mission – ill-prepared, overly ambitious and poorly supported – was a catastrophe. Like the Resistance, the Free French secret services accepted that losses were inevitable. But sacrifices had to be avoided wherever possible, and where they did occur they had to be worthwhile. So far, that had not been the case. In its first year the embryonic Resistance lost many militants at the hands of the Nazis and in return achieved very little. Some French honour had been saved, but the tiny groups remained isolated, dispersed and without any real influence.

To be anything other than a footnote in history, the Resistance had to change: it had to unite around a programme of action, become better armed and coordinate with intelligence and sabotage operations run from London. On 25 October, as France reeled with horror at the wave of hostage executions, the man who was to play a decisive role in carrying out this change walked into General de Gaulle's office in Carlton Gardens off the Mall, in the heart of London. He was the one-time prefect from Chartres, who in June 1940 had preferred suicide to dishonour. His name was Jean Moulin.

# 4

# *London Calling*

Jean Moulin's arrival in London changed everything. He brought with him one of the most precious wartime commodities: information. Moulin had first-hand knowledge of the situation in France, and he provided London with its first detailed description of the Resistance. At this stage of the war very few people made it from France to Britain. In the whole of 1940 and 1941, only six people were brought out of France by the RAF, all of whom were military personnel and only two of whom were French.[1] If ordinary people wanted to join the Free French, they had to make their own way. At the same time as Moulin left France, five young teenagers on a seaside holiday in the Pas-de-Calais hatched a hare-brained scheme to cross the Channel in two abandoned canoes. Jean-Pierre Lavoix, who was only seventeen years old at the time, recalled:

> In a carefully worked-out plan, we helped our parents pack as we were due to return home the next day. In the evening, we pretended to be very tired, and went up to bed as soon as it was dark. A few minutes later, we crept across the terrace, picked up our canoes in the courtyard, and climbed over the dunes and down to the sea.[2]

As they paddled through the dark, the swell got up and the boys were all terribly seasick. They were also terribly lost. For over a day they drifted in the Channel, reaching the English coast in the middle of the night, where they were arrested by the Home Guard and then interrogated by the Intelligence Service. Once their story had been verified, the five lads became overnight celebrities, fêted as examples of French courage and fighting spirit. They were eventually presented to Winston Churchill and his wife in the garden of 10 Downing Street. The press photos show five very smart young men in shorts, grinning and toasting Mrs Churchill and her husband, who is as pleased as Punch.

Moulin's journey to London was slightly less perilous – he travelled by train from the Free Zone, through Spain and Portugal, and then by RAF plane to London – but it was incredibly drawn out.[3] Moulin had been making preparations for nearly a year, beginning about three months after the fall of France, just before Vichy suspended him for being politically unreliable in November 1940. First, he got the Chartres administration to make him an identity card in the name of Professor Joseph Mercier. Then, using Mercier's ID, he was able first to get a passport, and finally a visa for the USA. A number of his political friends, including his pre-war boss, Pierre Cot, and the maverick left-winger Louis Dolivet, had recently moved to North America, and in December 1940 Moulin planned to join them.[4] But even with the passport and visa, Moulin still needed to get into Portugal, from where he intended to board a ship to America. Waiting for the necessary paperwork kept him hanging around in France for another nine months. He used that time to travel around the country, trying to discover as much as possible about the Resistance.

At some point Moulin changed his mind about leaving for the USA and decided instead to go to London, although he was still unsure whether he should work with de Gaulle or with British Intelligence. When he left France, Moulin carried with him a report on the state of the Resistance, much of which was based on hearsay – he was not able to meet any of the groups in the Occupied Zone and had to rely on information from some of his pre-war friends.[5] Surprisingly, none of them appears to have heard of – far less had any contact with – the Vildé group or even Christian Pineau's Northern Zone newspaper, *Libération*. Moulin had better luck in the Non-Occupied Zone, where he met Henri Frenay through an American priest, the Reverend Howard L. Brooks.[6]

Brooks had arrived in France in May 1941 to work for the US Protestant refugee charity, the Unitarian Service Committee (USC). But Brooks had also been commissioned by Cot and Dolivet to set up a 'communication service' that would inform the French population about the war, 'plans for a democratic world order, American determination to defeat Hitler, and . . . about the efforts of the Free Frenchmen'.[7] Dolivet had contacted the Free French and British Intelligence, inviting them to support Brooks' work,[8] but de Gaulle's enthusiastic reply came too late, while the head of MI6, 'C' (Sir Stewart Menzies), was concerned about Dolivet's politics and decreed that none of his agents should have anything to do with the left-wing French man.[9]

Brooks was in France for only three months, from May to August 1941. During this time he travelled throughout the Non-Occupied Zone and spent much of his time in Marseilles, where he worked in Varian Fry's Centre Américain de Secours (American Relief Centre). Fry helped thousands of refugees, including intellectuals and artists such as André Breton, Heinrich Mann and Marc Chagall, to escape to the US.[10] While in France, Brooks was unable to set up his 'communication service' because British Intelligence refused to forward any of his telegrams to Dolivet. When Brooks returned to the US, he wrote an eyewitness account of the situation in France, *Prisoners of Hope*, which helped popularize the French Resistance among the US public. Brooks' book contains excerpts from underground newspapers and heavily disguised descriptions of various Resistance members. Frenay appears as 'Michael Curtiss', a dark-haired French intellectual and author, whom Brooks says he had met in the US before the war.[11] Every detail is false, but Brooks' descriptions of Frenay's energy and his huge network of contacts ('he knew practically everyone in France who had anything to do with opposition to the Germans')[12] all ring true. Moulin makes a minor appearance under the guise of 'Émile Baron', a man who was intending to go to London. According to Brooks, he organized the meeting between the two future Resistance leaders, because Moulin 'would undoubtedly be useful as a courier'.[13]

During their discussion, Moulin took copious notes while Frenay explained the history and activity of his movement and described two underground newspapers from the Non-Occupied Zone that Moulin had not heard of (Emmanuel d'Astier's *Libération*, and *Liberté*, produced by a group of Christian Democrats around a professor at Montpellier University, François de Menthon). Above all, Frenay emphasized that they desperately needed regular contact with London. At the end, Moulin made a promise to Frenay: 'I intend to depart as soon as I can. If all goes well, I shall arrive in England towards the end of the summer.

I shall faithfully deliver your proposals – that I promise you . . . I shall have no trouble in being your advocate.'[14]

*

Moulin's train arrived in Lisbon on 12 September and he found a room on the fourth floor of a small hotel.[15] Two days later he went to the British embassy and asked to be taken to London. As proof of his real identity, he carried his prefect's card, hidden in several pieces, some behind the face of his travel clock, others in the handle of his suitcase. Moulin's first contact in Lisbon was with an 'assistant' to the British Military Attaché – in fact a member of the British Special Operations Executive (SOE).[16] SOE was a new secret military organization that had been created in a mad hurry after the fall of France; Churchill said its mission was to 'set Europe ablaze' through clandestine guerrilla activity. Although the origins of SOE lay in the British Intelligence community, MI6 and MI5 looked down on the new unit, considering it to be amateurish and a potential competitor, and throughout the war there was a continuous tension between SOE and the Intelligence organizations. This was aggravated as SOE began to recruit people in Occupied Europe. Moulin was exactly the kind of person they were looking for – intelligent, daring, highly knowledgeable about French society, and well connected to important people in French government and politics. But despite his potential importance to the British, Moulin had to hang around in Lisbon for over a month, repeatedly fobbed off with excuses about no transport being available. In fact the British were checking him out, although this was not done with any great urgency – an enquiry sent from Lisbon to MI5 on 15 October was eventually answered six weeks later with their usual laconic response in such circumstances: 'nothing known against'.[17]

Finally, on 19 October, Moulin was taken to Britain by an RAF flying boat.[18] After having been interrogated and debriefed for a couple of days at the MI5 London Reception Centre in the Royal Patriotic School in Wandsworth – the counter-intelligence control point for all immigrants – Moulin was next seen by Major Eric Piquet-Wicks of SOE. Piquet-Wicks had to try to convince Moulin that he should work for the British – one of Moulin's earlier interrogators had noted that 'SOE is interested by this man'.[19] But as Piquet-Wicks later recalled, Moulin would have none of it – for the time being:

> 'Do not let us waste time,' Moulin told me politely. 'I will see the General and his Services, for that is why I have come. I will also see the French Section [of SOE], and then I will know what I have to do.'[20]

The next day Moulin and de Gaulle met in the Free French headquarters at the end of Carlton Gardens.[21] By the time Moulin walked out of the front door he had decided to throw in his lot with the Free French. However, he was still not entirely won over by de Gaulle's leadership. Like many *résistants*, Moulin was suspicious of de Gaulle's political intentions, and of the right-wingers and ex-fascists who dominated the Free French.[22] When Moulin returned to France in the new year he confided his doubts about de Gaulle to François de Menthon: 'In his heart, what does he think about the Republic? I can't say. I know his official positions, but is he really a democrat? I don't know.' In a letter to Pierre Cot, Moulin implied that his support for de Gaulle was largely tactical: 'For the moment, we must be with de Gaulle. Afterwards, we'll see.'[23] He obviously said the same thing to his SOE interrogators, who summarized his view as follows: 'The matter of whether de Gaulle stayed or went could be settled afterwards.'[24]

Moulin's influence on the Free French and on the British view of the situation in France was immediate and long-lasting. His report on the Resistance, written while he was in Lisbon, had the precision and clarity typical of a high-ranking French civil servant. Pointedly addressed 'to the British authorities and General de Gaulle', it took as its starting point the fact that the Resistance supported 'the British cause and that of General de Gaulle'.[25] This emphasis on de Gaulle was a great surprise to the British – for over a year relations between the Free French and the British government had steadily worsened, and in the summer of 1941 they had reached breaking point. After the Free French were excluded from the peace treaty following the Allied victory in Vichy-controlled Syria, de Gaulle publicly accused the British of having a 'war-time deal' with Hitler to exploit France.[26] In response, Churchill claimed that de Gaulle had 'gone off his head', banned him from broadcasting on the BBC, issued secret instructions to stop him from leaving the country and even backed a half-hearted plot to oust him.[27] Moulin's arrival, and the news he brought, put a stop to this manoeuvring as the British realized they could not afford to do without de Gaulle – for the time being, at least.

Moulin called his report 'an SOS to London'. In it he described the scattered action of the small Resistance groups and warned what would happen if support was not forthcoming from London:

> If no organization imposes upon them some sort of discipline, some orders, some plan of action, if no organization provides them with arms, two things will happen:
>
> On the one hand, we shall witness isolated activities, born to certain failure which will definitely go against the common goal because they will take place at the wrong moment, in a disorganized and inefficacious manner and thereby discourage the rest of the population.
>
> On the other hand, we shall be driving into the arms of the Communists thousands of French men who are burning with the desire to serve . . .[28]

Given the spiral of Nazi repression that was engulfing the country following the attacks carried out in the Occupied Zone by Fabien and the Bataillons de la Jeunesse, this was particularly telling.

Moulin argued that the Resistance needed moral support, regular communications, money and, above all, arms. As one of Moulin's interrogators wrote after interviewing him on 4 November:

> Informant is strongly of the opinion that propaganda for de Gaulle as a symbol of resistance and, still more, strictly Gaullist propaganda are quite unnecessary. What is urgently necessary is to get down to the forming of paramilitary hard cores, everywhere if possible.[29]

However, Moulin was not suggesting either individual attacks or an immediate insurrectionary campaign:

> . . . the mere fact of giving money and arms to the movement is not designed to increase for the present the number and importance of

certain acts of violence. The object to be achieved is first and foremost to intensify propaganda and to organize eventual collective action for the future . . . there can be no question of aiming a revolutionary movement against the government of Vichy (at least not without previous agreement with London). The only question at stake is the fight against the Germans, and the men of Vichy are to be considered as opponents only insofar (and in such measure) as they help the enemy.[30]

Faithful to his promise to Frenay, Moulin was an advocate for the Resistance, but he also began to play a part more in keeping with his professional training as a government administrator, acting as an interface between the military men in London and the Resistance forces on the ground. To truly fulfil this role, he had to return to France.

\*

At around 3 a.m. in the morning of 2 January 1942 Jean Moulin jumped out of a twin-engined RAF Armstrong Whitley into the freezing black sky over the south of France somewhere between Avignon and Aix-en-Provence. Moulin was an athletic man – he was an enthusiastic skier and cyclist – and he had experience of keeping secrets both in his complex personal life, which featured a number of mistresses, and through his pre-war involvement in a secret government plot to supply the Spanish Republicans with French aeroplanes.[31] But he had no real preparation for the terror of the parachute jump or for the incredibly dangerous underground life he was to lead for the next eighteen months. A few weeks earlier he had undergone a weekend of parachute training in Manchester together with Passy, the head of Free French Intelligence, and he had been initiated into the essentials of underground 'tradecraft' (use of codes and so on), but that was all.[32] Moulin was dropped 'blind' – there was no one waiting for him on the ground; indeed, no one was expecting him back in France at all. Things started badly: due to a navigational error, Moulin and his two comrades were dropped fifteen kilometres from their intended landing site south of Avignon and became separated during the descent. Worse, Moulin came down in a frozen bog and was lucky not to drown or die of exposure, while the radio set was severely damaged on landing. For the next three months London heard nothing from him – they did not even know whether he had survived the jump.

During Moulin's time in London the war had changed dramatically. On 7 December the Japanese launched a surprise attack on the American naval base at Pearl Harbor in Hawaii, bringing the USA into the conflict. On the grand, strategic scale, the outcome was no longer in doubt. When de Gaulle heard the news, he told his intelligence chief, Passy: 'Now the war is won for certain.'[33] For de Gaulle, however, the entry of the US into the war meant that his relations with the Roosevelt administration became even more strained now that they were supposedly on the same side. Part of the problem was that, despite now being at war with both Japan and Germany, the Americans continued with their policy of trying to appease and influence Vichy. This disconcerted and irritated the Free French, and matters soon came to a head.

On 24 December 1941 Admiral Muselier of the Free French navy landed on two tiny Vichy-controlled French islands, Saint-Pierre and Miquelon, off the coast of Newfoundland. The takeover was bloodless and was greeted with enthusiasm, except in Washington. Roosevelt had rejected de Gaulle's proposal to take control of the islands; the fact that the Free French had gone ahead and deployed armed force not far from the US coast was seen as an example of the kind of fierce independence that Roosevelt loathed so much in de Gaulle. The US Secretary of State, Cordell Hull, publicly attacked the 'so-called Free French' and demanded to know how the Canadian government was going to restore Vichy's authority over the islands. But the US public did not share the administration's perception of de Gaulle. There was a huge outcry in the press, and Hull received piles of abusive mail addressed to the 'so-called Secretary of State'. The prospect of similar protests quickly dissuaded the British from supporting the US position, and eventually the row subsided, with the Free French firmly in control of this relatively insignificant outpost of the French Empire.[34]

Regardless of the rumbling conflict with Roosevelt, which continued until D-Day and afterwards, the involvement of the USA was ultimately of enormous benefit to the Free French. De Gaulle was right: victory was now merely a matter of time. The vast productive forces of the USA were bent

to the defeat of Nazi Germany and of Japan. In 1942 alone the USA produced 45,000 tanks, more than twelve times the number the Nazis had
used to attack the USSR. In 1941 Nazi plane production was 11,000 per
year; the US government ordered the production of 43,000 planes in
1942 and 100,000 in 1943.[35] In France the mood of the public began to
change rapidly. Three days after the Pearl Harbor attack, André Philip, a
university professor and one-time Socialist deputy, wrote in broken English
to the Reverend Howard Brooks, who was by now back in the USA:

> I am speaking with complete liberty, until now without incident. The
> mind is changing rapidly in France. The spirit of national resistance is
> growing every day and everywhere and expressing it quite openly,
> chiefly in the trains and in the movies. We are full of hope about
> 1942, which will certainly bring something new in the world, even if it
> is not yet the final decision.[36]

Despite Philip's optimism, the 'spirit of national resistance' he described –
conversations on trains and in cinemas – was hardly the stuff of decisive
opposition to the Occupation. In reality, the war was far from over.
Over the next four years, millions would struggle and die around the
world, and in France people would make fundamental choices. Some
would live and some would die; some would remain loyal to their
principles and some would betray them.

Even before Moulin's return, the disparate forces of the Resistance
had begun to shape themselves into something more coherent and
effective. In the Occupied Zone the Communist Party's turn to armed
struggle had placed itself at the centre of popular perceptions of the
Resistance. In the south, Liberté and Henri Frenay's organization had
fused and begun producing what became one of the best-known
Resistance publications, *Combat*. Emmanuel d'Astier's Libération
refused to join in, partly as a result of his personal animosity towards
Frenay, and partly because of the very different approaches of the two
groups. Libération was more left-wing and criticized Combat for its mil-
itaristic structure, arguing that most of Combat's recruits were
'proto-fascists'.[37] Furthermore, while Libération had recognized de
Gaulle's leadership from the summer of 1941, Combat continued to

prevaricate, hoping that Vichy might throw up a more suitable leader. Moulin's arrival eventually removed most of Frenay's doubts.

Because of these changes, Moulin's report on the state of the Resistance was incomplete and out of date even as it was being written. While he was out of the country, new publications had appeared on both sides of the demarcation line, such as the Paris-based *Défense de la France*, which concentrated on providing news, and the left-wing *Le Franc-Tireur*, set up in Lyons by Jean-Pierre Levy and named after the volunteers who had defended the Republic in 1870. Above all, the shot fired by Fabien in the Paris Métro at the end of August and the Communist Party's campaign of isolated guerrilla actions against the Nazis had transformed the situation. In these circumstances, Moulin's return to France was incredibly important. He had transmitted the Resistance's needs to London, and now he returned as de Gaulle's personal representative, carrying a letter from the Free French leader.

After briefly visiting his family in Montpellier, Moulin made his way to Marseilles. Using his new pseudonym – Max – he met Frenay and another leader of Combat, Maurice Chevance. Frenay later described the meeting to his comrade, Guillan de Bénouville: 'In the kitchen, next to the sink, he took out a handwritten letter. No one spoke a word; a handwritten letter from General de Gaulle.'[38] Addressing his letter to 'my dear friends' in the Resistance, de Gaulle wrote in an unusually personal, almost tender, tone:

> I know the work you are doing, I know your worth. I know your great courage and the immense difficulties you face. Despite everything, you must continue your work and spread your influence. We who are lucky enough to be able to still fight with weapons, we need you now and in the future. Be proud and confident! France will win the war, and she will welcome us in her soil. With all my heart, Charles de Gaulle.[39]

In the silence that followed, Moulin brought out his microfilmed orders. Chevance later recalled: 'I can see him now, taking a tiny scrap out of his waistcoat pocket, a small piece of paper that was hidden in a matchbox, and which you needed a magnifying glass to read.'[40] Despite his doubts about de Gaulle, Frenay was jubilant at the financial and material possibilities: 'Here at last was what we had so long awaited: contact with Free France, miraculous contact on the highest level! What a powerful spur this would be to our unity drive! We read pure joy in one another's faces.'[41]

But things were not as straightforward as Frenay hoped. De Gaulle was deeply suspicious of civilians with guns; Moulin's job was to persuade the Resistance leaders to separate the political, intelligence and military wings of the Resistance, with London controlling all military activities. This 'idea', as de Gaulle nicely put it, was in fact an order. Although de Gaulle's microfilmed instructions outlined a wide range of military actions, there was no scope for the Resistance to use its initiative. Not only were there extremely precise orders for how physical resistance should be carried out, the document finished with a final, terse declaration: 'Centralization and coordination will take place in London . . . All these operations will take place on the personal order of General de Gaulle.'[42] The Resistance could produce its underground papers and paint slogans on walls, but the decisive questions of the war – including the nature of the regime that would emerge after an eventual Allied victory – would be settled by force of arms, and de Gaulle intended to control the use of those arms on French soil. Moulin was to ensure that this happened.

Given that military action by the Resistance was still extremely rudimentary, there was no real reason for the Resistance not to accept de Gaulle's proposal. There were not even any obvious political reasons – no one had yet begun to conceive of the Resistance as an insurrectionary army. But Combat had been founded with the perspective of taking military action, and Frenay did not want to cede the initiative to someone on the other side of the Channel. Above all, Frenay's hostility to the idea of separating military and political action came from his realization that the *résistants* actually wanted to do both. Frenay's first, rigid, structure for Combat had been based on the kind of division de Gaulle had prescribed, but he had soon abandoned it as impractical.[43]

When Moulin first presented de Gaulle's vision of the Resistance, Chevance bristled at the idea that London knew best and argued back:

'Sure,' he said, 'in theory all this is perfect. But in practice it's utterly unfeasible. For example, we have, as you know, a certain number of

commando squads at our disposal. How can we possibly forbid them –
as this dispatch demands – to receive and distribute *Combat?* How can
we possibly order them not to transmit some important intelligence
report they've received?'[44]

In reply, Moulin repeated the arguments he had learned in London,
and the debate went round and round. By the time the meeting finished, it was beginning to get light. Moulin had to leave for another
meeting, and Frenay and Chevance went for a long walk around the
empty streets of Marseilles to discuss what to do. Given de Gaulle's real
political influence as a symbol of resistance, and the possibility of substantial financial and military support from Britain, they had no
alternative. As Chevance later put it:

> Everything revolved around the following question, which was fun-
> damental: What do we do? Do we become Gaullists? . . . That is, accept
> the financial means, the contact, the orders . . . Don't forget that
> London had the radio and that this means, this instrument, trans-
> formed, equalized, put everyone into the same Resistance. That was
> the importance of radio London and of the voice of the French. But
> in France, we did not have this kind of means. This was one of the
> main reasons that pushed us towards joining.[45]

The radio was partly a way of giving people in France a focus, a way that
everyone who was opposed to the Occupation could feel part of the
Resistance, either simply by listening to the BBC or by following its calls
to action, be they calls to demonstrate or to chalk up Vs. The BBC also
read out readers' letters – hundreds were sent each month, via the Non-
Occupied Zone, or through the neighbouring neutral countries (Spain,
Portugal or Switzerland).[46] These letters had a palpable effect on morale
in France, and reinforced confidence in the rest of the BBC's output –
if the letters were true, then the news must be, too. But the BBC's
broadcasts were also of more direct use to the Resistance – from autumn
1941 onwards, every evening the announcer would say 'And now, some
personal messages', and dozens of cryptic and often bizarre phrases would
follow, such as 'Esculapius does not like sheep' or 'Romeo is kissing Juliet'.

Some of these messages were deliberately meaningless, but others were precise instructions or messages to the Resistance – the Esculapius message indicated that supplies would be dropped near Chaumont, while Romeo told the Resistance that some correspondence from Toulouse had arrived safely in Switzerland.[47]

This system, dreamed up in summer 1941 by French SOE agent Georges Bégué, gradually turned from being a mere military necessity into yet another expression of the Resistance. The nightly sound of the surreal, impenetrable messages reassured the public that the Resistance was at work. They were also of direct use to the Resistance – demonstrating a material link with London by getting the BBC to broadcast a phrase chosen by a contact was often decisive in establishing the bona fides of the *résistant*. For example, Lucie Aubrac was able to use a BBC personal message to convince the State Prosecutor that the Resistance would indeed kill him if he did not free her husband from a Vichy jail.[48] For Frenay, Chevance and Combat, proof of the potential provided by Moulin's London link came within a few weeks, when the first supplies for Resistance in the Non-Occupied Zone dropped out of the sky on schedule. Whatever the doubts that everyone shared about de Gaulle, his links with the British military machine meant that he could not be ignored. And that meant that the man who represented those links – Jean Moulin – could not be ignored, either.

*

Moulin was not the only Free French agent in France at this time. Film producer Gilbert Renault, who had been a far-right political activist before the war and was one of the first people to join the Free French intelligence services, had returned to France in autumn 1940 to set up a series of intelligence circuits in the Occupied Zone. Under his code name, Rémy, Renault eventually recruited over 2,000 agents to his circuit, the Confrérie Notre-Dame (CND – Fraternity of Our Lady; the name was chosen by Rémy, a fervent Catholic, after he prayed at Notre-Dame des Victoires, a seventeenth-century church in Paris).[49] The circuit was highly effective – CND members played a key role in collecting and transmitting information that helped sink the *Bismarck* in May 1941, while a resourceful CND agent, 'Alex', bribed a German with six bottles of fine Sauternes wine in order to steal the plans of the Saint-Nazaire submarine pens, completing the intelligence survey of the installation begun by Boris Vildé's Musée de l'Homme group. When Alex arrived at Montparnasse station in Paris, carrying a large parcel containing the plans of all the Nazi Atlantic submarine bases, he first had to get through the police cordon at the end of the platform. Seeing an old lady struggling with a suitcase that was almost as big as she was, Alex offered to carry it for her. She accepted, and in return willingly carried his parcel. As Alex expected, he was stopped and her suitcase was searched, but she got through unhindered, together with the crucial plans.[50]

There was another link between Rémy's CND and the Musée de l'Homme group. When Vildé's organization was smashed by the Gestapo in spring 1941, one of its key members, socialist journalist Pierre Brossolette, remained free. A slim man with aquiline features and dark eyes, Brossolette was easily recognizable by his cleft chin and a streak of white hair – one of his nicknames was 'Pierre-le-Gris' ('Grey Pierre').[51] In the summer of 1941 Brossolette came into contact with Christian Pineau's Libération-Nord, but despite the fact that they were on the same political wavelength, Brossolette wanted to be involved in something more immediate, more practical, than simply producing a clandestine newspaper, no matter how dangerous that might be.

On a cold evening in November 1941 his friend Louis François was waiting outside the Parisian school near Port Royal, where Brossolette was a part-time teacher. As the two men walked down the Boulevard Saint-Michel towards the Seine, François explained that he was in contact with a Free French intelligence circuit, and that they wanted someone to write a monthly media report for London, describing the situation in the Occupied Zone, with the aim of guiding the propaganda output of the BBC. When he returned home, Brossolette excitedly beckoned his thirty-six-year-old wife, Gilberte, into their cramped bathroom so their two teenage children would not hear, and told her what had happened. Gilberte brushed aside his worries – 'Don't say any more. There's no need. You have to say yes. Finally we'll be doing something,' she said.[52]

Gilberte was slightly less enthusiastic when Rémy came to visit them at the end of the month. Although her first impressions of the secret agent were good – 'stocky and of medium height, a round face, clear skin and eyes, with a direct, confident and courteous manner'[53] – her confidence drained away when Rémy turned towards her and said: 'My real name is Gilbert Renault.' Despite this needless breach of security – the product of foolishness, overconfidence, or simply the desire to involve Gilberte – Rémy and Brossolette formed an immediate friendship, bridging the political gulf between them. As Rémy later wrote, 'From the first moment, I was conquered by his live intelligence and the kind of inner flame with which he seemed to be lit',[54] while for Brossolette Rémy was 'dynamic, enterprising. What he has set up is important, realistic, efficient and – who knows? – perhaps decisive.'[55] Brossolette threw himself into his work, writing fortnightly reports, and even joining the Free French in a ceremony in his apartment on 1 December.[56]

Moulin's report had given London a general picture of Resistance activities in the Non-Occupied Zone; Brossolette's regular correspondence now fleshed out the somewhat sketchy and out-of-date material they had received in October, and above all provided detailed accounts of what other groups were doing, particularly in the Occupied Zone. Up until this point, London had heard virtually nothing at first hand of how the French were reacting to the Occupation. Brossolette's close knowledge of the work of Libération-Nord meant that London, dominated by right-wing officers, began to hear the views of left-wing *résistants* who were linked to the underground trade unions, and as a result had a closer understanding of the feelings of ordinary working-class French men and women.

Brossolette's meetings with Libération-Nord brought him into contact with another fragment of the growing Resistance kaleidoscope, the Organisation Civile et Militaire (OCM – Civil and Military Organization). The OCM was a small group that recruited from among the right-wing upper middle class – military officers, businessmen, engineers, lawyers and university professors – and was very different from all other Resistance groups at the time. Instead of producing an underground publication, the OCM concentrated on the 'military' part of its name, through practical action – escape lines for French military prisoners and Allied airmen, caching arms or transmitting intelligence to the Vichy 'Deuxième Bureau' (Intelligence).[57] When it did eventually get round to setting out its positions, these were heavily influenced by the milieu of its founders, veering dangerously close to the anti-Semitism of Vichy's 'national revolution' at a number of points.[58] Once the contact with Brossolette provided the OCM with a direct link to London, they enthusiastically joined Rémy's CND.[59]

The bookshop on the Rue de la Pompe that Pierre Brossolette ran with his wife soon became a key meeting place for the Parisian Resistance. He would usher people into the cellar, where discussions could take place safely. It was at such a meeting, in February 1942, that Brossolette suggested to Christian Pineau that he should go to London to explain the state of the Resistance to the Free French. London was concerned that the wave of attacks being carried out by the Communist Party would weaken the Resistance in the Occupied Zone, he said. They wanted to persuade representatives of other Resistance organizations not to adopt this tactic. When Pineau heard he would soon be flown to London, he left Brossolette's bookshop full of excitement, 'almost choking on emotion and exaltation'.[60] But Pineau's comrades in Libération-Nord were less enthusiastic; some were worried that London might take control of 'their' movement, while others thought the whole thing was simply too dangerous.

Not everyone was so negative. Pineau's work with the Ministry of Supply took him into the Non-Occupied Zone, where he met André Philip, the Socialist ex-deputy who had corresponded with Pastor Brooks a few months earlier. Philip, whom de Gaulle admired despite their very different political traditions, saw that the trip could be turned to the advantage of the Resistance. He argued that Pineau should convince de Gaulle to produce a declaration of his political intentions; this could be a way of uniting the Resistance. This idea of putting pressure on de Gaulle soon caught on – Pineau's trade unionist comrades in the Occupied Zone decided they wanted a clear statement from the Free French leader about the role he saw for the trade unions after the Liberation.[61]

Pineau made the journey to London with François Faure ('Paco'), a forty-three-year-old businessman who was Rémy's second-in-command. Paco was in contact with the Communist Party, who had given him a message for London. They were prepared to throw their weight behind the Free French, they claimed, as long as they could retain their freedom of action, and they received substantial quantities of weapons. For the communists, this was partly a way of testing the water with the Free French, and partly a response to Moscow's growing interest in supporting de Gaulle, which was soon formalized by an agreement between de Gaulle and Molotov, signed in London in May 1942. Paco also brought with him a valuable piece of propaganda – the final testament of Gabriel Péri, the Communist deputy who had been executed as a hostage in December 1941. At the end of this document (Passy later described it as 'a magnificent letter of farewell'),[62] Péri wrote: 'I should like my fellow-countrymen to know that I am dying so that France may live . . . In a few minutes I am going out to prepare a future that will be full of song.' This moving letter became a key symbol of the Communist Party's sacrifice and was used to great propaganda effect in both Britain and the USA.[63] Péri's poetic closing phrase – 'des lendemains qui chantent' – subsequently became a well-known expression.

*

Early in the morning of 26 March 1942 Pineau and Paco arrived at a farmhouse near the hamlet of Saint-Léger-de-Montbrillais, not far from Chinon. The farmer, René, took them into a high-beamed, smoke-blackened room where there was a long oak table covered with local produce – butter, pain de campagne, rillettes and a saucisson – the like of which Pineau had not seen for months. The meal was washed down with two bottles of Saumur – a rather young 1941 ('drinkable') and a 1934 vintage ('excellent'). For Pineau, this was paradise:

> We ended the morning sitting in wicker chairs, set out in the farm-yard. The weather was warm, almost hot. There was not a cloud in the sky. In sixteen or seventeen hours, we could find ourselves miraculously transported from this typically French scene to Britain. The war, the Resistance, seemed so far away.[64]

Then it was time for lunch – meat, chicken, a 1921 red Champigny ('very good'), goats' cheese, crème au chocolat and, at around 5 p.m., a splitting headache. The solution? More Saumur – this time René's prize 1904 vintage. Finally, after supper – somehow they found space for supper – they listened to the BBC and heard the 'personal announcement' that indicated that their plane would arrive that night. At 11 p.m., they went out into a field as the reception team spread out torches in the shape of an inverted L. When the plane arrived, the plan was that the team would flash the agreed code signal and then turn on all the torches; the plane was supposed to land along a line sketched out by the vertical stroke, and come to a halt at the horizontal line – this plan had been devised in October 1940, scribbled on a tablecloth in Oddenino's restaurant in London, and was used until the end of the war.[65]

As a full moon rose into the clear black sky, lighting up the field, the warmth of the day vanished and the night became freezing cold. Huddled under a blanket to keep warm, feeling drowsy due to the combined effects of food and alcohol, Pineau began to doze off. When the plane finally arrived, just after midnight, he was fast asleep. Pineau got a shock when he woke up – the aircraft had overshot the final set of lights and had got stuck in the mud. The French reception committee, helped by Pineau and the passenger from London (who turned out to be Rémy, returning after a brief visit), had to heave for fifteen minutes before the plane was freed and turned around, ready to return.[66] Paco and Pineau jammed themselves into the narrow passenger cockpit, surrounded by reports from the CND circuit, the plane bumped along the field and then leaped towards the bright moon. They did not know it, but as they flew towards London, far below them on the coast of Brittany the raid on the Saint-Nazaire dry dock – Operation CHARIOT – was in full swing, as the explosive-laden HMS *Campbeltown* was rammed into the dock gates, the fruit of the work of both the CND and the Vildé group.

This was one of the first flights by the RAF 161 Special Duties Squadron that had been formed about six weeks earlier to provide the Free French and British intelligence services, SOE and the Resistance with a regular air link with France. As the war went on, these flights – which could take place only around the full moon and if the weather was clear – became vital for both the activities of the Resistance and for morale. Gifts would often be exchanged – cigarettes, whisky and food from Britain, champagne, fine wine, perfume and even freshly cut flowers from France.[67]

Like most of those trips, the flight that took Pineau across the Channel was made in a Lysander aircraft. These small single-engine planes, which could carry up to four people, were robustly designed so they could withstand harsh landings on bumpy fields, and so that they could take off and

land in a very short distance. Unarmed, and flying dangerously slowly –
a top speed of 180 mph – the Lysander was extremely vulnerable to
attack, but flying at night provided safe cover and only three of these
planes were shot down in over two hundred and twenty missions. The
main dangers were from trees and high-tension electricity cables, and
from cows and random pieces of farm machinery that were sometimes
inadvertently left in the fields. The other problem was getting lost – with
no navigator, and flying at night, getting to the landing site and back
again was not easy (even by the light of the full moon).[68]

Pineau's pilot was Flying Officer Guy Lockhart, a dashing twenty-
five-year-old who had been court-martialled from the RAF before the
war for flying so low over an aerodrome that the commanding officer
had to dive for cover. When war broke out, Lockhart rejoined the RAF,
flying Spitfires. In July 1941 he was shot down near Paris but managed
to get back to Britain via Marseilles and a march across the Pyrenees. A
year later, on his way to pick up Pineau again, Lockhart's Lysander got
stuck in a ditch near Macon and had to be burned; a few days later he
was exfiltrated via Narbonne.[69] After a brief period with SOE in 1943,
Lockhart rejoined the RAF.[70] His luck eventually ran out in 1944, during
a bombing raid over Friedrichshafen.

Dodging German flak, Lockhart flew Pineau and Paco safely to Britain.
At RAF Tangmere they were plied with whisky by the RAF personnel and
then taken to Bignor Manor, an Elizabethan building on the South Downs.
This house – owned by a member of MI6 – had recently become a staging
post for French visitors brought over to nearby Tangmere; hundreds of
Resistance members passed through during the war.[71] The lady of the
house, Mrs Barbara Bertram, was disappointed that Pineau and Paco,
having gorged themselves earlier in the day, were unable to finish the
slap-up meal she had prepared. 'It's the excitement,' they explained
politely.[72] The next morning they were taken to London, where Pineau
was given a false identity ('Major Garnier') and was told he had a private
dinner with de Gaulle at the Connaught Hotel at 8 p.m.

In the afternoon Pineau wandered the streets of London, window-
shopping – he eventually bought some coloured soap – and was amazed
at the pressing crowds, which he felt gave 'an extraordinary expression
of life and liberty'.[73] A few hours before his meal with de Gaulle, Pineau

had a meeting with Passy in the Duke Street headquarters of Free French Intelligence. The confrontation of a left-wing intellectual and a far-right militant should have produced fireworks. But instead, as with Brossolette and Rémy, it led to mutual admiration and a close working relationship.[74] Tied by the magic of friendship, the two men were pushed even closer by the Resistance and the tasks it required.

At the Connaught Hotel, Pineau was ushered into de Gaulle's presence:

> Without saying a word, he led me to an armchair, gestured for me to sit down, pushed a box of cigarettes towards me, sat down in his chair and then, looking me straight in the eye, spoke his first words: 'Now, tell me about France.'[75]

For half an hour Pineau explained the situation in as much detail as he could, but de Gaulle seemed perplexed by the main reason for his visit: 'When I mentioned that the Resistance wanted a sign from him, a message, a slight frown passed across his face. He was obviously quite surprised and had no conception of what I expected from him.'[76] De Gaulle then spoke, but did not respond to any of the points that Pineau had raised, simply ignoring Pineau's plea for some kind of declaration of his political intentions. Instead, the General talked about the internal politics of the Free French – about which Pineau knew nothing and cared less. De Gaulle also described his problems with the Allies, which for Pineau was a depressing revelation. De Gaulle made it quite plain that, for him, the Free French armed forces *were* the French Resistance. Pineau's morale plummeted even further as de Gaulle failed to ask a single question about the Resistance, or even a single personal question: 'Asking me if I'd had a good journey would have been trivial, but this journey was not like any other – at least for me; it might have merited some comment.'[77] After the meal, which was washed down with a bottle of Bordeaux ('excellent'), de Gaulle finally deigned to discuss the work of Libération-Nord and the other groups. Pineau suddenly realized what the problem was:

> . . . like Passy, he knew virtually nothing about the Resistance. His conception of 'France' was entirely military . . . He barely reacted to my descriptions of the dangers we faced, of the anxiety created by

occupation and repression. It was obvious that, for him, every soldier doing his job risked his life, and that there was no difference between the dangers faced by a tank-driver in the North African desert or someone carrying illegal newspapers in the Occupied Zone.[78]

In one sense, de Gaulle was right. Being killed is an occupational hazard for a soldier, as it was for members of the Resistance. But there was one major difference that the Free French could never understand: soldiers are conscripted, trained and act en masse, under orders. They are provided with weapons and equipment that can protect them, and if captured they are imprisoned. Resistance members were volunteers, isolated and often unarmed, living under the permanent tension of the threat of denunciation and discovery. Furthermore, they ran the risk not only that they might be killed, but also that they would be terribly tortured and, worse, that the same fate might befall their loved ones. From this point of view, the sacrifice made by members of the Resistance *was* greater than that of soldiers in the regular army.

Throughout the war, Resistance members, worn out by the dreadful dangers they faced and frustrated by the lack of resources, eventually became infuriated by what they perceived to be the ignorance and indifference of the Free French leadership. Meanwhile, de Gaulle, Churchill, Roosevelt and their respective political and military advisers became increasingly concerned about the potential threat the Resistance might pose to their plans for taking France into a post-war world. All sides therefore sought to dominate and channel the activity of the Resistance, in an attempt to keep its activities within what they considered to be appropriate limits. Claude Bourdet, a member of Combat, later tried to understand why things looked so different from either side of the Channel:

No doubt it was difficult, from London, to understand the unexpected nature of the problems faced by the Resistance. We ourselves discovered the nature and scale of the task bit by bit, empirically. To have imagined it, without living it every day, would have required a wide-ranging political culture, to have studied the history of revolutions, to more or less understand the meaning of revolutionary action. This was not the case with de Gaulle, nor the men who surrounded him.[79]

Pineau felt deflated. He was supposed to convince de Gaulle to take account of the views of the Resistance, but the Free French leader did not seem particularly interested in even hearing about the Resistance, never mind accommodating to it. Over the next few weeks de Gaulle and Pineau had several rounds of discussions. On some issues, like the promise of a future health service, Pineau persuaded de Gaulle to move to the left – de Gaulle no doubt considered this to be an easy way of gaining support; promises were for the future. But right until the very end of Pineau's stay in London, de Gaulle refused to budge over his conviction that the defunct Third Republic and the Vichy collaborators were as bad as each other. This was not merely an historical analysis; it had very real implications for the kind of France that de Gaulle wanted to emerge from the war. He would not countenance a return to the weak, party-dominated regime of the Third Republic, which he felt was directly responsible for the fall of France. Instead, he wanted a strong state, with a strong leader. This was more than enough to scare off many of the trade unionists and socialists in the Resistance who might otherwise support him. When Pineau pointed this out, de Gaulle brushed aside the issue in a way that showed he did not even understand what the problem was: 'Tell those brave people that I will not betray them,' he said, leaving Pineau feeling depressed and frustrated.[80]

Pineau had been in London for nearly a month. As the moon waxed, it was time for him to return to France. As well as endless political discussions, Pineau had undertaken a series of training sessions with British officers, learning how to encode and decode radio messages, how to choose appropriate sites for landings and parachute drops and what to do in case of a security breach. It had not all been hard work, however: he had long drinking sessions with British officers over various Bordeaux vintages (Château Gruaud-Larose 1920 was the best, they decided), he went out with Free French secretaries and frequented various dives and jazz clubs, dancing with girls until the early morning. His enthusiasm for these distractions became notorious, and steps were taken to ensure that subsequent visitors from France kept a lower profile.

Shortly before Pineau returned to France, his life took another dramatic turn. Passy asked him to work with Free French Intelligence and to set up two intelligence circuits, one in each zone. Swept away by his contacts with Passy and British Intelligence, Pineau had little hesitation in accepting the offer. This new task not only added a further layer of danger to his life; it also meant he would have to accept the new London line of keeping action and intelligence entirely separate, and abandon his work with Libération-Nord. As a result, he returned to France a changed man. He had left as the delegate of the Resistance in the Occupied Zone; he returned as a Free French secret agent. His uncertainties about de Gaulle remained.

Minutes before his Lysander left, Pineau received a new version of a speech de Gaulle was planning to make on the BBC. There were enough minor changes – a stronger critique of Vichy, some vague talk of the need for economic planning by the state – to make Pineau confident that his trade union comrades in France would be pleased.

But back in Paris Pineau felt the same kind of political vertigo he had sensed with de Gaulle. Just as the General did not understand the Resistance, Pineau's comrades did not understand the Free French. They were not impressed by what he told them about de Gaulle – when he read out the final, amended declaration, it was greeted with a stony silence. They felt the concessions were minor, that de Gaulle could not be trusted, and scolded Pineau for making too many compromises. Glumly, Pineau realized they were right. Even when it came to the one thing Pineau was certain they would appreciate – the money he brought with him – the gulf between them yawned once more, with the dyed-in-the-wool trade union committee men on one side, and the underground journalist turned spy on the other: when he handed the money over to Laurent, who acted as the treasurer for Libération-Nord, his comrade immediately offered to give Pineau whatever money he needed, in return for a receipt. Pineau was aghast at this absurd piece of routinism in such a dangerous context: 'Don't tell me you're going to ask people for receipts?' he asked. 'Of course,' came the indignant reply. 'I can hardly be Treasurer and not have my accounts up to date!'[81] The incomprehension was mutual, and total. The Resistance had a lot to learn.

# 5

# *Life and Death*

On a freezing cold evening at the end of January 1942 Henri Frenay sat alone in a small café in Lyons. He was completely dejected, unable to eat a single mouthful of his meal. The excitement of meeting Jean Moulin earlier in the month had been swept away: in the space of a few catastrophic days, forty-five members of Combat in the Non-Occupied Zone had been arrested by the Vichy police, including two of Frenay's closest associates – his lover, Berty Albrecht, and Maurice Chevance. Earlier that day, Frenay had lunch with Chevance;[1] now his comrade was in prison, and Frenay was touching rock bottom:

> I felt overcome with fatigue. Crushed, oh, I was utterly crushed! For the first time in my life I understood the full meaning of this word . . . One by one the faces of all those dear comrades rose up to haunt me. They seemed to be smiling. What could I do for them, my God, what could I do! I felt ashamed to be free, spared in the battle into which I had led them and in which they had fallen. Should not I too have been among them? It would have been so simple for me to surrender to the police, and I would have found such peace.[2]

Combat member André Koehl had been arrested near Clermont-Ferrand, his suitcase full of copies of the newspaper. In breach of the most elementary security rules, Koehl was carrying an uncoded list of names and addresses of Combat members. That was all the Vichy police needed. Frenay had sat in his room, stunned, as every hour brought reports of new arrests.

Worse was to come in the days that followed. The Combat group in the Occupied Zone was smashed by the Gestapo, who arrested forty-seven people in and around Paris.[3] Henri Devillers, a Combat agent who had been recruited in the autumn by Frenay and Berty Albrecht to carry information across the demarcation line, turned out to be an agent of the Abwehr, the Nazi counter-intelligence service. For three months the Gestapo had access to every piece of information that Frenay's group transmitted between the two zones. The arrested *résistants* – including René Parodi, who also worked with Libération-Nord – suffered a dreadful fate. After a period in French jails, they were deported to Germany under the sinister designation *Nacht und Nebel* (Night and Fog). This referred to prisoners who were to disappear without trace into the hell of Nazi Germany. Not even their relatives would know what happened to them. Eventually, in October 1943, the Combat prisoners were tried, and seventeen of them – including six women – were sentenced to a particularly brutal end: with one exception, they were beheaded with an axe in Cologne in January 1944. For the six women among the arrested, the death sentence was eventually commuted to life imprisonment, but at the end of the war only two made it back from the concentration camps.[4]

Devillers had no time to bask in his betrayal: in one of the strangest moments of the Occupation, he was immediately arrested by Vichy counter-espionage in the shape of the Travaux Ruraux (TR), led by Paul Paillole, one of Frenay's army colleagues and friends. The role of the clandestine TR – in breach of the armistice agreement with the Nazis – was to observe and harass foreign agents within Vichy France, including German spies. Devillers was promptly tried by a secret French military tribunal for communicating information to an 'enemy espionage organization' and was executed two months after his arrest.[5] With one hand Vichy was smashing a Resistance organization, with the other it was executing a man who provided the Nazis with information to do the same thing. This apparent paradox can be explained by the fact that Vichy was formally an independent regime, and by the existence of a small minority within the state apparatus who were hostile to collaboration.

After Frenay's moment of depression in Lyons, the Combat leader left for Annecy to discuss the crisis with François de Menthon, taking with him another of his lovers, Chilina Ciosi. To his amazement Berty Albrecht walked into the hotel where he and Ciosi were staying. Berty had been freed by the Vichy police to give Frenay a message: Henri Rollin, the head of Vichy police counter-espionage, wanted to meet him. Combat was still reeling from the wave of arrests, and Rollin's invitation could easily be a trap designed to finish the group off. Frenay's comrades finally agreed he should take the risk and meet Rollin, with the hope that something might be done for the dozens of Combat members who had just been imprisoned.

The next day, 28 January, Frenay entered Rollin's office in Lyons. Rollin, who was married to a Russian Jew, had written a fiercely anti-Nazi book and eventually joined the Free French in London. But at this point Rollin was apparently a Vichy loyalist who wanted Frenay to stop his activities. Neither Frenay nor Rollin budged an inch, but the interview ended with an invitation for Frenay to meet the Minister of the Interior, Pierre Pucheu, and a promise that Frenay would not be subject to Vichy surveillance for the time being.[6] The next day Frenay met Pucheu in his Vichy offices for ninety minutes. This was not a good idea. As well as being responsible for all anti-Resistance repression in France, the forty-two-year-old Pucheu was a far-right activist and one-time steel magnate who had bankrolled the fascist Parti Populaire Français.[7] Indeed, *Combat* never mentioned Pucheu's name without calling him a traitor. And now Frenay was in discussion with him.

Like Rollin, Pucheu argued that *Combat* should stop attacking the government, before reminding Frenay that 'These are not negotiations. I am simply giving you a warning before proceeding to repress your organizations with extreme severity.'[8] In response, Frenay asked for ten days free of police harassment, so that he could set out Pucheu's case to his comrades in Combat. That evening, in a final unreal twist, Frenay dined with Rollin and his wife in one of the smartest hotels in Vichy.[9] Frenay had one more meeting with Pucheu, on 6 February. For Combat, the point was to gain time – Frenay was convinced that the Vichy police knew enough details to round up the entire leadership if they wanted.[10] He read Pucheu a statement that criticized Vichy's anti-Semitic policies but suggested that if the government secretly provided the Resistance with information and changed its political line, then

*Combat* would be more measured. Pucheu asked for time to think about this unlikely proposition, and Frenay left. There was no further meeting between the two men. Frenay met Rollin one more time, on 25 February, to discuss the situation of the arrested members of Combat, virtually all of whom had been released as a result of the Frenay–Pucheu discussions, and had then immediately gone into hiding.[11]

Frenay's group appeared to have made a brilliant manoeuvre. They had gained valuable time that had been used to tighten up security and protect their members, and above all the arrested comrades had been freed. But this came at a terrible price, a price they were too naive to foresee.

Although the Resistance in the Non-Occupied Zone had not yet made any physical attacks on the Pétain regime, their continuous criticisms and their clandestine preparation for armed action represented a real threat. Frenay's discussions with Pucheu handed Vichy a golden opportunity to split the Resistance, which they seized in the first half of February by leaking news of the meetings to Frenay's Resistance rivals. In Paris Pierre Brossolette heard about the affair within a matter of days, and duly forwarded the news to Free French Intelligence, openly criticizing 'Fresnet' but without giving any indication of the context – there was no mention of the wave of arrests or of Combat's intention to bargain for the release of their comrades.[12] On 1 March Emmanuel d'Astier's *Libération* denounced 'petty schemes and petty betrayals' and poured scorn on 'those café diplomats who hoped to respond to the siren calls of Vichy'. Three weeks later *Libération* made a more open allusion to the affair, including a sotto voce appeal to doubting members of Combat:

> Among those Frenchmen and women who are fighting the Germans there are sincere and courageous people who thought they could negotiate with the government, having a strong hand to play. They will be fooled by Vichy, and their troops will abandon them.[13]

Although Moulin was eventually able to defuse the row and get both groups to publish a statement declaring their 'complete agreement' and their loyalty to de Gaulle, the damage was done, and the Resistance was permanently weakened.[14] Combat and Libération never truly fused, and rumours about Frenay's Vichy connections continued to circulate. In the middle of 1942 Christian Pineau and Free French Intelligence both suspected Frenay of being a Pétainist agent, and at one point Moulin was forbidden to have any contact with Combat, because London feared the group was manipulated by Vichy.[15] Moulin, however, staunchly defended Frenay, recognizing his fundamental loyalty and the vital role he played in the Resistance.[16]

\*

As the terrible winter of 1942 gradually ended, the Resistance in the Non-Occupied Zone began to realize the opportunity before it. Although Pucheu was determined to repress the Resistance 'with extreme severity', the movements in Vichy France still enjoyed a far greater freedom of activity than their counterparts in the Occupied Zone. At the same time as Frenay had been chatting in Pucheu's office, Frenay's comrades in the north were being thrown into prison, hostages were being executed with savage regularity, while the trials of Vildé's Musée de l'Homme group and of the members of the Bataillons de la Jeunesse were coming to their dreadful conclusions. If the Resistance movements in the Occupied Zone could act despite potentially lethal consequences, there was no reason for those in the south not to emulate them.

The first actions taken by Combat members were small beer compared with the assassinations and explosions carried out in the Occupied Zone. In 1941 Frenay had recruited Jacques Renouvin, a lawyer in his late thirties. Renouvin was a myopic bear of a man who had been a far-right street brawler in the early 1930s; now he wanted to use his physical talents and his taste for violent confrontation to serve the Resistance. With Frenay's enthusiastic support, Renouvin set up a series of 'Groupes Francs' – hit squads – whose role was to attack the most visible symbols of collaboration in the Non-Occupied Zone, beginning in his home town, Montpellier. In February 1942 the Groupes Francs blew up several recruiting offices for the Ligue Anti-Bolchevique (Anti-Bolshevik League), one of the main fascist groups that flourished in Vichy France. They then began intimidating kiosks that sold pro-Nazi publications. First they would send a letter signed 'Combat', inviting the owner to stop selling such material. If this brought no change, a second letter would be sent, warning of the consequences; if the owner continued to ignore such friendly advice, the kiosk would be blown up. In case anyone did not get the message, in Montpellier the comrades painted a huge reminder on the seventeenth-century aqueduct that dominates the city: COMBAT PUNISHES TRAITORS.[17]

These actions were the work of a very small and highly committed minority, but increasingly, ordinary people also wanted to protest. Recognizing this change, the key Resistance leaders in the Non-Occupied Zone decided to hold a series of demonstrations on May Day, to show the scale of opposition to Vichy and the Occupation.[18] Moulin contacted London and tried to persuade de Gaulle to support the campaign:

ALL RESISTANCE MOVEMENTS SUPPORT DEMONSTRATION STOP REQUEST GENERAL SPEAK ON RADIO TWENTY-SIXTH APRIL DATE LAUNCH OF MASSIVE CAMPAIGN OF LEAFLETS PAPERS ETC STOP AGREE IN PRINCIPLE BEFORE SEVENTEENTH APRIL STOP[19]

Although London agreed that de Gaulle would speak, there was no broadcast, either because de Gaulle was too busy finalizing his 'social' statement with Christian Pineau or because he was near comatose with a bout of malaria.[20] Whatever the case, Moulin was irritated: 'it was regrettable,' he said in a message to London, 'that the General had not launched the promised appeal on the occasion of the first common demonstration of workers and resistance movements. The movements had distributed 120,000 newspapers and 250,000 tracts for May 1st.'[21]

The effort paid off. In Marseilles tens of thousands of demonstrators poured into the Vieux Port; in Lyons, similarly large crowds marched through the centre of the city, to cries of 'Long live de Gaulle! Hang Laval!' Smaller demonstrations took place in Toulouse, Nice and Montpellier.[22] In Lyons and Marseilles there were violent confrontations with the police, revealing the intensity of popular opposition to the government. The demonstrations were even more successful than the Resistance had expected, partly because they coincided with a decisive shift in the politics of Vichy. After sixteen months waiting in the

Christian Pineau in 1945.

Claude Bourdet in 1945.

Gilbert Renault ('Rémy').

Pierre Brossolette.

André Dewavrin ('Passy').

Jean Moulin, in 1939.

Henri Frenay, the founder
of Combat, in disguise.

Emmanuel d'Astier
de la Vigerie.

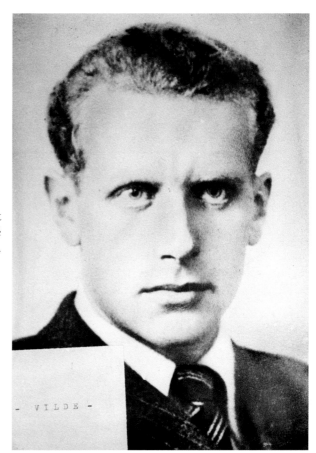

Boris Vildé, ethnologist and founder of the Musé de l'Homme group.

'Drawing Vs' – a child's drawing from the Nantes region, made during the war.

Major-General Edward Spears (left) and General Charles de Gaulle (right), June 1940.

Marshal Philippe Pétain (left) shakes hands with Adolf Hitler at Montoire, 24 October 1940.

Jean Cassou in 1953 at the launch of his book on the meaning of the Resistance, *La Mémoire Courte.*

Montage of Resistance newspapers.

Clandestine radio transmitter used in the north of France in 1942.

The prototype Westland Lysander. Aircraft flown into France were painted black.

wings, Pierre Laval had returned as Prime Minister. This change, which followed pressure from Germany, showed that the Vichy regime was truly nothing more than a tool in Hitler's hands. Two enthusiastic collaborators – Admiral Darlan and Pierre Laval, head of the military and head of the government respectively – now vied for power in Vichy. Pétain's pretence that he represented some kind of 'third way' between the Allies and the Axis, a tactic that had fooled many people, had been shown to be a delusion. As Jean Guéhenno wrote in his diary:

> By Hitler's will, Laval is the head of the government of France. The old man [Pétain] has handed over power and has turned into a ghost, even before he's dead . . . There are, in fact, two governments – a military power, in the hands of Darlan, and a civil power, in the hands of Laval. Perhaps the old man hopes to play one off against the other, and to preserve some degree of independence. What is certain is that France, and its 40 million citizens, does not want either of them. The Pétain government was backed by cowards. There is no one behind the Darlan–Laval government. Even the cowards are ashamed.[23]

\*

The May Day demonstrations proved that a traditional workers' protest could mobilize substantial numbers of ordinary people against the Occupation and against Vichy. At the same time, under pressure from Moscow to do all in its power to hasten an Allied attack on Nazi-occupied Europe, the Communist Party began to change its attitude towards de Gaulle, the Free French and the rest of the Resistance. On May Day the Communist underground newspaper, *L'Humanité,* called on its readers to build the 'Front National', a Communist-led front organization, 'which, from the Gaullists to the Communists, groups together all those French people who want France to remain French'. The declaration went on to recognize the Free French forces fighting with the Allies as 'representatives of France at war on the battlefield', and even called on French sailors 'to take their boats into the camp of General de Gaulle to continue the patriotic struggle which will restore France to its sovereignty and its grandeur'.[24]

Just as the Communists adopted Gaullist language, de Gaulle started to change his tone. In response to Laval's return to power, de Gaulle broadcast a call to arms that could have been lifted from a Communist leaflet:

> It is the duty of every Frenchman and Frenchwoman to fight actively, by all means in their power, against the enemy itself and against the agents of Vichy who are the accomplices of the enemy. These people are like the enemy: the French people should hound them, sabotage their plans and hate their leaders. National liberation cannot be separated from national insurrection.[25]

It was not only words that began to be shared. Shortly before leaving for London with Pineau in March, Paco had discussed with a Communist Party contact the possibility that the PCF would receive weapons and other materiel from London. Within weeks, the links were activated, beginning with discussions between the Free French agent Rémy and 'Joseph' (George Beaufils), a leading PCF member. These two men were very different – one was a royalist Catholic, the other a Communist atheist – but they struck up a strong friendship that lasted for decades.[26]

At the end of May the Free French decided to set up a permanent link with the Communists, and sent two men to France as part of Operation GOLDFISH. However, within a week one of the BCRA agents, Georges Weil, was arrested by the Gestapo and committed suicide by biting on the cyanide pill all agents were supplied with.[27] At the same time, many members of Rémy's CND circuit, including Paco, were arrested. The fragile link with the Communist Party was temporarily broken. Permanent radio contact with the Communist Party was finally established only in October 1942; even then, PCF security was so tight that it was often a month before a response was received.[28]

Despite the political differences between the Communists and the Free French, there was initially no sign of any discrimination against the PCF in terms of the resources sent from London. While Combat's monthly budget at the end of 1941 was a mere 30,000 francs a month,[29] in July 1942 the BCRA told the Communist Party they would receive 3 million francs – Rémy later gave them a further 2 million francs a month out of his own funds.[30] (The modern equivalents of these three sums would be around £6,000, £150,000 and £100,000 respectively.)[31] The PCF was also promised an 'important shipment of machine guns, pistols, explosives and grenades' which was so substantial it had to be sent by sea.[32] With the supplies from London, explosives stolen from quarries and weapons hidden during the summer of 1940, the Communists had access to large amounts of weaponry: in September 1942 the police in Rennes seized 300 kilogrammes of arms and explosives, while in October the Paris anti-terrorist brigade seized a major stash of about 2 cubic metres of cases containing Mills grenades, pencil-timer detonators and plastic explosives, all from London.[33]

Some of these weapons were employed in operations by an elite PCF hit squad made up of ultra-loyal party members, called the détachement Valmy (no connection with the newspaper of the same name). Tragically, the détachement Valmy was as much involved in settling accounts in paranoid Stalinist purges as it was in fighting the Nazis,[34] but in some cases it made good use of the British weapons. In particular, its activities began to change after an unprecedented mutiny by its members. In August 1942 the détachement met as a 'soldiers' soviet' and complained about the way in which they were being used by the Party, demanding to be allowed to attack the Nazis, like their comrades in the PCF's recently founded, broadly based fighting structure, the FTP. They got their wish. In the morning of 10 September 1942 the détachement carried out two Mills grenade attacks on German soldiers in Paris. Forensic examination of the shrapnel from these and other explosions left no doubt in the Nazis' minds: the Communists were being supplied with British weapons.[35]

This confirmed what the Nazis already suspected: the Communist Party was becoming more serious and professional, as the ramshackle Bataillons de la Jeunesse were replaced by the more effective FTP. As part of the overall rapprochement between the Free French (re-branded as the Fighting French in July 1942), the FTP proclaimed themselves to be 'the vanguard of the Fighting French on the soil of the Fatherland'.[36] The Nazi solution to the FTP threat was simple and brutal: more repression.

In summer 1942 SS General Karl Oberg, in charge of security in Occupied France, decreed that the adult male relatives of any convicted 'terrorist' would be sentenced to death, while the female relatives would be given forced labour.[37] On at least one occasion, this policy had its desired effect. Fosco Focardi, a member of the détachement Valmy, was instructed to plant a bomb outside a Paris cinema, the Rex, which was frequented by Nazi soldiers. But in the middle of the operation Focardi had second thoughts. As he later told the police:

> When Paris [his comrade] planted the bomb, which was due to go off in ten minutes, I realized that the attack could have terrible consequences. I thought, like each time in fact, that my brother, who is imprisoned in Poissy, could be taken as a hostage. Obeying a sudden impulse, I went and found the bomb and removed the detonator. I told my comrades that the times of the film had changed, so no one would be coming out of the cinema when we expected, which made the attack pointless.[38]

Most of the time, however, the dangers did not deter young people from taking arms against the Nazis. In spring 1942 five teenage school students from the Lycée Buffon in Paris decided to act, following the arrest of one of their teachers, Raymond Burgard, who had taken over the leadership of the *Valmy* newspaper (no relation to the PCF hit squad). Burgard was arrested during the Easter holidays; on the first day of term, the five young-sters organized a demonstration, involving children from other schools. Around a hundred school students took part, chanting Burgard's name and throwing leaflets in the air. Although the school authorities closed the gates to trap the demonstrators, everyone managed to escape – some by hiding in the cellars. But the five ringleaders were identified to the police and had to go into hiding; over the next few months they carried out a number of (rather ineffectual) attempted bombings and assassinations. Betrayed to the police, they were tried and sentenced to death. After the judge had passed sentence, he asked the five young men if they had any-thing to say. Pierre Grelot's reply summed up the courage, dignity and determination of his generation: 'I am proud to merit this sentence.'[39]

After several months in solitary confinement, the five lycéens were executed on 8 February 1943. Their final letters, written on the day of their execution, betray not the slightest bitterness, only a certain frustra-tion at leaving the battlefield when victory seemed to be in sight (one of the decisive events of the war – the German surrender at Stalingrad – had taken place the week before; the news had penetrated even into the heart of the Nazi prisons). As eighteen-year-old Pierre Benoît wrote:

> My dear parents, my dear friends,
> It is the end! They have just come to take us to the firing squad. Never mind . . . To die at the moment of victory is a bit annoying, but it does not matter! Things happen because of mens' dreams . . . Life will be beautiful. We are singing as we leave. Be brave! It's not so bad after six months of prison. My final kisses to you all, your Pierrot.[40]

Raymond Burgard was also sentenced to death. He was beheaded with an axe in Cologne in June 1944.

*

Imprisonment, torture and death were the fate of many *résistants*. One now-forgotten organization, Turma-Vengeance ('turma' is Portuguese for 'group'), paid a particularly heavy price, with nearly 600 members killed.[41] Vengeance was set up in January 1941 by two physicians, Dr Victor 'Vic' Dupont and Dr François Wetterwald. Three years later, both men were in Buchenwald concentration camp, betrayed by a Nazi agent within the organization. In 1941 Vengeance organized one of the most spectacular breaches of Nazi security, through the work of telecommunications engineer Robert Keller, known in intelligence circles as 'source K'. Sabotage of telecommunications equipment was punishable by death, but Keller – a father of four – nevertheless volunteered to intercept messages on the main Paris–Berlin cable. A house was rented in the Paris suburbs, right next to where the cable passed, and on 15 April 1942 Keller engineered a fault on the line; as expected, the Nazis called him in to solve the problem, which involved digging up the road in front of the house, with the approval of the watching Germans. In the middle of the cold wet night, Keller and his two technicians clambered into the trench and installed a complex wire-tap device which diverted the signal into the house. The next day the repairs were completed to the satisfaction of the Nazis, and messages were transmitted and received as normal. Except there was a team in the house transcribing everything and passing the material on to Vichy Air Force Intelligence and then on to MI6 in London.

After a few months Keller and his team had to move the operation to another suburb – the locals had become suspicious of the comings and goings and decided that the house was a nest of Gestapo agents who were listening to all the phone calls from the village. In the middle of December 1942 the second tap came online. However, within a week the Gestapo came to Keller's house to arrest him, but he was not at home. That evening, to prevent his wife from being harassed, Keller turned himself in. He had been betrayed to the Nazis by René Bousquet, head of the French police. Keller was deported to Bergen-Belsen, where he died.[42]

In retrospect, the existence of so many Resistance groups seems bewildering, and even wilfully counter-productive. At the time, however, the situation was more complex than this. The unification of the Resistance would eventually be a military necessity – if they were to strike effectively against the Nazis, then the highest degree of coordination would be required. But in terms of both security and politics, the scattered nature of the Resistance was a positive advantage. The presence of so many small, unconnected groups made it more difficult for the Nazis and Vichy to persecute them, and the effects of betrayal were inevitably less extreme as a result. Furthermore, the broad nature of the Resistance, with its wide range of voices, approaches and attitudes, showed that this was not a movement restricted to one particular section or region, nor was it the mere expression of a single individual or leadership. The Germans, Vichy and the French public all recognized that the Resistance represented something important and widespread. It was certainly not the voice of the majority, but its many voices had a moral authority that grew as the war progressed. Nevertheless, there was pressure for the Resistance groups to combine in one large organization. This was discussed throughout 1942, but there were major problems. Although Frenay was keen for Combat to fuse with Libération, Emmanuel d'Astier was utterly hostile, mainly due to his profound political and personal distrust of Frenay (this was mutual).[43] Many rank-and-file *résistants* found the whole situation deeply depressing, as did Moulin. As he wrote to London in August 1942:

We should not hide from the fact that in paramilitary terms we are in a period of acute crisis. Virtually everywhere, the militants want fusion. The lower-level cadres feel the same way, as most of them are fed up with a competition which, in certain regions, has turned into a self-serving squabble.[44]

For most of the year, progress on fusion was at a dead halt. First there was the Pucheu affair, which gave d'Astier more reasons not to budge. Then, in the second half of April, d'Astier suddenly left for London, without a word to Frenay or Moulin. D'Astier had hoodwinked SOE agent Francis Basin into giving him a place on the next Royal Navy submarine that surfaced in the Bay of Antibes, the P42 (HMS *Unbroken*).[45] After a two-week voyage – the submarine had other missions, including attacking a German convoy off Genoa – the P42 arrived in Gibraltar. Following intensive questioning by MI5, d'Astier was finally flown to London. When Basin realized that d'Astier had fooled him, he sheepishly contacted SOE and asked whether he should also send Frenay. 'No thank you, one is quite enough,' came the reply.[46]

Unlike Moulin and Pineau, d'Astier did not make a good impression on the Free French. Passy and d'Astier took an instant, visceral, dislike to each other. D'Astier could not see beyond the fact that Passy was a right-wing military man and a spy, while what really irritated Passy was not d'Astier's politics but his pretension: 'a mixture of a condottiere and Machiavelli . . . an anarchist in court shoes' was Passy's caustic description.[47] De Gaulle, however, was delighted with his visitor and decided to send d'Astier to the USA to drum up support. As a result, the leader of Libération spent nearly three weeks on the other side of the Atlantic.[48]

D'Astier's sudden departure was not entirely bad for the Resistance: practical coordination between the movements became much easier, simply because there were fewer rows. Furthermore, d'Astier's trip enabled the Resistance to get a measure of the full range of forces working in France under the control of London. The situation was unbelievably complex – there seemed to be almost as many intelligence services as there were Resistance groups. The Free French had two services – Colonel Passy's BCRA and a service under the orders of the Minister of the Interior – both of which sent people to France without telling the other. SOE had two separate and sometimes competing sections intervening in France – 'F', which ran the independent SOE circuits in France, and 'RF', whose circuits were linked with the Resistance. There was also an SOE section running escape lines ('D/F'), a separate British Intelligence escape service ('MI9') and a complex network of intelligence circuits run by MI6 and by Polish Intelligence. Predictably, in a war in which secret services jealously protected their own patches, d'Astier's suggestion that a coordinating committee should be set up to make things simpler was dismissed out of hand.

This lack of coordination produced confusion and led to some embarrassing mistakes. SOE's 'F' section came a cropper when it swallowed some of the fantasies of André Girard ('Carte'), a forty-year-old artist who claimed to have a large group of 'apolitical' and deeply anti-Gaullist *résistants*, together with a substantial intelligence network. This was music to London's ears, and SOE soon provided Carte with vast amounts of money and arms and even his own British-based radio station, Radio Patrie, which claimed to broadcast from within France.[49] Girard had contacts with Vichy Intelligence, including with Henri Rollin of Vichy police counter-espionage,[50] and a number of minor Vichy officers, but his group never really spread outside the privileged and comfortable region of the Côte d'Azur. Nevertheless, Carte managed to persuade the deputy leader of 'F' section, Major Bodington, that his group involved leaders of the Vichy army, and that he could mobilize up to 300,000 troops. 'F' section believed this because they were desperate to work with an armed group that was not under the influence of de Gaulle. However, Girard's increasingly bizarre behaviour led to splits within his small organization and growing suspicions in London, while the careless loss of a set of uncoded file cards carrying details of the circuit's members soon led to the arrest of dozens of people. After the war, SOE's official historian wrote diplomatically that 'it is impossible to separate the bluff from reality' in the Carte affair.[51] At the time, SOE's verdict was rather sharper. For over three months at the beginning of 1943 'F' section tried to get Girard to come to London to explain himself; for over three months Carte repeatedly made excuses. When he finally arrived they decided that he was 'virtually mad' and forbade him from returning to France.[52] He was eventually dispatched to the USA, where he lived until his death in 1968.

Free French operations were equally chaotic. Moulin complained to London about the way in which ex-Prime Minister Édouard Herriot 'had been contacted nineteen times by nineteen different agents, each of whom claimed to be the sole legitimate representative of de Gaulle'.[53] This reflected badly on the Resistance and made it much more difficult to plan and carry out work seriously. Things got so bad that at the end of August 1942 Moulin sent a furious message to London:

INFORM YOU THAT ONLY SERIOUS DIFFICULTIES HAVE ENCOUNTERED IN MY WORK COME FROM GAULLIST AGENTS STOP IF ISSUE NOT SETTLED IMMEDIATELY WILL REGRETFULLY ASK YOU TO ACCEPT MY RESIGNATION STOP IN THIS FIELD DISORDER IS EXTREME STOP.[54]

Moulin did not resign, even though the situation was not resolved, mainly because there was no easy solution. Some attempts to find an answer verged on the bizarre. To ensure that Resistance and intelligence work did not interfere with each other, London helpfully suggested that Moulin should give Pineau two different code names – one as head of Libération-Nord ('Berval') and the other as a BCRA agent ('Francis'), and that when Moulin met 'Berval' the pair would have to ignore everything that they had decided when Moulin met 'Francis'.[55] This did little to ease Moulin's frustrations, or to convince him that London had any real understanding of what life in the Resistance actually involved.

*

There is a popular image of the Resistance which could be from a comic book – a man in a black leather jacket laying explosives on a railway track, accompanied by a woman in a beret carrying a Sten gun, the pair of them on the run from the Gestapo. Those things did exist, more or less, for some people, some of the time. But for the leaders of the Resistance, this was not their everyday life. True, they lived in permanent fear of betrayal or discovery. But apart from that, their lives were remarkably humdrum – neither Frenay nor Moulin harmed anybody during their time as *résistants*. Claude Bourdet, a leader of Combat, later recalled his situation, cleverly mixing the prosaic and the dramatic:

> At root, my own life, until I was arrested, was that of a kind of civil servant, a bureaucrat writing memos and sitting on committees; nothing distinguished it from the life of an ordinary bureaucrat except its precarious state, a habit of looking both ways when leaving a building, and the frequent presence of an automatic pistol under my left arm.[56]

Moulin's life was not much different. When Daniel Cordier, aged twenty-two, was parachuted into the Non-Occupied Zone in July 1942 to act as a radio operator, Moulin decided he needed a secretary, and gave Cordier the job. The young man, a slight elf-like figure, was appalled to find that de Gaulle's personal representative in France was living in a miserably small room near the station. As befitted his apparent taste for secrets and mystery, Moulin had two lives – his clandestine existence in Lyons, where he was known as 'Max' or 'Rex', and an official, public existence in Provence, where he was registered as a retired civil servant. Together with a young woman called Colette Pons, who may have been his lover, Moulin owned an art gallery in Nice – they made a tidy living selling early-twentieth-century paintings, including works by Renoir, Utrillo and Dufy. Apart from his sister, no one knew the full extent of the link between the respectable ex-prefect and the Resistance leader.

Cordier was soon able to put some order into Moulin's life, providing him with appropriate and efficient support. Cordier's memories of their daily routine in Lyons are strikingly clear:

> Very early in the morning, I began running around, on foot and by tram. First I would meet Limonti, who would give me the letters that had been collected that morning. At 7 o'clock I would be in Moulin's apartment – he lived in a small room on the Place Raspail . . . I would bring him the morning newspapers, bread for his breakfast that I had bought with his ration tickets in a boulangerie. When I got there, his landlady would have already made him a cup of the ersatz coffee that he would drink before looking at the papers I had given him – requests for meetings, various papers, notes produced by the services

or the movements, underground leaflets or newspapers. Moulin began by reading the telegrams that I had decoded in the night, and the reports that would arrive periodically from London. Seated at his small table by the window, smoking his first cigarette, he read rapidly, took notes, then dictated or wrote his reply . . .

I would see Jean Moulin in the evening and give him an account of the day. Sometimes, I had to see him during the day. For example, when he went to a meeting, I would carry the documents, which I would give to him immediately before he went into the meeting so that, as far as possible, there was no compromising material on him or in his room. At the end of the meeting he would give them back to me, to be destroyed or filed, if required, in a small archive that was kept in a friend's apartment.[57]

Every day Moulin would meet members of Combat, Libération and Le Franc-Tireur – the three main groups in the Non-Occupied Zone – to discuss everything from military actions to the latest political developments. These meetings would sometimes take place in a safe house. Lyons was ideal for this, as many of the apartments in the city centre are built on hillsides, with narrow passageways or *traboules* going between them, so it is possible to enter a *traboule* on the ground floor of one building and leave it on the top floor of another. Although there were rarely cinematic chases through this maze, the *traboules* gave a justifiable sense of security. When meetings were held outside – Moulin liked to talk while walking in Lyons' public parks – Resistance tradecraft dictated that no one would wait at a rendezvous. The safest procedure was to arrange to meet on a particular street at a given time; one *résistant* would walk down the street in one direction, while the contact walked in the other. That way, no one drew attention by hanging around.[58]

Elsewhere, the Resistance involved physical effort as well as the constant strains and worries of clandestinity. FTP leader Charles Tillon was based in Limours, south-west of Paris, in the rural area known as Hurepoix. He had to use a bicycle to get to the various underground meetings that took place in the region, and this was not a pleasure:

Both physically and morally, 1942 was the hardest of my life. Riding around on a bike required just as much exhausting vigilance as a meeting on the Métro ... As I criss-crossed the region, between Limours, Palaiseau and Arpajon in Hurepoix, I became a strong cyclist. When the weather was fine, I would ride about with a small box of paints on my carrier-rack, as a way of justifying to the neighbours that I was an artist and explaining why I was always out and about. After a while, Colette and I got a tandem and would ride as far as Versailles.[59]

One of Moulin's main achievements was creating joint services to aid the Resistance movements. The first service he set up, in April 1942, was the BIP (Bureau d'Information et de Presse – Press and Information Service), which acted as a clearing house for material from and for the Resistance, circulating articles to the underground press, or to the press abroad, in particular in the UK and the USA. This was not just a matter of providing raw material; it was also a way of 'spinning' the news from the Resistance, of presenting it in the best possible light in France and elsewhere. The BIP was particularly important because, for most of the time, the underground press was the most tangible sign of the Resistance. To produce their papers, each group had to organize a complex network of printers, all of whom ran terrible risks to carry out their work.[60]

The creation of these common services (others included radio contact with London, and a pickup service for air and sea liaisons with Britain) was partly a reflection of Moulin's professionalism. The existence of common, centralized services was also a way of unifying the disparate Resistance groups in practice, even if they maintained their separate existences. And because that unification took place under Moulin's control, it was a way for him to put his personal stamp on the shape and outlook of the Resistance.

Probably the most important service Moulin created was the Comité Général d'Études (CGE – General Study Committee), set up in July 1942. Made up of bureaucrats and administrators (mayors, prefects, engineers, railway staff and so on), the CGE was to 'advise the government at the Liberation, proposing the first measures that need to be taken; it should, therefore, from today, begin studying projects concerning the future political, economic and social regime of the country'.[61]

This was Resistance on a scale that Frenay and his like could never have imagined. Moulin was already thinking about the post-war world, even before the war was halfway over, while the initial vision of Frenay and most of the other Resistance leaders went no further than driving the Nazis out of the country and settling accounts with Vichy.[62] Part of the reason for this lack of political ambition was that the fall of France had revealed the failure of the mainstream political parties, none of which were able to muster the political will to prevent the debacle, or even to oppose the installation of Pétain. Both the Free French and most of the Resistance movements were deeply suspicious of the political parties, and were downright hostile to the idea that they might re-emerge. The movements were concerned that their hard-won position would be usurped, while de Gaulle was wary of politicians and was tempted to see his role as that of a military saviour – a modern-day Bonaparte.

Moulin was opposed to the idea of any political party simply waltzing in and taking over the Resistance, but he was politically astute enough to realize that the population would soon want more complex answers to their problems than simply getting rid of the Nazis. If the parties were the only forces that had such responses, then they would inevitably gain influence. The CGE solved this problem in two ways. First, it gave the Resistance a political programme that would be a benchmark for any party that wished to join the movement, and, second, it would bind the Resistance and the Free French to a common vision of the future. Given Moulin's socialist past, and the general political evolution of the Western European population during the war, the eventual form that programme took was left-wing, although it stopped far short of threatening the existence of capitalism.

During the course of the war, the CGE gradually became a kind of shadow state, a parallel structure that would be able to step in and take over when Nazi power collapsed. But a future state needed not only a government and policies, but also personnel. From the second half of 1942, the Resistance began to organize ordinary civil servants, employees of the main nationalized companies and members of the police force and the gendarmerie in a common service called NAP – Noyautage des Administrations Publiques (Infiltration of Public Administrations). This was a different form of Resistance: members of NAP passed information to the

Resistance and the Free French, and sat in the wings, waiting to take over when Vichy collapsed. The Resistance recognized that NAP contained the danger that some high-ranking civil servants could continue to carry out Vichy's reactionary and anti-Semitic policies at the same time as almost literally having a 'Get Out of Jail' card when the Resistance triumphed. Although there were some notorious cases of such cynicism, NAP played a vital role in the period around D-Day, disrupting Vichy's control over the country, in particular in the Post Office and the railways, and ensuring that the state did not simply collapse with the disintegration of Vichy.

\*

The most dangerous part of the work carried out by Moulin and the other Resistance leaders involved crossing the demarcation line that separated the two zones. A few people, like Pineau, or the traitor Devillers, could sometimes use their jobs as a reason to travel across the zones. Others, like Moulin, had preserved their secret identity and could travel on their real ID, but they needed an official permit (an 'Ausweiss') to cross the line, and this grew increasingly difficult as the war went on. So most *résistants*, most of the time, had to take a risk. That involved either travelling by train on forged papers or using one of the many clandestine crossing points.[63]

This could be relatively simple. At Chalon, in Burgundy, the demarcation line was marked by the river Saône, with the bridges controlled by sentries. Following Brossolette's instructions, Christian Pineau crossed the line here in 1942, together with a group of other clandestine travellers:

Around twenty people were gathered in a small café, like any provincial café, with its counter covered with bottles of apéritifs, its dark wooden tables covered in marks, its straw chairs. They were not the usual clients to be found in this kind of establishment. There were women, their faces twisted with worry, bored children, and a few men, their noses stuck into their newspaper, who looked alarmed when the door opened.[64]

The actual crossing was almost romantic. The passengers embarked on a small flat-bottomed boat, which then floated out on to the river: 'all that was missing was a lamp hung on the stern, a guitar and a mandolin,' remembered Pineau.[65]

At around the same time, Rémy had to cross into the southern zone, in the pitch dark of a February night. No boat for him; he had to strip naked, wrap his belongings in an oilcloth and wade across a freezing stream which was deeper, broader and stronger than he expected. Halfway across, he stumbled and the bundle fell into the water, drenching everything. When he finally scrambled on to the other bank, he did not have the energy to dress in his soaking clothes, and simply pulled out his coat from the sodden bundle and wrapped it around his exhausted and shivering body. As he walked across the frozen, boggy field towards a farmhouse where he would be welcomed, the ice repeatedly gave way beneath him, plunging his legs into freezing mud. At the farmhouse he had to stop the old lady of the house from immediately taking his soaking coat from his shoulders, for fear of embarrassing her by his nudity. Eventually, his modesty protected by a clean pair of warm corduroys, he sat down to some welcome hot soup.[66]

Crossing the demarcation line could also go horribly wrong. In May 1942 Henry Labit, a twenty-one-year-old BCRA agent, was parachuted into France for his second tour of duty. Before he left he was interviewed by SOE and BCRA officers who were so concerned about his youth and his 'latent foolhardiness' they emphasized that 'his venture was no historic encounter between cowboys and Indians – action from which he could shoot his way to freedom was not asked of him; what was required was that he should renew his Calvados contacts, that he should lay the groundwork for military intelligence concerning enemy troop and transport movements in the area, and that the basis for small sabotage groups should be laid'.[67]

Early in the morning of Sunday 3 May, Labit parachuted blind into the countryside south of Bordeaux. He was on his own and carried a radio transmitter in a suitcase. Unfortunately, the bus service he expected to get to Bordeaux did not run on a Sunday, so he took the rash decision to get a train, even though this meant crossing the demarcation line at

Langon. At the crossing point, Labit was searched. As he held out his papers, a spare, blank set fell to the ground – they should have been stashed somewhere safe, but they were there in his pocket. Their suspicions aroused, the Germans took him into the Customs shed, where they asked him to open his suitcase. Realizing the game was up, Labit took out his revolver, killed the two guards and fled. Chased by the Nazis, he soon found himself surrounded and decided to swallow his cyanide pill to protect his contacts. He died on the spot, but he unwittingly endangered the life of his fiancée and her family: he was carrying a letter from his girlfriend, Ginette, and she and her mother were interrogated by the Abwehr for several days before being released without charge.[68]

Sometimes – often? – survival hinged on chance. In February 1942 Jacques Baumel, only twenty-three years old and one of Frenay's closest assistants, travelled from Lyons to Paris on a night train. Following the best Resistance tradecraft, he sat huddled in a damp, smelly and overcrowded third-class carriage, where the police checks were less rigorous. Hidden in his suitcase was too much money to be easily explained and, mixed in with sheaves of innocuous papers, precious coded lists of names and addresses. Not the kind of thing you wanted to be caught with, especially when all you had to prove your identity was a set of badly forged papers.

Some time after 2 a.m., his body swaying to the rattle of the train, his face pressed against the freezing cold window, Baumel heard the French ticket inspector say to another passenger, in an unusually loud voice: 'I don't know what's got into the Jerries tonight, but they're checking papers like I've never seen before.' Baumel went rigid with fear and found it hard to breathe. He felt the ticket inspector looking at him and slowly turned around. The inspector stared at him hard, said in a flat voice, 'Just as well they don't check the toilets', and then moved down the carriage. Baumel's heart started pounding. Should he trust the inspector or not?

Finally, Baumel got up, went to the toilet – passing the inspector as he did so – and locked the door behind him. He sat there above the simple hole in the floor, the railway track flicking past below, holding his papers in his hand, ready to rip them up and throw them into the dark. He heard voices, German mixed with French, then footsteps, stopping outside the locked toilet door. The handle was suddenly and violently wrenched up and down repeatedly. Hypnotized, Baumel stared at the handle like it was a snake. Then he heard the ticket inspector's voice: 'It's out of order.' The handle was wrenched up and down again, and then came the sound of feet moving away. The seconds slurred by as Baumel's head reeled. There was a soft knock at the door and the inspector whispered: 'He's gone.' Baumel opened the door and slipped out. The inspector gave Baumel a nod, locked the door from the outside and moved down the carriage. They never saw each other again. Baumel went back to his seat, his heart frozen, vomit surging at the back of his throat, and tried to sleep. He could not.[69]

\*

Ordinary people also found the Nazi Occupation a dangerous and terrifying time. RAF bombing raids on industrial sites posed a permanent threat to the surrounding populations, although the French seem to have taken this in good heart, at least at the beginning. On 4 March Jean Guéhenno wrote in his diary:

> Yesterday evening, in the moonlight, the British bombed the Renault factory at Boulogne-Billancourt. A massive, continuous bombardment, the first that we have really experienced. To get a better view I went with Vaillant to the Place des Fêtes, but even there we couldn't see much. Only rockets, the gleam of fires from the other side of Paris and twice, above the Place, two aeroplanes like shadows against the clouds. We talked with people. No one was angry. Most of them could not hide their jubilation. The Occupying Authority did not even sound a warning. There were 500 dead, and another 500 injured. At 2.00 this afternoon the sirens went off; for no reason, of course. The Occupying Authority was having a bit of fun. Tomorrow morning, 20 hostages will be shot.[70]

Even the people directly under the bombs seemed resigned to their fate. Six weeks after the Renault raid, Liliane Jameson went to Nanterre, a western suburb of Paris, and talked to families who were preparing to leave their homes:

Without hatred, without acrimony, the families who live in the small houses around the Fiat and Simca factories are preparing to leave, saying they'll come back when it's all over. Leaflets are dropped during the raids to explain the importance of destroying the factories that work for 'them', thanking people who are transmitting information, encouraging the population to resist but to be prudent, and presenting the excuses and regrets of His Majesty's government to the affected families.[71]

As Resistance activity grew, so did Nazi reprisals. For example, in April 1942 in the Paris region, as well as the execution of hostages, curfews were imposed, bars and cinemas were shut and wine was banned in restaurants.[72] At the same time, restrictions on the food supply made life increasingly difficult, especially for women as they trailed around the shops trying to find food. This Parisienne's fruitless experience from a morning in 1942 was typical:

7h30 – To the baker's. Buy bread. There will be biscuits at 11h00.
9h00 – It is a meat day today, but the butcher says there won't be any until Saturday.
9h30 – To the dairy shop. No cheese before 5 p.m.
10h00 – To the tripe shop. My ticket is number 32, I will be served at 4 p.m.
10h30 – To the grocer's. There will be vegetables at 5 p.m.
11h00 – Back to the baker's. There are no biscuits left.[73]

The most dramatic and murderous expression of the Occupation was what happened to the Jews.[74] In January 1942, at the Wannsee conference in Berlin, the Nazis launched their chilling plan to exterminate the Jews, and throughout Occupied Europe their collaborators put this into operation. France was no exception. In August 1941 the activities of the Bataillon de la Jeunesse had been used as a pretext to arrest over 4,000 Jews in Paris. They were taken to what was effectively a prison camp – a half-finished housing estate in Drancy, to the north of the capital. In March 1942 the first railway convoy left Drancy for Auschwitz, although no one at the time realized what would be the fate of their passengers.[75] Elsewhere in France, foreign Jews were interned in appalling conditions that had lethal effects. The camp at Gurs in the south-west was notorious. In July 1942 Julius Koppel, an internee in the camp, described his surroundings – 51 men slept on the floor of his draughty, windowless hut; there were often over 20 deaths a day, and of the 6,000 Jews who were imprisoned with him, 1,000 were already dead. A total of 3,000 Jews died in the camp during the war.[76]

In June 1942 all Jews in the Occupied Zone over six years old were ordered to wear a yellow Star of David marked with the word *Juif* and were subject to curfew; in July they were banned from public places – cinemas, main roads, libraries, parks and gardens, phone boxes, cafés and restaurants, swimming pools, etc. – and had to ride in the last carriage of the Métro. In Paris the population seems to have gone out of their way to express their solidarity with the Jews, and some young people even wore yellow stars with their own slogans ('Breton', 'Aryan', 'Honorary Jew'). This touched the Jewish population, and made the growing horror slightly less appalling. In July 1942, Hélène Berr, a twenty-one-year-old Jewish Parisienne, wrote in her diary:

And then there's the sympathy of people in the street, on the Métro. Men and women look at you with such goodness that it fills your heart with inexpressible feeling. There's the awareness of being above the brutes who make you suffer, and at one with real men and women. As the misfortunes are heaped up, this connection deepens. Superficial distinctions of race, religion and social class are no longer the issue – I never thought they were – there is unity against evil, and communion in suffering.[77]

Nevertheless, these empathetic gestures had no effect on the full horror of the Holocaust. On 16 and 17 July 1942 one of the most infamous events of the whole Occupation occurred in Paris. Under the command of René Bousquet, the Parisian police force rounded up 3,031 Jewish men, 5,802 women and 4,051 children from Paris. Around half of these – 6,900 – were herded into the Vélodrome d'Hiver or 'Vél' d'Hiv', a covered cycling stadium in the fifteenth arrondissement, where they were held for several days with virtually no food or water, before being sent to internment camps in Drancy, Pithiviers or Beaune-la-Rolande. From there, the convoys began to rattle their way to Auschwitz, at the rate of nearly one a week. During the Occupation, a total of 75,721 Jews were deported from France. Only one in thirty returned.[78] Seven months later, the appalling scene was repeated, this time in Marseilles, where on 22 and 23 January 1943 6,000 people were arrested in an 'anti-Resistance raid', and nearly 800 Jews were deported to Sobibor extermination camp. The operation was again commanded by René Bousquet.[79]

Sometimes, the arrest of Jews had a veneer of good manners, but it was always terrifying and devastating for all those concerned. On 1 August 1942, fourteen-year-old Renée Ferdinand-Dreyfus witnessed her father, Jacques, a civil servant who had won the Légion d'Honneur, being taken from their house in Montfort-l'Amaury, a small village about forty kilometres west of Paris. As she wrote in her diary:

> At about 7, I was sewing with Geneviève. I stepped into the garden and saw two gendarmes. I asked them what they wanted and they said, 'Mr Dreyfus knows what it's about.' That made me terribly anxious, and I went running upstairs where I found my aunt Chevrillon looking so anguished (I will never forget the look in her eyes) that I understood. In our room, Alice and Claudine were crying. 'You know,' Alice told me, 'they're taking Daddy.' His suitcase was packed and he left with the gendarmes. He will leave at dawn tomorrow for Drancy. We all went to the gendarmerie to say good-bye to him.[80]

Jacques Ferdinand-Dreyfus was deported to Auschwitz on 31 July 1943; his family never saw him again.

The Vél' d'Hiv round-up was soon a cause célèbre for the Resistance. An article in *Défense de la France* described the horror, detailing the conditions inside the Vél' d'Hiv, including graphic descriptions of children being taken from their mothers. You can almost feel the author's pen trembling with rage:

> The odious yellow star had already shown that German domination is taking us rapidly back to the darkest days of the barbarism of the

Middle Ages . . . With the latest measures taken against the Jews, we are sinking even lower. Those who have ordered these measures are forever condemned in the eyes of all human and divine justice . . . We hesitate to use the term bestiality, because a beast does not separate a female from its babies. This is a case of human intelligence entirely in the service of Evil, using all its resources to aid the global triumph of evil, of cruelty, of filth.[81]

Although no one realized that virtually all of these people were going to their deaths, the danger was obvious, and over the next few months the plight of the Jews became a recurring topic for the Resistance. On 13 September Moulin wrote to London: 'The arrests of foreign Jews and their handing-over to the Germans and the repulsive measures taken with regard to Jewish children, initially unknown to the general public, are beginning to raise public opposition.'[82]

The Resistance, too, began to change. When Henri Frenay began the movement that eventually turned into Combat, he was deeply tainted by the casual, corrosive anti-Semitism of the French right wing. In October 1942, in an article entitled 'The Jews, Our Brothers', *Combat* showed quite how much the Resistance as a whole, and Frenay's movement in particular, had altered:

Foreign Jews, the vanguard of French Jews and indeed, quite simply, of the French, victims of Hitlerian persecution, are experiencing a painful martyrdom. Their martyrdom and their persecution make them more dear to us. All those who suffer at the hands of the Germans, be they Jews or not, be they Communists or not, are our brothers. Their German or French butchers will one day be brought to account . . . There is no Jewish racial problem, no question of Jewish 'blood', for the simple reason that the supposed 'Jewish race' is, as all serious ethnologists recognize, as mixed as the French 'race' or the German 'race' . . . This Jewish community is a constituent component of the French national community, just like all the other religious, cultural or regional communities.[83]

One of the most moving expressions of this realization of the full horror of anti-Semitism was a series of powerful pamphlets, focusing solely on the fate of the Jews. One of these brochures, duplicated in about 10,000 copies in Paris and subsequently printed in Lyons, Nice, Toulouse and Grenoble, reproduced a letter thrown from one of the trains going from Drancy to Auschwitz at the end of July 1942. It was written by a woman, Sarah, and was addressed to the concierge of her apartment block in Paris, who was looking after Sarah's two children:

> Épernay, 27-7-42
>
> I do not know if this letter will get to you. We are in a cattle-wagon. Everything has been taken from us, even the most essential toilet items. For a three-day journey we have hardly any bread, and a tiny supply of water. We have to go to the toilet on the floor, men and women, with no privacy. One woman is dead. When she was dying I called for help. She could have been saved. But the wagons are sealed and no help came. Now we have to put up with the smell of death. We are threatened with being beaten and shot. My sister and I are keeping up each other's morale and we still have hope. Kisses to you all – the children, the family and our friends. Sarah.[84]

It is not known what happened to Sarah or her children.

*

During these tragic events, London was focused on abstract and petty squabbles that nonetheless had a direct effect on the Resistance. The military and financial resources that the British were prepared to send to France depended in part on their perception of the Free French. Relations between the British government and de Gaulle were fluctuating, to say the least. In June 1942 Churchill publicly praised the action of Free French troops led by General Koenig at Bir Hakeim in the Syrian desert, where they resisted Rommel's Afrika Korps 'with the utmost gallantry'.[85] In a private conversation with de Gaulle he said Bir Hakeim was 'one of the finest feats of arms in this war'.[86]

A few weeks earlier the Allies had shown a less positive view of the Free French when their troops invaded French Madagascar without even informing de Gaulle, and decided to leave the Vichy governor in charge of the island. De Gaulle was furious, and rightly questioned the attitude of the Allies – and in particular of the Americans. After a month of rows and bitter reproaches, during which de Gaulle threatened to take all his people off to Moscow, and even told his closest aids that 'The Free French adventure is over', Churchill once again managed to placate de Gaulle. Nevertheless, the tensions with the Allies remained and would grow as the prospect of an Allied invasion of France came closer.[87]

In these circumstances, de Gaulle realized that he had to strengthen his influence over the Resistance, and especially over its left wing. The growing importance of the Resistance was shown by the widespread demonstrations that took place in the Non-Occupied Zone on 14 July 1942, following calls made on the BBC and initiated by Moulin. Towns like Grenoble, Limoges, Chambéry, Nice, Montpellier and Toulon all saw crowds of several thousand protesters, singing the 'Marseillaise' and showing their opposition to Vichy.

The two largest demonstrations took place in Lyons and Marseilles. In Lyons, 100,000 people marched around the town for five hours before clashing with the police. In Marseilles the demonstration was equally large, but less peaceful: fascists opened fire on the demonstration and killed six people. Despite this tragedy, the day was an incredible success, surpassing even the May Day demonstrations, and showed that the Resistance had real popular support.[88] Two days later, however, Vichy and the Nazis made it clear that they had no intention of changing their policies in the slightest, and launched their round-up of the Jews.

Part of the reason for the growing influence of the Resistance was that Pineau's long discussions with de Gaulle had paid off. As luck would have it, de Gaulle's 'social' declaration was broadcast the day after Laval declared he wanted the victory of Germany and announced that French workers would go to work in Nazi Germany in return for the liberation of a few French prisoners of war. This heightened version of collaboration contrasted with de Gaulle's speech, which promised a national assembly elected by the whole population (including women's suffrage for the first time), stated his support for democracy and for the first time used the Republican slogan *Liberté, Egalité, Fraternité!*

These gestures did not satisfy everyone in the Resistance, however.

Pineau's comrades in Libération-Nord were furious when the BBC claimed that all the Resistance movements backed de Gaulle's declaration, when in fact they were less than impressed by parts of it. Others were more open in voicing their doubts. *Le Franc-Tireur* loyally reproduced de Gaulle's declaration, but added a warning for the future:

> We have previously stated, and we repeat it here, that we are entirely with General de Gaulle in his struggle to liberate the country; but we will be against him once liberation has occurred if, against all his previous declarations, he considered setting up a dictatorship which we would not be any better able to accept from a General than we have been from a Marshal.[89]

The underlying tension between de Gaulle and the Resistance was set out in that article. De Gaulle had tried to ignore the Resistance, but it had proved itself to be far more important than he imagined. To increase his influence over the Resistance, he had taken a political step towards its ideas, but that might not prove enough.

# 6

# *United, Divided, Betrayed*

At ten o'clock in the morning of 17 April 1942, a group of army officers walked nonchalantly along the parapet of the rocky fortress of Koenigstein, high above the river Elbe, deep in the heart of Nazi Germany. Koenigstein was a prison, and they were prisoners. When the coast was clear, one of them brought out a long cable, tied it to a metal bar in the rock and gave the other end to a dapper, grey-haired man in his early sixties, who was sitting on the parapet with his legs hanging over the edge. As he held tight on to the cable, his comrades slowly lowered him into the void. Once he reached the bottom, the cable was hauled back up and General Henri Giraud of the French army, imprisoned since the fall of France, picked up his walking stick and shuffled into the undergrowth.[1]

Giraud's dramatic escape had been planned for over a year by Vichy Intelligence in cooperation with his wife – the plans had been transmitted to Giraud using a subtle code in her letters, while the cable had been carefully hidden in four cans of tinned ham.[2] Hitler took the breakout as a personal affront, and called on Giraud – who had allegedly promised not to escape – to surrender immediately. But by the time 'wanted' posters were plastered all over Germany, Giraud had safely reappeared in Vichy France, to a huge fanfare of publicity and the intense embarrassment of Pétain and Laval. Giraud became a hero: ordinary French people were overjoyed that the Führer's nose had been put out of joint, while important sections of the French army, uncomfortable with collaboration but too rigid and disciplined to follow de Gaulle, felt that here was a leader who could save their honour. Despite German protests, there was no question of handing Giraud back to the Nazis. The British were equally excited and asked Giraud to come to London. MI6 telegrammed Marie-Madeleine Fourcade's ALLIANCE intelligence circuit:

HAVE LEARNED HEROIC ESCAPE OF GENERAL GIRAUD STOP . . . WOULD BE MOST HAPPY IF YOU WOULD AGREE TO CONTACT HIM TO DISCOVER HIS INTENTIONS STOP WOULD HE SERVE AGAIN STOP IF SO WHERE STOP[3]

Fourcade did as she was asked, but her agent reported that Giraud had no intention of going to London. On the other hand, if the British would kindly supply Giraud with money and material help, and put him in contact with the various Resistance groups in Occupied Europe, the General was prepared to become leader of the European Resistance. London's reaction is not recorded.

The Resistance, too, soon discovered that Giraud had a very inflated view of his own role. In summer 1942 Claude Bourdet of Combat was sent to persuade Giraud to join the Free French. He explained the role and structure of the Resistance organizations in some detail; in response, Giraud gave a long, condescending account of the various 'cards' he claimed to hold – the French army, the Resistance and, of course, the 'tiny' Free French armed forces. All of these, proclaimed Giraud, were elements he would deploy as he saw fit, in his role as the leader of the European Resistance. Amazed, Bourdet took his leave. François de Menthon had a similar experience when he asked Giraud what he thought about the social issues being raised by the Resistance, which had begun to influence de Gaulle. The General smiled:

Social questions are irrelevant. Believe me, I know. When I was governor of Metz there were some major movements among the workers, some strikes. I posted machine guns at each corner of the city and things settled down pretty sharpish.[4]

The differences between Giraud and the Free French were soon common knowledge. On 20 May Bernard Pierquin, a Parisian medical student, wrote in his diary: 'Giraud's refusal to join de Gaulle in London is worrying. It appears that the two men cannot stand each other, either militarily or politically. This will continue.'[5] Pierquin was right. The conflict between Giraud and de Gaulle, played off against the background of manoeuvres and disputes with the Allies, in particular with the United States, lasted over a year.

Sensing how the war would be won, Giraud wanted to work with the Americans, and by July he was in discussions about the planned Allied invasion of North Africa (Operation TORCH).[6] The USA was attracted to Giraud because he was not de Gaulle, whom they loathed and distrusted because he was so independent and obdurate, and because they hoped that the French army's support for Giraud would ensure the success of the invasion. If Giraud was involved in the action, the Allies reasoned, the Vichy troops in the region might be persuaded not to fight.

But Giraud proved just as unrealistic in his dealings with the Americans as he had been with the British and with the Resistance. First he demanded complete control of the operation, then he insisted that the US delay the operation so that an Allied bridgehead could be established on the French Mediterranean coast. Finally, he wanted to be told of the launch date ten days in advance.[7] Marie-Madeleine Fourcade, who had to transmit Giraud's demands, described them as 'a sort of strategic delirium'.[8] The Americans apparently agreed with her. Giraud's dreams were simply brushed aside – they would humour their stooge only so much and they would not give way on any of these points. They were, however, quite happy to agree to his insistence that the Free French should not be involved at all.[9]

At the beginning of November Giraud was brought out of France on a British submarine, through the work of the ALLIANCE circuit. But a terrible price was paid – while ALLIANCE transmitted information about Giraud to London, Marie-Madeleine Fourcade and the whole ALLIANCE leadership were arrested. Then a chance event led the Americans to change their plans, and Giraud's importance began to fade.[10] When Operation TORCH began early in the morning of 8 November, Admiral Darlan, the head of Vichy armed forces, was in Algiers visiting his sick son. Contacted by the Americans, he responded positively, making it plain that he was open to discussions with the Allies. Darlan was a far bigger fish than Giraud, and the

Americans decided to make the Vichy admiral their ally.[11] Giraud, sidelined, sat out the invasion in Gibraltar.

Operation TORCH was the first indication that the Allies could turn the tables on Hitler. Over 100,000 American and British troops and 100 ships took part in the invasion, which involved a massive parachute drop and five simultaneous amphibious landings along nearly 1,000 miles of the North African coastline. In Algiers, right-wing Giraudist army officers (including Emmanuel d'Astier's brother), together with civilian members of Combat, led an uprising to help the operation, but the seizure of the city was still a bloody affair. Throughout French North Africa, Vichy forces fought back against what they saw as an invasion, not liberation. But Darlan played his role to perfection, persuading his men to surrender, and within three days the fighting was over. With US backing, Darlan, the man who had been Pétain's heir apparent, the enthusiastic leader of Vichy's anti-Semitic and profoundly reactionary 'National Revolution', was now in charge of French North Africa. For years, the US had been hoping to persuade Vichy to change its politics and join the Allies. The second half of their hopes had now been partly fulfilled; the first half no longer seemed to matter.

As Darlan took over in Algiers, Hitler acted rapidly to meet the potential threat from the south. On 11 November the Wehrmacht swept towards the Mediterranean, smashing through the demarcation line, completing their occupation of the whole country and destroying Vichy's pathetic claims to independence. Many people expected the Vichy army to react. In Lyons eighteen-year-old Denise Domenach was sent home from school early because the headmistress feared there would be a battle in the city when the Germans arrived. Denise and her friends took this as an invitation to go and watch. They made their way to the centre of Lyons, Place Bellecour, the largest square in Europe:

> . . . we bumped into a load of *gardes mobiles* who were blocking the Rue
> Victor-Hugo and parallel streets. It was impossible to get to [Place]
> Bellecour, but we sensed that's where it was all happening. We argued
> with them, but had no luck. Finally, Jacques Benon and I took our
> chance when the cops weren't looking (although God knows there
> were plenty of them) and we got to the end of the Rue Victor-Hugo

and there we saw with amazement that the Place Bellecour was full of German vehicles. I don't know what we expected, but we felt suffocated ... After wandering around town, our heads blazing, we decided to go home. Beforehand, we went through a *traboule* right to Place Bellecour and walked dignifiedly through the German sentries, all the time fearing that we would be pistol-whipped for our disobedience.[12]

There was no battle in Lyons, or anywhere else. All the hopes that the Allies – and some parts of the Resistance – had put in the Vichy armed forces came to nothing. The absurd claims of Carte that 300,000 soldiers were ready to fight were revealed to be a pipedream. Even when there were real forces on the ground, nothing happened. Ever since the fall of France, sections of the army had been stockpiling arms out of sight of the Nazi weapons inspectors who were supposed to ensure that Vichy abided by the armistice agreements. Sixty-five thousand firearms, four hundred pieces of artillery and tons of ammunition had been hidden all over the Non-Occupied Zone, while hundreds of armoured vehicles had been ingeniously constructed in tractor factories.[13] Like King Arthur's army, these weapons were supposed to be used when the time came. But when the time did come, and the Nazis were storming towards the sea, the Vichy army did nothing. The sole exception was General de Lattre, whose brief and small-scale rebellion ended in a cell. Worse, the army rejected the pleas of Combat and Libération to give them the weapons. Frenay wrote a furious letter to General Picquendar of the Vichy army:

> The army's weapons belong to the nation and not to you alone. It is your duty to give them to those who will use them for the liberation of our homeland. If through your stubbornness they fall into the enemy's hands, you shall answer before the courts of our liberated land, and I myself shall be your accuser.[14]

There was no reply. When Laval ordered that all clandestine arms should be handed over to the Nazis, the lions of the military meekly complied, with virtually no exceptions.[15] The most ignominious symbol of this spinelessness came in Toulon, where the French navy refused to sail out of the clutches of the Nazis and instead scuttled itself at the dockside, going down without a fight. Only one vessel escaped: the submarine *Casablanca* and her crew made for Algiers to join the Free French.

\*

The determination of the Allies to short-circuit de Gaulle during Operation TORCH showed the Free French that they could expect few favours when it came to the liberation of France. On 20 November André Philip – de Gaulle's new Interior Minister – met President Roosevelt in Washington. The President stoutly defended his support for Darlan and conjured up a stark vision of what he intended to do when the Allies arrived in Europe:

> I did the right thing to support Darlan – I saved American lives . . . what's important for me is to get to Berlin. I don't care about anything else. If Darlan gives me Algiers, long live Darlan! If Laval gives me Paris, long live Laval! . . . When we get to France, we will have the power of an occupying force. I cannot recognize de Gaulle, because that would undermine the rights of the French by imposing a government on them . . . By right of occupation, the Americans will remain in France until free elections are organized.[16]

When Philip pointed out that the French would not tolerate an American occupation any more than a German one, Roosevelt grew impatient: 'I will speak to the French people on the radio and they will do what I wish,' he snapped.[17]

The American attitude caused massive consternation in France. On 15 November Jean Moulin sent a furious telegram to London:

> INFORM AMERICAN AND BRITISH GOVERNMENTS IN NAME OF RESISTANCE MOVEMENTS IMPOSSIBLE TO EXPLAIN TO FRENCH WHY ALGIERS LANDING NOT IMMEDIATELY ACCOMPANIED BY RESTORATION OF REPUBLIC . . . WHY FRENCH NATIONAL COMMITTEE NOT YET INSTALLED IN ALGIERS WHY ALLIED RADIO FRIENDLY TO PETAIN . . . VERY BAD IMPRESSION WILL SOON BECOME SCANDAL[18]

In turn, SOE sent the British Foreign Secretary, Anthony Eden, an alarming report, warning him that the Darlan deal had 'produced violent reactions on all our subterranean organizations in enemy-occupied countries, particularly in France where it has had a blasting and withering effect'.[19] For the Resistance, there must have seemed little point in fighting for liberation if the Allies were simply going to put the enemy back in charge. Eden alerted the Cabinet that 'the present regime [in Algiers], even though it fights the Axis, is rooted in falsehood. Darlan is Vichy, and Vichy is the rule of those same wealthy and selfish interests which ruined France'.[20] By mid-December Churchill and Roosevelt began to get cold feet as they were repeatedly attacked in the press for their collusion with Darlan and his Vichy cronies.

Then, on 24 December, the Allies got an unexpected Christmas present. Bonnier de la Chapelle, a monarchist *résistant*, burst into Darlan's office and shot him in the stomach.[21] Two hours later, Darlan was dead. The next day, SOE and BCRA toasted his passing with champagne,[22] while Churchill later admitted that the assassination 'relieved the Allies of an embarrassment'.[23] But the Allies simply replaced one embarrassment with another: determined to keep de Gaulle at arm's length, they put Giraud in charge of French North Africa. Giraud soon proved to be as much a Vichy man as Darlan had been. Despite promises to repeal anti-Semitic legislation and to get rid of the Vichy administrators who had put it in place, Giraud did nothing. Indeed, it took three months and tremendous pressure before he could bring himself to repudiate Vichy and declare that he was a democrat.[24]

Eventually, after several months of manoeuvring and politicking in Algiers, London and Washington, the Allies grudgingly accepted that de Gaulle and the Free French were the legitimate political representatives of the vast majority of the French population, and from autumn 1943 Giraud gradually slipped from the stage of history. De Gaulle won this struggle not simply because he was more wily, arrogant and plain stubborn than the naive and deluded Giraud, but because he was backed by the Resistance and a growing section of the French population.[25]

\*

After the German invasion of the Non-Occupied Zone on 11 November 1942, life got far more difficult for the Resistance. The relatively lax security procedures employed by the groups in the southern zone had previously been merely a cause of irritation for the more experienced *résistants* from the north. Now they had become literally lethal. There was virtually no chance of sympathetic treatment from the Vichy police or counter-intelligence services – anyone within the Vichy state apparatus who retained even the slightest shred of self-respect realized they had to resign their post.[26] As in the northern zone, the Vichy police generally obeyed their new masters, while the army proved spineless. The Vichy state was completely rotten, its human components utterly corrupted by collaboration with the Nazis.

Although the Allies still did not fully appreciate the true nature of Vichy, ordinary people – even those not involved in the Resistance – understood the reality of collaboration only too well. In June 1942 Janet Teissier du Cros, a Scot living in the Non-Occupied Zone, gave birth to a boy, Nicolas. Shortly afterwards she was overwhelmed by an apocalyptic vision of the world her son would grow up in:

> Never, it seemed, would we emerge from the mists of gloom and despair. I saw the Nazi occupation spreading like a pool of filthy oil on a lovely patchwork counterpane. One after another the patches of beautiful faded cretonne that represented in my mind the countries of Europe had been stained and had lost their character . . . Even if Germany should end by losing the war, the harm done would be lasting. Traces would persist of the anti-Semitism, cruelty and corruption they brought wherever they went; the dishonesty that had become a part of patriotism would linger on as a habit. What sort of gift had I given Nicolas?[27]

Nevertheless, for a few days after the Nazi invasion, there was a period of uncertainty that helped some *résistants*. In August 1942 Christian Pineau had been arrested on the beach near Narbonne, as he was about to leave for London.[28] While the Nazis marched southwards, Pineau was moved in the opposite direction, transferred from a military prison in Montpellier to an internment camp near Limoges. Just before Pineau left the prison, news came through of the invasion; the governor said to him: 'Well, you'll just have to escape.' Which is exactly what he did, jumping from the train.[29] Six weeks later, exhausted and at the end of his tether, Pineau had a hurried meeting with his wife, who had recently given birth to their son. Then he left for London. He had not been able to see his baby, nor did he know if he ever would. Shortly after he returned to France, Pineau was arrested again, this time by the Gestapo. By the end of the year he was in Buchenwald concentration camp.

Marie-Madeleine Fourcade, who had been arrested following the exfiltration of Giraud, was lucky enough to be dealt with by some of the few Vichy policemen who were opposed to the Nazi invasion. Thrown into the l'Evêché prison in Marseilles, Fourcade was eventually taken to her house for further detailed questioning. There, without their Gestapo minders, the police officers agreed that she could make fake versions of her radio transmission documents, in order to deceive the Nazis who were now demanding to take over the investigation. The three policemen then drove her to Avignon and freedom – boldly stopping at the prison on the way to pick up her jewellery. Yet Fourcade was under no illusions. Far from being a sign of the future, the bravery of those three men represented the past. As she later recalled:

> Gone was the illusory unoccupied zone and its relative oases. Farewell, Vichy policemen, with your easy-going instincts. Now operating over the whole territory, the Abwehr and the Gestapo had suspended their rivalry to advance like a steamroller of deadly efficiency. The Abwehr with its subtle infiltration methods was the demoniacal intelligence. The Gestapo with its arrests, tortures and killings was the blind, bestial force. We should have to brave them with our poor weapons and on our forefathers' soil for a very long time yet. The terrible year was about to begin.[30]

Despite the real threat posed by the Nazi occupation of the south, the Resistance was in relatively good shape. A few months earlier, in London, a huge step towards unifying the Resistance had been taken at a meeting of the groups in the Non-Occupied Zone. Jean Moulin, Jean-Pierre Levy of Franc-Tireur, Frenay and d'Astier were all invited, but not all of them arrived. Frenay and d'Astier managed to leave France from Port-miou, one of the stunning Mediterranean fjords or *calanques* that line the coast between Marseilles and Cassis.[31] Things did not go so straightforwardly for Moulin and Levy. They stayed overnight in a hotel near Macon, cycled for six kilometres, crossed the Saône in a small boat and then waited by the side of the MARGUERITE landing field. But thick fog prevented the Lysander from landing. Levy wrote: 'Thus began a week of waiting, in which the same scene was played out night after night: mist, rain, no plane.'[32] With the moon waning, the air pickup was eventually cancelled, and Moulin and Levy went south to Anthéor, near Cannes, where a submarine was to deliver a load of weapons as well as pick up Moulin, Levy and a number of other leading Resistance members. Once again, nothing went right. Léon Morandat was in charge of security:

> The submarine surfaced in the wrong bay, so we spent the whole night under the viaduct at Anthéor. I was up to my chest in the water, flashing signals with an electric torch every quarter of an hour. When day broke, we had to disperse.[33]

Moulin and Levy's journey was eventually abandoned.

Despite the absence of Moulin and Levy, the London summit set up a Coordinating Committee that would meet in France with a delegate each from Libération, Combat and Franc-Tireur; the chair – Moulin – would have the casting vote. But although the committee strengthened the scattered forces of the Resistance, it also became yet another way of reinforcing London's domination: 'in military terms the Coordinating Committee is under the orders of General de Gaulle, within the framework of the Allied strategic plan' it was agreed.[34]

London's determination to control all military action in France was made even clearer in the discussions about the need for a unified command of the embryonic armed wing of the Resistance in the Non-Occupied Zone, the Armée Secrète (Secret Army). The Secret Army was Frenay's brainchild, and he understandably wanted to be its leader. Equally understandably, this met with outright opposition from d'Astier and the Free French who were suspicious of Frenay's ambitions. Frenay therefore proposed that General Delestraint, a sixty-three-year-old retired officer, should lead the Secret Army.[35] This was agreed unanimously: d'Astier was relieved that the new leader was not Frenay, de Gaulle was content to have a military man in charge, while Frenay thought that he could manipulate the naive Delestraint, who had no experience of clandestine work, nor any links with the Resistance.

The instructions de Gaulle issued to the Secret Army were a continuation of the orders he had given to Moulin nearly a year earlier. Large-scale military activity was forbidden except in conjunction with an Allied invasion, and it would be approved only 'at an appropriate moment'. The only immediate action that was permitted was sabotage, and even here London did not give the Resistance a free hand. 'Orders will be sent,' said de Gaulle, while generously allowing the Resistance to attack power stations in the meantime.[36] De Gaulle wanted complete control over the Resistance's military action and, for the moment, the Resistance leaders were happy with that.

What they were not happy about, however, was Moulin. D'Astier complained to de Gaulle that Moulin behaved like 'a petty civil servant', while Frenay bridled so much at Moulin's role as the voice and hand of de Gaulle that he threatened to split the movement. 'What will happen if we cannot agree with Rex [Moulin]?' asked Frenay. De Gaulle replied: 'You will come here, and we will try and find a solution.' 'And if that proves impossible?' pursued Frenay. 'Well,' said de Gaulle, 'in that case, France will have to choose between you and me!'[37]

In every respect, Moulin stood above the Resistance leaders. He was General de Gaulle's personal representative, he had a vision that was broader and more far-reaching than those of Frenay, d'Astier and the others, and he had a top civil servant's irritating habit of getting his own way. All these things caused clashes. The most consistent source of conflict was the question of money and resources, over which Moulin had sole control. London was now sending large sums of cash to the Resistance, but it was Moulin who decided how much should be allotted to each group. He even controlled radio contact between the Resistance and London – throughout the war, Frenay did not have his own radio operator, but instead had to go through Moulin. All these problems inevitably led to jealousy and spiteful recriminations, making Moulin the focus of the fears and frustrations felt by the whole Resistance.

These squabbles with Moulin – organizational, political and personal – were amplified by the terrible strains of life under Nazi Occupation and provided a pathetic and poisonous backdrop to the tragic events that soon unfolded.

\*

In the middle of January 1943, BCRA agent Rémy and a tall, gaunt man got into a fishing boat at Pont-Aven in Brittany and hid under a false floor. The gaunt man had been told to bring nothing, not even a tooth-brush. Rémy, however, cluttered their cramped hiding place with New Year presents for de Gaulle – a box of soil from Lorraine, an 1816 vin-tage bottle of cognac which had allegedly belonged to a Russian general who had fought Napoleon and a metre-high azalea bush covered in pink flowers, bought in Paris for Mme. de Gaulle. After transferring to a British ship off the Isles of Scilly, the two men and their unlikely bag-gage were taken to London.[38]

Rémy had risked everything to bring his passenger across the Channel. He had repeatedly disobeyed orders from his BCRA superior, Colonel Passy, to stay in France. Not only had Rémy ignored Passy's threats ('IN CASE OF DISOBEDIENCE ON YOUR PART I WILL TAKE ALL NECESSARY STEPS' telegrammed Passy), he had even demanded that de Gaulle change his travel plans as a result ('INSIST GENERAL AWAITS ARRIVAL BEFORE LEAVING FOR WASHINGTON STOP MY PRESENCE NECESSARY FOR CERTAIN MEASURES STOP AM CERTAIN OF YOUR APPROVAL').[39] Rémy was both right and wrong. His passenger was indeed of enormous importance, but Passy never forgave him, and ensured that Rémy did not carry out any further mis-sions in France.

The gaunt man was Fernand Grenier, a Communist Party deputy who had been a hostage in the Chateaubriant prison camp and was now the Communist Party's delegate to the Free French in London. As Grenier explained on the BBC in a classic piece of hyperbole, his mis-sion was to bring to de Gaulle 'the support of tens of thousands of our comrades . . . who each day risk their life in the unceasing struggle against the hated Nazi invader'.[40] Grenier was also instructed to secure more arms and money for the Communist FTP and, on a more strategic level, to pressurize de Gaulle into making a compromise with Giraud. Not only did the PCF feel there was little to choose between two reactionary generals, Moscow wanted to resolve the issue as quickly as possible, to hasten the Allied invasion of Western Europe. And as always, the French Communists followed Moscow's lead. But whatever the manoeuvres that lay behind Grenier's arrival in London, the Gaullists seemed genuinely enthusiastic at the prospect of working with the Communists. As Grenier put it in a message to his comrades: 'HAVE SEEN GENERAL DE GAULLE AND PHILIP STOP THEY ARE ENCHANTED WITH MY SUPPORT AND WILL ENSURE PUBLICITY'.[41]

The decision of the Communist Party to rally to the Free French was the fruit of a long series of negotiations, first with Moulin and then with Rémy.[42] Although the British and the Free French knew of these discussions, the first sign of how successful they had been came when Grenier turned up in London. The Communists had a reputation as the most combative of the Resistance organizations and, after the USSR's victory over the Germans at Stalingrad at the end of January, they bathed in the reflected glory of Moscow's military might. The real impression of Resistance unity created by the PCF's support for the Free French was reinforced on 26 January 1943, when, following weeks of work by Moulin and Frenay, Libération, Combat and Franc-Tireur publicly formalized the existence of the Coordinating Committee that had been set up at the London meeting in September, by announcing the creation of an umbrella organization, the Mouvements Unis de la Résistance (MUR – United Movements of the Resistance).

Moulin's ambitions were even greater, however. He wanted to create a national resistance leadership that would include not only the Resistance movements but also the trade unions, and – most controversially – the old political parties. Combat leader Claude Bourdet was scornful of this last suggestion: these parties, with the exception of the Communists, were 'the living dead' who had been silent since 1940. Worse, by resuscitating these 'fossils', the Resistance would hinder the reorganization of the French political landscape that everyone agreed was necessary.[43]

Moulin considered that the return of the parties was inevitable, especially given that the Allies wanted the Free French to show they had the support of the French population and their political representatives. In these circumstances, Moulin felt, it was best to act pre-emptively, thereby creating conditions that were as favourable to the Resistance as possible. Although de Gaulle agreed with Moulin's analysis, Frenay and d'Astier, who had neither Moulin's vision nor de Gaulle's guile, were strongly opposed. They were supported by Pierre Brossolette, who was not just hostile to the old political parties but also wanted to strengthen the power and influence of de Gaulle. As he declared in November 1942:

> We have arrived at a period of concentrated capitalism throughout Europe, and soon, perhaps, in the whole world. Either the Trusts will be the masters of the country, or the country will be the master of the Trusts. That is why we need a strong executive . . . we need an élan, a voice, a mystic, which will enable the whole of France to cooperate, to go forward, together, towards a new political life . . . There is only one possibility, one guarantee of that, and that is the Fighting French, as represented today by General de Gaulle.[44]

Frenay expressed similar ideas in the pages of *Combat*, as he evolved further from his narrow-minded military origins:

> In no case will we tolerate in France the kind of sinister pantomime that has taken place in North Africa, in which the spoils of the victory to come would be confiscated to the benefit of the abject Vichy regime . . .
> One leader, one symbol: DE GAULLE.
> One idea: LIBERTY WITH HONOUR.
> One system: SOCIALIST REPUBLIC AND DEMOCRACY IN ACTION.[45]

The clashes between Moulin and the Resistance were growing in number and in importance. To the outside world, the Resistance appeared unified. The reality was somewhat different.[46]

*

In February 1943 Moulin and General Delestraint flew to London, where Moulin argued that the Free French and the Resistance should incorporate the political parties. As usual, he won. Ten days later he left for France, the sole passenger in Lysander 'D for Dog', carrying a suitcase full of tobacco and British food.[47] The pilot, Squadron-Leader Hugh Verity, later recalled: 'I had just one passenger outbound. He was a Frenchman of some authority, I judged by his bearing, although he wore a very ordinary suit and overcoat and a felt hat.'[48] But there was fog over the landing ground near Bourges, and Verity had to fly back to Britain with Moulin still on board. At this point the situation became dangerous, as Tangmere aerodrome was also fog-bound. After eleven landing attempts, and with fuel running low, Verity decided he had to land come what may. Unable to see anything in the thick fog, which glowed orange from the light of flares along the runway, Verity misjudged the plane's altitude and crunched into the ground. The Lysander's undercarriage snapped off and the aircraft skidded along nose first, the propeller twisting out of shape as it gouged into the soil. Verity recalled:

> I turned off the petrol and ignition, threw off my helmet, safety harness and parachute straps and clambered out. I was concerned about my unfortunate passenger stuck up there in the rear cockpit with the little ladder unhelpfully far from the ground and at the wrong angle. I was very relieved that there was no fire . . . My distinguished passenger managed to slide his roof back (and up) and climb out. I helped him to jump down. It had been a truly disastrous trip and I apologized profusely in my best French. He could not have been more charming and even went to the length of thanking me for 'a very agreeable flight'.[49]

Two nights later Verity and Moulin tried again, with no greater success – this time a danger signal was flashed from the landing ground – but with a less dramatic flight back. As a result of these problems, Moulin had to wait until the next moon before he could return to France. The enforced stay in London was undoubtedly useful for Moulin's physical state – he had been operating underground without a break for nearly fourteen months, far longer than was advisable. As time wore on, complacency and mistakes became ever more likely, and ever more lethal.

When he did eventually return to France – on the same plane as Christian Pineau and General Delestraint[50] – Moulin was charged with setting up the Conseil National de la Résistance (CNR – National Resistance Council),[51] which would involve both the Resistance movements and the political parties. London was determined to limit the influence of the Resistance movements – only those groups that had a publication, an armed wing and an intelligence-gathering role would be admitted to the CNR. As a result, *Défense de la France* – which was only a newspaper and at this stage was opposed to armed action[52] – was excluded, despite having the largest circulation of any of the underground publications (by 1944 *Défense de la France* was printing 440,000 copies of each issue).

Moulin's new mission to create the CNR provoked more conflict with those in the Resistance who were already chafing under his leadership. To make matters worse, de Gaulle had made him a minister with responsibility for Resistance work in the whole of the country. The final addition to an already explosive mixture was the presence in France of Pierre Brossolette (code-name 'Brumaire'), who had recently joined Free French Intelligence (the BCRA). Brossolette had been ordered to convince some of the groups in the old Occupied Zone – Libération-Nord, OCM and the Communists – to set up military wings under the direct control of the BCRA.[53] These intense discussions were accompanied by a flurry of nearly eighty telegrams to London, which received virtually no response. Brossolette therefore decided to use his initiative, and set up a Resistance coordinating committee for the northern zone, deliberately excluding the political parties, in clear breach of the position agreed in London.[54]

The Free French were furious, and André Philip sent a blistering telegram to Passy, Brossolette's superior, who was also in France: 'BRUMAIRE PROPOSITIONS . . . INCOMPATIBLE WITH DECISIONS HERE STOP BRUMAIRE GONE BEYOND MISSION LIMITS STOP DO NOT COMPROMISE RESULTS OF DISCUSSIONS HERE . . . DELAY ANY DECISION UNTIL ARRIVAL OF REX [Moulin].'[55] But Brossolette simply ignored these orders and went ahead.[56]

Shortly after returning to France, Moulin confronted Passy and Brossolette in an apartment on the Avenue des Ternes, on the west side of Paris.[57] The atmosphere was electric. Also present were Moulin's old friends Meunier and Chambeiron, who claimed in the meeting that Brossolette thought Moulin was power-hungry. Brossolette explained that he had been misinterpreted, but to no avail. Moulin began to shout. He attacked Brossolette for putting his own ambition before the unity of the Resistance, and criticized Passy for not ensuring that his subordinate obeyed orders.[58] Passy later recalled that Moulin was shouting so loudly that he had to be told to calm down, as there were Germans in the building:

> . . . it was tragic to think that the Gestapo might be in the room above, next door or below us, and that these verbal fireworks might lead to the capture of two men who had worked so hard for their country. The shouting carried on for a good quarter of an hour. I admit that I wanted only one thing: to leave, as I had the impression I was sitting on a powder keg. Thankfully nothing serious happened and we all left in one piece, although there was no conclusion to the debate. A wave of disgust swept over me and it took the fresh air to bring me back to life.[59]

Once again, Moulin won. Within days Brossolette and Passy were packed off to London while Moulin's view that the old parties and the trade unions had to be represented in a national Resistance leadership gradually took hold. However, Moulin still had to cope with a campaign of criticism from his comrades. Frenay complained to de Gaulle that Moulin always took London's side and that he knew nothing of the real life of the Resistance organizations, having only ever met their leaders. Frenay concluded by threatening 'a serious conflict' if the Resistance was not given greater independence from both London and Moulin.[60] At the same time, d'Astier arrived in London and complained of 'the danger to the Resistance and to its future development caused by the installation of a system that would lead to the bureaucratization and sterilization of the movements'.[61] In reply, Moulin wrote to de Gaulle explaining the need for centralization, ironically using terms that were close to the hearts of Brossolette and Frenay and which reveal de Gaulle's overwhelming influence over the Resistance:

> I consider that you should consider yourself more as a leader of a party than leader of a government. What is your task, apart from liberating the country? You will have to take power against the

Germans, against Vichy, against Giraud, and perhaps against the Allies. In these conditions, those who rightly call themselves Gaullists must have, and in fact do have, only one political leader: you.[62]

The vast majority of Resistance members knew nothing about these arguments. The rows over the role of the political parties, the niggling over various internal structures, all took place only at the highest level. As Claude Bourdet later put it: 'none of us had heard of all these proposals which, we should not forget, involved a tiny fraction of the Resistance, a few sectors that were linked to London, and that's all.'[63] The rank and file would no doubt have been horrified by the squabbling and venom, and would have despaired at the way in which their leaders were distracted from the task at hand. If such debates were lost on the Resistance, they would have seemed even more obscure to the French population. At this point in the war, the Resistance still had little effect on the lives of ordinary people. The Occupation was a crushing weight, but people were convinced that deliverance would come from developments on the international stage. In the meantime, they thought, there was nothing to do but wait.[64] During the course of 1943, that attitude began to change.

*

On 27 May 1943 the CNR, Moulin's brainchild, met behind the closed shutters of a first-floor flat on the Rue du Four, on the Left Bank in Paris.[65] Even d'Astier, Levy and Frenay had signed up, although Frenay refused to be a delegate and d'Astier and Levy were in London. There were sixteen men at the meeting – eight for the major Resistance movements (five from the north), six for the political parties and two for the trade unions. The Communist Party effectively had two delegates (their own, and the representative of the Front National), while most of the other parties were what Bourdet had described as the 'living dead'. Moulin, of course, was in the chair.

At the beginning of the meeting, Moulin read a message from de Gaulle which explained that after the liberation of France the CNR would be 'the primary representation of the desires and feelings of all those who, within the country, had participated in the struggle'. It would therefore be the 'indispensable instrument' for de Gaulle's government-in-waiting to 'exercise its duties within the country and help it to express the rights and interests of France with regard to the foreign powers'. In other words, the CNR – and therefore the Resistance – would be entirely subordinated to de Gaulle. For its part, the CNR adopted a single resolution – co-authored by Moulin – which called for the creation of a provisional government, with Giraud as the head of the 'resuscitated French army', but with de Gaulle ('the soul of the Resistance in the darkest days') as the undisputed leader. The Communists initially demurred, but after some heated debate, during which Moulin had to ask the participants to keep their voices down, the resolution was adopted unanimously.

Many years later, de Gaulle was quite clear about Moulin's importance in bringing the Communist Party on board:

> Precisely because he had the reputation of being a prefect who was left wing – and even close to the Communists . . . he could not be rejected by them. His mission was to reintegrate them into the national community. He was the best person for that. He was as straight as a die. A right-wing prefect like Bollaert could never have succeeded. It was Moulin, more than any other, who made it possible to bring the Communists on board, as part of the Free French organization, and thus to control them. Without the CNR, there would not have been *a* resistance, but *several* resistances. At the Liberation, there would not have been a united people, but a divided country. We would not have stopped the Communists from holding parts of the territory.[66]

The existence of the CNR, and its clear support for de Gaulle, helped put an end to the complex wrangling between the Allies, Giraud and the Free French. But in either a cock-up or (more likely) a piece of wartime spin by the Gaullists, the founding of the CNR was announced on the BBC over two weeks before it actually took place. Despite the irritation and confusion this caused in France – the members of the CNR understandably suspected that they were being manipulated[67] – it apparently helped push Giraud and the Allies into finally accepting de Gaulle's dominance.[68] The Allies were not completely convinced, however. The

British tried to censure broadcasts about the meeting,[69] and even after de Gaulle arrived in Algiers at the end of May, Churchill and Roosevelt continued to snipe at him.[70] But with public support in Britain and America clearly on the side of the Free French, both leaders eventually had to bow to the inevitable. At the end of August the Allies recognized that de Gaulle's Comité Français de Libération Nationale (CFLN – French Committee of National Liberation), the latest re-branding of the Free French, governed the French colonies and liberated territories (it was still not recognized as the French government-in-exile).

Had Moulin been able to create the CNR a year earlier, it is highly unlikely that the Allies would have been impressed. At that time, the Resistance was simply too small and ineffective to have any weight in the context of a world war involving millions of men and machines. The existence of a small make-believe Resistance 'parliament' would probably have provoked no more than a condescending smile on the faces of Roosevelt and Churchill. But by the middle of 1943 the Resistance had changed completely and was becoming a vital factor in Allied planning. Paradoxically, this fundamental shift came about through the desperation and short-sightedness of the Nazis and their Vichy stooges.

In June 1942 Laval announced that French men and women would be encouraged to work in Nazi Germany, in return for the liberation of French prisoners of war. But only 17,000 skilled workers left voluntarily (the Germans wanted 150,000), so in September Vichy decided men aged eighteen to fifty and single women aged twenty-one to thirty-five had to carry out work 'in the superior interest of the nation'. The interests of 'the nation' and those of the Nazis turned out to be exactly the same, so 200,000 workers were shipped off to Germany.[71] There were protests all over the country as workers went on strike against the new law, blocked the railway lines taking people to Germany and fought with the gendarmes and the Nazis.[72] But the hunger of the Nazi war economy was boundless: with so many men fighting on so many fronts, the Nazis needed even more workers. In February 1943, Vichy therefore obediently set up the Service du Travail Obligatoire (STO – Obligatory Labour Conscription): all men aged between eighteen and twenty would have to work in Germany for two years. 250,000 men were due to be sent to work for the Nazis in the space of a month.[73] One fascist bright spark – Dr Hermes, head of censorship in Paris – predicted that the new policy 'would, by itself, disorganize the army of resistance'.[74] He could not have been more wrong.

Faced with the prospect of going to work in Germany for two years, many young men simply took to the hills. There they looked to the Resistance to feed them, protect them, organize them and arm them. The Resistance leaders soon sensed the potential in the situation and began to bombard London with calls for help. On 6 March, d'Astier sent de Gaulle a personal telegram; its excited and exaggerated tone captures the mood of the time:

FRANCE THREATENED WITH BEING EMPTIED OF ALL ABLE-BODIED MEN IN TWO WEEKS STOP AWAIT YOUR CALL FOR VIOLENT AND TOTAL RESISTANCE STOP HAVE DECIDED TO TAKE UP REPEAT TAKE UP IMMEDIATE ACTION STOP HOPE TO PRODUCE UNANIMOUS MOVEMENT OF DISOBEDIENCE AND REVOLT STOP REQUIRE HELP AID AGENTS AND ARMS[75]

The Swiss press reported that there had been a 'rising in the Haute-Savoie' (the mountainous border region), and the BBC soon picked up the story, praising the 'légion des montagnes' ('mountain legion'). It appears that at least several hundred young men were holed up in the area, desperate for food and weapons.[76] Following a series of increasingly agitated messages from France, and with the enthusiastic support of Moulin, RAF planes tried to drop supplies but were apparently prevented by bad weather.[77] Over the next few months, more and more young men decided simply not to go to Germany. A new word soon entered the French language, a Corsican term for mountainous scrubland – *maquis* – describing both the place where groups of men were living in the mountains as well as the groups themselves. With amazing rapidity, the maquis soon spread throughout the country; as the British historian Rod Kedward has put it, 'the concept did not exist in January 1943; it was everywhere by June'.[78] As the concept became a reality, the Resistance began to change completely.

*

The appearance of the maquis heightened tensions within the Resistance. Virtually all the Resistance's money came from the Free French. The Resistance simply could not survive on its own funds – the general population was poor, it was dangerous to ask for money openly and enormous sums were required to pay full-time workers and produce large numbers of newspapers and leaflets. In turn, de Gaulle and his colleagues relied completely on the UK and the US to provide them with money. (This point was not lost on Roosevelt, who suggested that Churchill should threaten to cut off funds to bring the French leader to heel.)[79] When the cash arrived in France, it had to go through Moulin. This inevitably led to frustration, as he was unable to satisfy everyone's needs.[80]

Combat, which had a large number of full-time workers to support, was particularly vulnerable to financial pressures. In February 1943 US Intelligence, the OSS (Office of Strategic Services), offered Combat 10 million francs a month (more than the budget for the rest of the Resistance put together) in return for military intelligence. Frenay accepted the proposal, which involved channelling the money through Switzerland. Both sides were being disloyal: Frenay should have let Moulin know what he was up to, and the Americans were encroaching on British and BCRA territory – any military intelligence that Combat could collect should have gone to London.

When Moulin finally learned what was going on – two months later – he was furious as it threatened his control over the Resistance, and weakened the links between the *résistants* on the ground and the Free French. Although the 'Swiss affair' was soon condemned by all the Resistance leaders (except Frenay), Moulin realized that he could make something of the issue. In May he sent a report to London, insinuating that Frenay's link with the USA made him an ally of General Giraud, and using the affair to appeal for more money. His message concluded:

Nef [Frenay] has just received the first 10 million [francs] from the Americans. At the same time, I am unable to meet the most elementary needs, having no money left. Yet again, I am sending you an SOS. The responsibility of the Fighting French is very great. This situation must be remedied as soon as possible.[81]

Although Frenay accepted Moulin's dominance, on 19 May he wrote to de Gaulle, threatening a split if sufficient funding was not forthcoming.[82] Frenay's attitude was not simply based on an argument over money – above all, it was a question of politics and of military strategy.

De Gaulle and Delestraint, like the British and, to a lesser extent, Moulin, thought the Secret Army should merely give the Allies a helping hand, by a campaign of sabotage and harassment.[83] Frenay had a different view. Two letters written in April and May 1943 outline his ideas:

> Liberation and revolution are two aspects of the same problem that are indissolubly linked in the minds of all our members . . . A revolutionary army appoints its leaders and does not have them imposed . . . We have not forged an army . . . In reality we have created groups of partisans who want to fight even more for their liberties than against the invader.[84]

> In no case can these men be compared to the soldiers of a regular army, even if they are members of the AS [Secret Army]. The relative degree of discipline they display is much more like that of a revolutionary army, and that is only right, because one of the missions of the AS is to participate in the seizure of power.[85]

Frenay realized that this could mean a major conflict between the Resistance and de Gaulle. As he put it to Moulin:

> You seem not to realize what we really are – a military force and a revolutionary political expression. If on the former point, and with the reserves I expressed at our last meeting, we consider ourselves to be under the orders of General de Gaulle, on the second point we retain our full independence.[86]

Frenay was not Lenin. He was not arguing for a socialist revolution to overthrow the capitalist class. But he sensed that the Resistance, through its solidarity and its mobilization of growing numbers of people, could produce something more than a return to pre-war normality. These feelings were heightened by the appearance of the maquis – many *résistants* now felt that the time had come for immediate action, not for playing the waiting game. They even gave de Gaulle's orders ('attendre' – 'wait') a scornful name – 'attentisme' ('prevarication', 'temporization') – implying that was all London could offer in the way of military strategy. Although de Gaulle and Moulin had repeatedly tried to assert Free French control over the Resistance, they had not been able to resolve the key problem. The Resistance, growing in size and confidence, did not necessarily want the same future as de Gaulle.

*

Before the Resistance could reach that future, it had to survive. As 1943 went on, life became increasingly difficult. At the end of January the head of Combat's hit squads, Jacques Renouvin, was arrested at a railway station in the Limousin. Having led armed actions throughout Vichy France, including the sabotage of the Hispano-Suiza aero-engine factory in Toulouse, Renouvin was a key target for the Nazis. Probably his most spectacular stunt was the simultaneous destruction of ten government offices in the Non-Occupied Zone on 29 July 1942.[87] Betrayed by a Nazi infiltrator, Renouvin was swiftly taken to prison near Paris where he was tortured. Desperate to save him, twenty of his comrades travelled to the capital and worked out a daring plan to free him. But they in turn were arrested, and Renouvin was soon deported to the Mauthausen concentration camp, where he died in January 1944.[88]

Escape was sometimes possible. So, too, was revenge. At the beginning of April two radio operators of the PAL circuit were arrested near Paris, together with their liaison agent, a young student named Louis Goron ('Gilbert'), who immediately talked to the Gestapo. Within a few days a further twenty people were arrested, including 'Pal' himself, Jean Ayral, a twenty-one-year-old who was in charge of parachute supply operations in the northern zone. Ayral was bold, and lucky – he charged his guard, knocking him over, and then ran out through the front door of the hotel where he had been held by the Nazis. With his cover blown, Ayral was ordered back to London. But before leaving he worked out who was responsible for the disaster and got the information to

'Médéric', the head of the hit squad run by a small Resistance group called Ceux de la Libération (Those of the Liberation). In July the SOE closed their file on the affair with a curt note: 'Goron was eventually liquidated by Médéric in May 1943.'[89] Behind that laconic description there was a grim reality. As Ayral wrote in his diary:

> Gilbert's parents suspected something was wrong but said nothing. Gilbert was pale, the car drove towards the Meudon woods. Médéric and Gilbert were in the back seat. Two shots were fired and Gilbert crumpled over, hit in the head and heart. Médéric and the driver carried Gilbert's body to the edge of the woods, where it was discovered the next day.[90]

The first half of 1943 brought a vicious wave of repression against the Resistance. In March the Nazis stumbled on a mine of information following the arrest of Resistance members in Lyons – a suitcase containing the archives of the MUR and of the Secret Army. In total, 137 documents containing 163 names, many of them uncoded, fell into the hands of the Nazis.[91] Among these papers was a copy of a letter Frenay had sent to OSS in Switzerland as part of the 'Swiss affair', in which he described in precise detail the organization and activities of the Resistance. This find was deemed to be so important it was immediately brought to Hitler's personal attention. The Nazis now had an accurate picture of the whole of the Resistance, with the exception of the Communist Party. In particular, they now knew that the leader of the Resistance was 'Max'. He was the man they most wanted to capture.

Three weeks earlier, the Resistance in the northern zone had been hit by the arrest of Moulin's right-hand man, Henri Manhès. Moulin was alarmed – not only had he lost one of his key links with the Resistance groups in the north, but, as he confessed to his sister one night in the family home: 'I gave Manhès some photos so he could get a new identity card made for me. The Gestapo might have found them, either on him or in his desk. They turned his apartment upside down, and even cut the legs off chairs, looking for papers.'[92]

At the heart of the Nazi web that was being spun to catch 'Max' was twenty-nine-year-old Klaus Barbie, a member of the Sicherheitsdienst

(SD), the SS intelligence service, and head of the Gestapo in Lyons. Despite his unprepossessing appearance – he was 'a rather run-of-the-mill, slightly vulgar young man' according to Lucie Aubrac[93] – Barbie's campaign against the Resistance and against French Jews was terrifyingly effective. Moulin could sense Barbie's presence; he could almost smell the danger. On 7 May 1943 he wrote to de Gaulle, fearing the terrible consequences were he to be captured, and pointing the finger at Frenay:

> I am now hunted both by Vichy and by the Gestapo who, in part due to the methods of some members of the [Resistance] movements, know everything about my identity and my activities. As a result, my task is becoming increasingly hard, while the difficulties are becoming increasingly numerous. I am quite decided to hold on as long as possible, but if I am killed, I will not have had the time necessary to train my successors.[94]

Meanwhile, Barbie crept closer. On the morning of 9 June General Delestraint went to Mass in a Paris church, before setting off for La Muette Métro station, where he was due to meet René Hardy, who was in charge of Resistance work on the railways.[95] When Delestraint got to the rendezvous, he was arrested. The Nazis had known of the planned meeting for nearly two weeks, ever since Combat member Henry Aubry had left an uncoded message for Hardy in a Lyons letter box that had been 'blown' by the Nazis, following the betrayal of a young Resistance member, Jean Multon. Although Aubry soon learned that the letter box had been blown, he did not warn Delestraint or anyone else. Arrested by the SD, Delestraint was interrogated and eventually sent to Dachau, where the SS executed him in April 1945, days before the Allies liberated the camp.

News of Delestraint's arrest hit the Resistance leadership badly. Frenay was furious and left for London almost immediately afterwards. Pierre de Bénouville was so concerned about Frenay's state of mind that he hid some terrible news from his comrade. De Bénouville had just heard that Berty Albrecht, Frenay's lover and fellow leader of Combat, had committed suicide in Fresnes jail two weeks earlier. Fearing that the news would destroy Frenay, and wanting his friend to focus on picking up the pieces after Delestraint's arrest, de Bénouville let Frenay get on the plane to London without telling him Berty was dead. Frenay finally discovered the awful truth two months later.[96]

When Moulin learned of Delestraint's arrest, he immediately dispatched a handwritten letter – his last – to de Gaulle, putting the entire blame for the disaster on Frenay and the long-running campaign against himself and Delestraint that had been organized by Frenay, d'Astier and the other leaders.[97] He further insisted that the name of Delestraint's successor should be kept secret from all the leaders of the Resistance to avoid a repetition of the squabbling and the security leaks. There was no reply from London.

Delestraint was not the only victim that day; unaware of the danger, Hardy had taken the train to Paris – followed by the traitor Multon and the sinister Robert Moog, a French Gestapo agent.[98] Arrested en route and taken to Gestapo headquarters in Lyons, Hardy later admitted that he agreed to 'work for Barbie', although why, and what exactly that involved, remain unclear.[99] A week later Hardy was released. It can be assumed that from that moment onwards he was at the very least tailed by the Nazis. Elementary tradecraft dictated that anyone who was arrested should be isolated from all Resistance activities – they would probably be followed, and they might have been 'turned'. But the handful of Resistance members who knew that Hardy had been arrested did nothing. Not only did he return to his duties, he even turned up unannounced at a Resistance summit meeting to choose a replacement for Delestraint, held on 21 June, in a doctor's surgery in the Lyons suburb of Caluire. A meeting that included Jean Moulin.

Everything about this meeting was wrong. Despite the presence of so many Resistance leaders, there was no armed security group outside. And although Hardy's presence was entirely unexpected – he was pushed into attending by Combat member de Bénouville, probably to ensure that the new head of the Secret Army would be amenable to the action-orientated views of Combat – no one seems to have thought there was any problem when he appeared. Raymond Aubrac, who had been released by the Nazis five weeks earlier, came to the meeting with Moulin, when he also should have been kept at arm's length. Finally, Moulin and Aubrac spent thirty minutes in the centre

of Lyons, waiting for a comrade who was to accompany them to
Caluire. They should have abandoned the rendezvous after ten to fifteen minutes, but against all the rules they waited. And although
Moulin and his comrades turned up at Caluire forty-five minutes late,
the five Resistance leaders were still waiting for them. In an ultimate
bizarre twist, because Moulin and Aubrac were so late, the doctor's
housekeeper thought they were patients and ushered them, perplexed, into the waiting room, where a number of genuinely sick
people were sitting. The two men sat there, uncertain what was
happening. Then Barbie and his Gestapo agents burst in, arresting
everyone, including the Resistance members in the room above.[100]

The Nazis were overjoyed. They had inflicted a terrible blow on the
Resistance. They knew that one of their prisoners was 'Max', but at first
they did not know which of the men it was. Eventually, they discovered.
Over the next two weeks Moulin was beaten and tortured almost to
death by Barbie, but he was never broken. Fatally injured at Barbie's
hands, Moulin was eventually transferred to Germany, but died en
route. The last of his comrades to see him alive was Christian Pineau,
who was being held in Montluc prison in Lyons on his way to
Buchenwald, his real identity and his true role still hidden from the
Nazis. At six in the evening of 24 June, Pineau was called out of his cell
and told he had to shave a prisoner who was lying on a bench:

Imagine my stupefaction, my horror, when I realized that the man
lying down was none other than Max Moulin. He was unconscious, his
eyes were sunken as though they had been pushed into his head. On
his temple there was a nasty purple wound. A slight moan escaped
from his swollen lips . . . Suddenly, Max opened his eyes and looked at
me. I am sure he recognized me, but he must have found it difficult
to understand why I was there. 'Water,' he murmured . . . I leaned
towards Max, uttered some stupid, banal words of comfort. He spoke
five or six words in English, but his voice was so broken and stuttering
that I could not understand. He drank some of the water I gave him,
then lost consciousness again . . . Max Moulin remained stretched
out on the bench where, no doubt, 'they' were going to leave him for
the night. I never saw him again.[101]

*

The events at Caluire have fascinated French readers and writers for over sixty years, with every possible theory being advanced to explain why the meeting was raided and who identified Moulin as 'Max'.[102] After the war, Hardy was tried twice for allegedly betraying Moulin and the others and was acquitted both times, committing perjury on the first occasion. When Klaus Barbie was eventually brought back to France in 1983 and tried for war crimes, he threatened to make all sorts of 'revelations' about the affair, but the wizened and unrepentant fascist shed no further light on events.

It seems unlikely that we will ever know the truth. In a way, it does not matter. The meeting was betrayed, Moulin was murdered and the others were arrested and were subject to appalling and inhuman treatment. The Nazi machine rolled over these brave men and crushed them. The Resistance, however, continued.

# 7

# *The Maquis*

The railway line south from Limoges snakes through the small town of Eymoutiers, following the Vienne river, hugging the wooded hillside. About four kilometres west of Eymoutiers, the railway crosses the river on a high viaduct. Here, at around two in the morning of 13 March 1943, the Resistance carried out one of its first pieces of large-scale sabotage. Later in the week, a rail convoy of Service du Travail Obligatoire (STO) labour conscripts was due to leave Eymoutiers for Nazi Germany. The nine men gathered that night at the foot of the viaduct were determined to stop the convoy. They carefully loaded a home-made pipe bomb into a gutter that ran into a pier, attached a long fuse and retired to a safe distance. About twenty minutes later there was a massive explosion, and the pier came tumbling down, leaving an enormous gap between the two parts of the viaduct, bridged pathetically by two thin lines of rail, like a child's toy. The STO convoy was cancelled.[1]

The attack was the work of a small group led by Georges Guingouin, a thirty-year-old teacher. Guingouin was a charismatic local Communist leader who from the very beginning of the Occupation had run into difficulties with the Party high-ups, because of his determination to fight the Nazis and his refusal to accept the ambiguous position that marked the PCF's politics in the early phase of the war. Even when the Party leadership had swung behind the idea of resistance, Guingouin's independence and his unorthodox methods continued to irritate his comrades. Thrown out of his job for being politically unreliable, harassed by the Vichy police, Guingouin found himself hiding in farmyard outhouses, duplicating leaflets in sheep pens and storing the paper and ink in haylofts.

In December 1942 Guingouin single-handedly blew up a hay-baler at Eymoutiers railway station. At that time the Resistance was centred on the cities, where it was easier to hide and where the large population provided a ready stream of recruits. Guingouin's focus on the country-side seemed perverse, but in fact it was remarkably prescient. Although destroying a single hay-baler in an obscure rural town did not have the slightest effect on the Nazi occupation, it was a powerful symbol for the local farmers. The baler was a tiny part of the Nazis' policy of stripping France of all its material wealth. Farmers had to bring their hay to the station, where it would be baled up and transported to Germany. In return, they received far less than its worth; if they needed hay to feed their animals, they had to buy it back – at a higher price, of course.

Guingouin's symbolic act began the process of winning the rural communities over to the Resistance. As STO was extended to include farm workers, rural families were deeply affected as their sons and employees faced the choice of going to Germany or taking to the hills. Although only a small minority of the young men from rural commu-nities joined the maquis (most either hid with friends and family or went to Germany), the Resistance in the countryside was not the anony-mous action of faceless men as it was in the cities, but instead became the work of people who, directly or indirectly, were known to the com-munity. Despite its deeply conservative traditions, the French countryside would play an important role in the development of the maquis, and in support of the Allied advance after D-Day.[2]

*

By the end of summer 1943 the Resistance had changed substantially. Moulin was dead, Delestraint had disappeared into the hell of the concentration camps, while Frenay and d'Astier were out of the fray – first in London and then in Algiers, where de Gaulle's new govern-ment-in-waiting, the Comité Français de la Libération Nationale (CFLN), made its headquarters in the summer, and eventually set up a Provisional Constituent Assembly in September. At the same time, the headquarters of the Mouvements Unis de la Résistance (MUR) moved to Paris.[3] The absence of the early Resistance leaders removed poisonous personal antagonisms and gave the 'second wave' of leaders room to get on with the job.[4]

Meanwhile, the term 'maquis' had slipped into the language, and there were at least 13,000 *maquisards* scattered around the country, virtually all of them young men under twenty-five, most of them working class.[5] The rapid expansion of the maquis, which took everyone by surprise, made nonsense of all the careful plans made by the Free French and the Allies. The diagrams of the internal organization of the Resistance, drawn up with typically French Cartesian precision, littered with acronyms and rigid structures, literally had to be torn up. With the appointment of Delestraint in spring 1943, London had gained control of the Secret Army, ensuring that there would be no widespread military activity without its approval. But now there was a far less disciplined set of men, with no military training or organization, threatening to take action outside de Gaulle's control. The running conflict between London and the Resistance over the separation of military and political forces now looked completely irrelevant when there were thousands of bored young men in the hills, most of whom wanted to fight.

Furthermore, even in the southern zone, would-be *résistants* now had a choice about which Resistance group they wanted to be involved in – through the Franc-Tireurs et Partisans (FTP), the Communists had begun to extend their influence across the old demarcation line, challenging the influence of the Resistance groups of the MUR. Virtually all the maquis groups ended up aligning themselves either with the MUR or with the FTP. Although some *maquisards* made a strictly political choice, for most it was a question of tactics – some maquis even switched their allegiance overnight. The FTP were committed – at least on paper – to immediate action by small, highly mobile groups, while the MUR tended to follow Moulin's original view of the maquis as a kind of fortress, a way of preserving troops for a future battle. As FTP leader Charles Tillon later put it, the choice was whether the maquis should be 'drops of mercury or tin soldiers'.[6]

By the end of the summer the MUR, the Free French and the Allies all realized that they were in danger of losing the initiative to the Communists. There was no possibility of stopping the maquis from forming; all that could be done was to ensure that they were well supplied and did not act rashly. On 31 October 1943 a Resistance report concluded:

> One of the best . . . ways of creating cohesion and a team spirit in the camps and of keeping morale high, is action. It trains the *réfractaires* [men fleeing STO], gives them experience, and helps stop individual actions, most of which are misguided. All those in charge of military action must be fully aware of this necessity: as a result, they must use as many maquis *réfractaires* as possible when they carry out missions. Winter is approaching: we will not keep our men unless they are sufficiently equipped, appropriately fed and unless they have weapons to defend themselves and have the impression that when they act they are useful to our cause. Otherwise we will see the camps dissolve.[7]

Georges Guingouin had sensed this several months earlier, and at the beginning of May 1943 he organized a more traditional piece of sabotage: the destruction of the Wattelez rubber recycling facility near Limoges. In April three RAF bombing raids had failed to put the plant out of action, and it continued to produce up to twenty tons of rubber per day, all of it used for German vehicles and weaponry. Members of Combat in Limoges had been commissioned to attack the factory, using information from a sympathetic worker in the plant, Henri Granger. But shortly before they were due to act, the Nazis smashed the local Combat group, so Granger contacted Guingouin instead.[8] In January Guingouin's *maquisards* stole 1.4 tons of explosive from a mine; some of this was used in the attack on the Wattelez plant. Guingouin played a key role in the Wattelez operation, cycling fifty kilometres with the explosives on his back. Using SOE pencil timers – slow-acting chemical fuses about the size of a pencil – a five-man squad led by Guingouin cut the phone wires leading to the factory, planted their bombs at two sites on either side of the buildings and left. Six hours later there was a huge explosion and the plant was put out of action for five months.[9]

At the time of the Wattelez operation, Guingouin's group had grown from the handful of men who blew up the viaduct to over a hundred. By 1944 they were several thousand strong and controlled an extensive region of 2,500 square kilometres around Eymoutiers.[10] They lived in a camp in the middle of around seventy square kilometres of dense forest near Châteauneuf. The location was a tightly controlled secret, known only to the *maquisards* and to two locals who provided food. Although the forest teemed with game, feeding all those men turned out to be difficult. Initially, they had to make do with a frugal diet of potatoes and water. This proved dangerous when their water source became polluted and the camp was struck with an outbreak of dysentery. Drinking fresh water was banned, and the maquis reverted to old rural habits, drinking wine as the only safe source of liquid. Supplies had to be brought into the camp at night: sacks of rye, potatoes and smoked ham would be left at the edge of the forest, and were then carried into the camp in the pitch dark, along rocky and winding paths.

These problems were faced by all the maquis that sprang up around the country, most of them in the remote and hilly areas of the Massif Central, in the foothills of the Pyrenees and in the mountains of the Jura in the east. In every case, survival required the aid of the local community. Without support, the maquis would collapse. In January 1944, near Puivert, south of Carcassonne, a group of young men was reduced to living on onions for eight days before finally dispersing, beaten by starvation.[11] Guingouin's group was luckier – and better organized. Like many of the maquis, they carried out raids on the camps of Vichy's compulsory youth service, the Chantiers de la Jeunesse, which provided food, equipment and potential recruits, and on town halls, where thousands of ration tickets could be stolen. Guingouin was given sugar and cheese by Mme. Ribéras, a shopkeeper at Sussac, and was helped by two young women, Anna Coisac and Marcelle Legouteil, who rode their bikes around the region, acting as liaison agents. Above all, he and his comrades could rely on a network of farms to provide shelter during their missions.[12] This was a risky business: although none of Guingouin's *maquisards* were caught the night they blew up the viaduct, the police did raid the farm of M. Fermigier in the village of Bujaleuf, because he had sheltered two of Guingouin's team the night before. Fermigier – 'a notorious Communist,' said the police – was arrested and deported to the Nazi camps. He never returned.[13]

Elsewhere, support for the maquis and the *réfractaires* drew in previously respectable members of the community. In spring 1943 Georges Gillier, a

Protestant pastor in Mandagout, an isolated set of tiny villages that spill down a steeply wooded mountain in the Cévennes, found himself making fake ID cards. In a scene repeated in towns and villages all over France, Pastor Gillier was given a rubber stamp from a bank and got to work:

> With a razor blade I lifted off the words without destroying the individual letters, and with other letters from other old rubber stamps I composed 'Mairie de Nîmes – Gard' and stuck them on with solution from a puncture repair outfit. It wasn't perfect, but I was able to stamp over 100 false identity cards with it, several of which enabled people to get out of tight corners.[14]

Food and safety were vital concerns, but the key problem for the maquis – and for the Resistance as a whole – was how to get weapons. Although explosives could occasionally be stolen from quarries and mines, and there were caches of small arms that had been hidden after the debacle of June 1940, the only substantial source of weapons was London, and that required connections with either SOE or the BCRA. Even when London had approved the operation, the process of actually getting the supplies to France was surprisingly complex – it required twenty-three separate steps on the British side to organize a parachute drop, from agreeing the drop site with the RAF and arranging for the password to be broadcast on the BBC, through the complex logistics of finding, packing and loading the materiel, culminating in a parachute blossoming in the night sky somewhere over France. On the Resistance side, a reception committee had to be organized, securely transported to the drop site despite the curfew, and finally the materiel had to be found and then moved to a safe storage site. And everything depended on the weather. Cloud over the target could put an end to the operation at the last minute.[15]

Notwithstanding these difficulties, a substantial amount of materiel was sent to France – even if a large proportion of it ended up being captured by the gendarmes or German troops (SOE's arbitrary assumption was that ten per cent of all materiel would be captured, ten per cent would be lost in transit, twenty per cent would be used for immediate purposes and the remainder would be stored by the Resistance).[16] With the appearance of the maquis, the amount of materiel dropped in France increased sevenfold in the second quarter of 1943, rising to nearly 150 tons (1,361 containers and 236 packages). Those matt black containers were about the size of a man and carried up to 180 kilogrammes of weaponry, explosives and ammunition. Nine months later, in the run-up to D-Day, the figure had increased a further six times to nearly 1,000 tons.[17] This was still nowhere near enough.

The Resistance sometimes used subterfuge to get the weapons they needed. Guingouin suspected that neither the British nor the Free French would want to arm a Communist-led maquis, so all his contacts with the local SOE circuit, HECTOR, went through a frontman, Charles Gaumondie. As a result 'Hector' (Maurice Southgate) thought the maquis was run by 'Colonel Charles' and had no idea that the monthly drops he organized were going to Guingouin. There seems to have been no ill feeling, however – after the war, the UK awarded Guingouin the King's Medal for Courage in the Cause of Freedom.

Although most maquis groups carried out their operations independently, sometimes there had to be coordinated action with other Resistance groups. In the second half of January 1944 an attack involving the maquis, SOE, a BCRA intelligence circuit and the local MUR was launched against the Ratier aero-industry factory at Figeac, a small town of around 5,000 people 150 kilometres east of Bordeaux. The plant made sophisticated variable-pitch aircraft propellers – it was one of the largest such factories in the world, and each week it churned out enough airscrews to equip over fifty Heinkel bombers.[18] A series of small-scale RAF raids had failed to damage the factory, which was only a kilometre from the town centre – sufficiently close for a carpet-bombing raid to produce substantial civilian losses and therefore to be out of the question. Yves Ouvrieu, a local teacher and member of the GALLIA intelligence circuit run by the BCRA, had the idea of destroying the plant from the ground.[19]

The attack was planned with the aid of SOE operatives and local MUR maquis leader Jean-Jacques Chapou. Once the explosives had been parachuted in, they were made into plastic charges in Jean Verlhac's cheese shop near the town of Martel; they then had to be transported sixty kilometres to Figeac. Because of the German patrols, maquis member Dédé

Saint-Chamant, disguised as a pastry chef, carried the explosives to the van in a basket covered with a white cloth. On the night of 19 January, with the help of the Figeac Resistance, the van was driven through the factory gate, using keys provided by a supervisor. The bombs, armed with SOE pencil timers, were positioned around the bulky presses, and the group fled. Shortly afterwards a series of huge explosions smashed the presses and machine tools, killing one *résistant*, blowing out windows in nearby houses and causing a huge fire. The plant was out of action until the end of the war. Infuriated by the attack, the Gestapo and the SS launched a series of raids in the region, arresting people they thought might have been involved and ordering all males aged sixteen to fifty-five to gather in the town square. They were all eventually released, and none of the group who carried out the attack was ever caught.[20]

The shattered Ratier plant became a local attraction: the day afterwards, fourteen-year-old Pierre Feigl wrote in his diary:

During the night of Wednesday to Thursday, members of the Maquis blew up the Ratier factory in Figeac after first stealing tobacco and gasoline. There was only one death. The most important machines were destroyed. (8 explosions). This afternoon I did not go out for a hike. I visited the Ratier factory buildings, then, after running some errands, I went to the dentist who told me that I had a good set of teeth.[21]

Given that the Gestapo were swarming all over the town, young Pierre would have done better to stay out of sight. His name was in fact Klaus Peter Feigl, and he was a German Jew, armed with false identity papers. His family had fled Germany to escape the persecution of the Jews, baptizing Peter a Catholic on the way in order to protect him, and finally arriving in France in 1939. In the summer of 1942, as Vichy began to organize mass round-ups and deportations, Peter's mother arranged for him to travel south, where he became one of thousands of Jews who were hidden in the Protestant enclave of Le Chambon-sur-Lignon in the hills between Lyons and Nîmes. In September 1943 Peter and four other young refugees were sent a hundred and fifty kilometres to Figeac, to attend the College Champillon boarding school. Throughout this period, Peter wrote a diary addressed to his parents – he did not know that they had both been deported to Auschwitz-Birkenau and would never return. As the situation in Figeac took a turn for the worst, Peter was moved first to Clermont-Ferrand before eventually being smuggled over the Swiss border in May 1944.[22]

The bravery and humanity shown by the people of Le Chambon-sur-Lignon were other forms of resistance. Their actions did not involve blowing things up, shooting Germans or producing underground newspapers, nor were they intended to kick the Nazis out of France; they were simply about saving people from humiliation, victimization and deportation. In Le Chambon this kind of resistance was inspired by a somewhat dour Protestant pastor, André Trocmé. Even before the round-ups of Jews had begun in the summer of 1942, Trocmé and his fellow Protestants were hiding hundreds of young Jews, simply because, as he put it, 'We do not know what a Jew is. We know only men.'[23] When the Vichy police came to Le Chambon to arrest Jews, Trocmé sent messengers to the outlying farms where the refugees were hiding, ordering them to flee into the woods until the danger had passed. For three weeks the police remained in Le Chambon, managing to arrest only two people, one of whom was later released because he was not Jewish enough. But for Trocmé, rightly, losing even one of his charges was a tragedy. As he said in a sermon at the time: 'It is humiliating to Europe that such things can happen, and that we the French cannot act against such barbaric deeds that come from a time we once believed was past.'[24] Trocmé and his parishioners did act, and saved up to 5,000 Jews from the Holocaust.

*

For the young *maquisards*, hiding out in the woods might have been fun at the height of summer, but in the cold and wet of winter it became more difficult, and far more dangerous. The maquis needed to be safe – bare trees and snow made the men more visible – and they needed to be warm. To avoid being tracked in the snow, Guingouin broke his maquis up into several groups, each small enough to move down the valleys and stay in farm buildings. In a series of raids on warehouses and on the Chantiers de la Jeunesse, Guingouin equipped his men with a winter uniform – leather jacket, sheepskin gilet, green trousers, thick socks, white scarf and helmet.[25] Like all the maquis leaders, Guingouin wanted his men to be disciplined – giving them a uniform not only strengthened their feelings of comradeship, it also reinforced the popular impression of the maquis as a serious military force. In July 1944, shortly before the liberation of the Cévennes, Janet Teissier du Cros saw a parade of *maquisards* pass through her village:

> They wore the dark green uniforms that had recently been looted from government stocks, badly cut and badly fitting, a little reminiscent of Robin Hood with their big hoods as protection from the rain. The young men's thin, set, badly shaven faces were marked by the strain of constant danger, lack of sleep and underfeeding; but they all had the same look of having an inner purpose to sustain them.[26]

The most celebrated of these maquis public appearances took place on 11 November 1943 in Oyonnax, a small industrial town in one of the valleys of the Jura, near the Swiss border. The local maquis was founded by Henri Petit, known at the time by his pseudonym, Romans. His SOE comrade, Richard Heslop, described him as 'of medium height, stocky, with a chin that jutted out, and a pronounced nose. His hair was slightly touched with grey, he looked you straight in the eyes, and possessed the sort of personal magnetism peculiar to natural leaders of men.'[27] A reserve officer in the French Air Force, Romans-Petit initially intended simply to protect *réfractaires* who were fleeing STO. By the middle of 1943 there were a series of maquis camps in the Ain, led by Romans-Petit and set up completely independently of the MUR, FTP or SOE. These woodland camps had to be at least sixty-strong to be viable but were deliberately dispersed – they were at least two hours' march apart to reduce the risk of discovery. Realizing that the young men he was recruiting desperately needed military training, Romans-Petit set up a leadership school in the hills above Montgriffon, south-east of Oyonnax. Despite genuine hardship – the *maquisards* ate lots of carrots and got meat only twice a week – there was a real enthusiasm to learn both theoretical and practical skills even though, at this stage, weapons were scarce. Romans-Petit recalled:

At the beginning of July we got our first Sten machine gun, which made us extremely happy. We took it apart and assembled it over and over again, night and day. We even organized competitions between the students to see who was the fastest.[28]

From mid-July the Ain maquis began to get food and money via the MUR Secret Army and in August received the first parachute drops of arms. But even with money and weapons, the maquis needed to be able to move about: safely isolated from the enemy, they were also far from the targets they wanted to attack. For Romans-Petit, it was essential that his men should get in and out of an operation as quickly as possible, and the steep slopes of the Jura meant that it was not feasible to copy Guingouin and simply ride bicycles. The Ain maquis initially used gas-driven lorries, but they were severely underpowered and could barely make it up the steep mountain roads when loaded with men and stolen equipment. The maquis eventually managed to steal two petrol-driven lorries and on 28 September, with the aid of the MUR and the complicity of the local gendarmes, they raided an army depot close to Bourg-en-Bresse, the largest town in the département. Without a single shot being fired, they stole several tons of food – enough to keep them going for nine months.[29]

Those same vehicles were used for the meticulously planned 11 November stunt, when the maquis paraded in military formation through the streets of Oyonnax. They chose the town because there was no German garrison, and the heads of both the police and the gendarmerie were working with the Resistance. The maquis threw the Nazis off the scent by declaring they would organize demonstrations throughout the sprawling département, in defiance of Vichy's ban on all commemorations. In Oyonnax, the maquis first took control of the roads leading into the town and then occupied the post office and the fire station as well as the gendarmerie and the police station. To the amazement and joy of the local population, over 200 *maquisards*, wearing a uniform of leather jackets, berets and white scarves, walking boots and pale socks, marched smartly through the town, their weapons over their shoulders – they had practised the drill repeatedly in the mountains and were now near perfect.

At their head was Romans-Petit, in full Air Force dress uniform, accompanied by a colour guard of seven men surrounding the tricolour, all wearing impeccable white gloves (these had proved incredibly difficult to find). The procession arrived at the War Memorial, where Romans-Petit laid a wreath in the shape of the Gaullist double-barred cross of Lorraine, bearing the inscription 'To the victors of 1914–18, from the victors of tomorrow'. There was a minute's silence, the 'Marseillaise' was sung and a joyous crowd surrounded the *maquisards*. Then, as suddenly as they arrived, they disappeared back into the mountains.

Although there was no immediate response from the Nazis, a month later, in nearby Nantua, over a hundred men were arrested and deported, while the local Secret Army leader was shot dead. Reprisals continued in neighbouring Haute-Savoie – in winter 1943–4, German troops burned down around 500 farms.[30] Nazi policy was to respond to displays by the Resistance with crushing force, both to smash its organizations and demoralize its supporters.

The demonstration had an impact far outside the region, partly because Romans-Petit had a distinctly modern eye for propaganda: the whole event was filmed by André Jacquelin (Romans-Petit worked as a publicist before the war). The cine film was long thought to have been lost, but it has recently reappeared. The grainy black and white images show the *maquisards* marching through the town to the beat of a drum, with the crowd applauding them. Jacquelin's stunning photos were printed in his swankily produced underground paper, *Bir-Hakeim*, and were soon reproduced in both the UK and the USA.[31] In one of the most audacious stunts carried out by the Resistance, a spoof edition of the Lyons daily newspaper, *Le Nouvelliste*, was printed and sold in news kiosks, with a full description of the demonstration on the front page.[32] The Oyonnax parade was important because of its symbolism – it looked just like any Armistice Day commemoration from before the war. The message was that the Resistance, not Vichy, represented the continuity of the French state, which they were reclaiming on the streets of Oyonnax. The Occupied became the Occupiers, and even if the magic lasted only a few minutes, there was the promise that it would happen again, throughout the country, this time permanently.

Georges Guingouin's maquis went even further in asserting its power. By the targeted destruction of machines involved in the Nazi exploitation of the French countryside, Guingouin had shown that he sided with the farmers against the Vichy collaborators. He continued along the same line in September, when Vichy tried to requisition twenty-four cows for exportation to Germany; the maquis intervened and returned the cattle to their owners. Three weeks after the Oyonnax demonstration, members of Guingouin's maquis turned up when the Vichy food requisition board attempted to seize a crop of potatoes. The price set by Vichy – 1.25 francs per kilo – was simply too low for the farmers to survive. The *maquisards* demanded that Vichy pay 4 francs per kilo; when the officials refused, the *maquisards* simply stopped the requisition from taking place. In response to food scarcities and rising food prices in the shops, Guingouin published a series of official-looking declarations, fixing retail prices 'by order of the Prefect of the Maquis', and insisting that children and invalids be given priority access to the dwindling milk supplies. Thanks to the work of a sympathetic printer, the Vichy-loyalist regional daily newspaper, *Le Courrier du Centre*, unwittingly carried an article publicizing Guingouin's order. Vichy was furious and closed the newspaper down for a month as a punishment.[33]

Not surprisingly, Guingouin's measures were hugely popular with the population, if not with some traders. When M. Trochet, a shopkeeper from the village of Domps, refused to abide by the new prices, Guingouin sent him a very official-looking letter from the 'Prefect of the Maquis' ('Sir, I have been informed that my officials have received complaints about your behaviour . . . I hope that you will not make it necessary for me to take further steps against you . . .') and fined him the difference (2,000 francs). A declaration to this effect was also posted on Trochet's door with the warning 'Anyone who removes this declaration within the space of eight days will leave themselves open to the most severe penalties'. Trochet, desperate not to have anything more to do with 'them', pleaded with the gendarmes to leave the declaration in place.[34]

What Vichy presented as extortion by 'bandits' was in fact the embryo of an alternative state in the Limousin. This was intuitively recognized

by the local population, and, as the Occupation wore on, public acceptance of the Vichy gendarmes dwindled away. Even Vichy police
Intelligence ('Renseignements Généraux') admitted as much:

> Overall, the population is favourable to 'the maquis'. The peasants
> will not or do not want to speak, either out of support for the *réfrac-
> taires*, or through fear of reprisals. Their reticence makes
> investigations much more difficult.[35]

For example, over a hundred people witnessed a maquis ration ticket
raid at Terrasson, but no one would speak to the gendarmes, while
during a similar raid at La Coquille the population actually applauded
the *maquisards*.[36] As a result of all this activity, on 24 March 1944 the prefect declared Guingouin's region of the Haute-Vienne département to
be a 'no-go area', implicitly accepting the maquis' control.[37] Outside
this area, Nazi reprisals were vicious – on 2 April, 145 of the 148 houses
in Rouffignac were burned down. During the four years of the
Occupation, the Nazis killed 822 people in the Haute-Vienne and
deported 1,200.[38]

Guingouin's attitude was shared by most of the Resistance, which
saw how its activities could shape the future of the country. De Gaulle
had said that national liberation would be inseparable from national
insurrection: for the Resistance, including the Communist Party, 'insurrection' meant that the population as a whole would take direct action
to free themselves and at the same time to create a new government,
rather than relying on the Allies. De Gaulle was well aware that any
such insurrection could pose a threat to the France he wanted to create.
Hence the importance of controlling the men with the guns. In June
1944 Michel Brault, the head of the Service National Maquis, summed
up the potential of the maquis, which he had no intention of simply
handing over to de Gaulle:

> There will be no Liberation without insurrection . . . National insur-
> rection is the only way of ensuring independence and giving the
> French population the political representation it desires. It would be
> particularly dangerous if we had complete confidence in foreign

military commanders, in foreign political envoys and in officers
from a French colonial army, expecting them to put in place a
Republic and to enable the French people to express themselves . . .
The immediate action we demand and which we are daily intensify-
ing is a form of training for the insurrection . . . It is less a question
of the immediate strategic value of these actions than of training the
fighters of the insurrection.[39]

*

Guingouin was extremely popular with the ordinary people of his
region, but not with his Communist Party comrades. The Party recognized his abilities and his influence – a PCF apparatchik declared:
'Guingouin is very popular and loved by the masses . . . All his men and
his subordinates listen to him and have a great confidence in him . . .
He has the stuff of a great leader.'[40] But for the PCF leaders, his independence and his influence made him deeply suspect – he had opposed
the Party's equivocal line faced with the Occupation in 1940, and there
was nothing more threatening for the leadership than someone who
had proved the Party wrong. So in spring 1942 Guingouin was removed
from his Party positions and dismissed as 'the madman who lives in the
woods'. Then, in 1943, they took far more drastic steps.

Guingouin was warned that a regional FTP leader was trying to convince Limousin maquis members to leave, saying, 'if Guingouin
continues his activities, we will be obliged to kill him'.[41] FTP leader
Émile Planteligne recalled:

> Between the end of 1942 and the beginning of 1943, difficulties
> developed between Georges Guingouin and the 'inter-regional
> commander', who was a delegate of the Central Committee. Relations
> got worse during the sabotage of the binder and Guingouin's actions
> against requisitions . . . Sanctions were envisaged, up to the physical
> destruction of Guingouin.[42]

They were not only envisaged; they were acted on. Pierre Lerouge, a veteran of the International Brigades, was sent into the maquis to kill

Guingouin. Eventually, Lerouge told his new comrades why he was there and was summarily kicked out. Despite the failure of this attempt, the Party was still intent on ridding themselves of this troublesome *maquis-ard*. In September 1943 PCF leader Gabriel Faure told a meeting of regional Communist leaders: 'You should also know that we have received an order from the Party to liquidate Guingouin' because he was an 'enemy of the Party', an agent of British Intelligence who received weapons from London.[43] Thanks to the local support for Guingouin, these threats came to nothing.

Other PCF militants unjustly accused of treason were not so lucky. In October 1942 the naked body of a young woman was found in the Rambouillet forest, south of Paris. She had been shot through the head. Sixty-five years after her death, two French historians finally identified her as Mathilde Dardant, a liaison agent for clandestine PCF leader Jacques Duclos.[44] She was murdered by the détachement Valmy, the group of ultra-loyal PCF members who in 1942 and 1943 assassinated various 'traitors' – real and imagined. Their superiors suspected Dardant, with no justification, of being a security risk.

The 'case' against Pietro Tresso, a fifty-year-old founder of the Italian Communist Party, was clearer: he was a Trotskyist.[45] Tresso was arrested in 1942 after a police swoop on the Centre Américain de Secours in Marseilles founded by Varian Fry, which Vichy claimed was a 'Trotskyist conspiracy'.[46] In September 1943 Tresso and four comrades – Albert Demazière, Pierre-Georges Salini, Jean-Noël Reboul and Abraham Sadek – were transferred to Le Puy-en-Velay prison, where many inmates were hard-line Stalinists. Shortly after they arrived, a breakout was organized by a young guard, Albert Chapelle, who was in contact with SOE.[47] At 11 p.m. on 1 October Chapelle cut the telephone wires and then plied the guards with drink. After freeing all seventy-nine political prisoners, he pressed the guards to join the maquis (none of them accepted the invitation). In the biggest prison escape of the Occupation, the inmates fled with two light-machine guns, a Sten gun, eight automatic pistols and a substantial amount of ammunition, and over 32 million francs from the prison safe, for which Chapelle duly signed a receipt in the name of the Resistance.

After they escaped, there was a gruelling two-day march into the hills to join the hard-line PCF 'Wodli' maquis. At the maquis camp, the five Trotskyists were threatened and, when one of them escaped on a trip to find wood, the remaining four men were imprisoned in an abandoned farmhouse. Then, after a few days, they were simply taken out, shot and buried on the hillside. Absurdly, the *maquisards* were told that the men had been planning to shoot their guards and poison the water supply. The order to kill them had in fact come from the PCF leadership, via Léon Mauvais, who was also involved in the attempt to eliminate Guingouin.[48]

The full truth, deliberately hidden by the PCF for decades, came to light only in the 1990s.[49] The Party denied that there had been any cover-up and explained there was no question of criticizing 'men who were prepared to die for the anti-Nazi cause'. For the PCF, the fact that the *maquisards* were determined anti-fascists would always provide them with an alibi for having killed fellow *résistants* because of their political opinions.[50]

Communist members of the Resistance did indeed show remarkable bravery, and many of them paid a terrible price for their courage and convictions. After the war, the PCF described itself as 'le parti des 75,000 fusillés', suggesting that 75,000 of its members had been executed during the Occupation. This was a rather tasteless exaggeration – there were not even 75,000 executions for the whole of the Resistance – but it underlined the sacrifice made by the Party and its members.[51] One of the episodes that sums up the courage of the Communist resistance was the Main d'Oeuvre Immigrée (MOI – Immigrant Workforce). By 1942 and 1943 the FTP groups in Paris, Lyons, Toulouse, Marseilles and Grenoble were entirely composed of MOI members, many of them young Jews from Eastern Europe.[52]

The most important FTP-MOI group was based in Paris; its military leader was a Ukrainian Communist, Boris Holban.[53] Although there were never more than a few dozen active FTP-MOI members in Paris at any one time, in the first half of 1943 they carried out ninety-two armed actions. Forty-three of these were attacks against Nazi troops, as against sixteen in the second half of 1942.[54] Not all of these actions were successful, and many involved at most killing an individual soldier, but they were nonetheless a powerful irritation for the Nazis. At the end of

1942 the Gestapo smashed one of the four MOI detachments in Paris, and as the number of attacks increased in 1943 they began systematically to harass what remained of the Jewish community in Paris. By July only eight members of the second MOI detachment remained.[55]

In response, the MOI raised the stakes and focused their attention on leading Nazis. On 28 July they bombed the car of General Schaumburg, the Nazi commander of Paris. But the MOI's information was out of date – Schaumburg was not in the car. Indeed, he was no longer in charge of the capital and was not even in the country.[56] Two months later the MOI was more successful in its attack on SS General Julius Ritter. Although Ritter was in charge of the hated STO, Holban, who planned the attack, later declared the MOI had not realized who their target was – they discovered his name in the press after the assassination, which was a bloody affair.

Shortly before nine in the morning on 28 September 1943 a four-man hit squad was waiting outside Ritter's apartment in the sixteenth arrondissement. The first shots were fired as Ritter got into the car but missed; as he tried to flee, he was shot twice in the stomach. At the same time, the chauffeur and the bodyguard were shot dead. Ritter, still alive, tried to get up, so one of the MOI members came over and pulled the trigger again. But the gun did not go off, so he pulled out a knife and stabbed the Nazi in the chest. The four men then walked calmly off, leaving their victims in the street, covered in blood.[57]

In June 1943 Holban was replaced as military leader of the FTP-MOI.[58] His successor was a man who has become synonymous with the whole history of the MOI: Missak Manouchian, a thirty-seven-year-old Armenian. Within five months of his appointment, Manouchian and virtually all the FTP-MOI members in Paris were arrested. The police, who had been tailing Manouchian for nearly twelve weeks,[59] got their lead from an MOI member, Joseph Davidovitch, who agreed to betray his comrades. Betrayed in turn by a policeman who was a member of the Resistance, on 28 December Davidovitch was lured to a meeting in a Resistance safe house south of Paris, where an MOI squad led by Holban confronted him with the allegations. Davidovitch confessed everything and was shot. Over forty years afterwards, Holban recalled the events:

One of us read our conclusions to him before he was executed. Once this grisly and sad encounter was over, we had to act to ensure that the safe house was not compromised and that the tenants were not exposed to any consequences – a safe house was particularly valuable to the Party. What happened next was a nightmare. In the middle of the night, under curfew (it was around three in the morning), six armed men dragged the body. If we had met a routine patrol, we would have been done for. Exhausted, we arrived at a piece of waste-land, dumped the body and did our best to cover it. At six in the morning, with curfew over, we finally left. Only the gun remained in the house. In pairs, we got on the train back to Paris.[60]

This might seem callous and brutally unjust, but this was a war. As Holban later pointed out, 'We must not judge [Davidovitch] with today's eyes and with today's attitudes. At the time, it would have been simply inconceivable to have let him live.'[61]

The fruits of Davidovitch's betrayal were soon plastered on the walls of Paris, in one of the most notorious pieces of Nazi propaganda. To drive home their victory over the MOI, the Nazis published a poster with a lurid red background – hence the name by which it is known, 'L'Affiche rouge' – featuring photos of ten MOI members, each carefully described as 'Polish Jew', 'Hungarian Jew' or simply 'Armenian', together with pictures of derailed trains and bodies riddled with bullets. 'Liberators?' ran the text, 'Liberation by the army of crime!' In February 1944 Manouchian and twenty-two of his comrades were subjected to a show trial in Paris and were executed (the one woman, Olga Bancic, was denied the chance of dying with her comrades, and instead was deported to Germany, where she was beheaded in May). In total, Davidovitch's betrayal led to the capture and execution of sixty-eight *résistants*. As a result, the FTP–MOI was effectively wound up, merged into the broader Parisian FTP, which had a less audacious – or fool-hardy – guerrilla orientation.

Although the Affiche rouge's portrayal of the Resistance as foreign Jewish criminals satisfied the Nazis and comforted the Vichy collaborationists in their anti-Semitism and xenophobia, it had the opposite effect on the general population. The sacrifice made by these immigrants touched and shamed the French, and even Vichy's police intelligence service noted that there was a growth in sympathy for the Resistance after the appearance of the Affiche rouge.[62] The French did not consider the MOI as terrorists, but instead agreed with Manouchian, who in his farewell letter to his wife, written the day before his execution, proclaimed that he was 'a volunteer soldier in the Army of Liberation'.[63]

\*

When the Germans invaded the southern zone in November 1942, the Italians invaded Corsica and the region south-east of the Rhône. The Vichy administration on Corsica simply handed over power, in a political and military collapse that the islanders found deeply shocking. The Italian occupation of the island was one of the densest of the whole war: 80,000 soldiers were sent to dominate a population of around 180,000 – a ratio of nearly 1:2. Around ninety per cent of Corsica is mountainous and unpopulated scrubland: the original maquis. Ironically, there was no maquis on Corsica, in the sense of semi-permanent camps of *résistants,* but the inaccessible regions of the island did play a vital role in the rapid development of the Resistance, as a result of which Corsica was the first part of France to be liberated.

In January 1943 the Free French made their first serious attempt to coordinate the Corsican Resistance. On 7 January, shortly after midnight, a British submarine surfaced off the coast of Corsica and dropped an inflatable dinghy containing a twenty-eight-year-old Corsican BCRA agent called Fred Scamaroni, accompanied by a radio operator and a sabotage expert.[64] The operation was doomed from the start. Local peasants stole the radio crystals, arms and the substantial sum of money the three men had brought with them. The radio operator, Hellier, was unreliable: he said it was impossible to make contact with London, drank too much and proclaimed he was going to give himself up.

Worse still, Scamaroni was not the only operative on the island: a month earlier, General Giraud's intelligence bureau in Algiers had set up Operation PEARL HARBOR, and had made contact with the local

Resistance, which was dominated by the Communist-led Front National, and claimed to have 3,000 members organized in 115 villages. Scamaroni had a series of discussions with the FN leaders, but, reasonably enough, they were not prepared to hand over the command of their men.

Thanks to lax security, Scamaroni's presence on the island soon became known, and in March 1943 Hellier was arrested in a bar in Ajaccio by the Italian secret police, the OVRA. Scamaroni was warned of the arrest – he had time to send a cable to London – but refused to take to the hills. 'A captain does not abandon his army in the moment of greatest danger,' he said.[65] After intensive interrogation, Hellier broke down and took his captors to where Scamaroni was hiding. The young man was arrested, dreadfully tortured and then, in the night of 19 March, he committed suicide by severing an artery in his neck with a thin piece of wire.[66] The Gaullist Resistance in Corsica was in tatters, leaving only the Front National, supported by Giraud's Operation PEARL HARBOR.

The FN's strong clandestine structure – no group had more than five members – and its mobilization around national and social issues gave it a depth of support that Scamaroni could only have dreamed of. As on mainland France, the FN and the PCF organized housewives' demonstrations to protest against food shortages – the Italian occupation had increased the population by over forty per cent.[67] At the same time, the Italians inadvertently handed over leadership of the Corsican people to the FN when they arrested 110 elected representatives and deported them to Elba. With the traditional parties decapitated, the population – and the tiny Gaullist Resistance forces – rallied to the FN. To support the movement, Giraud sent an agent from Algiers, the gendarme Paul Colonna d'Istria, who was soon joined by several other Giraudist agents. Backed up by substantial support from the British – there were over sixty arms drops, either by parachute or by sea, containing tens of thousands of weapons – the FN and its 'military adviser', Colonna d'Istria, created a huge network of armed partisans, based in the scattered villages and hamlets of the gorgeous Corsican mountains, but sometimes living in caves, their weapons stashed in the maquis.[68] All this was hidden from de Gaulle and the Free French, who were focused on their politicking in Algiers.

On 10 July the Allies invaded Sicily. Mussolini was overthrown and imprisoned (he was subsequently rescued by the Nazis, and was eventually killed in April 1944). Although the Italian forces on Corsica began to waver, they showed no respite in their campaign against the Resistance. Paradoxically, OVRA repression became even worse after the fall of Mussolini – several leading FN members were arrested, tortured and executed during the summer, even as some Italian officers, such as Colonel Gianni Cagnoni, secretly joined the Resistance. But Cagnoni's courage was rare. During the summer, General Magli, the Italian commanding officer who would go over to the Resistance at the very last minute, continued with business as usual, refusing to commute the death sentences of FN members such as the schoolteacher Jean Nicoli, who was shot in the back at 7.30 a.m. on 30 August in a particularly brutal execution, together with two of his comrades.[69]

In response to the OVRA offensive, Colonna d'Istria insisted on a complete overhaul of all security measures – codes, addresses, pseudonyms – and introduced a highly decentralized command system which made the Resistance less susceptible to OVRA attacks, and also made its activity richer and more flexible. In his memoirs, Giraud ungenerously – but not untruthfully – contrasted the organizational abilities of his agent, Colonna d'Istria, with those of the martyred BCRA operative:

> If the unfortunate Scamaroni had been more professional, if he had been as discreet as Colonna d'Istria, he would have lived to see the liberation of his little country.[70]

Towards the end of August 1943 it became clear that the Italian army was about to be defeated by the Allies. At a secret meeting held in the night of 27 August, the Corsican Front National decided that when the Italians surrendered, they would launch an insurrection. The FN's PCF leaders wanted to seize the opportunity to liberate the island and to put pressure on the Allies to open a second front in Europe that would directly confront the Germans, relieving the pressure on the USSR. To put the final finishing touches to the plan, the FN leader, Arthur

Giovoni, was taken by the Free French submarine *Casablanca* to Algiers, where he met Giraud on 4 September, returning to Corsica two days later. Neither de Gaulle nor his entourage knew of this – any more than they knew that the Allies and the Italians had already agreed peace terms. On 8 September the Allied-Italian peace treaty was made public; contacted by Colonna d'Istria, General Magli let it be known that he would support the Resistance.[71]

The next day the Allies landed near Naples; in response, the Wehrmacht occupied Rome and the north of Italy. In Corsica fighting broke out between anti-fascist Italian soldiers and German troops, and the Resistance launched an insurrection in Ajaccio. There was an enormous demonstration, in which the leaders of the Front National stood on the roof of a van, while the crowd waved flags, threw rice and chanted: 'Corsican patriots, take arms against Hitler! Italian soldiers, join us against the enemy of Europe!'[72] As the revolutionary carnival came to a close, Colonna d'Istria sent a frantic message to Giraud in Algiers: 'REBELS MASTERS OF AJACCIO STOP ITALIANS PASSIVE STOP FIGHTING IN BASTIA STOP CORSICA CALLS FOR HELP FROM THE ARMY'.[73]

At this point Giraud finally informed de Gaulle and the Free French leadership what was happening. De Gaulle was furious at having been kept in the dark, but eventually agreed to Giraud's proposal to send troops to the island, despite his fears that there would be a bloodbath, and his irritation that Giraud had allowed the Communists to play such a dominant role. As the Resistance fought the Germans and some hardline fascist Italian units, a small force of around 6,000 Free French soldiers left Algiers for Corsica, one hundred and nine of them crammed into the claustrophobic space of the submarine *Casablanca*, which arrived on 13 September. The next day two Free French ships, the *Fantasque* and the *Terrible*, arrived in the port of Ajaccio, to be greeted by huge celebrating crowds. The liberation of Corsica was in full swing.

The German high command, alarmed by the developments in the Mediterranean, soon decided that their troops would be better employed on the Italian mainland, and gave the order to evacuate both Sardinia and Corsica. On 12 September General von Senger und Etterlin of the 90th Panzer Division, stationed in Sardinia, took his

20,000-strong division across the Strait of Bonifacio and headed for Bastia and for the Luftwaffe aerodromes on Corsica, from where they would be evacuated. The French rebels now had to deal with tens of thousands of German soldiers and hundreds of tanks.[74] But within three weeks, Corsica was free. In scores of small-scale operations, the Free French soldiers – spearheaded by the commandos of the Bataillon de Choc, commanded by General Gambiez, and by Moroccan and African troops from the French Empire – supported by Resistance fighters based in the maquis and by anti-fascist Italian units, harried the Germans northwards through the island. The Nazis were eventually chased to their bridgehead at Bastia, where, with air support and far superior numbers, they were able to embark for Italy. In total, the liberation of Corsica left 75 French soldiers dead, 245 Italians and around 1,000 Germans.[75]

De Gaulle's fears about the role of the Communist Party in the Corsican events proved unfounded. Although the Front National declared itself the sole police force on the island, and effectively took civilian power, this revolutionary fervour was short-lived.[76] De Gaulle insisted that one of his loyal staff members, Charles Luizet, should be installed as Prefect, and the Front National made no complaint. Far from launching a purge of the Corsican state, the FN allowed many of the old Vichy staff to remain in office.[77] With elections deemed impossible by de Gaulle, a Comité de la Libération was formed, a coalition of Resistance forces which ran the island until the end of the war.

For the Communists the Corsican events were a huge propaganda coup. They had shown their legitimacy as a key force in the Resistance, and their loyalty to the Gaullist project. Their task now was to build on that position in the struggle to liberate mainland France. For Giraud, the liberation of Corsica was a pyrrhic victory. He took the credit, but he also paid the price. De Gaulle was convinced that Giraud's self-proclaimed political naivety was a terrible liability, and his secrecy had shown that even in military matters he could not be trusted. With the keen support of the Free French leadership, the CFLN, which Giraud had also kept out of the loop, de Gaulle was soon able to remove his rival from power, barely a month after the French tricolour flapped in the Mediterranean sky.[78]

The liberation of Corsica, desired by the population, but not by the Free French or by the Allies, was a kind of dress rehearsal for what could happen on the Continent if the French were left to their own affairs. For the Allies, still suspicious of both the Communists and de Gaulle, it also represented a situation they did not want to see repeated. The outcome was not so far from what they – and de Gaulle – wanted, but the danger had been substantial. A population in arms, mass meetings and demonstrations, Communists in power – this was not how Churchill, Roosevelt or de Gaulle saw the Liberation of France.

# 8

# *Hopes and Fears*

The liberation of Corsica convinced many people in mainland France that the Allies would soon be launching an all-out invasion. There was no such plan, but the Allies deliberately fuelled speculation as part of an elaborate deception. In April 1943, when it became apparent to London and Washington that for logistical and military reasons there could be no invasion of Northern Europe before 1944, the Allies decided, in Churchill's words, 'to pin down the enemy in the west by keeping alive the expectation of invasion'.[1] This operation, code-named COCKADE, fooled the Germans into expecting attacks on Boulogne, Brest and Norway. Men and machines were sent on pointless manoeuvres in the British countryside, carefully constructed dummy aeroplanes and land-ing craft were deployed in strategic sites, while double agents fed the Nazis misinformation about the size, location and destination of Allied forces.[2]

The Resistance was soon caught up in the general excitement. Between July and September 1943 there were 327 parachute drops of arms and money by the RAF, twice as many as in April to June.[3] While these operations were mainly intended to support the growing number of men in the maquis, they also suggested that the invasion was close. One of the many people who became convinced that D-Day was not far off was SOE agent Francis Suttill, who ran a sprawling intelligence and sabotage circuit (PROSPER),[4] which had about a thousand French mem-bers, including a substantial number of Communists. In May 1943 Suttill returned from London certain the invasion would take place in the coming weeks and put the whole circuit on alert.[5] But in a little over a month PROSPER was in ruins, blown apart by a series of indiscretions and bad luck, with still no sign of D-Day on the horizon.

On 21 June 1943 the Nazis arrested two Canadian SOE agents shortly after they arrived in France. The two men carried uncoded messages and new radio instructions for Suttill's radio operator, Gilbert Norman. Within two days Norman was arrested, followed by Suttill – they had been tailed by the Gestapo for weeks. In the period that followed, between 400 and 1,500 French members of the circuit were arrested. In terms of *résistants* deported and executed, the collapse of the PROSPER circuit was the biggest single blow suffered by the Resistance.[6] From the outset, much of the circuit had been built on sand – many of the early members were linked to the CARTE circuit, whose files had been seized by the Nazis at the end of 1942, while the SOE operatives themselves seem to have been careless about security. Worse, at the beginning of January 1943 SOE sent Suttill a new air drops supervisor, Henri Déricourt. Déricourt was in fact working for the Nazis; all of the information that went through his hands, from the details of the landing drops to the personal letters sent by SOE agents, was handed over to the Germans.[7] Although Déricourt was not directly responsible for the collapse of PROSPER, he gave the Nazis a route to the heart of SOE's operations, weakening the work of the Resistance.[8]

The story of PROSPER came to an ignominious conclusion when, after a series of interrogations by the Nazis, Norman, or perhaps Suttill, apparently made a 'pact' with their captors, and agreed to reveal the location of the circuit's weapons dumps in return for a promise that no other members of the circuit would be executed. As might have been expected, the Nazis did not keep their promise, and in 1944 and 1945 all the key members of PROSPER were killed.[9]

Some writers and *résistants* have argued that London knew all along that the PROSPER circuit was insecure, and cynically used it to misinform the Nazis about the date of the Allied invasion, thereby sacrificing several hundred French members of the PROSPER circuits and the British SOE operatives themselves.[10] Governments and military commanders in the Second World War regularly killed civilians and sacrificed soldiers to pursue strategic aims, but there is no proof that this was the case with PROSPER. Although Suttill was certain in May 1943 that the invasion was imminent, there is no evidence that he had been manipulated – it is more likely that, like millions of French people who took the growing number of Allied bombing raids as a sign of approaching invasion, he simply believed what he wanted to believe.[11]

Whether D-Day was around the corner or not, the Resistance still had to resist. A key way of gaining support from the population and weakening the Nazis' grip on the country was to stop the departure of young men to Germany under STO. On 14 October 1943 *résistants* in Paris attacked the STO office on the Rue des Francs-Bourgeois where the files on 100,000 STO candidates were kept. They intended to set fire to the building – without the names, men could not be called up. But their plan failed, so instead they stole around 65,000 files, saving tens of thousands of young men from deportation.[12] Five months later, half a ton of documents were stolen from the STO offices in Cahors and thrown into the river Lot by a watermill in the centre of the town. The mill wheels churned up the documents and left an enormous mess along the banks of the river, attracting the amused interest of passers-by and showing the effectiveness of the Resistance.[13]

At around the same time, a small group of FTP and Combat members destroyed the central STO files held in the Place Fontenoy in Paris, just behind the École Militaire. Helped by a civil servant who worked in the STO offices, they entered the building pretending to be a maintenance team. After pistol-whipping the young lad who was guarding the room where the files were held, they smashed down the door. Léo Hamon, who led the operation, recalled:

> We spread out our banana-shaped incendiary devices, then lit a match, and the whole place went up like a dream. We got out of the room, picked up the lad, who was still a bit stunned, shook him and said, 'Go on, get the hell out of here!' Then we hurried out . . . We made our way towards our car, still trying not to look as though we were running, and then the cry went up: 'Fire!' So we pelted off in the car, past all the official drivers waiting for the high-ranking administrators, and crossed Paris with the barrels of two pistols pointing out of the rear window, ready to shoot at anyone who tried to follow us.[14]

The group made a clean getaway, and Hamon was thoughtful enough to send a food parcel to the young man they had knocked out, together with a brief note that concluded: 'You risked your life – next time, make sure it is for, and not against, France. Get well soon.'[15]

For the Allies, action against STO was useful because it disrupted the Germans' industrial plans – as far as London and Washington were concerned, the main role of the Resistance was to carry out military and industrial sabotage. In the summer of 1943 SOE agent Harry Rée came up with a novel approach – he got the bosses to help. On 16 July 1943 there had been a catastrophic RAF raid on the Peugeot plant at Montbéliard-Sochaux, near Besançon, which left the factory intact but killed 110 civilians and seriously injured another 154. The British were desperate to stop production at Sochaux, which made tank parts and components for the new Focke-Wulf night-fighter plane. Rée was able to meet the head of the Peugeot company and convince him that the RAF would stop trying to destroy the plant if they would help the Resistance sabotage production.

Even before Rée arrived on the scene, the Sochaux plant was causing the Germans problems. Although the Peugeot company had been enthusiastically pro-Vichy at the beginning of the Occupation, by the autumn of 1942 management had changed their attitude. A number of factors – workers refusing to do their job properly, anti-German feeling in the population and the bosses' desire to protect their investments from Nazi expropriation – had led to some spectacular delays. For example, out of 100,000 cylinder heads ordered in November 1941, only 1,000 had been delivered by July 1944, while in May 1942 the Nazis complained that sixty per cent of the Peugeot 2T vehicles were useless because they had faulty clutches. Following the agreement with Rée, Peugeot management turned a blind eye to eighteen major sabotage operations, some of which put key parts of the plant out of action for several months.[16]

SOE tried to repeat the tactic at the Michelin tyre plant in Clermont-Ferrand. On 11 March 1944 SOE agent Pearl Witherington reported that after negotiating for five months she had been unable to convince Michelin management to let her Resistance contact, Villiers, sabotage the plant. Worse, Villiers' sabotage leader had been arrested when he tried to set fire to the factory. Witherington was scornful of Michelin's motivations and drew the necessary conclusion:

> They refuse to believe the RAF will have time to bomb Clermont-Ferrand before an allied landing,' she told London. 'In the meantime they are working turning out material and making money . . . They are playing for time . . . I hate to suggest this bombing of MICHELIN but Villiers and I think it would give the management a lesson and force Villiers' hand if Clermont-Ferrand were bombed.[17]

Three weeks later, following an RAF raid, she reported:

> Michelin was well pin-pointed and destruction complete in main factory. People in Clermont say many of the incendiaries were duds. Casualties: about 16 killed and 20 injured.[18]

Attacks on vital targets could sometimes lead to terrible reprisals. On the night of 1 April 1944 the Resistance blew up the railway line at Ascq, near the Belgian border. A train carrying around 400 men and 60 armoured vehicles of an SS Panzer Division was derailed, but none of the troops were hurt, and only minor damage was done. Nonetheless, the Nazis immediately went on the rampage, killing the stationmaster and one of his workers. The soldiers were then sent into the town where they knocked on the doors, demanding the men get out of bed and help repair the railway, promising the women that their menfolk would soon return. Shortly after the events, one anonymous survivor described what happened next:

> We were made to walk for about 15 or 20 minutes until we went through a hole in the fence onto the railway line, beaten with rifle-butts as we went . . . There were German soldiers, with a machine gun, on the ground by the track . . . I thought we were going to be put on to the train. As I walked, I saw around 20 or 25 bodies on the ground, and I realized we were going to be shot. We walked a few metres more. The man at the head of our group was a gamekeeper; he was shot at point-blank range by a German. I saw him fall – I was

fifth or sixth in line. That was the signal for the Germans by the railway to start shooting. I leaped forward and fell to the ground, holding my head in my hands. The shooting carried on. Then everything went quiet. The Germans were walking up and down the path. After a moment, another group of prisoners arrived. They passed barely one metre from my feet and then the shooting began again. After this round of shots, I heard two victims still breathing; a German must have heard them, because there were two shots right next to me. I was kicked twice in the ribs and once in the shoulder, as though to make sure I was dead . . . Eventually a locomotive came and took the train away – it seemed to take forever. I could still hear noises and the sound of Germans on the track. I still didn't dare move. Then a comrade in front of me began to crawl away. I was afraid that the Germans might see him and come and finish us off, but I did the same. Together with a third man we crawled through the fields to the Rue Mangin. Then I fled to the other side of the village.[19]

In total, eighty-six men, aged between fifteen and seventy-five, were killed that night.[20]

*

The existence of Resistance operations against the railways raises the question of what was done to stop the deportation of the Jews. The answer is shamefully short: nothing. Eighty-five rail convoys of Jews left France for the concentration camps, transporting over 70,000 people to their deaths, including 10,000 children. Not one train was stopped or even significantly delayed. Amazingly, this is not only true for France; it is also true for the whole of Occupied Europe, with two exceptions.[21]

This inaction may seem incomprehensible, but such responses flow partly from the hindsight of history. Today the Holocaust is often seen as the overwhelming feature of the Second World War, but the Allies did not fight the war to save the Jews – indeed, at the time few were aware of the vast extermination plan the Nazis were putting into place. The vicious anti-Semitism was plain for all to see, and only the hopelessly naive could suppose that the convoys of deported Jews were heading anywhere pleasant, but the appalling reality was literally unimaginable. It was known that people died in concentration camps – of starvation, beatings, overwork or disease – but not that the Nazis had built a machine for murdering millions of people.

When news gradually began to leak out about the horror of the camps, it was rarely believed. In May 1942 reports reached London from Poland, describing the extermination of whole Jewish villages by gas, but these were generally considered to be an exaggeration.[22] In October 1942 *J'accuse*, a small newspaper produced by the 'French forces against racist barbarism' (one of many guises adopted by the Jewish section of the MOI), published an account of what was happening, written by someone working for the Germans:

> You should know . . . that all Jews who are deported are killed as soon as they arrive in the camps. They are killed by gas. I heard from an officer that 11,000 people deported from France were killed in this way.[23]

Nearly fifty years later, Trotskyist *résistant* and concentration camp internee David Rousset recalled his own reaction:

> I think it was in 1943 that I first had information about the existence of the gas chambers. I refused to publish it because I did not believe it . . . It was only when I arrived in Buchenwald that I understood that, in fact, anything was possible and that, effectively, the gas chambers were not quite so incredible . . . my response was the same as that of most people – we simply did not believe that such things were possible.[24]

This was not a failure of the imagination, but a psychological defence mechanism for people faced with overwhelming horror. Pierre Francès-Rousseau was in a camp linked to Auschwitz; even when he was made to sort through the clothes and shoes of those who had been gassed, he could not bring himself to accept what was taking place.[25]

Those who did accept the horrific reality had doubts about whether they should make it generally known, for fear of the terrible demoralizing effect the news might have. The editor of *J'accuse*, Adam Rayski, recalled that he and his comrades had 'a substantial internal debate' before deciding to publish what they had heard:

> We were seized by doubt: would the effect of this information on the Jewish population not be disastrous? Would it provoke a reinforcement of resistance, or a despairing collapse of morale? If people panicked when they heard this, would the *résistants* be able to deal with it? Would they succeed in driving out fear and transforming despair and pain into the determination to fight?[26]

Rayski soon realized there was nothing to lose, and that the population had to be mobilized. In March 1943 the MOI publication *Notre parole* ('Our Word') set out seven tasks for every Jew, man or woman, old or young, in Occupied France. They were: leave home; hide the children among sympathetic French people; join a Resistance organization; if caught by the Nazis, resist or flee; organize demonstrations and barricades in the French camps; try to escape from the convoys; organize sabotage in the German prison camps. The article concluded with a rousing call to action:

> Use every hour of your life to wound the Hitlerian beast! Strike it wherever you can! Smash the machines! Destroy all produce! Join the partisans! Arm yourselves and fight for the destruction of the brown-shirted barbarians, if you do not want to be destroyed yourselves! This is the fighting programme of each Jew who does not want to walk into Hitler's abattoir. This is the programme that can be summarized in these words: STRUGGLE AND VENGEANCE![27]

But although many young Jews did join the Resistance, there was no wave of action along the lines called for by the authors of *Notre parole*, and the Jewish Resistance organizations never involved more than around two thousand people.[28] In fact deportation was not used only against the Jews – the trains that left France also carried tens of thousands of *résistants* (over 88,000 in total). There was, however, a terrible difference in the survival rate: only three per cent of Jewish deportees made it back, as against fifty-two per cent of the *résistants*.[29] The Resistance did virtually nothing to stop any types of deportation (and, strikingly, none of the Jewish Resistance organizations ever called for such action). The lack of action against the convoys of deported Jews did not reflect a French indifference to Jewish suffering.

What could seem at best as passivity and at worst as callous indifference towards *all* deportees can be explained by the weakness of the Resistance and by the scale of the deportations. As shown by Georges Guingouin's destruction of the railway line near Eymoutiers, stopping a train would have been straightforward; the real problems would have begun afterwards. Each convoy of deportees carried around a thousand people. Once freed from the cattle-wagons in which they had been locked, they would have to be clothed, fed and sheltered for the duration of the war. When the STO trains were stopped from leaving, freed workers simply went home for the night. However, deportees from the Drancy transit camp could have come from anywhere in the country and would have to be hidden either in the countryside or in willing households. That would have required an elaborate underground infrastructure that the Resistance simply did not possess. Even maintaining the maquis – groups of fit young men who had volunteered for gruelling conditions – was extremely difficult. As a result of all these factors, it seems that the Resistance never even considered the possibility of stopping a convoy.

Nevertheless, we know of two attempts to stop deportations, each of which, while small in scale, was significant. Léon Bronchart was a forty-four-year-old train driver from Brive who was a member of Combat and was involved in Jacques Renouvin's Groupes Francs. On 31 October 1942, at Montauban station, north of Toulouse, Bronchart was told to drive a train of 'political internees' (this was the Vichy term for Jews and others who were not members of the Resistance) who were being transferred towards Limoges.

> I immediately made up my mind and refused to drive the train. The stationmaster, the depot manager, the deputy depot manager, an

inspector, all came to the engine to talk to me. Despite the advice, the coaxing, the warnings and the threats, I continued to refuse; when I had enough, I shut the locomotive down.[30]

Someone else was found to drive the train, and in December 1942 Bronchart was disciplined and fined by his managers. Then, on 29 January 1943, he was arrested in Brive for possessing copies of *Combat* – the same day as his comrade Jacques Renouvin was captured, also in Brive. Sentenced to deportation, Bronchart was sent first to Buchenwald, then Dora, where he helped sabotage the V2 rockets the prisoners were making, before finally arriving in Bergen-Belsen. After the war, he was given the title of 'A Righteous Among the Nations' for saving Jewish families in Brive.[31]

A far more effective and dramatic operation to save Jews occurred in Belgium in April 1943. This was the only known organized attempt in the whole of Occupied Europe to stop the deportation of Jews. Belgian Jews were herded into a concentration camp in Mechelen near Antwerp and housed in an old barracks. By the end of the war, over 26,000 Mechelen inmates had been deported to Auschwitz, all of them Jews, apart from 365 Gypsies. Nearly 16,000 of them, including virtually all the children, were gassed as soon as they arrived in Auschwitz. Conditions in the Mechelen camp were appalling. The Nazis subjected their prisoners to systematic humiliation and degradation, drawing swastikas on Torah scrolls and religious books, making Hasidic Jewish men cut off their distinctive hairstyles and repeatedly threatening people with dogs.[32]

In early 1943 a young Jewish Communist called Hertz Jospa hatched a plan to attack one of the rail convoys and free the deportees. The Belgian Resistance felt the plan was 'too daring and too dangerous'[33] – they thought such an operation would require at least twenty men armed with grenades and firearms to hold off the Nazi guards, and the Resistance would then have the responsibility of looking after hundreds of refugees. However, one of Jospa's comrades, Youra Livchitz, a handsome young Jewish physician, was enthused by the idea, and managed to persuade some *résistants* to give him a revolver. Meanwhile, Jospa began to organize support for the operation. Twenty thousand francs were collected, enough to give each freed deportee fifty francs – the price of a tram ticket.[34] Coincidentally, Communist prisoners in the Mechelen camp were planning to escape when the next convoy left. With the help of a secretary who worked in the camp, the Communists manipulated the list of deportees so they would all be in the same wagons. When a message was smuggled into the camp, announcing that the convoy would be attacked, the prisoners gathered the saws, files and knives they had been hiding. Then, on 16 April, the inmates were told the next convoy would be leaving three days later, on the eve of Passover. The Nazis had planned it so that over 1,600 Jews would spend one of the most important days in their religious calendar riding in cattle-wagons towards their death.

Despite having only three days' notice of the operation, Livchitz was able to persuade two young men to join him: his childhood friend Jean Frankelmon, a Communist actor and musician who had fought in Spain, and Robert Maistriau, four years younger, who had gone to the same school. Neither had previously been involved in any action against the Occupation. Armed only with the revolver, a torch covered with red silk and some bolt-cutters, the three young men rode off on their bicycles to the place Livchitz had decided would be the site of the attack. As Maistriau later recalled: 'We felt a mixture of adventure, a desire to help and also to cause trouble for the Germans. At that point, nothing could have stopped me. We were full of hope.'[35]

At ten o'clock on the evening of 19 April, right on schedule, Convoy 20 pulled slowly out of the Mechelen camp on its way to Auschwitz. Thirty wagons long, hauled by a huge Type 44 locomotive, the convoy carried 1,631 people, including 262 children, many of them travelling without their parents. The oldest person, Jacob Blom, was ninety years old; the youngest, Suzanne Kaminski, had been born in the camp less than six weeks before. Her short life would end in the Auschwitz gas chambers. Even before the train arrived at the spot where Livchitz and his comrades were waiting, two young men and a woman had escaped, having broken through the bars of the small windows and jumped to safety. That was just the beginning.

As the train chugged around a curve, the driver saw the red warning lamp Livchitz had placed in the middle of the track. He slammed on the brakes, bringing the convoy to a halt with a terrifying mixture of scream-ing metal and hissing steam that paralysed Maistriau with fear. He gathered his wits and ran to the last wagon, cut open the lock, slid back the door and called on the prisoners to jump out. There was an argument, as some deportees shouted: 'It's forbidden: The Germans will kill us.' Hena Waysng, a thirty-year-old woman in the wagon, remembered what happened:

> All of a sudden, the train stopped. We didn't know what was happen-ing or where we had stopped. In the wagon, people started shouting, pushing. Then a passenger who was by the narrow window shouted: 'Over here, over here!' A young *résistant* opened the door and gave money to those who were in front and shouted: 'Get out, get out!' I was frightened and I didn't dare jump. But in a flash I realized that my two sons would always be on their own if I didn't have the courage. So I jumped.[36]

Meanwhile, Livchitz was firing from the bushes, convincing the German guards at the front of the train that they were being attacked by a large group of partisans. Eventually, the soldiers realized that they were in no real danger and men were sent out to chase Livchitz, who very sensibly fled. Maistriau and Frankelmon freed seventeen deportees, gave each of them fifty francs and showed them how to get to the nearest tram sta-tion. Once their charges were safe, the two young men returned to where they had hidden their bicycles and rode off, exhausted. Livchitz, unable to get to his bike because of the Germans searching for him, had a two-hour walk home.

Eventually, the train steamed off, but all along the way, thanks to the work of the Communist partisans, it leaked prisoners as people escaped through doors and windows, using the equipment the partisans had smuggled on board the train. Twenty-three people were killed either when jumping or as the German guards shot at them, but in total two hundred and thirty-one more men, women and children escaped from the convoy. Exactly as the Resistance had feared, many of the escapees had little choice but to throw themselves on the mercy of local people.

But the Belgians proved more welcoming than many expected – amazingly, not one of the deportees was denounced.

Things did not go so well for Livchitz and Frankelmon, both of whom were betrayed and arrested later in the year. They were executed in 1944. Before he was finally captured, Livchitz gave another bravura display, managing to escape from Gestapo headquarters after hours of torture – he overpowered his guard, put on the Nazi's uniform and walked calmly out of the building. Of the three young men, only Maistriau survived the war.

The story of Convoy 20 was unique. The combination of an attack by a handful of brave men, a well-planned escape by the deportees and amazing luck all round was never repeated. But the date of the attack was significant: by coincidence, it also marked another moment in the Jewish fight against Nazi barbarity. On the other side of the Continent the Jews of the Warsaw ghetto began the final phase of their heroic but doomed uprising against the Nazis. Around 13,000 Jewish residents of the ghetto died, while the surviving 50,000 were deported to the camps. The ghetto itself was razed to the ground by the Nazis, and a concentration camp was built on the site.

French Jews may not have launched an uprising like their comrades in Warsaw, or even carried out an attack like that on Convoy 20 from Mechelen, but they were intensively active in the Resistance, both as individuals and as an organized force.[37] Several Resistance leaders were Jews – for example, Jean-Pierre Levy, Raymond Aubrac and Daniel Mayer – while most of those in the MOI were Jews, as the Nazis did not fail to point out during the 'Affiche rouge' trial of the Manouchian MOI group at the beginning of 1944.

Jews also carried out their own specific forms of resistance. One of the most important was related to the first of the seven instructions published by *Notre parole* in March 1943: 'hide the children'. Some infants, like Peter Feigl in Figeac, were hidden by refugee charities. Up until 1941 the Oeuvre de Secours aux Enfants (OSE – Charity for Children's Aid – the French branch of a Jewish organization that traced its origins back to the pogroms of tsarist Russia) looked after 850 children in its centres. But then, under new legislation, its work was entirely taken over by the tame Jewish Council set up by Vichy (the

Union Générale des Israélites de France – UGIF). What should have been havens for needy children had turned into traps.

The Nazis and their Vichy collaborators knew where the homes were and had lists of all the children, while the UGIF lulled the children into a false sense of security, urging them not to run away.[38] On 20 October 1943 the children's home at La Verdière, near Marseilles, was raided by the Gestapo; the director, Alice Salomon, and the forty children in her charge were all deported to Drancy. Finally realizing the danger, the OSE began to empty the homes, dispatching children to stay with sympathetic French people, or smuggling them over the border into Switzerland. In Limoges the homes were requisitioned by the prefecture, thereby taking them out of the UGIF circuit that was being preyed on by the Gestapo.

After the Nazi invasion of the southern zone in November 1942, the French départements to the south-east of the Rhône river were occupied by the Italians. Until late 1943, when the Nazis took over following the Italian capitulation, conditions for Jews in these regions were less dangerous than elsewhere in France.[39] Among those who fled there was Sabine Zlatin, a Polish Jew who worked at a children's home in Vichy France, and who took the forty-two children in her charge to the relative safety of the Italian-occupied zone. At the beginning of summer 1943 they arrived in Izieu, a tiny village fifty kilometres due south of Oyonnax. The site was idyllic – high on the hillside overlooking the Rhône Valley, there was not only sufficient accommodation for the children but also a farm that could provide food. Then, on 6 April 1944, all hope was extinguished. The Gestapo arrived, sent from Lyons by Klaus Barbie. Forty-four children and seven staff members were arrested. All of them, except for one classroom assistant, were killed by the Nazis.[40]

There were other organizations that helped Jewish children hide from the glare of Nazi eyes – the MOI group Union des Femmes Juives (Union of Jewish Women) hid a hundred children in the Parisian suburbs or in the countryside, while an informal body called Entraide Temporaire (Temporary Welfare), a product of Parisian high society, helped save dozens of children.[41] There were also hundreds of spontaneous acts of generosity as ordinary people looked after children threatened with death simply because they were Jewish.[42] The precise number of Jewish children saved is unknown, but the figure ran into the tens of thousands.[43]

\*

It may be difficult to accept, but the raid on Izieu and the massacre at Ascq, indeed all the appallingly brutal acts of the Nazis, were often carried out by normal people. While the Nazi leaders were crazed anti-Semites, motivated by fear, lurid fantasies and hatred, many of the rank-and-file soldiers who did the dirty work were 'only following orders'. This classic defence has been repeatedly used to try and avoid personal responsibility in terrible events, from Nazi Germany to Abu Ghraib. As a legal and moral defence it is risible, but it is based upon an element of truth: armies – and especially conscript armies – are not homogeneous blocks. They are composed of men and women who may not always agree with the instructions they are given; the best of the soldiers may refuse to carry out morally indefensible orders, even at the risk of their own lives. Under such circumstances, armies can split. This was the hope behind one of the boldest pieces of Resistance action, which occurred when left-wing groups attacked German soldiers not with bullets but with ideas.

The Communist Party, which had substantial contacts with conscript German soldiers who had once been in the German Communist Party (KPD), set up a special section, the Travail Allemand (TA – German Work), with Czech Communist Artur London at its head. The TA produced a German-language bulletin, *Soldat im Westen* ('Soldier in the West'),[44] which called on soldiers to support the Resistance, emphasized the successes of the Red Army on the Eastern Front and reported protests by Wehrmacht troops. To get the newspaper into the hands of ordinary soldiers, *Soldat im Westen* was thrown over barrack walls, or left in cinemas, cafés and restaurants. As a result of this work, small groups of anti-fascist soldiers were set up in the Navy Ministry, in the St-Germain-en-Laye barracks to the west of Paris and in the Bordeaux submarine base.

As the fighting grew worse on the Eastern Front, some German soldiers serving in France but due to be redeployed to fight the Russians, preferred to desert rather than go to their death, and were welcomed into the maquis or the FTP. Others did their duty, but went east armed with passes from the TA, which gave them free passage through the Russian lines.[45] Realizing the potential threat to the stability of their army of occupation, the Nazis were desperate to smash the TA, and in 1942 they arrested Artur London and deported him to Mauthausen concentration camp. His place was taken by Otto Niebergall, an exiled KPD member who in September 1943 set up the Comité Allemagne Libre pour l'Ouest (CALPO – Free Germany Committee for the West) in Paris. Many CALPO members went on to play a courageous role after parachuting into Germany with the American OSS. Most of them were killed while carrying out their mission of trying to undermine the Reich from within.[46]

The Communists were not the only ones to try and influence German soldiers. In 1943 Martin Monat, a thirty-year-old German Trotskyist living in Paris, produced a bulletin called *Arbeiter und Soldat* ('Worker and Soldier'),[47] and his comrades in Brest organized a group of German soldiers around *Zeitung für Soldat und Arbeiter im Westen* ('Newspaper for the Soldier and Worker in the West').[48] This was laboriously typed on to stencils by the young André Calvès, who later recalled:

I haven't forgotten the tiresome chore of typing a stencil in a language you don't understand. Furthermore, I typed in an underground hiding place in the garden, near to the house. It wasn't very comfortable, but it was pretty well fitted out . . . You got in by a small hole that led into the bottom of a pit. This entrance was hidden by a piece of wood covered with mud. If someone thought of snooping about and lifted the lid that covered the pit, all they would have seen would have been a few old tins. Of course, you had to be young to get into the hiding place. But it was good, and it was never discovered.[49]

Tragically, Calvès' hiding place was safer than the meetings with the Germans, and in October 1943 twenty-seven soldiers and sailors were arrested. One of them had talked to the Gestapo and the group was smashed. Ten soldiers were shot, Robert Cruau, the twenty-two-year-old leader of the Brest group, was executed by the Gestapo and sixteen Trotskyists were deported, several of them never to return.[50]

In September 1943 the idea that sections of the German army could fracture along class or national lines turned from hope into reality. At the time, the 13th Waffen SS Battalion was billeted in Villefranche-de-Rouergue, forty kilometres south of Figeac. The battalion was composed of over 1,000 young Bosnian Muslim and Croatian conscripts, but was led by German SS officers. On the night of 17 September some of the conscripts mutinied and shot several of their officers, but instead of immediately joining the maquis (they were in contact with local FTP members) they first attempted to rally the rest of their comrades. With the help of the battalion imam, the remaining SS officers were able to turn the tables on the mutineers, who had neither the guns nor the numbers necessary for victory. There was a bloodbath that lasted several days, and around 150 mutineers were killed. Desperate to avoid the mutiny spreading to other SS battalions, the Nazis immediately transferred the remaining soldiers first to Germany and then back to Yugoslavia, where they were used against Tito's partisans.[51]

Although none of the anti-fascist mutineers of Villefranche-de-Rouergue escaped to join the maquis, this did happen in the Cévennes. A number of anti-fascist Germans – some of them deserters, others exiled KPD members who had fought in the Spanish Civil War and had sought refuge in France after the triumph of Franco – had taken to the hills in November 1942, when the Nazis swept aside the demarcation line and invaded the southern zone. Towards the end of 1943 they joined the small maquis created by François Rouan (code-name 'Montaigne') in Jalcreste, a remote, heavily wooded area sixty kilometres north of Montpellier. Rouan, a twenty-nine-year-old civil engineer who had fought in the Spanish Civil War, had been expelled from the PCF in 1934 for being a Trotskyist. Despite this potential political flashpoint, one of the anti-fascist Germans – Otto Kühne, who had been a KPD Reichstag deputy before Hitler came to power – became Rouan's second-in-command.

At the beginning of February 1944 the 'Montaigne' maquis was joined by six German Communists who had been staying in Séderon, a village about a hundred kilometres away. One of the six, Max Dankner, aged thirty-two at the time, later recalled a conversation on their train journey towards the maquis:

> There were some railway workers in the carriage; they were eating and chatting, without seeming to pay any attention to us. They complained about the war, about Hitler . . . then they began to talk to us, at first prudently, then more and more openly. There was a good contact between us and when they heard that we were joining the maquis and that we had fought in Spain, they were very supportive. Having invited us to share their food, they then offered us some wine and we drank to the end of the war. When the train came to our stop, we said our goodbyes and parted good friends. They wished us success in our fight against fascism and promised to do their duty, too.[52]

\*

Some *résistants* refused to let hope die, even when those they loved most were in the hands of the Gestapo. In June 1943 Raymond Aubrac was arrested at Caluire, along with Jean Moulin. Only six weeks earlier, his wife, Lucie, had bluffed the Lyons prosecutor into freeing him following an earlier arrest, and shortly afterwards she had spirited a group of *résistants* from a guarded hospital by posing as a nurse.[53] Raymond was again in severe danger, so once again Lucie used her audacity and guile. This time, she walked right into the lair of the beast, knocking on the door of Klaus Barbie's office at Gestapo headquarters in Lyons. She asked for her husband under his cover name, 'Ermelin', describing him as her fiancé, and played innocent when Barbie told her that he was a 'terrorist'. Explaining that she was pregnant (which was true) and that 'Ermelin' had promised to marry her, she asked Barbie to let the two get married, as a way of maintaining contact with Raymond. Heartless, suspicious, or both, Barbie refused point-blank and Lucie, her eyes streaming with real tears, staggered out of the building.

Seven weeks later Lucie's luck changed. In mid-July Barbie left Lyons and did not return until December. As a result, Raymond Aubrac was kept in Lyons rather than being transferred to Paris like the rest of the Caluire detainees. Lucie repeated her 'abandoned fiancée' routine, this time with a Wehrmacht colonel, whom she courted with gifts of Lyons silk. This ruse enabled Lucie to see 'Ermelin' on a number of occasions, and, by her mere presence, reassure him that the Resistance was trying to free him. After one of these meetings, on 21 October, a group of *résistants* led by Serge Ravanel, which included Lucie (by now six months pregnant), attacked the truck carrying Raymond and other *résistants* back to prison. In the ensuing firefight, Raymond and one of the attackers were wounded, but all fourteen prisoners were able to escape.[54]

On the night of 8 February 1944 the Aubracs, together with their first child, Jean-Pierre, were due to fly to London. They had been waiting for a plane for months – bad weather had repeatedly delayed them – and Lucie was by now only days away from giving birth. But when the twin-engined Hudson aircraft touched down near Bletterans in the Jura mountains, it got bogged down in the wet ground. The pilot, Flying Officer Affleck, realized that it would not be possible to take back all the passengers – who included a stranded British airman and Claude Serreulles, de Gaulle's delegate to the CNR – and several sacks of vital messages. There were discussions as to who should fly back, or even if the plane should be destroyed, before a solution was found:

> . . . everyone from the neighbouring village came out and got busy round the plane. But neither the horses nor the bulls that were brought on to the field by the locals could get the plane free. On the advice of the pilot and Paul Rivière [the ground-side head of the operation], we dug two trenches and inserted sloping planks which would enable the plane to get free. We were worried that it would get stuck again after a few metres. Day was going to break soon and Affleck, moved by the stoicism of the Aubracs – including their little boy, wrapped in his blankets – finally agreed to take them back if the plane was freed. We had been there since 23.45 . . . At 2.00 in the morning the engines roared again . . . the plane hopped over the hedges and flew off; everyone hugged and congratulated each other.[55]

Four days later, in the middle of a London air raid, Lucie gave birth to a baby girl.

Shortly afterwards, a rather different escape took place, again with the help of the RAF. At eleven o'clock in the morning of 18 February 1944, three waves of RAF Mosquito bombers, protected by Typhoon fighters, took off from RAF Hundson in Hertfordshire. The nineteen Mosquitoes skimmed the Channel waves at nearly 300mph – flying dangerously low to escape detection by the new German radar stations – and then screamed over the flat, snow-covered terrain of northern France, heading for Amiens prison as part of Operation JERICHO.[56]

Amiens jail was crowded with the normal inhabitants of prisons everywhere – petty criminals, thieves and murderers. It also housed scores of *résistants*, including Dr Antonin Mans and Raymond Vivant of the OCM, Jean Beaurin, who worked for the SOSIE circuit as a saboteur, and two MI6 agents, Robert Beaumont and Maurice Holleville. At noon the first of the Mosquitoes reached the prison and dropped its bombs, followed in close succession by the other planes. Within ten minutes there were gaping holes in the north and east walls of the prison. As shouting and screaming replaced the thunderous noise of exploding bombs, and the planes roared off into the smoke-filled sky, hundreds of prisoners poured out of the jail into the surrounding streets and fields. Forewarned of the attack, many *résistants* fled to freedom, although Dr Mans preferred to stay and tend the wounded.

Tragically, over a hundred prisoners had been killed. Despite the dead and injured – who included Robert Beaumont as well as twenty-eight-year-old Group Captain Pickard and his navigator, twenty-two-year-old Flight-Lieutenant Broadley, who were shot down by the Germans – the attack restored French morale by showing the power of the Allied military machine and its concern for the fate of the *résistants*. Dominique Ponchardier, head of the SOSIE circuit, who was involved in planning the operation on the French side, later called it 'the most beautiful act of Franco-British solidarity in the whole war'.[57]

Probably the most important result of the raid was its direct effect on the intelligence received by the British. The *résistants* who disappeared into the backstreets of Amiens or who hid in the villages of Picardy helped

re-form the shattered intelligence circuits in the region, providing valuable information about the Nazi V-weapons that were aimed against
Britain. Finally, by focusing German attention on the north of France,
which the Allies were still pretending would be the site of their invasion,
Operation JERICHO may also have helped deceive the Nazis about the
true location of the D-Day landings, now less than fourteen weeks
away.[58]

Most Allied-inspired escapes were far less dramatic and involved not
*résistants* but downed Allied airmen. Shortly after the outbreak of war,
London set up a section of the Secret Intelligence Service specifically
charged with organizing the return of British servicemen – MI9.[59] On its
own, MI9 could not do a great deal to ensure the safe return of their
comrades; they needed the active and extensive cooperation of the
French. In this way, assisting Allied pilots in what were known as 'escape
lines' became another form of resistance.

One of the most effective MI9-run escape lines in France was the 'Pat
O'Leary' line, based in Marseilles but which had contacts all over
France. The line had been set up by a Scottish officer, Captain Ian
Garrow, who found himself trapped in Marseilles after the fall of France.
Rather than escape himself, Garrow spent the next year helping over
fifty British servicemen return to Britain. After Garrow's arrest in the
summer of 1941, 'Pat O'Leary' took over the command of the organization, and it became known by his name. O'Leary claimed to be an
evading French Canadian airman; in fact he was a Belgian army doctor
named Albert-Marie Guérisse, who had been working for MI6 when he
was stranded in southern France in April 1941. Over 600 Allied
airmen – among them Guy Lockhart, who flew Lysanders into France –
were saved by the Pat O'Leary line.[60]

At the same time as the O'Leary line was getting into its stride,
another escape line – COMET – was created by a young Belgian woman
called Andrée de Jongh. With contacts spreading from Belgium down to
the far south-west of France, COMET was able to perform some astonishing feats. One was the return of all seven crew members of an RAF
heavy bomber, who had parachuted to safety near the Dutch border
and, thanks to COMET, arrived in Gibraltar a week later (this rapidity
gave rise to the line's code name). De Jongh accompanied virtually

every one of her charges – in the space of 16 months, she crossed the Pyrenees 35 times, taking 118 evaders to safety.

When de Jongh was arrested as she prepared to leave with another group, she decided to tell the truth about her role, to protect her comrades. But the Nazis refused to believe that she was the organizer of the line, because she was a woman. Interrogated twenty times, Andrée was eventually deported to Ravensbrück concentration camp. Within a month, another hundred members of the line were arrested, and yet new recruits were found and the organization continued to function right up until the Liberation. Altogether around 800 people were involved, many of whom were arrested. A hundred and fifty-six of them were either executed or died in the camps or in transit. As a result of this price, 700 Allied servicemen were helped, 288 of them making the long trip to Gibraltar.[61]

The main work of the British Secret Service in France involved the collection of intelligence.[62] Probably the most important of the intelligence circuits was ALLIANCE, set up by Commander Georges Loustaunau-Lacau in 1940. As a loyal military man who retained strong illusions about Pétain, Loustaunau-Lacau was deeply suspicious of de Gaulle, so he put his growing intelligence circuit at the disposal of MI6. After the arrest of Loustaunau-Lacau in July 1941, the circuit was run by Marie-Madeleine Fourcade ('Hérisson' – hedgehog). Her MI6 handlers at first had no idea that 'POZ 55' – her radio code name – was a woman, and Fourcade carefully hid the fact in her transmissions.[63] They finally discovered she was not 'the moustachioed officer we imagined' in December 1941, when Fourcade met British Intelligence officers in Madrid, having been spirited over the border hidden in a mailbag.[64] The Germans were only slightly better informed: when they were hot on her trail, they asked for the whereabouts of 'Mrs Harrison' – they mistook her code name for a British surname.[65]

Other MI6 intelligence circuits were the product of joint French and British initiatives. For example, the JADE-FITZROY circuit was set up by Claude Lamirault ('Fitzroy') a twenty-two-year-old on the far right of French politics. Lamirault escaped to London in October 1940, and parachuted back into France four months later, charged by MI6 with setting up a military intelligence circuit. His first recruit was his wife, followed by an ex-army colleague, Pierre Hentic, who was at the opposite end of the political spectrum. Despite their political differences, the two men worked closely together. Hentic took photos of the German military aerodrome at Boissy-l'Aillery near Paris, using a camera hidden in a bag, and was soon in charge of the circuit's extensive air contacts with Britain.[66] Within a year the circuit extended to all the major ports of the Occupied Zone and had sub-circuits on the railways and in the Post Office. In 1942 and 1943 JADE-FITZROY was repeatedly targeted by the Nazis, and in December 1943 Lamirault was arrested and deported to Dachau.

Gilberte Champion, a thirty-year-old woman whose eldest son was looked after in a British boarding school while she worked for the circuit, was one of the JADE-FITZROY radio operators. She was arrested in Lyons in April 1943 and held incognito for three months, during which time she was regularly interrogated by Klaus Barbie. She later recalled Barbie going into the cell next door to interrogate a Jewish prisoner:

> The cell door opened, he didn't pronounce the prisoner's name, he said, 'So, have you decided to talk? You're a bastard,' and he took out his revolver . . . He said, 'You dirty Jew' and so on . . . I heard the prisoner say, 'Please, don't kill me, I'll tell you everything, I'll tell you everything, don't kill me,' and then, at the same time, bang, bang, and it was all over. The next day, I quickly asked the person who brought the soup round, 'Next door?' and was told, 'We tidied everything up, it's finished.' Barbie had killed him, he had shot him. We lived bathed in terror.[67]

Gilberte was eventually deported, first to Mauthausen and then to Ravensbrück. With over 700 members, the JADE-FITZROY circuit saw 217 arrests; 82 of its members were either killed or died in the camps. As Gilberte discovered, the fact that the circuit members worked for the British made life even more difficult in the camps – not because of the Nazis, but because of the other inmates. Each group of *résistants*, in particular the Communists and the Gaullists, would look after themselves. The MI6 agents, seen as being outside the Resistance, were told to ask instead for help and support from imprisoned British soldiers and operatives.[68] In the hell of the camps, the situation was so appalling that 'even the basic solidarity between people fighting on the same side broke down. For those unfortunate enough to experience these terrible conditions, this was one more reason to pray for the Allies and the Resistance to smash the Nazis once and for all.

# 9

# *A Duty to Kill*

As 1943 drew to a close, the mood in France was bleak. The war seemed to have reached new heights of destruction: Allied bombers were pounding German cities to rubble, dropping tens of thousands of bombs in enormous raids involving up to 1,000 aircraft. Bombs were also dropped on French cities, killing thousands in the Paris region and in Toulon. The hopes of an Allied invasion had evaporated: determined Nazi resistance in Italy was hindering the Allied advance, and there was no sign of a second front on France's Mediterranean coast. Parisian student Bernard Pierquin wrote in his diary:

> The reality is becoming painfully apparent: a new (and final) winter will take place under the Nazi yoke. The immense hope of September has evaporated. In Paris, everyone is depressed: we hoped for the rapid return of the people who have been deported, the prisoners. That's all finished.[1]

In a lethal counterpart to the bloody events that were taking place around the world, the Resistance was hit by waves of arrests, as traitors and tortured prisoners gave information to the Nazis. Sometimes prisoners tried to play for time, hoping against hope that they could somehow dupe the Gestapo, or at the very least limit the damage they were causing. In the harsh world of the Resistance, their names, such as Roland Farjon or André Grandclément, both of the OCM, became bywords for betrayal.[2]

Most dangerous of all, Vichy and the Nazis now had another weapon at their disposal in their fight against the Resistance: the Milice. This paramilitary fascist militia, created by the Vichy government, mobilized the most reactionary sections of the population – mainly shopkeepers, professional people and fundamentalist Catholics – in a brutal anti-Semitic and anti-Communist crusade against the Resistance.[3] In November 1943, after the Resistance assassinated the chief of the Lyons Milice near Annecy, the fascists organized a revenge attack. One member of the Milice said to another in a tapped phone call: 'Do you have any Jews up there? Which hotels are they in? Give us the names of the most important of them.' In the raid that followed, three suspected *résistants* and three Jews were killed.[4] Despite the pro-Nazi role of the Milice, some ignorant and foolish young men who did not want to go on STO labour conscription felt they had a new alternative – joining the Vichy Milice instead of the Resistance maquis. They ended up fighting on the wrong side.[5]

Cranking up the machine of repression in January 1944, Pétain appointed Milice leader Joseph Darnand as the Vichy Secretary General for Law and Order. Darnand now had control over 45,000 gendarmes, 6,000 gendarmes mobiles and 25,000 members of the hated Gardes Mobiles de Reserve (GMR), as well as up to 30,000 members of the Milice. Vichy also set up special military courts to try 'all those individuals accused of having committed an assassination or a murder, or having attempted an assassination or a murder, committed with arms or explosives, to support terrorist activity' – in other words, virtually everyone involved in the Resistance. With such broad terms, the perfunctory judicial process (there were no lawyers involved at any stage) meant there was virtually no chance of being acquitted. If guilty, the defendant was to be immediately executed.[6] Paradoxically, the repression revealed the weakness of the Vichy state. The collaborationists could no longer rely on the police, gendarmes and army to impose their will, so they had to create new structures with which to enforce their authority. Coupled with the growth of Resistance activity and a shift in the attitude of the population in some parts of the country towards support for armed resistance, the conflict between the Resistance and the maquis began to create something like a civil war mentality.

Even before the military courts were created, the Resistance was subject to a terrible campaign of repression. In September 1943 sixteen-year-old Henri Fertet was condemned to death for shooting a German Customs officer near Besançon. A few hours before his execution, he wrote a last letter to his parents, settling his 'affairs' – reminding them that one school friend owed him a packet of cigarettes, that another still had his book on prehistoric humans, and asking them to return a copy of *The Count of Monte Cristo* to yet another. Henri's letter concluded:

> I will die for my country. I want a free France, and happy French people. Not a proud France, but a hard-working, honest France. The French should be happy, that's the main thing. Farewell, death is calling me, I do not want a blindfold, nor to be bound with ropes. I embrace you all. It is hard to die . . . A thousand kisses. *Vive la France.*
>    A condemned man, H. Fertet
> PS Sorry about the spelling mistakes, no time to reread.[7]

In a speech at the Albert Hall in London, Pierre Brossolette explained the effect of such terrible losses:

> . . . after the initial shock, after a period of torpor, we return to battle even more determined, because it is now not only a question of victory, but also of revenge. And with these victims, inspired by their example and their sacrifice, the nation will also resist. Because the violence of German repression tells us something: it tells us the battle is close, and, through the battle, it announces victory.[8]

The sombre, determined mood of the times was captured by a popular song, 'Le chant des Partisans', which had been recorded earlier in the year in London by Anna Marly. In English, the lyrics seem flat and brutal; in French, sung by a trilling female voice to a Russian tune that is both mournful and powerful, accompanied by a pulsing guitar, they were a rallying cry on a par with the bloody words of the 'Marseillaise':

| | |
|---|---|
| Ohé partisans, | Hey, partisans, |
| Ouvriers et paysans | Workers and peasants |
| C'est l'alarme! . . . | The alarm has sounded! . . . |
| | |
| Ohé les tueurs | Hey, killers |
| À la balle ou au couteau | With bullet or with knife |
| Tuez vite . . . | Kill swiftly . . . |
| | |
| Ami, si tu tombes | Friend, if you fall |
| Un ami sort de l'ombre | A friend will come from the shadows |
| À ta place | To take your place |
| | |
| Demain, du sang noir | Tomorrow, black blood |
| Sèchera au grand soleil | Will dry in the sunshine |
| Sur les routes. | On the roads. |
| | |
| Sifflez compagnons . . . | Whistle, companions . . . |
| Dans la nuit, la liberté | In the night, freedom |
| Nous écoute. | Listens to us. |

Broadcast on the BBC, printed up as sheet music and dropped into France, 'Le Chant des Partisans' was sung in the maquis and the concentration camps – the lyrics both comforted and enthused the *résistants*, and gave the rest of the population a melodramatic glimpse of the dark reality of the struggle.[9]

In November and December 1943 there was no need for a song to communicate that reality to the citizens of Grenoble. On 11 November, while the maquis was parading through the streets of Oyonnax, sixty kilometres due south the Vichy police and the Nazis arrested around 600 people at the end of a banned rally at the Grenoble War Memorial. Over 400 demonstrators were deported, of whom only 120 returned after the war. Within two days the Resistance retaliated, attacking a massive Nazi arms dump on the edge of the city. The operation had initially been launched five days earlier – Aimé Requet of the Grenoble MUR had planted explosives, set to explode in the middle of the night of 6 November. But the fuses failed, and, faced with the possibility that they could go off during the day, killing dozens of French workers, Requet went round and removed them all, despite the risk that they might explode at any moment. On 13 November he tried again, setting the timers for 11 p.m. That night, his commander, Louis Nal, sat at home, listening, waiting, as first eleven o'clock passed, and then midnight:

> I felt utterly discouraged. Suddenly – I couldn't believe it – a brilliant flash lit up the sky at the same time as an incredible explosion ripped through the air. The operation had succeeded. The arsenal had exploded.[10]

For the next three hours there was explosion upon explosion as several hundred tons of munitions went up. Windows were smashed in a 500-metre radius, blocks of stone were hurled hundreds of metres and the explosions were heard 100 kilometres away. When the Germans realized that this was a Resistance operation, they began to attack people on the streets – some of whom had left their damaged houses. Ten people were killed by the Germans that night. Over the next few days the Nazis and the Milice carried on with the killing spree, murdering a further eleven people, including the leaders of Combat and Franc-Tireur.[11]

In revenge, Nal organized another attack. Early in the morning of 2 December an anti-Nazi Polish Wehrmacht conscript planted explosives in a German barracks; fifty Nazi soldiers were killed and another hundred were injured.[12] In reply there were yet more murders by the Milice, including the assassination of René Gosse, Professor of Mathematics at the University of Grenoble, who was killed with his son. The pair were arrested and then found the next day on the side of a road, each with a bullet in the back of the neck. The Resistance tracked down their killer and left his body at the same place.[13]

By the end of the winter, even the most non-violent sections of the Resistance recognized that the new combination of Milice brutality and Nazi repression called for a determined response. *Défense de la France*, the mass-circulation underground newspaper whose journalists had initially opposed armed action, published an editorial entitled 'A Duty to Kill':

We are not obsessed with murder. In fact, we are obsessed with a peaceful and happy life, in which we can create, build and love. But those who want to stop us from living must die! . . .

Our duty is clear: we must kill.

Kill the German to cleanse our territory, kill him because he kills our own people, kill him to be free.

Kill the traitors, kill those who betray, those who aided the enemy. Kill the policeman who has in any way helped arrest patriots.

Kill the men of the Milice, exterminate them, because they have chosen to hand over French men and women, because they have embraced betrayal. Shoot them like mad dogs on the street corners. Hang them from the lampposts, following the example of Grenoble. Destroy them like vermin.

Kill without passion and without hate. Never torture or inflict suffering. We are not butchers, we are soldiers . . .

*If you dare not risk your life, it loses its value, and we will do nothing to defend it.* But if you carry out the duty of war, we will be brothers in arms. French men, French women, look into your hearts and answer this:

*Do you want to live or die?*[14]

Resistance actions became increasingly widespread, no longer the prerogative of the Communist-led FTP or MOI. For example, the 'Special Section' of Turma-Vengeance blew up a fifty-ton railway crane used to lift derailed and damaged trains. On a smaller scale, Bernard Chevignard, the thirty-year-old leader of the Special Section, carried out audacious operations against German troops, stealing their uniforms and their vehicles, in order to carry out further attacks with impunity. Chevignard was finally cornered at the end of August during one of his regular raids to steal uniforms from the changing rooms of a floating swimming pool moored in the Seine. Pursued by an irate French crowd who took him for a thief, he was arrested by the police under the eyes of his sister, who was waiting for him with a getaway bicycle. Chevignard was executed on 15 March 1944, together with his young sidekick, betrayed by a Gestapo infiltrator.

At the beginning of December 1943 Vengeance organized a training school in a decaying château in the small Normandy village of Cérisy-Belle-Étoile. François Jacquemin, a twenty-year-old student at the time, recalled how the first half of the school was devoted to weapons use and to physical training, while in the second part they discussed more theoretical issues such as the origins of the war. To reinforce their cover story that they were a charity devoted to physical education, they marched through the village in their PE gear, singing the Vichy anthem 'Maréchal, nous voilà!'[15] Jacquemin later recalled the end of the school: 'In the morning of the 10th, full of enthusiasm, we went our separate ways, without imagining that so many of us would soon die, in front of the firing squad, in the battles of the Liberation or in the Nazi camps.'[16]

\*

Although the *résistants* were desperate to fight and the maquis was growing, the Resistance was rudderless. Moulin had dominated the Resistance and the Secret Army through his exclusive contact with London and by his relentless centralization. All his effort was aimed at the creation of a Gaullist government after the Liberation, as shown by his close work with Delestraint, whom de Gaulle had named as head of the SA.[17] After the arrests of the two men in June 1943, things drifted. De Gaulle and the Free French had always been ambivalent about the Resistance; distracted by the politicking in Algiers, they paid no serious attention to the question of finding a replacement for Moulin.

Without Moulin's strong leadership to keep the Resistance tied to the Free French, the movements began to reassert their independence. On 23 July 1943 the MUR and some of the small Resistance organizations set up a 'Central Committee', which deliberately excluded all the political parties (including the Communists, the FTP and the Front National) and which sought to control all armed action.[18] In response, de Gaulle's delegate to the northern zone, Claude Serreulles, set up a rival CNR 'Bureau', composed of the Front National, the PCF, the CGT trade union, Ceux de la Résistance, the OCM and Libération-Nord, which also claimed control over the maquis and the Secret Army. This was a straightforward power struggle over the leadership of the Resistance, but the contending parties were aligning themselves in an unexpected way. The

Parisian Gaullists had united with the Communist Party, while the Resistance movements had the support of Colonel Passy's BCRA, in the shape of Pierre Brossolette, who was sent back to Paris in September 1943.[19] In reality, the BCRA wanted the leadership of the Resistance to be weak and fragmented, so that Free French Intelligence could dominate it.

Brossolette had arrived back in France in September 1943, together with his close friend, SOE agent 'Tommy' Yeo-Thomas. Brossolette was supposed to act as a liaison for Émile Bollaert, de Gaulle's new delegate to the CNR,[20] while Yeo-Thomas was to report on the situation of the Secret Army and the maquis.[21] Brossolette's aim – with Passy's full support – was to exploit the lack of direction at the head of the Resistance and bring about the kind of changes in its organization and control that he had tried to produce during Moulin's absence earlier in the year. De Gaulle had conspicuously passed over Brossolette when the question of Moulin's replacement had been discussed – hardly surprising, given that Brossolette was viscerally opposed to the inclusion of political parties in the Resistance leadership, which was at the heart of de Gaulle's strategy for gaining the support of the Allies. Brossolette and Passy now hoped that while the Free French leadership was focused on its struggle with Giraud, and there was no one with Moulin's vision or authority to oppose them, they could get their way.

As soon as Brossolette and Yeo-Thomas arrived in Paris, their relations with the Parisian Resistance leaders became extremely strained. The immediate flashpoint was Brossolette's scathing criticism of what he saw as the lax security procedures of Claude Serreulles ('Sophie'). As Claude Bourdet recalled, even Serreulles' appearance was a provocation:

> He was a tall lad, with an air of British elegance; his Savile Row suits, the tiny collars on his well-fitting shirts – not forgetting his umbrella – made him look like a City gent, straight out of the pages of *Punch*. We found his easily recognizable appearance both amusing and alarming. We were wrong, because the Gestapo seems not to have paid much attention to looks, and Serreulles was not in any greater danger than those of our comrades who looked like real conspirators, with their leather jackets, hats pulled down low and their sunglasses . . .[22]

Yeo-Thomas was less charitable than Bourdet, and in his SOE debriefing complained that Serreulles had 'a most dangerously self-satisfied frame of mind . . . overconfidence oozed from every pore'.[23] Serreulles breezily dismissed such worries; as Yeo-Thomas reported it, the French considered 'we had grossly overstated the dangers of clandestine work and that we were both timid and possibly scared . . . Our friends openly showed us that they considered our insistence on the security angle quite childish.'[24] But within three days of Brossolette's arrival, one of Serreulles' closest colleagues was arrested, and shortly afterwards his secretariat was raided by the Gestapo. Four months' worth of uncoded archives, containing all the messages that had gone back and forth to London in that time, were seized. As a result, nine *résistants* were arrested.[25]

Whether or not Serreulles' behaviour was responsible for the Nazi raid, the reality was that the Gestapo were getting closer, and everyone was making mistakes. Yeo-Thomas recruited two liaison agents who at first appeared merely feckless but turned out to be Gestapo spies; he was followed on a number of occasions (he had to shoot one of the men who was tailing him, and then dump the body in the Seine), and he left some of his effects and 125,000 francs in a 'safe' apartment, all of which were found by the Gestapo when they raided it.[26] In this context the furious tone of the correspondence from Yeo-Thomas and Brossolette seems ill-advised. In a letter to Passy, Brossolette called for the immediate recall of Daniel Cordier (Serreulles' secretary), complaining of the 'disorder' and 'cliques' that were weakening the Parisian Resistance leadership and arguing that if Cordier remained in post it would be 'catastrophic'.[27] Yeo-Thomas supported this view and even argued that Brossolette ('Briand') should be given full command, before signing off in a typically jocular manner:

SOPHIE AND SECRETARY APPEAR FOLLOWED AND IN DANGER HAVE WARNED THEM REPEATEDLY IN VAIN STOP ENERGETIC MEASURES REQUIRED TO SAVE SITUATION CONSIDER PASSY BE REQUESTED TO GIVE BRIAND MEANS AND AUTHORITY TO TAKE MATTERS IN HAND AND AVERT DISASTER DOT THERE IS NO TIME TO WASTE DOT GREAT LIFE IF YOU DONT WEAKEN NOT ARF TOM [28]

A few days later Yeo-Thomas went even further:

RECOMMEND IMMEDIATE RECALLS OF SOPHIE AND SECRETARY WHO ARE
OBSTRUCTIVE DETRIMENTAL TO IMPROVEMENT SITUATION AND SECURITY
DOT BEAR HEAVY RESPONSIBILITY FOR RECENT ARRESTS DASH WILL RETURN
WITH EVERY JUSTIFICATION OF MY REQUEST STOP[29]

Brossolette's second mission in France was turning into a disastrous repetition of his first, exacerbating conflicts within the Resistance rather than overcoming them. Passy responded by instructing the Resistance to cut off all relations with Serreulles and Jacques Bingen, who was de Gaulle's delegate to the southern zone, because they were deemed to be unsafe.[30] Furious at this attack on their integrity, Serreulles and Bingen fought back. Serreulles wrote to Passy, complaining of his 'criminal sabotage' and insisting that he restrain those of his 'collaborators who are losing their heads'; Bingen wrote to leading Free French figures, demanding a public apology and calling for an enquiry to discover how such a 'warning' had been issued. He got no reply. As Brossolette and Passy fiddled, the Resistance – or at least its Parisian leadership – was on the point of imploding and the Free French did not even notice.

The Gaullists, now divided between London and Algiers, were focused on completing their victory over Giraud and on manoeuvring with the Allies. As a result, Resistance leaders often found that their messages went unanswered, and they did not get the moral and logistical support they needed.[31] When de Gaulle eventually turned his attention to the problem created by Brossolette, his solution was designed to preserve his own authority. Emmanuel d'Astier and Henri Frenay had been removed from the Resistance by making them ministers in de Gaulle's government-in-waiting. The same tactic was now applied to Brossolette, who was proposed as a delegate to the makeshift Free French parliament that sat in Algiers. In what at first looked like an even-handed decision, de Gaulle ordered Serreulles, Bollaert and Brossolette to return to London by the November moon, at the same time as SOE recalled Yeo-Thomas. But in a clear disavowal of Brossolette and Passy, and in a confirmation of his decision to appoint Bingen, the delegate to the southern zone was allowed to remain in France.[32] Brossolette and

Passy's attempt to gain control of the Resistance had failed a second time.

*

Despite receiving clear orders from London, Brossolette initially refused to go back. When he eventually presented himself for a return flight, there was a disaster – one of the two Lysanders sent out had to turn back because of bad weather, and the other was shot down by German anti-aircraft fire, killing the pilot and the two passengers.[33] The safe house near the landing site, where Brossolette had been staying, was raided the following day, and the liaison agent who was due to meet him was arrested. Brossolette's luck was running out, and the Nazis were closing in.

Yeo-Thomas was eventually brought out on a flight from Arras on 15–16 November – the pilot had orders to bring him back by whatever means necessary, conscious or not[34] – but things were not so straightforward for Brossolette, Bollaert and Serreulles. For six weeks appalling weather prevented them from leaving by air. Having failed to leave on the plane that took the Aubracs to London in February, Serreulles finally flew back at the beginning of March, through an old friend who worked for MI6 and got him a place on one of their flights.[35] Brossolette and Bollaert eventually decided to travel by sea, but storms wrecked the fishing boat that was due to take them. On 3 February 1944 the pair were arrested at a routine roadblock in Brittany, simply because they did not have the requisite papers for the coastal region. They were taken to Rennes prison, but the Nazis had no idea who the two men really were – their fake IDs aroused no suspicions. In Britain and France the race began to save them.

In London Passy was utterly distraught when he heard of his comrade's fate. Jacques Soustelle recalled:

> I can still see Passy, completely overwhelmed, his eyes full of tears, asking me to leave for France: he hoped that the Gestapo would not have recognized 'Brumaire' [Brossolette] and that we could save his friend. He wanted to risk everything to save him.[36]

Yeo-Thomas felt the same and persuaded SOE that he should undertake one more mission to France, to get Brossolette out of jail before the Nazis discovered who he was. On 24 February Yeo-Thomas parachuted back into France and was soon in contact with the Resistance, organizing an escape operation. The plan they finally settled on – Yeo-Thomas travelled to Rennes to scope out the situation – involved three *résistants* disguised in Nazi uniforms, claiming they had come to the prison to transfer Brossolette and Bollaert; they would then overpower the guards and take the two men to freedom.

Meanwhile, behind the prison walls, Brossolette was equally active. The very day he arrived in the jail, he was able to smuggle a message to his comrades in the Resistance – in total he managed to send fourteen letters. Having got wind of Yeo-Thomas' arrival, he asked the Resistance to organize a safe house in Rennes and to send him chloroform and two metal saws.[37] Then, a little over a month after Brossolette was imprisoned, his letters suddenly stopped. A week later the situation took a dramatic turn. The Nazis interrogated Brossolette and Bollaert for the first time; they addressed Brossolette by his real name and brushed aside his claims to be 'Paul Boutet'. Somehow, his cover had been blown.[38]

On the evening of 19 March Brossolette and Bollaert were taken to Gestapo headquarters on the Avenue Foch in Paris. After being interrogated and beaten, they were then transferred to Fresnes prison, outside Paris. On 21 March they were again taken to the Gestapo building and again they were brutally interrogated. As this was happening, scarcely a kilometre away Yeo-Thomas – who thought the two men were still in Rennes – had a rendezvous at Passy Métro station at eleven in the morning. When his contact failed to turn up at the bottom of the stone steps leading to the station, Yeo-Thomas broke all his well-learned rules of tradecraft and hung about, waiting. Suddenly, the Gestapo arrived – they had arrested his contact earlier in the morning – and captured Yeo-Thomas. Stripped, interrogated and repeatedly beaten, Yeo-Thomas was about to take the dose of cyanide hidden in his ring when the Germans noticed and stopped him. After more beatings, they took their torture techniques to another level of depravity. Yeo-Thomas was taken into a bathroom, and his head was pushed backwards into the water-filled bath:

I was helpless. I panicked and tried to kick, but the vice-like grip was such that I could hardly move. My eyes were open, I could see shapes distorted by the water, wavering above me, my lungs were bursting, my mouth opened and I swallowed water. Now I was drowning. I put every ounce of my energy into a vain effort to kick myself out of the bath, but I was completely helpless and, swallowing water, I felt that I must burst. I was dying, this was the end, I was losing consciousness, but as I was doing so I felt the strength going out of me and my limbs going limp. This must be the end . . .[39]

But the whole point of water-boarding is not to kill, but to make the victim think they are dying, over and over again. Yeo-Thomas was repeatedly tortured in this way as the Nazis beat him with rubber truncheons and asked for information about his Resistance contacts and the location of SOE weapons dumps. Then, on 22 March, he was taken to the Avenue Foch for further interrogation, where he was beaten and hung from his manacles for hours on end. He almost cracked.[40]

About an hour after Yeo-Thomas arrived at Gestapo headquarters that day, Pierre Brossolette was taken up to the fifth floor of the same building for another bout of interrogation. Suddenly, as his captors' attention was turned, Brossolette ran over to the window and climbed down onto the balcony on the floor below. He then calmly put one leg over the balcony rail, then the other, and in a final gesture of victory stepped out into the air, falling four storeys to the ground. He died of his injuries ten hours later. Yeo-Thomas was only a few rooms away but knew nothing of the death of his friend. He had to endure several more weeks of torture and interrogation before he was put on a train to Buchenwald. Bollaert was also sent to the camps. He had been in post for five months.

As Yeo-Thomas was arrested, another episode in the Nazi offensive took place on the other side of Paris. On the night of 17–18 March 'Médéric' (Gilbert Védy), the hard man of Ceux de la Libération, had been dropped on a beach in Finistère. In the middle of 1943, while in London, Médéric had come to know Yeo-Thomas well. The two men had a similar taste for audacious action, and hatched a madcap scheme to kidnap Admiral Doenitz, commander-in-chief of the German navy, and bring him back to Britain.[41] Médéric had returned to France from Algiers, where he was a member of the Provisional Consultative Assembly, to take over as head of Ceux de la Libération after its leader had been shot by the Nazis in an ambush. But on 21 March Médéric was arrested in Paris, betrayed by someone within the Free French movement.[42] When first questioned, Médéric tried to persuade the policeman to help him, but this failed and Médéric was sent for interrogation by the hated Commissar David, head of the 'anti-terrorist' Brigade Spéciale of the Paris police. Taunted by David, Médéric replied with words that later became famous – 'You'll see that a French man knows how to die' – and then bit on his cyanide pill. His brother, Maxime Védy, had been executed by the Nazis two weeks earlier.

To complete a miserable month for the Resistance, Claude Bourdet, Frenay's right-hand man in Combat, was arrested on 23 March. A liaison agent had been arrested on the Swiss border, carrying papers that eventually led the Gestapo to one of the Parisian offices of the Resistance, where Bourdet was waiting for a meeting. Bourdet was interrogated, then deported, finally ending up in Buchenwald. Shortly afterwards, Frenay, now ensconced in Algiers as Commissar for Prisoners, Deportees and Refugees, received a belated letter from his comrade. Bourdet described the bloody offensive by the Nazis and the Milice, little imagining that he would soon be a victim:

> Forain, our top man in Toulouse, was nabbed a few months ago. We found him in a wood with his head blown off by a grenade . . . People of varying importance are being arrested everywhere. The Milice has assassinated Dr Valois, whom I wanted to make a regional chief, as well as his assistant, Bistozzi, a university professor. At the same time they murdered Professor Gosse.[43]

In the space of a year, the shape of the Resistance had changed completely. The leadership had been shattered – Frenay and d'Astier were abroad; Berty Albrecht, Moulin, Manouchian, Brossolette and Médéric were dead; Pineau, Renouvin, Delestraint and Bourdet had all been deported; Jean-Pierre Levy was in a Parisian jail, his cover still intact – while repeated waves of repression and betrayal had condemned hundreds of rank-and-file *résistants* to death or deportation. More important, however, by spring 1944 a decisive step towards the unification of the Resistance and its consolidation as an independent fighting force had been taken.

*

Having failed to gain control of the Resistance through Brossolette's attempt to destabilize the Parisian leadership, the Free French tried another tack. De Gaulle appointed fourteen men to act as Délégués Militaires (DM – Military Delegates) to the various regions, supposedly to help the Resistance. Under orders from Passy, they were in fact to assert control over the Secret Army and the maquis. They would do this by 'decentralizing' command from the centre to the regions, where they would be able to dominate local Resistance leaders and would monopolize contact with the vital supply lines from London. But the choice of men was catastrophic, and their behaviour soon aroused the scorn of the Resistance. In January 1944 Pascal Copeau, a young leader of Libération, wrote of one of the DMs, an ambitious man who apparently desired to be the 'French Tito':

> . . . he is a complete lightweight and his activity is quite insufficient. After spending a whole month in Switzerland, a few weeks after he arrived, he then spent a 'holiday' at the end of the year with his wife in Switzerland and has now – God knows why – decided to go to Spain and then on to Algiers, leaving behind him a well-meaning but completely inadequate replacement. These military men are not much more serious than their BCRA.[44]

To resolve the issue, Jacques Bingen suggested that the Resistance Central Committee set up a Commission Militaire d'Action ('COMAC') to unite – not control – all the armed organizations, from the Communist FTP to what later became known as the Organisation de Résistance de l'Armée (ORA – Resistance Organization of the Army) – those turncoat sections of the Vichy army that had put their faith first in Pétain then in Giraud and now realized that the time had come to ally themselves once and for all with the Resistance.[45] At the beginning of February COMAC created a common command structure for all the armed Resistance organizations in France, called the Forces Françaises de l'Interieur (FFI – French Forces of the Interior). FFI soon became synonymous with the Resistance as a whole, and the initials were seen all over the country – on armbands, on flags and on commandeered vehicles, as well as scrawled on walls and stamped on leaflets.

The inclusion of the Communist-led FTP in the FFI was particularly important. The FTP was the largest military organization in the Resistance. As Corsica had shown, the French Communists would be loyal participants in the liberation of the country, so long as they were accorded some recognition and positions of power. The leadership of the Communist Party, following Moscow's strategic calculations, accepted that its ambitions should be limited to the creation of a national army, the strengthening of the FTP and a purge of traitors and collaborators within the state apparatus.[46] Communist leader Maurice Thorez made this clear in January 1944, when he stated 'the Communists are not thinking of taking power, either now, or after the liberation'.[47] Revolution might have still been the dream of rank-and-file Communist Party members and the nightmare of the right wing of the Resistance, but Stalin and his loyal followers would have none of it.[48]

De Gaulle took more than six weeks to react to the creation of COMAC, but when he did, on 10 March 1944, his attitude could not have been plainer. COMAC, he declared, 'is not a command structure' but instead would carry out 'inspection and supervision'.[49] In other words, the armed action of the Resistance was to be controlled from Algiers, not Paris. The Resistance simply carried on as before, focused on taking action against the Nazis. So total was the rejection of de Gaulle's attempt to take control that on 13 May 1944 the CNR took COMAC under its direct authority and proclaimed quite simply: 'It is the supreme command structure of the FFI.'[50] The whole of the Resistance – the movements, the parties and even Moulin's CNR – was taking a stand against de Gaulle's attempt to control it.

The fact that two of the three voting members of COMAC were Communists (Pierre Villon and Maurice Kriegel) has led some *résistants* and historians to suggest that this represented a Communist coup over the Resistance. But not only did COMAC have the full support of the CNR – an organization set up by Moulin and entirely within the Gaullist mould – the third member of COMAC was right-winger Jean de Vogüé, and it also included as non-voting members General Revers of the ORA and a young Military Delegate, Jacques Chaban-Delmas.[51] The truth is, COMAC and the CNR represented the views of the vast majority of *résistants* – who, after all, did not have to obey COMAC if they did not want to. They wanted to take immediate action and were deeply distrustful of the attempts by London and Algiers to hold the Resistance back. The conflict between the Resistance and de Gaulle, which had been rumbling on for years, had finally come into the open.

Even the most committed Gaullists found their allegiances shifting. In August 1943 Jacques Bingen had left London full of hope and excitement. As he wrote to his mother shortly beforehand:

My departure, which is a completely unexpected opportunity, may help France as much as many soldiers. I hope that before my end, I will have rendered many of these services. Finally there is the additional desire to avenge so many Jewish friends who have been tortured or assassinated by a barbarism such as we have not seen for centuries. One more Jew (there are so many of us, if only you knew) will have taken his part – and more than his part – in the Liberation of France. There you have it, dear Mother, that's why I'm leaving, fully aware of the danger, and having weighed the risks.[52]

But there were dangers in France that he could not have imagined, which threatened not only his life but also his loyalties and his political convictions. A friend who was with him the day before he climbed into the Lysander that would take him home later recalled:

I will never forget his last afternoon in London, full of humour and nervous excitement. Vitia Hessel and I walked with him under a radiant blue August sky, from St James's Park to the little house in Dorset Square that was the departure point for flights out. It was here that he received SOE's 'Holy Communion' – a rubber-coated cyanide pill. He was great company and a charming man, this Jew who did not believe in God but who believed in de Gaulle; this brother-in-law of the boss of Citroën who believed that the Liberation would lead to the construction of a mass Labour Party that would unite the socialists of Léon Blum and Daniel Mayer and the new forces of the Resistance. He appeared to be a dilettante who hid his anxiety under a nonchalant lightness of being and found his fulfilment in action.[53]

Bingen's enthusiasm, and his political commitment to de Gaulle's strategies, were soon undermined by the cruel realities of underground life. By April 1944 he felt completely isolated and abandoned by the Free French. Bitterly aware that Passy and the BCRA were still spreading rumours about his alleged security breaches, at loggerheads with his masters and 'for the first time feeling my life is really threatened', he wrote a final despairing testament, addressed both to his friends and to de Gaulle. He described his treatment as 'scandalous', and advised de Gaulle to take more care with the men he appointed.[54]

Less than a month later Bingen travelled to Clermont-Ferrand, where he was met by a liaison agent who was unwittingly accompanied by a Gestapo spy. Early the next morning Bingen was arrested by the Nazis but managed to escape. He ran through the town and hid in a doorway, but a French woman hailed a passing German lorry and pointed out where he was hiding. Recaptured, Bingen swallowed his cyanide pill and died shortly afterwards. The whereabouts of his body are still unknown.[55]

*

As part of their preparations for the eventual invasion of France, the Allies needed to find out how strong the maquis really was. In mid-October 1943, six months before his arrest, Yeo-Thomas had visited the maquis near Cahors and in the Ain and was extremely impressed – the men were far more organized and disciplined than he had imagined. As he explained to London: 'These organized maquis can, properly supported and armed, provide us with formidable and efficient support on D-Day.'[56]

At a meeting of the six regional maquis leaders in the southern zone that took place in November 1943, Yeo-Thomas heard repeated complaints from the maquis that they did not receive sufficient weapons, that they were poorly armed.

In truth, without proper Allied logistical support the maquis could not fight. The leader of Region 6 said: 'we can scare people, that's all ... our maquis do not yet have machine guns ... in the town of Clermont-Ferrand we have 3,000 men, but only 35 machine guns.' Region 2 was slightly better off – they had 7 heavy machine guns (which they had stolen), 151 rifles, 2 machine guns which were used solely for demonstration purposes and 4 or 5 cases of grenades, while Region 3 had a few dozen rifles, around 40 machine guns that had been hauled out of the water and a heavy machine gun with no ammunition.[57]

In reply, Yeo-Thomas could only repeat the classic British explanation: the bombing raids on Germany took valuable planes and pilots away from other missions, such as supplying the Resistance. He had been promised that the explosives that filled most parachuted containers would be replaced by weapons. This was a common request from the maquis, and reflected a difference in conception – the Allies wanted to use the maquis for sabotage purposes, which required explosives; the maquis wanted first to survive, and then to fight, which above all required guns. However, as Yeo-Thomas frankly admitted, 'that is a promise – will it be kept? I have no idea.'[58]

At the beginning of 1944, as planning for D-Day became intense, the Allied high command began to take the Resistance seriously for the first time. Meetings took place in North Africa between Henri Frenay and the American Assistant Secretary of War, John J. McCloy, and between Emmanuel d'Astier de la Vigerie and Winston Churchill. Frenay impressed McCloy with his arguments in favour of coordinating the actions of the Resistance and the Allies following D-Day, while d'Astier argued for a substantial increase in weapons drops to the maquis. Churchill swung behind d'Astier's request, partly because of strategic considerations (a substantial growth in Resistance activity in south-eastern France would help the planned Allied landings on the Mediterranean coast), partly because of his own enthusiasm for guerrilla warfare and partly because of the personal impression made by d'Astier. As Churchill told Roosevelt:

This is a remarkable man of the Scarlet Pimpernel type and fairly fresh from France, which he has revisited three or four times. He has made very strong appeals to me to drop more arms by air for their resistance movements. I hope to be able to do more in February. He says that in Haute Savoie, south of Geneva between Grenoble and the Italian frontier, he has over 20,000 men all desperate, but only one in five has any weapon. If more weapons were available, very large numbers more would take to the mountains. As you know, I am most anxious to see a guerrilla *à la Tito* started up in the Savoie and in the Alpes Maritimes . . . He is a fine fellow, very fierce and bitter but one of the best Frenchmen I have struck [sic] in these bleak times.[59]

On 27 January Churchill invited d'Astier and leading figures from SOE to a meeting of the War Cabinet, and agreed to double the supplies to the Resistance – but only to the maquis in the south-east. Groups in central and northern France got nothing extra because their needs did not coincide with the immediate Allied strategic interest.[60] At the same time, Emmanuel d'Astier's brother, Free French Air Force General François d'Astier, discussed the role of the Resistance with General Eisenhower, who had recently been appointed Supreme Commander of the Allied Expeditionary Force for the invasion of Europe, in charge of OVERLORD.[61] After a complex series of negotiations between London, Washington and Algiers – including a man-to-man discussion with de Gaulle, in which Eisenhower did much to overcome the traditional US hostility to the French General – Eisenhower's Supreme Headquarters, Allied Expeditionary Force (SHAEF), took into account Resistance activity in its planning for D-Day (it also took over command of SOE). Unlike Churchill, Eisenhower's interest in the Resistance was neither romantic nor limited to south-east France – he wanted a surge of Allied-controlled action to support his troops when they landed in Normandy.[62]

The changing attitude of the Allies towards the Resistance was soon felt in the south-east corner that so interested Churchill. The Haute-Savoie region around Annecy was the focus of intense Resistance activity, largely inspired by Romans-Petit, head of the maquis in the neighbouring Ain département. By the beginning of 1944 the Haute-Savoie maquis was under the leadership of a young lieutenant, 'Tom' Morel, supported by SOE and BCRA agents.[63] Faced with a huge rise in maquis activity in the region, Darnand decided to send the Milice to reimpose Vichy's authority by destroying the 'terrorists'. On 2 February the BBC broadcast a warning:

> Attention the maquis! Attention the Haute-Savoie! Calling the Haute-Savoie maquis, SOS, SOS. The Oberführer Joseph Darnard has decided to launch a massive attack, tomorrow 3 February, against the patriots hiding out in the mountains of the Haute-Savoie . . . Soldiers without uniform in the maquis of the Haute-Savoie, there is not a minute to spare – you must take up your defensive positions.[64]

As the Allied invasion loomed closer, the Milice and the Vichy state were like rats in a trap – increasingly vicious and desperate, unable to find a way out.[65] The Resistance and the Free French had made it quite clear that there would be no quarter, no amnesty, no pardons after the war. Pierre Pucheu, the Minister of the Interior, had left Vichy when he saw the way the wind was blowing, just after the Allied invasion of North Africa. He arrived in French North Africa in May 1943, just in time to see his supporter, General Giraud, lose out in the struggle with de Gaulle. In March 1944 Pucheu was tried for treason, found guilty and executed – de Gaulle refused to pardon him: saying 'I owe it to France.' Maurice Schumann, speaking on the BBC, had warned the collaborators in October 1943: 'From now on, whatever you do, it is too late to buy your way to freedom.'[66] The same approach was taken in the Haute-Savoie, as the BBC directly addressed the Vichy officials involved in the operation, using their names, threatening them with terrible retribution: 'Each drop of blood that tomorrow, perhaps through your actions, runs in the ravines and gorges of our Haute-Savoie will fall on your heads.'[67]

As the repression increased in the valleys, hundreds of *résistants* climbed up into the deep snow, to join the maquis on the Glières plateau, high above Annecy.[68] In the shadow of the Haute-Savoie alps, the Glières is a vast region of about 70 square kilometres, situated at 1,500 metres above sea level, a region with no human habitation save a few chalets suited only for the summer months – an 'icy desert', as FTP leader Charles Tillon put it.[69]

Soon there were up to 600 men on the plateau – members of the FTP, Spanish immigrants who had fought in the Civil War, members of the

Secret Army – all of whom needed to be fed, sheltered and supplied with clothes and weapons. Although four RAF planes parachuted fifty-four containers in the night of 13 February, and drops of around fifty tons arrived a month later, the men were doubly vulnerable: they were still poorly armed and, against all the rules of guerrilla warfare, they were now grouped together, isolated in a single place instead of being spread out and able to melt away into the countryside. London soon became alarmed, and the BBC urgently advised the maquis to disperse: 'Today's France already has too many martyrs. Tomorrow's France will never have enough soldiers' came the message.[70]

Despite the dangers, the maquis felt confident that, with sufficient supplies, they could hold out until the Allied invasion, which surely could not be far off. The narrow paths leading up to the plateau were easily defendable and would be blocked with snow for weeks, impassable to any but the most determined groups of men. Morale was incredibly high, despite the cold and the lack of supplies. As one of the men later remembered:

Something amazing happened. We had been outlaws, but on the plateau we felt like free men. You got carried away with enthusiasm. Something different, an atmosphere of solidarity, the birth of a community, a new relation between officers and soldiers.[71]

As an expression of this spirit, at the beginning of March the BCRA agent on the Glières sent a bold but ominous message to London: 'We have decided to occupy the plateau, which is impregnable, and to have as our motto "Live free or die".'[72]

But Vichy and the Nazis were equally determined. Hundreds of Gardes Mobiles de Réserve and members of the Milice were sent to the foot of the plateau, and during February and March there was a series of bloody skirmishes.[73] The Germans grew impatient and decided to intervene, repeatedly sending the Luftwaffe to bomb the plateau, reinforcing Darnand's Milice with three infantry batallions (around 7,000 men) and artillery support. The final attack came on 27 and 28 March. Although 300 *maquisards* managed to escape, another 149 either died in the fighting, were killed in the terrible reprisals that continued for weeks as *maquisards* were hunted down or executed after perfunctory trials, disappeared into the concentration camps or were toyed with in cruel, lethal games. In scenes of barbarity that were typical of the Nazis, prisoners were allowed to run across fields, before being mown down like rabbits.

For the Communists and the FTP, Glières demonstrated the dangers of trying to gather *maquisards* together in one place – 'a monstrous error in strategic conception,' they wrote – and the correctness of their fluid and highly mobile conception of guerrilla warfare.[74] British views were only slightly kinder: the SOE agent in charge of the Glières maquis, Richard Heslop, later claimed he always thought it was 'nonsensical . . . madness, a glorious stupidity'.[75] Despite the awful losses and the strategic errors, because of the terrible sacrifice involved and the unity shown by the different sections of the Resistance, Glières came to symbolize French determination to liberate the country, whatever the cost. This played an important role as the Vichy Minister of Information, Philippe Henriot, made a series of broadcasts pouring scorn on the maquis and their deaths, while carefully avoiding all mention of the involvement of the Nazi troops. While this might have played well in Vichy, it was entirely counterproductive in the Haute-Savoie, where the broadcasts actually helped strengthen local support for the Resistance. As Romans-Petit later put it, 'Glières a été une défaite des armes, mais une victoire des âmes'[76] – 'Glières was a military defeat, but a victory for our souls.'

\*

The Resistance in France was not only asserting its military independence: it also flexed its political muscles. While de Gaulle and the Free French played at parliament in Algiers, in France the Resistance set out the shape of the country that would be built on the ruins of Vichy. Two years earlier, Christian Pineau had spent days trying to persuade de Gaulle and his advisers to make some kind of 'social' declaration to the Resistance. Throughout the intervening period, Resistance groups had published programmes, declarations and charters designed to put flesh on their opposition to the Occupation.[77] None of them had much meaning, for the simple reason that they were plans for the future, not

for the present. With D-Day almost literally within reach, that was beginning to change. In April the CNR simply bypassed de Gaulle, the CFLN
and the Provisional Consultative Assembly, and published its own
'Action Programme of the Resistance', which it then politely sent to de
Gaulle, for information.[78]

Four months in the writing, and the subject of many heated debates,
the Action Programme began by making it plain who the Resistance
thought would be in control of the 'national insurrection' which, as de
Gaulle had put it two years earlier, was 'inseparable' from national liberation. The insurrection 'will be led by the CNR', they declared. Even
though such action would not take place immediately but 'as soon as
political and military circumstances permit' and 'under the authority'
of de Gaulle's CFLN, it was clear that the Resistance would be in control. Among the measures that the CNR wanted to see applied 'as soon
as the country is liberated' were 'true social and economic democracy', 'the broadest possible democracy' through universal suffrage, the
establishment of an economic plan, 'support for cooperatives in production, buying and selling', 'the right to work', guaranteed spending
power and the creation of a fully fledged welfare state, including retirement pensions, a health service and unemployment benefits. All these
were slogans shared by the Communists and the Socialists, and made
perfect sense to a substantial proportion of the French population,
even if they must have caused raised eyebrows in Algiers, London and
Washington.

The conclusion of the Action Programme demonstrated the distance
travelled by the Resistance since 1940, and quite how far they now were
from the ideas of the Free French, who wanted a 'strong state', a single
party and a providential leader:

> . . . we will found a new Republic which will sweep away the pro-
> foundly reactionary regime set up by Vichy and which will give the
> popular and democratic institutions the efficacy that had been taken
> away from them by the organs of corruption and treason that existed
> before the capitulation. In this way there will be a democracy which
> will unite continuity of governmental action with real control by the
> elected representatives of the people.[79]

Before the Resistance could hope to put this programme into action, however, there was another force it would have to reckon with: the Allies. Britain, America and the USSR remained deeply distrustful of de Gaulle and the Resistance, and were undecided whether the Free French should play any role at all in governing the country after the Liberation.[80] Not only was de Gaulle unpredictable and difficult to manipulate; he was also profoundly hostile to the Allied plan to dismember the French Empire, which spread from Vietnam and New Caledonia to vast tracts of North and West Africa.[81] (Even the CNR Action Programme did not propose to make the colonies independent, but merely to give them more democratic rights.)

Recent events in Lebanon, which was under French control, had done nothing to reassure the Allies on this point. De Gaulle's delegate to the region had responded to a Lebanese declaration of independence by arresting the government, dissolving the parliament and crushing protest demonstrations. Faced with Allied protests and British threats to send troops, the Free French freed the imprisoned politicians.[82] This was too little, too late, and at the Tehran conference (28 November to 1 December 1943) Roosevelt, Churchill and Stalin (de Gaulle, having no real forces to bring to the table, was conspicuous by his absence) agreed that the US and British armed forces alone would be responsible for liberating France, through Operation OVERLORD, which would be launched in May 1944. There was to be no independent role for the Resistance or for the French people as a whole.

Right up until D-Day, the Allies did not want to see the French control their own country after the Liberation. Instead, they planned to impose AMGOT (Allied Military Government of Occupied Territories), replacing one military occupation with another. De Gaulle, ferociously opposed to this, was equally hostile to the Resistance and its plans for independent action. The Allies and de Gaulle both wanted to keep control of the situation, and would do all in their power to ensure the population did not take any initiatives. And that included the Resistance and its idea of a national insurrection. The outcome of the three-way struggle between the Resistance, the Free French and the Allies, which opened up after D-Day, would decide the future of France, and of the whole of Europe.

# 10

# 'There Was Never a Time Like It'

Early in the morning of 6 June 1944 Marie-Madeleine Fourcade of the ALLIANCE intelligence circuit was in London packing her bags for her return to France when she heard the sound of aeroplanes:

> I opened the window and the noise became deafening, but not a single searchlight swept the sky nor had the air-raid warning sounded. It was possible to see the aircraft flying in massed formation above the sleeping capital. They flew over in a never-ending stream. Holding my breath and looking steadily in the direction of Nazi Germany, I could see, beyond the barbed wire sealing the frontiers, beyond the prisons, the dawn that was bringing to our enslaved friends the first glimmer of their victory.[1]

It was D-Day, and Operation OVERLORD – the biggest military operation in history – was under way. An invasion fleet of nearly 7,000 vessels, including 3,000 landing craft, backed up by 12,000 aircraft, was making its way across the rough Channel seas towards five Normandy beaches on the Bay of the Seine, each designated by code names that have since gone down in history: UTAH, OMAHA, GOLD, JUNO and SWORD.

On that first day, around 150,000 men were landed or parachuted into Normandy. Thousands died, their blood draining into the soil of a country that many of them had never seen before. The news of the landings ran through France like an electric shock. Bernard Pierquin, by now a junior doctor in a Parisian hospital, was riding to work:

I was on my bike, going past the Jardin des Plantes on the Rue Buffon, when a young woman ran across the road towards her husband, shouting out, 'It's happened. They've landed!' In the early-morning silence, it was deeply moving.[2]

Since the beginning of spring 1944 the Resistance and the Allies had been planning what would happen when the landings finally took place, and had drawn up four national sabotage plans – VERT, VIOLET, BLEU and BIBENDUM – each corresponding to a different Resistance target (railways, telecommunications, electricity and troop transport). Late in the evening of 5 June, as the invasion fleet was preparing to leave, the BBC's French service crackled with 'personal messages' – 200 were broadcast in the space of 15 minutes – instructing the Resistance to activate the plans.

The level of Resistance action was proportionally on the same massive scale as OVERLORD. Within twenty-four hours, the railway network had been paralysed by up to 1,000 acts of sabotage carried out by the Resistance and by SOE circuits. Locomotives were destroyed, trains were derailed and bridges were blown up, reducing rail traffic by fifty per cent. Fifty-one trains stuck in a traffic jam around Lille were easy pickings for Allied aircraft, and with nowhere for trains to go, Parisian mainline stations were closed, bringing the shock of the invasion into the heart of the capital.[3] The attacks on the railways were so vital to the Allies because ninety per cent of the German army was still transported by rail or horse. By fragmenting the rail system, the Resistance and SOE disrupted the Nazi riposte and gained valuable hours for the men fighting for their lives on the Cotentin peninsula of Normandy. Over the next six months, millions of men and machines surged into France, including British SAS 'sticks', who acted alone or with the Resistance, and 'Jedburgh' teams composed of three officers (an American, a Briton and a Frenchman), whose role was to liaise with the Resistance and the advancing armies.[4] They came first from the west, then, in August, from the south, as the long-awaited Allied landings on the Mediterranean coast took place. Through their bravery and sacrifice, these men would eventually drive the Nazis out of France – the Allied armies, not the Resistance, created the conditions for the Liberation of

France.[5] But throughout the summer, the Resistance continued to play a vital role, shaping the momentous events that shook the country.

Over the next few months the Resistance grew enormously. With news of the landings came an immediate shift in the place, role and perception of the Resistance. For four years *résistants* had given up life and liberty in the painstaking construction of underground movements, many of which had little connection with the majority of the population. They had struggled to unify their forces, squabbled with the Free French over the separation of military and political activity and argued over who commanded the Resistance. All that faded away as the prospect of liberation arrived. As one *maquisard* from the Grenoble region put it on hearing of the Normandy landings: 'The underground Resistance is over! Open Resistance begins!'[6]

Hundreds of thousands of men and women who had previously remained at home – out of fear, uncertainty or simple ignorance as to how to join the Resistance – put on armbands emblazoned with FFI (Forces Françaises de l'Intérieur) and helped liberate their country. Four years earlier, Arthur Koestler had predicted with cynical accuracy what form the Liberation would take. 'When the scales of success turn in favour of England,' he wrote, 'the barricades will emerge from the pavements of the towns of France, the snipers will appear behind the attic windows, and the people will fight as in the old days – but not before'.[7]

As the summer wore on, all the main cities were liberated and ultimate victory became increasingly certain, the risks of resistance declined and attitudes towards latecomers to the struggle became correspondingly more scornful. These tardy fighters were called *résistants du mois de septembre* or, in the case of those soldiers who paraded about in carefully preserved uniforms that had not seen service since June 1940, the *naphtalinés* ('the mothballed'). But in the initial weeks after D-Day, the outcome was still extremely uncertain. German resistance to the invasion remained strong throughout June and July, and only a narrow strip of land in the far north-west of the country was free of Nazi domination. Those who resisted in June ran terrible risks.

On the evening of D-Day, de Gaulle broadcast to France, warning the population not to launch any 'premature insurrection'.[8] Despite this instruction, all over the country people took the announcement of the invasion as a call for action. The miners of Toulouse immediately went on strike to celebrate the landings, and the Republic was declared from the town hall balcony of the small industrial town of Annonay. Neither of these actions led to any major response, but elsewhere the reaction was more brutal, a chilling contrast to the joyous hopes of the population. A few hours after news of the landings broke, a group of youngsters heard that a maquis was being set up in the hills above Saint-Chinian, north of Narbonne. Wildly enthusiastic, they seized some lorries, bread and supplies and took off. At Fontjun, on the outskirts of Saint-Chinian, they bumped into a German patrol. Five of them were killed instantly, while a further eighteen – including a woman and her husband – were arrested, taken to the prison at Béziers and shot the next day.[9]

That was nothing compared with the horror that occurred in the region around Limoges. On 8 June the industrial town of Tulle, capital of the Corrèze, was seized by an FTP maquis unit commanded by Jean-Jacques Chapou, who had been involved in the raid on the Figeac aero factory the year before. Chapou had left the Secret Army for the FTP because he was impatient for action; now he had it in spades. When news of the D-Day landings came through, the Communist leadership of the FTP ordered his unit to seize Tulle as part of their hoped-for national insurrection – Limoges was to become 'a base for resistance and attack'.[10] At the same time, the FTP tried to convince Georges Guingouin to send his maquis against the German garrison in Limoges to the north, but he rejected the idea as foolhardy.[11] Chapou was more disciplined (or less astute) and on 7 June, armed with Sten guns, mortars and a bazooka, his unit launched a messy, ill-prepared attack on the Nazis and their Milice stooges. During vicious fighting, over fifty German soldiers were killed, and some Nazi prisoners were subsequently executed as Gestapo agents or torturers.[12] The next day, a tricolour flew over the FTP headquarters, and, with the exception of a small group of Germans holed up in a school, the town was liberated, accompanied by scenes of general rejoicing. But this did not last for long.

Unknown to Chapou, that morning the 2nd SS Panzer Division 'Das Reich' – 15,000 men and over 1,400 vehicles – had roared its way out of Montauban, north of Toulouse. It had instructions to head for the region around Limoges and continue the vicious 'anti-terrorist measures' it had been pursuing in the south.[13] The massive armoured column moved north through the Lot and the Corrèze, past Cahors and Souillac, heading for Brive, not far from Tulle. With the phone lines cut, a member of the ALLIANCE circuit in Cahors made a desperate attempt to warn the *résistants* further north of the threat, but the message did not get through.[14] All along their route, the Nazis were repeatedly attacked by small, poorly armed groups of *résistants*, leaving fifteen German soldiers dead and over thirty wounded. In return, dozens of *maquisards* were killed – the Nazis draped the body of one of their victims across the front of a half-track as the column ploughed into Brive, giving a terrible warning of what was to come.

As the Das Reich division arrived in Brive, its commander dispatched a reconnaissance group composed of 500 men, half-tracks and armoured vehicles with 75-millimetre guns, eastwards towards Tulle.[15] They arrived at dusk, completely unexpected.[16] There was a brief but terrifying firefight which left scores of dead – twenty-six *maquisards* and seventy Germans – and then the Germans retook the town in a matter of minutes.[17] The *maquisards* withdrew, obeying their orders to avoid any engagement with Nazi troops. As Chapou put it that evening in his report on the FTP's actions: 'The Tulle operation took place. It was a failure.'[18] Less laconically, FTP commander Elie Dupuy recalled the view from the hills above Tulle:

> . . . it was like something out of Dante's inferno. Flares were fired from all directions, while the sound of machine-gun fire, cannons and the explosions of shells drowned out everything else. Tired and beaten, our commanders and our men saw all their efforts, their sacrifices and their hopes evaporate in a matter of minutes.[19]

The Nazis were appalled at the number of their dead, and at the way the Tulle garrison had been militarily humiliated by the *maquisards*, whom they despised as terrorists.[20] Enraged, the Germans took a dreadful revenge. Early the next morning 3,000 men were assembled in the town square, and at the end of the afternoon the Nazis announced they would hang 120 of them, one by one, from balconies and telegraph poles around the town. By 7 p.m. they had hanged ninety-nine innocent men, aged between seventeen and forty-two. Then, for reasons which remain unclear, the killing stopped. The Nazis may simply have run out of rope.[21] A further 311 men were taken to Limoges, and 149 were then deported to Dachau; only 48 of them returned. In total, 200 civilian men died as a result of the Nazi attack on Tulle.[22]

Even worse was to come. On 10 June a regiment of the Das Reich was ordered to deal with an alleged maquis group that was supposedly holding a German officer captive in Oradour-sur-Glane, around twenty kilometres north-west of Limoges. Early in the afternoon the armoured column arrived in the sleepy village and the entire male population was ordered into the central marketplace, while the women and children were herded into the church. There was no maquis group, and there was no captured German officer. Nevertheless, over the next three hours an appalling massacre took place. The men were machine-gunned and the village was set on fire. Marguerite Rouffanche, aged forty-seven at the time, had hidden behind the church altar with her two daughters and her grandson. The only woman survivor of the day's events, she later recalled the horror:

I gathered up my children and took shelter behind the sacristy. The Germans burst in and began machine-gunning the interior of the church . . . There were screams of terror and pain and women and children fell where they were. My daughter was killed at my side.

More Germans came in carrying straw trusses, chairs and benches and logs of wood. These caught fire from flames coming up from the basement. My hair and dress began to burn. I ran through the flames to get behind a high altar. By luck there was a small ladder there. I climbed up and got out of the church through a small window. I fell to the ground on a heap of brambles. At the same instant a woman who had been near me sought to escape as I did, and she had a seven-month-old baby with her. She threw the baby out of the window, shouting to me to catch it. As she shouted, the Germans opened fire and killed her. Her name was Mme. Joyeux.

I don't know what happened to the baby. I was too far away to catch it. The Germans saw me and started to shoot. I was hit. A bullet

fractured my shoulder blade, another pierced my thigh. My two legs
were badly burned, and then I was hit again in my right side. I fell
down and played dead. I lay there for hours . . . At about five o'clock,
people from a neighbouring village, who had heard what happened,
came by to look for any survivors and found me. Seven members of
my family were killed in the massacre of Oradour.[23]

In total, 642 inhabitants of Oradour were murdered, including 205 children. It was the worst massacre of civilians to take place during the
Occupation.[24]

*

The extent of uncoordinated popular action in the wake of D-Day, and
the risks run by ill-armed and ill-prepared *résistants*, led the Free French
to try to stop the wave of action. BBC broadcasts called on the population to prepare for a long struggle and to temper their efforts, while on
10 June General Koenig – the nominal Free French head of the FFI –
sent an urgent message to all Resistance forces:

PUT MAXIMUM BRAKE ON GUERRILLA ACTION STOP CURRENTLY IMPOSSIBLE
TO SUPPLY ARMS AND AMMUNITION IN SUFFICIENT QUANTITIES STOP WHER-
EVER POSSIBLE BREAK OFF ATTACKS TO ALLOW REORGANIZATION STOP
AVOID LARGE GROUPINGS FORM SMALL ISOLATED GROUPS[25]

This decision resolved the argument that had raged between the Free
French and the Communists over whether the maquis should be composed of guerrilla groups or were simply a kind of parking lot for the
future French army. The Free French had apparently accepted that the
Communists were right. The news came too late for the two largest
maquis in the country, both of which would pay an appalling price.

From April 1944 the Secret Army had been gathering its forces at
Mont Mouchet in the Auvergne, to the growing irritation and alarm of
the Nazis. On 10 June around 2,500 *maquisards* were attacked by
German troops. Outnumbered and above all outgunned, the maquis
fell back to a reserve position, but this, too, was attacked, and by dawn

of 12 June the Nazis were in control of the whole forest area that had
been the realm of the maquis. A hundred and twenty-five *maquisards*
died in the fighting.[26] Far to the east, in the region of Grenoble, similarly tragic events were unfolding in the mountainous region known as
the Vercors, a huge 1,700-square-kilometre plateau composed of a series
of villages and hamlets, protected by high chalk cliffs.

Since the beginning of 1943 there had been a maquis in the Vercors
that, like the maquis of the far smaller Glières region to the north, was
dominated by military officers. In Jean Moulin's first plan for the
maquis, the Vercors played an important role because of its size, prox-
imity to Grenoble and the main north–south communications routes,
and the existence of a suitable area that could be used as an airstrip. By
1944 regular radio transmissions and exchanges of personnel led to a
high level of contact between the *maquisards*, the Allies and the Free
French in Algiers. And yet, somewhere along the line, wires got crossed,
messages were forgotten and the Vercors maquis drifted off the Free
French radar, with disastrous consequences.

On the night of 8 June Colonel Marcel Descour, the commander of
the maquis, ordered the plateau into 'lockdown' as part of what he
thought were his orders from Algiers. All roads to the plateau were
blocked as the Vercors became the first part of France outside the Allied
beachhead in Normandy to be liberated.[27] Over the next month thousands of young men and women from the surrounding area joined the
maquis, which swelled from nearly 400 strong on 6 June to over 4,000.[28]
Under the combined leadership of military officers and local socialist
politicians, the Vercors became a liberated zone, declaring itself a
republic.[29] To increase the impression – and the reality – of a new state,
*maquisards* were given uniforms, and all the apparatus of a mini state was
created – an official newspaper, a functioning legal system and even a
prison camp for collaborators and German prisoners. At one point the
Free French sent a Commissar of the Republic – veteran *résistant* Yves
Farge – to visit the liberated territory. In a particularly bold – even
provocative – gesture, every morning a large tricolour flag was raised at
Saint-Nizier, clearly visible to the German garrison that occupied
Grenoble in the flat valley below. Even more so than in the Glières four
months earlier, the atmosphere was infectious: for *maquisard* Yves

Perotin, 'The life of liberty in the tiny Republic was like nothing else . . .
For the first time, the air was cleansed of all traces of treason, and yet
the virtual state of siege made the situation stifling.'[30]

Although morale was high, something was wrong. Weapons and ammunition were in worryingly short supply – increasingly so as new *maquisards*
flocked to join the original group. With no sign of the hoped-for Allied
landings in the Mediterranean, it became apparent that there might be
little difference between a fortress and a trap. Colonel Descour claimed
that 'our aim is to free as much of the country as possible by slowly enlarging our "free zones" by slow and patient progress', but nothing of the sort
was happening.[31] The Nazis and their Vichy stooges were locked out of the
Vercors, but the *maquisards* were locked in.

Radio calls to Algiers demanding reinforcements led to the arrival of
a small group of thirteen American commandos, who trained the
*maquisards* in the use of mortars and bazookas, and helped them attack
two German armoured convoys. French officers were also parachuted in,
together with a number of SOE agents, some of whom could not speak
a word of French.[32] Finally, on 14 July – Bastille Day – 107 USAAF B-17
'Flying Fortress' bombers dropped 1,000 containers of vital supplies on
to the plateau, with the parachutes touchingly coloured in the red, white
and blue of the French flag. But the Luftwaffe, well aware of the operation, repeatedly strafed and bombed the drop site and fire-bombed the
neighbouring village, preventing the *maquisards* from collecting even
half the containers. As a result, although the Vercors maquis now
possessed around 1,400 Sten guns and 1,700 rifles, plus nearly 80 anti-
tank weapons as well as machine guns and revolvers, around half the
*maquisards* were still unarmed and, crucially, there were no heavy
weapons and no artillery. Increasingly desperate messages from the
Vercors demanded more weaponry, more troop reinforcements and a
raid on the nearby Nazi aerodrome that served as a base for German
reconnaissance and attack operations. There was no response.[33] On
the evening of 20 July the political leader of the maquis, Eugène Chavant,
sent a final, furious message to Algiers: 'IF NO AID WE AND POPULATION WILL
CONSIDER ALGIERS CRIMINAL AND COWARDLY REPEAT CRIMINAL AND COWARDLY'.[34]
For reasons that remain unclear, no action was taken.

The end began the next morning, when 10,000 Nazi troops attacked the plateau. The scale of the operation – the largest German attack on the Resistance in the whole of Western Europe – indicates how worried the Germans were about the maquis. At first the defenders held their own, but on 24 July 200 crack SS troops landed in gliders, right in the heart of the plateau. The tide of battle soon turned, and within two days the order was given to evacuate the plateau. *Maquisards* and civilians fled as best they could, but the fury of the Nazis was terrifying. The civilian population of Vassieux-en-Vercors was massacred and the town was almost completely destroyed. On 27 June thirty-six wounded *maquisards*, hiding in a cave that doubled as a hospital, were coldly assassinated. Only one man – an American – was spared, while the nurses were deported to the concentration camps. Nazi atrocities knew no limits – there were appalling gang rapes, and one woman who had helped SOE was disembowelled and left to die.[35] For days, *maquisards* hid out in the hills, desperate to escape, while the Nazis hunted them down like animals. In total, 326 *résistants* and 130 civilians were killed in the assault. The tragedy of Vassieux was eventually added to a list of Nazi atrocities that formed the French case in the Nuremberg trial of Nazi war crimes, along with the massacres at Ascq, Tulle and Oradour.[36]

The reasons why the Vercors maquis did not receive the support it needed have been repeatedly debated over the last sixty years, with explanations that vary from military stupidity on the part of the local leaders, squabbles between rival Free French services to simple forgetfulness in Algiers. Behind these alternatives lurks a bitter but real truth: the local maquis leaders launched their 'republic' because they mistakenly thought that military support was imminent, either in the form of Allied landings in the south or of substantial supplies and reinforcements. The Allies could have supplied the maquis with the artillery they required, and the men with the skills needed to operate it. But the Vercors was not an immediate Allied priority, and above all the Allied and Free French commanders remained deeply suspicious of the Resistance and consistently refused to supply the maquis with heavy weapons. Giving handguns to potentially undisciplined forces was bad enough; there could be no question of providing them with artillery.

The terrible events of June and July 1944 showed the limits of the military power of the Resistance. The *résistants* could not defend themselves against the might of the German army, and, even worse, they were unable to guarantee the safety of the civilian population when the Nazis decided to inflict horrendous repression. The tragically unequal struggle between the Nazis and the Resistance, in which underground newspapers and minor sabotage actions were wielded against the murderous terror of the Nazi machine, had turned into something unimaginably nightmarish.

*

The Allied commanders knew that the Liberation of France would not be straightforward. Total air superiority meant they were able to construct their bridgehead on the beaches, including the massive artificial 'Mulberry' harbours, which were towed across the Channel. But after an initial hesitation caused by the absence of the German commander Rommel (who was on holiday) and by Berlin's continued conviction that the real Allied invasion would take place near Calais, the Nazis threw everything into holding the Allied advance in Normandy. For over a month they succeeded, and the Allies were unable to break out of the Cotentin peninsula, despite the heroic sacrifice of thousands of soldiers.

Behind the front line, in liberated territory, a semblance of normality broke out, despite the endless eastward stream of troops, armoured vehicles and aeroplanes. The Allies had assumed they would have to impose a military government, but virtually immediately, the Free French showed that they enjoyed at least the acquiescence of the local population. In the run-up to D-Day the Allies had again displayed their scorn for de Gaulle – they told him of the imminent invasion only on the evening of 4 June (the first warning messages to the Resistance had been broadcast four days earlier!) – and they still refused to recognize the recently declared French Provisional Government.[37] But on 14 June they allowed de Gaulle to visit Normandy for the day. He went on a brief walkabout in Bayeux, which had been liberated a week before, and got an enthusiastic, if not overwhelming, reception. After the Free French leader returned to Britain, his Commissaire de la République took over as the civil authority without a whisper of opposition. As the London head of OSS Research and Analysis, Crane Brinton, put it in a report written from Normandy at the beginning of September:

> The transition from the Vichy government to what I shall call for convenience the Provisional Government has been effected in Normandy, and indeed throughout the West, with great smooth-ness . . . Vichy has faded away, like Lewis Carroll's Cheshire cat, but not even the leer has remained.[38]

The relative ease with which the Free French were able to take over was not primarily due to massive popular support for de Gaulle. The Free French had carefully prepared an alternative administration that could take the place of local Vichy personnel. These new local leaders – Commissaires de la République – were supported by Comités Départementaux de la Libération (Departmental Committees of Liberation), which had been set up in every region. Their job was to control local Resistance groups and ensure that the decisions of the new administration were implemented.[39] Faced with military reality, the Vichy personnel accepted the new situation. As the American historian Robert Paxton put it:

> When the Vichyite local authorities were dispossessed or vanished, de Gaulle wanted them replaced neither by anarchy, Communist *francs-tireurs* partisans from the hills, nor an American military govern-ment . . . In retrospect a certain harmony of interest in an orderly transition appears in both Algiers and Vichy, a harmony drowned out at the time by more conspicuous discords.[40]

Eisenhower and Montgomery enthusiastically embraced the possibility of handing over power to effective and – in their eyes – reliable French personnel rather than using their precious troops to police a whole country. The real obstacle, however, was Roosevelt, who hated and mis-trusted de Gaulle, wary of his personal politics and his ambition for a renewed and strengthened France. Public opinion in both Britain and the US was pressing for official recognition of de Gaulle and the Free French, but Roosevelt was obdurate. Churchill, unwilling to do anything to upset his powerful ally, obediently followed suit. After his successful visit to Bayeux, de Gaulle travelled to the USA, where, after four years of continual conflict, the Provisional Government was grudgingly and only partially recognized as 'the working authority for civilian administration in the liberated areas of France'.[41]

The reality of public and Resistance acceptance of de Gaulle's power did not mean that the job of the Resistance was over, or that the rumbling tensions between the Resistance and the Free French had entirely evaporated. In the heat of the action after D-Day, the differences over who controlled the military action of the Resistance – was it Algiers or was it the Resistance itself? – had largely been forgotten. But as the summer went on, the question threatened to undo the fragile French unity. Paradoxically, the immediate source of these conflicts was the success of the Allied advance. In those areas of Normandy that were liberated by the Allied armies, power was neatly handed over to the Free French representatives. But at the end of July the military situation began to change. First, the Allies finally broke out of the Cotentin peninsula. Then, on 15 August, they defeated a German counter-attack in the 'Falaise pocket', south of Caen, opening the road eastwards. On the same day the long-awaited Allied Mediterranean landings took place, as 150,000 troops disembarked on the coast around St-Tropez.[42] Hitler described it as 'the worst day of my life', and immediately gave secret orders to his commanders to withdraw all German troops to the east of Paris, beginning a retreat that ended nine months later in Berlin.[43]

The collapse of Nazi rule in France came incredibly quickly. For four short weeks in August and September there was an ecstatic summer of liberation, as the whole of the country, with the exception of the north-eastern region around Alsace-Lorraine, was freed. The full story of these tumultuous events is extremely complex, and can only be fully told in a series of detailed 'micro-histories'.[44] Put simply, in the wake of the Nazi withdrawal, the Resistance took power, often without any intervention of Allied troops. The Allied invasion forces headed eastwards from Normandy and north from Provence; the whole southern and western part of France – around half the surface area of the country south of the line Nantes–Dijon–Avignon, including major cities like Bordeaux, Toulouse, Montpellier, Perpignan, Clermont-Ferrand and Limoges – was left to its own devices. Of 212 major French towns, eighty-four per cent were liberated without much fighting by the Resistance, either because the Allied armies did the job for them or because the Germans simply left.[45] In over thirty major cities, however, there were insurrections that threatened to destroy the unity of the Resistance, and to lead to a very different outcome from that hoped for by the Allies. The most symbolic of these events took place in Paris.[46]

\*

A month after D-Day, Marie-Madeleine Fourcade was finally transported back into southern France to continue her intelligence work with the ALLIANCE circuit.[47] Within a few days she was encoding information from a high-ranking Nazi officer explaining that there was a plot to kill Hitler and demanding to negotiate with General Koenig of the Free French. Fourcade was bemused – 'The Nazis were all going mad,' she thought.[48] Shortly afterwards, she was arrested by the Germans and found herself in a prison cell in Aix, waiting for the Gestapo interrogation she deeply feared. Fourcade then remembered how, according to a fanciful tale told by her father, Indo-Chinese burglars supposedly oiled their bodies and then stripped naked so they could escape from the clutches of their would-be captors. At around midnight she slipped off her silk dress, rolled it into a ball and gripped it with her teeth, then took off the rest of her clothes and managed to get her head through the bars of her ground-floor cell:

> . . . the pain and the fear of failure made me perspire profusely, which helped my skin to slip against the iron. After my neck, I got one shoulder through, then my right leg. Squeezing my hips through was sheer agony. The pain was appalling, but I knew that once the head is through the rest of the body will go, while the pain I felt would be nothing compared with what would be in store for me with the Gestapo.[49]

Amazingly, she not only got through the bars, but also managed to escape the patrols in the surrounding streets, and strolled off, barefoot, to safety. By early August she was in Paris, refusing calls from London to return, but instead collecting information from ALLIANCE

members in the capital. To underline Fourcade's total commitment to
the secret world of intelligence, she played absolutely no role in the
momentous events that shook the capital in the second half of August.[50]

Even before the Allied breakthrough on 15 August, the Nazis had
begun to evacuate all the key German command centres from Paris.[51]
On 8 August Charles Braibant noted in his diary:

> They're moving out, it's for certain . . . This afternoon, I saw lorries in
> black and green camouflage remove all the paperwork and the office
> equipment. I watched the spectacle with great pleasure.[52]

But although the smell of retreat wafted on the summer air, the business
of Nazi horror continued as usual. On 15 August, on the orders of the
new Nazi commander of the capital, General von Choltitz, 3,000 *résistants* were assembled on the 'quai aux bestiaux' ('animal platform') at
Pantin railway station, to the east of Paris.[53] They were herded into a
train, 170 to each cattle-wagon, and deported to Buchenwald and
Ravensbrück; 2,080 prisoners were then transferred to the Ellrich camp;
only 27 returned. For those who remained in France there was the permanent threat of death. Two days after the train had left Pantin, the
mutilated bodies of thirty-five *résistants* were discovered by a waterfall in
the Bois de Boulogne. Hoping to get weapons, they had walked into a
Gestapo trap, were shot and then had grenades thrown at them.[54]

As Nazi rule gradually collapsed, Vichy breathed its last. In a series of
cynical and sordid manoeuvres, the leading collaborators attempted to
negotiate with the Allies and de Gaulle. Laval came to Paris and tried to
inveigle Édouard Herriot, who had been Prime Minister three times
before the war, into providing a fig-leaf of respectability to his attempt
to save his skin. Herriot would have none of it, and Laval's plan collapsed. Pétain – still in Vichy – was even more pathetic, as he tried to
transmit his powers directly to de Gaulle via a series of intermediaries.
There was no response. On 17 August Laval was carted off by his masters
as they fled eastwards; Pétain suffered the same fate shortly afterwards.[55]

The atmosphere in Paris had begun to change a month earlier. On
14 July there were huge illegal demonstrations to celebrate Bastille
Day – over 100,000 people marched through the city. Although German

soldiers fired in the air to disperse the crowds, the French police stood by and did nothing. The apparatus of Occupation was cracking. The next blow to the Nazis came on 10 August, when railway workers in the Paris region began a strike with openly political aims. As a leaflet put it: 'To make the Hun retreat: strike. To win our demands: strike. For the complete and definitive liberation of our country: strike.' Within two days over half the 80,000 railway workers were on strike, and the rail system ground to a halt.[56] Then, on 15 August, the Parisian police, furious that their comrades in the Parisian suburbs had been disarmed by the Germans, went on strike. The same policemen who had participated in the round-up of Jews in 1942, who had arrested *résistants* and handed them over to the Nazis, now decided to act, just in time to save their reputation – and their skins.[57]

The situation in the capital was growing desperate. There was virtually no gas or electricity, little food, the Métro was closed and now there was no effective police force.[58] But although the road to Paris was open, Eisenhower was not interested in liberating the capital. Despite its political and emotional importance to the French, Paris had little military significance. The relatively small German garrison could easily be contained and left to stew in its own juices, like the pockets of Nazi soldiers on the Atlantic coast, holed up in Brest or Saint-Nazaire. Eisenhower's task was to destroy the Nazi army as quickly and effectively as possible, and liberating Paris would distract from that objective.[59] As General Omar Bradley, commander of the US 12th Army Group, put it:

> Paris represented nothing more than an inkspot on our maps, to be bypassed as we headed toward the Rhine. Logistically, it could cause untold trouble, for behind its handsome façades there lived four million hungry Frenchmen. The diversion of so much tonnage to Paris would only strain further our already taut lines of supply. Food for the people of Paris meant less gasoline for the front.[60]

The Allies felt Paris could wait. The Resistance did not agree.

On 19 August the national Resistance leadership (the Conseil National de la Résistance) and the Comité Parisien de Libération (the city-wide liberation committee) both called for an immediate insurrection in the capital, despite the ferocious opposition of one of de Gaulle's Military Delegates, General Chaban-Delmas.[61] De Gaulle's instructions to his men had been absolutely plain. At the end of July he had sent a telegram to his personal delegate, Alexandre Parodi, instructing him to ensure order and to maintain his authority over the Resistance:

> Always speak loud and clear in the name of the State. The numerous acts of our glorious Resistance are the means by which the nation fights for its salvation. The State is above all these manifestations and actions.[62]

But in the reality of the hot Parisian summer, de Gaulle's instructions were useless. Chaban-Delmas and Parodi were in danger of being completely overtaken by events. Reluctantly, they decided to rally to the majority position. Despite their fears that the insurrection would lead to a repetition of the Paris Commune (the city-wide revolution of 1871), they placed all their forces under the command of the Communist regional FFI leader, Colonel Henri Rol-Tanguy. Rol-Tanguy was in turn under the orders of the Commission Militaire d'Action (COMAC), set up in February to act as the Resistance military leadership, much to the irritation of the Free French.

Early on the morning of 19 August, Rol-Tanguy got on his bike, his saddlebag bulging with copies of the call for insurrection, a makeshift uniform from the Spanish Civil War and a machine gun, and headed for his secret headquarters. As he rode past Notre-Dame, he heard the sound of the 'Marseillaise' coming from the Préfecture de Police, facing the cathedral. Unknown to the FFI commander, the striking policemen had seized their headquarters, even before the call for insurrection had been posted on the city walls.[63] Later that afternoon the Comités de Libération in the Paris districts occupied town halls, government buildings and collaborationist newspaper offices. Barricades sprouted in the northern and eastern parts of the capital, where the Resistance was strongest, and through which the Nazis would have to pass if they tried to retreat. Few of these barricades would have posed any problem to a German tank, but they enabled the population to participate in the insurrection, and they also exerted a powerful symbolism, recalling the events of past Parisian revolutions.

Simone de Beauvoir remembered that morning:

When I woke up I leaned out of my window. The swastika was still flying over the Sénat, housewives were shopping as usual in the Rue de Seine, and a long queue had formed outside the baker's shop. Two cyclists rode past shouting, 'The Préfecture's fallen!' At the same moment, a German detachment emerged from the Sénat and marched off towards the Boulevard St-Germain. Before turning the corner of the street the soldiers let loose a volley of machine-gun fire. Passers-by on the Boulevard scattered, taking cover as best they could in doorways. But every door was shut; one man crumpled and fell in the very act of knocking, fists drumming at the panels, while others collapsed along the sidewalk.[64]

The violence observed by de Beauvoir emphasized that the insurrection would not be straightforward. Although the crack Nazi forces had left Paris, von Choltitz still commanded 20,000 troops, plus around 80 tanks and 60 pieces of artillery.[65] The Resistance, on the other hand, had only 600 handguns shared among 20,000 *résistants* and hundreds of thousands of Parisians.[66]

Despite the lack of weapons, the insurgents soon took one of the key buildings in the city – the Hôtel de Ville. Early in the morning of 20 August a small group led by Léo Hamon entered the office of the Prefect of the Seine and declared: 'In the name of the Comité Parisien de Libération and the Provisional Government of the Republic, I take possession of the Hôtel de Ville.' Amazed, the Prefect asked Hamon for his papers. 'We've got out of the habit of that kind of thing,' was the laconic reply. After a brief verbal exchange in which the Prefect accused the insurgents of 'acting like children', the 'children' arrested the members of the Paris municipal council to protect them 'from legitimate popular anger' and took control of the building.[67]

But no sooner had the insurrection started than it was undermined. In a series of secret meetings, Parodi and Chaban-Delmas emphasized the extremely unfavourable balance of forces, and argued for a ceasefire between the Resistance and the Nazis. It is still not known who thought up this proposal, which was brokered by the Swedish consul in Paris, Raoul Nordling. But the impact on the insurrection was plain: as well as potentially preventing unnecessary bloodshed, the ceasefire broke the rhythm of the movement so feared by the Gaullists and gained time for the arrival of the Allies. Far worse, however, the agreement allowed the Germans to take their troops safely out of the capital. After twenty-four hours of confusion, in which orders and counter-orders were issued – many of them gleefully ignored by the *résistants* on the ground, who simply wanted to get on with the business of fighting the Germans – the ceasefire was officially broken. In reality, it had never been fully obeyed.[68]

*

From 21 August the insurrection was commanded by Rol-Tanguy from a vast bunker complex twenty-six metres underneath Place Denfert-Rocherau, built by the government before the war, and which had its own air conditioning, power supply and dormitories. The telephone lines were intact, and there was continual communication between Rol-Tanguy, the Préfecture and the Hôtel de Ville although, unsurprisingly, the chain of command down to the forces fighting in the streets was not always particularly effective. The Resistance newspapers took over the presses of the collaborationist print media, producing hundreds of thousands of copies, bringing many Parisians into contact with the Resistance press for the very first time. There was even a Resistance radio station – Radiodiffusion de la Nation Française. Although on the first day it broadcast only French classical music and the 'Marseillaise', it was soon relaying FFI communiqués and broadcasting interviews with leaders of the insurrection.[69] In the streets of the capital, ordinary people joined in the fighting. In his diary, Parisian Jean Galtier-Boissière noted with humour:

> Urban warfare is less risky and more picturesque than war in the countryside; you can go home to eat, with your rifle; everyone in the district is at their windows, watching and applauding you; the dairy-shop, the fruit-seller and the bistro all offer you free rounds. If only the cinema was there, glory would be complete.[70]

In fact the cinema was there, in the heart of the insurrection. Film professionals recorded the whole event on celluloid, and as soon as the city was liberated the rushes were rapidly edited into a thirty-minute black-and-white newsreel, *La Libération de Paris*. This striking film provided the people of Paris – soon followed by the rest of the French and by cinema-goers in Britain and the USA – with a powerful view of the insurrection as it happened. It also fixed iconic scenes in the popular imagination – armed *résistants* inside the Préfecture, crouching behind smashed windows; a Molotov cocktail attack on a German lorry, its soldiers spilling onto the road, covered in flames; joyous Parisian men, women and even children building barricades, digging up paving stones and chopping down trees.[71]

Not all the events of the insurrection were so picturesque. On 22 August a German tank shell exploded in the Grand Palais and set fire to the glass-roofed building, which was housing a circus. One of the circus horses, stabled behind the building, was killed; within an hour hungry Parisians had flayed it to the bone, taking the precious meat off to their homes or the black market.[72]

Despite the scenes of enthusiastic crowds fixed on film, the fighting in Paris was real urban warfare – messy, chaotic and sometimes horrifying. Tortured bodies of *résistants* were found dumped in the street with their eyes gouged out, the skin stripped from their hands.[73] In return, insurgents ignored cries from German soldiers, trapped in their burning vehicles, desperate to be put out of their agony – 'Let them roast like pigs' was the reply.[74] Soldiers were stabbed with kitchen knives, German snipers and Vichy *miliciens* were summarily executed in the street. The Communist Party's distinctly un-internationalist slogan 'À chacun son boche' (Everyone get a Hun) was being realized in the most bloody fashion.

Young André Calvès, who had come to Paris from Britanny to help his Trotskyist comrades, had joined an FTP brigade, wisely hiding his true political opinions from the FTP's Communist leaders. Based in the nineteenth arrondissement, Calvès' unit was at the forefront of some of the fighting, although what went on was not always heroic:

There were Germans in the road. One of them, a young lad, turned the corner. He had his rifle pointing towards the sky and was watching the roofs. Suddenly, he saw me. I could swear he smiled. The situation was quite funny. We were about three metres away from each other.

He brought his rifle down. I fired. He fell in the street. We couldn't even get his weapon as his comrades were behind him.[75]

Sometimes Calvès and his comrade Jo had the impression they were being used:

The cops brought us a member of the Milice who had just killed two men: 'Hey, FTP – you can kill this bastard.' Jo spoke out – 'You're always careful, you cops, aren't you? After all, the Germans might end up back in charge.' They didn't reply. We shot the *milicien* in front of the post office. People applauded. It was understandable, but it was still sad.[76]

Just up the road from the post office where that incident took place, a deep railway cutting passes through the Buttes-Chaumont park. On 22 August two other members of the nineteenth arrondissement FTP brigade, Madeleine Riffaud and her young sidekick, Max Rainat, got a phone call telling them that there would be a German troop train passing through. They rushed out, armed with what they had to hand – a few grenades and boxes of fireworks and flares. The explosions were loud, colourful and very effective – the *résistants* were able to immobilize the train and take eighty German prisoners.[77]

All over the capital, insurgents got weapons where they could. Rifles, handguns and grenades were stripped from fallen German soldiers, while the most successful raids saw *résistants* making off with Nazi lorries, artillery pieces and even tanks. The lack of weapons remained the biggest problem for the insurgents. Despite the fears of de Gaulle's representatives, Rol-Tanguy had no intention of seizing power for the Communist Party, or of creating a new Commune. He was well aware of the threat posed by the continued presence of the Nazi forces in the capital, and the need for well-armed military forces to come to the aid of the insurrection. His orders finished with this instruction to all FFI forces in the region: 'OPEN THE ROAD TO PARIS FOR THE VICTORIOUS ALLIED ARMIES AND WELCOME THEM HERE.'[78]

To convince the Allies to turn their attention to Paris, both the Resistance and the Free French sent messengers through enemy lines.

Chaban-Delmas and Parodi, deeply worried that they would lose the initiative to the Resistance if the insurgents took control before the Allies arrived, were particularly desperate to ensure that aid came quickly. But when the message finally got through, on 22 August, it was due to the bravery of Rol-Tanguy's right-hand man, Roger Cocteau ('Gallois'), who finally arrived at General Patton's headquarters early that morning. Gallois explained the situation in the capital – or at least, the situation as he had left it thirty-six hours earlier – and emphasized that the low morale of the German garrison made the city ripe for the taking. Finally, he asked the Americans to parachute weapons to help the insurrection and immediately to send their tanks towards the capital. The US commanders refused to do either, but sent Gallois to see General Leclerc, commander of the French 2nd Armoured Division ('Division Blindée' – 2nd DB). Following discussions between Eisenhower and General Bradley, it was agreed that Leclerc should immediately move his men towards Paris.[79]

This was no spur-of-the-moment decision – the 2nd DB (entirely armed with American weapons) had been chosen for this role at the beginning of the year when the Allies began planning for the period after D-Day. Acutely aware of the potential political importance of French soldiers liberating the capital, the Allies cast around for an appropriate formation among the ranks of the Free French. The reasons behind their eventual choice of the Leclerc division are surprising and have only recently come to light. Apart from a series of logistical considerations, the American and the British generals (with the support of de Gaulle) wanted a division that was '100 per cent white', with no soldiers from the French colonies, or one that could be made to be so without reducing its numbers too greatly.[80] The Allies and the Free French were not explicitly racist; rather they thought that for the population of Paris to identify with their liberators, the troops involved should all be white (no such segregation was thought necessary for the populations in Provence, who welcomed the Free French armies with their African and Arab soldiers). In the case of the 2nd DB, shearing the division of its colonial troops would have meant removing twenty-five per cent of its total muster. In the end, it appears the 2nd DB was left intact, not only with its African and Arab troops but also with several hundred foreign fighters – above all Spanish Republicans who had fled Franco, as well as Italians, Americans and even anti-fascist Germans.[81]

*

Early in the morning of 23 August the 2nd DB – 16,000 men, 4,200 vehicles and 200 tanks – set off for Paris. All along the route, they kept Henri Rol-Tanguy and the insurgents informed of their progress.[82] By the afternoon of 24 August the French were fighting in the southern suburbs of Paris, alongside American troops. To keep up morale in the capital, a small Piper plane was sent swooping low over the Préfecture, where it dropped a message to the insurgents: 'General Leclerc says: Hold on, we are coming.' Two hours later Leclerc ordered Captain Dronne, at the head of a small scout group composed of three tanks and eleven half-tracks, to enter the capital. The final phase of the liberation of Paris had begun.[83]

Shortly after 9 p.m., having met no opposition, Dronne's column arrived in the courtyard of the Hôtel de Ville to be greeted by Georges Bidault, the head of the CNR, and André Tollet, the leader of the Comité Parisien de Libération. Not long afterwards, a similar but more official meeting took place at the Préfecture, where de Gaulle's representatives, Parodi and Chaban-Delmas, greeted Captain Dronne. All through the evening, the Resistance radio announced the imminent arrival of the Free French column. Now they were in the centre of the capital. Speaking to the radio listeners, Parodi said: 'I have in front of me a French captain who is the first to arrive in Paris. His face is red, he is grubby and he needs a shave, and yet I want to embrace him.'[84] All over the city, the church bells rang out.

In Rol-Tanguy's underground bunker, there was an outbreak of joy which did not amuse the stern Colonel Henri. His wife, Cécile, who acted as his secretary, later recalled:

When we heard that Dronne had arrived, all the women went a bit mad and had a pillow fight to celebrate. It just happened, and we had a great time. It didn't last long – maybe ten minutes. But the next day, when Henri heard about it, when people said, 'Ah! If only you'd seen

Madame Rol!', he had a real go at me! 'A colonel's wife does not have pillow fights . . .' I didn't think it was that bad . . .[85]

The next morning, 25 August, the rest of the Leclerc division arrived in the capital, together with General Barton's US infantry division. This time they were met by stiff resistance from the German troops. Around Invalides there was a series of firefights that saw French tanks destroyed and French soldiers killed – Second Lieutenant Bureau died an hour after telephoning his father to say he would soon be home.[86] Fierce fighting at the École Militaire left fifty German soldiers dead before the group finally surrendered. As the fighting stopped, at the other end of the Champs-de-Mars a tricolour flag flew from the top of the Eiffel Tower.

While the 2nd DB was on the move, the Swedish consul, Raoul Nordling, tried to broker a peaceful settlement. The German commander, von Choltitz, had received orders from Hitler to leave the city a pile of burning ruins but was apparently unwilling to do so – from the outset, he could have smashed the occupation of the Préfecture by sending in tanks and blasting the building to rubble, but he had not. Although von Choltitz was an unrepentant Nazi, he may have been thinking about what would happen after the war was over – better to be remembered as the man who allowed Paris to survive than as the person who oversaw its destruction. By 25 August it was obvious that the Germans were beaten, and von Choltitz was mainly concerned about not being captured by the Resistance, fearing mistreatment. After much fighting in the streets, the German commander finally left his headquarters at the Hôtel Meurice and was taken to the Montparnasse railway station, where General Leclerc had set up his headquarters.

The surrender was signed at around 3 p.m., in a railway-staff billiard room in the presence of the commanders of the 2nd DB, as well as Chaban-Delmas and two Resistance leaders – Rol-Tanguy for the FFI and Kriegel-Valmiront for COMAC. After Leclerc and von Choltitz signed the surrender, Kriegel-Valmiront, supported by Chaban-Delmas, pointed out that the Resistance should also sign the surrender document, given their role in the insurrection. Leclerc – who had not heard of Rol-Tanguy until that morning – dictated a second version, putting the name of the FFI leader before his own.[87] The Occupation of Paris was over.

Two hours later de Gaulle entered the capital. After seeing General Leclerc at Montparnasse and complaining that he had allowed Rol-Tanguy to sign the surrender document, de Gaulle made his way to the War Ministry, which he had left four years earlier.[88] After a brief battle of wills, in which de Gaulle insisted that the Resistance should come to meet him, he eventually bowed to political reality and made his way to the Hôtel de Ville, where he was greeted by Georges Bidault, head of the CNR, in front of an excited crowd of insurgents. While Bidault spoke movingly of the Resistance, paying homage to his predecessor, 'Max' (Jean Moulin) – 'On this day of triumph I remember him with pride and tenderness' – there were no words of recognition from de Gaulle. In his speech, de Gaulle did not mention the CNR or the Resistance, nor did he thank them for their decisive role in the insurrection. Instead, the Free French leader emphasized the need for national unity, brushing aside the catastrophe of collaboration as the work of a 'few unhappy traitors who gave themselves over to the enemy and who are tasting or will taste the rigour of the law'. He did make a rare recognition of the importance of popular action, but it was swamped by his mystical invocation of 'France':

> Paris! Paris humiliated! Paris broken! Paris martyrized! But now Paris liberated! Liberated by herself, by her own people with the help of the armies of France, with the support and aid of France as a whole, of fighting France, of the only France, of the true France, of eternal France.[89]

As de Gaulle was about to step on to a window sill of the Hotel de Ville and appear in front of a wildly enthusiastic crowd, Bidault invited him to declare the Republic – just as in previous Parisian insurrections.[90] De Gaulle knew his history, and had no intention of unleashing forces he might not be able to control:

> 'No,' he replied, 'the Republic has never ceased to exist. In their turn the Free French, the Fighting French, the French Committee of National Liberation have incorporated it. Vichy was always, and remains, null and void. I am President of the government of the Republic. Why should I proclaim it?'[91]

In the heat and noise of the Hôtel de Ville, buzzing with the excitement of insurrection, de Gaulle had outlined the basis of his power, and how he saw the future.

Other things were happening that evening. All along their route, the 2nd DB had been the happy recipients of the usual gifts of a grateful female population – kisses, hugs, phone numbers. That night, as they camped in the Jardin des Plantes in the centre of Paris, the soldiers of the 2nd DB received some extra attention. According to woman soldier Suzanne Massu:

> That first night, everything was quiet in the Jardin des Plantes . . . or at least, almost quiet . . . from all around there were stifled sighs and ticklish giggles. Many Parisian women were too charitable to let our lads spend their first night in the capital alone.[92]

The next day saw a triumphal, chaotic march down the Champs-Elysées, as de Gaulle, accompanied by members of the Free French army, marched to the acclaim of hundreds of thousands of Parisians. Resistance leaders were also present, but de Gaulle was careful to claim the limelight – when Bidault seemed to be getting too close to the front, the General allegedly turned and said: 'Monsieur – step back a bit, please.'[93] People climbed on to lampposts and on to roofs to get a better look at the man whose voice they had heard through four years of Occupation. There were banners, flags and placards, and, stretching right across the broad avenue, a huge banner in Spanish Republican colours, a welcome sight for the Spanish members of the 2nd DB. At first de Gaulle was furious at the chaos and irritated by the fact that the FFI fighters were not neatly lined up in best military formation, but he relaxed slightly as he realized the size of the crowd and the warmth of the reception. He later recalled his impression of the immense wave of humanity that surrounded him: 'It's the sea,' he wrote.[94]

Photos of the beginning of the demonstration show a young black man, his arm in a sling, breaking through the crowd and coming up to de Gaulle and Bidault. This was twenty-two-year-old Georges Dukson, who had been wounded when fighting with the FFI in the seventeenth arrondissement, earning the nickname 'the lion of the seventeenth'.

Now a minor celebrity, he had bet his friends he would be with de
Gaulle on the march, and by a combination of fame and cheek he had
won.[95] At one point, when the crowd yet again stopped the cortège
from moving forward, de Gaulle noticed a young *résistant*, one of the
thousands who had risked their lives in the fighting. The young man
wore an FFI armband, had a cigarette hanging from his lips and was
mad with joy. De Gaulle beckoned him over and spoke a few words into
his ear; the *résistant* returned to the edge of the crowd. 'What did he say
to you?' he was eagerly asked. 'Don't smoke on the procession' was the
reply.[96] There were other unscripted moments – at various points along
the route to Notre-Dame, where a celebratory Mass was held, shots rang
out, causing the crowd to scatter, even in the cathedral itself. Whether
these were the acts of desperate members of the Milice firing from the
rooftops or of trigger-happy members of the Resistance, as de Gaulle
suggested, will never be certain. The film images of the march capture
the striking combination of joy and panic as the crowd dashed for cover
at the sound of gunfire.

Around 2,000 Parisians died in the struggle to liberate Paris, along
with perhaps 800 *résistants* (FFI and police) and over 100 Free French
and American soldiers.[97] Like the dead, the credit for the Liberation
was shared – the Allied advance had shaken the German garrison and
made the insurrection possible; the Parisian *résistants* had rightly sensed
that the time was ripe to free the city and wound the Nazis by defeating
their soldiers; while the Free French army had provided the weight to
put an end to the fighting. For de Gaulle, the outcome could not have
been better. Acutely aware of the power of symbols, de Gaulle had been
able to enter Paris as a hero, surfing on the wave of a popular uprising,
but firmly based on the traditional power of the army. In the heroic days
of August a new French myth had been forged; at its heart was the tall
man in a uniform, the man who had consistently belittled, ignored or
undermined the Resistance, yet had finally ridden it to power.

\*

In the evening of 25 August, after the Nazi surrender was signed, there
was fierce fighting as dozens of Resistance groups tried to take the SS

barracks in the Place de la République. Twenty-two-year-old Michel Tagrine, the young violinist who had foolishly taken his instrument with him on the 11 November demonstration in 1940, was a member of the St-Just FTP brigade, along with Madeleine Riffaud and André Calvès. Tagrine insisted on joining the operation, even though he was wounded. He was shot dead at the very end of the attack, one of the last Resistance victims of the Parisian insurrection.[98]

Madeleine Riffaud later recalled the events, still inflamed by the feeling of liberation after sixty years:

They were firing proper shells at us on the Place de la République. We were fighting floor by floor, dropping grenades through the windows. It lasted all day and I lost one of my best men, Michel Tagrine, to a bullet fired after the surrender. But you cannot understand how wonderful it was to fight finally as free men and women, to battle in the daylight, under our own names, with our real identities, with everyone out there, all of Paris, to support us, happy, joyful and united. There was never a time like it.[99]

# 11

# *Aftermath*

Paris is not France, and, despite the scenes in the capital, France was not liberated. On the same day that Parisians were overcome with joy as the Nazis surrendered, the inhabitants of Maillé, a small town forty kilometres south of Tours, were screaming in terror. A group of German soldiers – still not identified, over sixty years later – killed eighty adults and forty-four children and destroyed or damaged eighty per cent of the town's buildings.[1] Even Paris was not completely secure – the Germans attempted to retake the city a few days after the surrender was signed, mounting a vicious counter-offensive from the east that was beaten back by the Allies. All over the country the Nazis carried out massacres and arbitrary shootings as they withdrew. Thirty prisoners were executed as hostages in Rodez, nineteen *résistants* were assassinated in Carcassonne, while over a hundred prisoners were taken out of Montluc prison and shot, their bodies then burned.

This last massacre led to a terrible twist in the roles of the Resistance and the Nazis. Fearing that the remaining 1,200 *résistants* in Montluc jail would also be shot, the regional Resistance leaders wrote to the German commander of Lyons. They pointed out that they held 752 German prisoners who would suffer 'very serious consequences' if there were further atrocities; in the meantime, eighty German prisoners would be executed as a reprisal for the killings of the Montluc prisoners. Two days later the eighty Germans were duly shot.[2] The next day, 24 August, with the American army only thirty kilometres away, the left wing of the Lyons Resistance launched a general strike and insurrection in the working-class suburb of Villeurbanne. But Allied progress was slower than they hoped, and after two days of fighting the insurgents were forced to accept a ceasefire – the Nazis stopped their reprisals in return for the dismantling of the barricades. Although fighting continued in nearby Oullins, the Resistance was threatened by a disastrous internal power struggle as the Free French loyalists sought to calm the determination of the FFI *résistants* and contradictory orders were issued, confusing the fighters on the ground.[3] The city was finally saved through one of the few actions where US and FFI forces fought side by side in a textbook battle. On 1 September, in boiling late-summer heat, several hundred US troops and *résistants* held off the 11th Panzer Division at Meximieux, twenty kilometres to the north-east of Lyons, opening the road for the main US force to advance.[4]

As the Americans closed in on the city the German garrison withdrew, dynamiting the bridges over the Rhône and the Saône behind them. Although the US troops were not supposed to enter Lyons – their objective was to chase the German army back to Berlin – on 3 September some Special Operations units made their way through the pouring rain to the centre of the city. Their commander, Major Alfred Cox, recalled:

> Somehow or other we got out in front of the attacking Maquis who were still forming up, and had to fight our way through the wildly cheering crowds to get where we wanted. We reached the Cathedral overlooking the city just about as the first Maquis and French Army unit arrived at the river bank below us, and for half an hour enjoyed the spectacle . . .[5]

Journalist Andrée Viollis reported the event in a local newspaper:

> I can tell you, the FFI looked proud when you compare them to the green-uniformed cowards who fled. And then, the shouting got even louder – there were some firemen carrying two men on their shoulders, men wearing khaki uniforms, their faces red, smiling white-toothed smiles. They were Americans. The first we'd ever seen! This time, nothing could stop the crowd – they grabbed the men, kissed them all over. And there they were, covered in lipstick. And when some policemen came to save them, they got kissed too. We

were all a bit mad. And all the time it was bucketing down. If it had been sunny, who knows what would have happened! And they say that the people of Lyons are cold![6]

As the Allied armies drove the Nazis back, the same scenes of joy were repeated in town after town in the northern and eastern parts of France.[7] But in the other half of the country, where there were no Allied soldiers, the Resistance was left to its own devices and events sometimes took an unexpected turn. In Toulouse, everything went more or less according to plan – at first. On 19 August, while the Resistance called for an insurrection, the Nazi garrison began to withdraw, burning buildings and destroying the telephone exchange as they left. Attacked by Resistance groups, the Nazis fought back, killing thirty-five *résistants* and gravely wounding Jean Cassou, one of the founders of the Musée de l'Homme group, who was now Commissaire de la République in Toulouse.[8] On the night of 20 August Resistance reinforcements arrived, and by the next day the Germans had fled. In celebration, there was a demonstration of around 30,000 people on the Place du Capitole, in front of the Hôtel de Ville.

But that was only the beginning. While delirious crowds crammed into the centre of the city, the workers in the SNCASE aviation plant hastily repainted a D.520 fighter that was due to be delivered to the Luftwaffe and sent the plane, now sporting Free French markings, roaring into the sky in a sign of victory. Because the managers of SNCASE had collaborated with the Nazis, the workers had no confidence in their bosses' commitment to producing aircraft for the Allied war effort. So they simply took control of the factory. On 23 August they broadcast a blood-curdling declaration, announcing their intention of increasing production of aircraft and armaments, and warning that there would be no slacking in the fight to ensure that the Nazi armies were destroyed:

The better we are armed, the fewer lives will be lost. The military command of the SNCASE FFI group will not tolerate any mistakes. The factory is militarized: any mistakes in work will be considered as treason and will be judged by the Factory Committee. Everyone to work, with passion! Long live France and the IVth Republic![9]

In the heady excitement of the Liberation, workers' liberation committees soon controlled all the major workplaces of the region – arsenals, engineering companies, banks and even prisons, but above all the whole of the aeronautical industry.[10] The director of one aero factory complained that the committee in his company was 'slowly transforming itself into a soviet. It asks for information on stocks, on the state of supplies, on what remains, etc. It also asks for the keys to all the offices.'[11] Soon there were rumours of people being strung up from the lampposts around the Place du Capitole, of bodies being thrown in the river Garonne, and of the city having been taken over by a soviet. Because there were no Allied troops for hundreds of kilometres, Toulouse came to represent the nightmares of those who feared that liberation would turn into revolution.

De Gaulle was determined that there would be no revolution, in Toulouse or anywhere else. To stop that happening, he had to get control of the men with the guns. Throughout the war, he fought to ensure that armed action in France remained under his command. He had largely failed, and the country was now teeming with hundreds of thousands of armed *résistants*, many of whom were not impressed by traditional military authority, especially given the poor record of the French army four years earlier.[12] As one Free French senior officer reported gloomily:

> In many towns, French officers, appointed to military regions . . . have shown themselves to be not up to the task. Most of them have done nothing more than put on their uniforms, which they abandoned during the hard years of the German occupation, believing that the sight of their stripes would be enough to regain the respect which had sadly been lost . . . many FFI groups, and in particular the FTP, still refuse to recognize the authority of these officers, and in some cases insult them quite basely.[13]

De Gaulle needed the government to have complete control over all the levers of power. He not only wanted to take the guns out of the hands of civilians and to restore order and discipline in society; he also had one eye on the post-war international balance of forces. In his plans for rebuilding France as a world power, a reorganized and strengthened

French army would have to play a role in the destruction of the Nazi armed forces. That meant getting the Resistance fighters under his discipline and into the ranks of the armed forces. The long-running dispute between the Free French and the Resistance had reached its highest and most decisive level. There could be only one winner.

De Gaulle acted with almost indecent haste – on 28 August, when the hangovers from the Liberation of Paris had barely faded and half the country had yet to be liberated, he ordered the dissolution of the national leadership of the FFI and of COMAC, the military leadership of the Resistance. After a brief stand-off, COMAC accepted the dissolution of the regional FFI leaderships in return for the fusion of FFI fighters with the Free French army. By the end of November over 200,000 FFI members had joined up and were fighting their way to Berlin – almost twice as many soldiers as in the regular Free French army.[14] The Resistance called this '*l'amalgame*', a reference to the fusion of batallions of revolutionary soldiers and the regular army during the French Revolution.[15] But instead of the traditional army officers losing their influence, as in 1793, the opposite happened: the officers of 1940 were allowed to keep their rank, no matter what their behaviour during the Occupation, while FFI officers were strictly selected, and the rank-and-file FFI soldiers simply obeyed orders. The *amalgame* of 1944, unlike its predecessor, strengthened the forces of conservatism.[16]

On 9 September de Gaulle created the first government of liberated France, and included CNR chief Georges Bidault and Communist FTP leader Charles Tillon as a gesture to the Resistance and a way of testing its intentions. He then immediately embarked on a tour of the main cities of the south to reinforce his personal authority and press for the disarmament of the Resistance. The result was a series of clashes between de Gaulle's profound attachment to order, discipline and authority, and the disorganized and improvised nature of Resistance power in the regions. On 14 September, in Lyons, the Commissaire de la République dutifully outlined the programme of visits and dinners that had been worked out for the official visit, each involving different sections of the Resistance. De Gaulle looked doubtful and asked when he would meet the city authorities. 'But they are all in prison, General,' was the reply.[17] The following day de Gaulle was in Marseilles, where he

Fake identity card for Alliance intelligence circuit leader Marie-Madeline Fourcade, in the name of Marie Suzanne Imbert.

Lucie Aubrac during the war.

Georges Guingouin in maquis
winter uniform, 1943–4.

The railway viaduct near Eymoutiers, destroyed by Georges Guingouin's
maquis in March 1943.

Workers in the town of Romans take action to prevent a train of labour conscripts leaving for Germany. Most of the men in uniform are Vichy *gardes mobiles*.

Anti-Resistance cartoon produced by Vichy. 'Monsieur Ballandard' was a character in a comic strip that appeared in the anti-Semitic newspaper *Le Pilori*.

Survivors of the Turma-Vengeance group at a ceremony after the war. Centre, in overcoat, Victor Dupont; on his right (without hat) François Wetterwald. The names of many of the people in the photo are unknown.

Young maquisards from Saint-Eugène, south-west of Dijon, about to be executed. 28 March 1944.

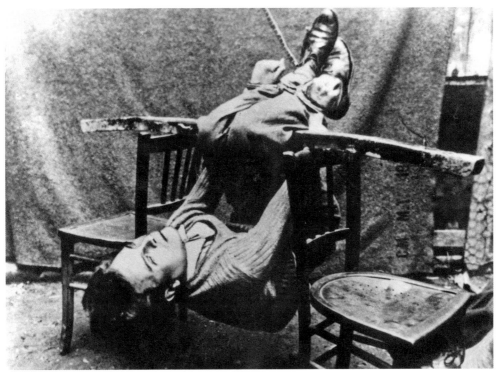

Man being tortured in a Gestapo building in the Paris suburbs.

The Conseil National de la Rèsistance in Paris, August 1944. Among those in the picture are Georges Bidault (centre), Pascal Copeau (fifth from left), Daniel Mayer (sixth from right) and Jean-Pierre Levy (fifth from right).

Nazi propaganda poster attacking the 'Groupe Manouchian' in 1944. Known in France as 'L'Affiche rouge' (the red poster).

Maquisards in the Vercors, 1944.

Resistance fighters during the Liberation of Paris, August 1944.

The Liberation of Paris, August 1944.

Parisians build a barricade, August 1944.

Resistance fighters in Toulouse, 20 August 1944.

watched a victory parade of FFI fighters. Lucie Aubrac recalled his reaction:

> There was an amazing parade of *maquisards* wearing tattered clothes. Real *sans-culottes*! Most of them had their collars open. It was very hot. And they had flowers in the barrels of their rifles. They were pulling a German armoured car on which were perched some young women in skimpy dresses. They were shouting and waving flags. De Gaulle took all this very badly. He just sat there, muttering 'What a farce!'[18]

The most significant clash came in Toulouse. Shortly before de Gaulle arrived, the movement in the factories was nipped in the bud following the appointment of the new Aviation Minister, the Communist Charles Tillon. The workplace liberation committees were dissolved in return for the creation of toothless 'mixed production committees' that would supposedly improve production 'in the interest of the whole nation' but would have no executive role.[19] As the Toulouse militants took a step back, de Gaulle pressed home his advantage and told the Resistance leaders that he would not tolerate the ramshackle nature of the forces in control of the city. During the parade to celebrate his visit, he was appalled to see a group of conscript Russian soldiers who had come over from the German army, followed by an armed contingent of Spanish Republicans, while the undrilled FFI troops made him appreciate the virtues of traditional military discipline.[20] To ensure that the Toulouse FFI followed his ultimatum – join up or disarm – he put a military governor in command of the city and ordered a loyal regiment of Algerian fighters to be stationed there.[21] Finally, de Gaulle took action against what he perceived to be Allied interference in the city. Conspicuous on the parade was a 1,500-strong maquis group commanded by a British SOE agent, George Starr ('Hilaire'), who had run the WHEELWRIGHT circuit in the region for nearly two years. According to the philosopher A. J. Ayer, an SOE officer in Toulouse at the time, Starr was as influential as any of the local FFI leaders.[22] This apparently irked de Gaulle profoundly, for he attacked Starr as a 'mercenary' and ordered him to leave the country. Within a week, Starr was back in London.[23]

A month later US OSS agent Crane Brinton toured southern France to test the Parisian rumours 'that those parts of France in which there are no Allied forces were prey to disorders of all kinds'.[24] With communication lines still severely disrupted – the railways in particular took months to be reconstructed – there was plenty of room for rumour to grow. Having heard that Toulouse was in the grip of a workers' council, he found the truth to be somewhat different:

> I need hardly add that when we got to Toulouse we found the town as quiet as a southern French city ever is, the civilian authorities duly installed and the FFI under the command of a French general.[25]

In many ways de Gaulle's trip to the apparently rebellious southern cities was a turning point. Although his evident scorn for the Resistance disappointed and dismayed those who had made such sacrifices – indeed, it was partly intended to have such an effect – he received an ecstatic response from the public wherever he went. This was not only a popular vindication of his personal position; it also indicated that the Resistance was still very much a minority affair, just as it had been throughout the war. De Gaulle wanted order, the population wanted peace and quiet, while what exactly the Resistance wanted was not at all clear. It was not even certain that there was such a thing as 'the Resistance' any more. Although the war in Europe had nine months to run, and hundreds of thousands of people would die before it was over, the tide of battle had turned, and by mid-September the Germans were pushed back to the eastern corner of the country, behind a line from Metz to Mulhouse. With the job of driving out the Nazis done or about to be done, the Resistance began to fall apart. It appeared that nothing could hold back de Gaulle.

The French leader was faced with two remaining problems. Aero-industry plants in the Paris region were now affected by the movement for workers' control – at the Caudron factory, for example, a committee ensured not only that the workers had enough food to eat but also that the factory had enough supplies to continue making military aircraft.[26] This embryonic class conflict was easily extinguished when the government enacted some of the demands of the CNR Action Programme, nationalizing sectors of the economy and creating workers' committees in every company.[27] The final challenge was to consolidate government power in the regions. The Free French had always opposed Resistance plans to create local liberation committees, fearing they would lead to a breakdown of central authority. In the tumultuous events after D-Day, de Gaulle lost that struggle and there were now Resistance-led committees all over the country organizing food, water and electricity supplies, and keeping order through their armed police force, the Milices Patriotiques.[28] Furthermore, many of these local committees wanted to retain their power in the face of central authority.[29] With the support of the old Resistance leaders like Emmanuel d'Astier, who were suspicious of the Communist-inspired Milices and wanted to see central authority restored, the government declared that the Milices Patriotiques were 'private structures' and banned them from carrying arms.[30] There was opposition from sections of the Resistance – *Franc-Tireur* newspaper asked, 'Why disarm the people?' – but although the Communist Party organized a series of protests, they significantly did not withdraw Charles Tillon from the government. All this went over the heads of most people, who were simply not interested in who controlled the weapons. They wanted to know where the food, heat and light were coming from, and could not see a connection between the two issues.

The death knell of the Resistance came when the government announced that the newly appointed parliament, the Consultative Assembly, would include seats for the Resistance, in particular for all the members of the CNR.[31] With its leadership incorporated into national politics, the Resistance saw its local power disappear as elections were announced for municipal councils, while the Communist Party accepted the dissolution of the Milices Patriotiques. In return for this concession, de Gaulle amnestied Communist leader Maurice Thorez, who had spent the war in Moscow. In January 1945 the Communist Party's acceptance of the new situation in the country was made explicit when Thorez thundered the Communists' commitment to 'one army, one police, one administration'.[32] De Gaulle had won.

*

Popular images of the Liberation are dominated by the events that occurred in many towns in the immediate wake of Liberation, known in

France as *l'épuration* – the cleansing. A mixture of shameful score-settling and a desire to see justice done after years of oppression, the *épuration* is often reduced to its most macabre spectacle – the shaven heads of women who were deemed to have 'collaborated' with the enemy, often in a sexual sense. Although this punishment was first meted out under the Occupation, it was mainly inflicted during a few weeks in August and September 1944. Exactly how many victims there were is unknown; all over the country there were examples of women being systematically humiliated in public: their heads were shaved and often they were tarred and feathered or painted with swastikas. The baying crowds – frequently composed of people who had played no part whatsoever in the Resistance – expressed an atavistic desire for revenge that, in a spasm that was almost Freudian, focused on women. On the scale of the horrors committed during the Occupation, the *tondues* (shaven women) were small beer, but they revealed the complex mixture of joy, relief, guilt and self-loathing that characterized many people's attitude to the Liberation.[33]

More serious was the summary justice that was doled out to collaborators and *miliciens* – the *épuration sauvage* (wild cleansing). This period of the *épuration* has given rise to some truly fantastic claims. In 1961 the right-wing anti-Gaullist historian Robert Aron stated that between 40,000 and 100,000 summary executions were carried out in the name of the Resistance. Research by French and American historians has substantially reduced the figure – it is now accepted that there were around 9,000 'extra-judicial' executions by the Resistance, of which eighty per cent took place during the Occupation. Many of those executed before the Nazis fled were collaborationist gendarmes and policemen who were acting against the Resistance.[34]

Even these figures seem terribly high, viewed from a time of peace when many countries – including France – have abolished the death sentence. But it needs to be put into context. Around 100,000 *résistants* were killed during the Occupation: they were the true martyrs of the period. This was a time of war: those collaborators who faced the firing squad might have been carrying out terrible deeds only a few hours before. The justice system was in tatters – all the French judges except one had sworn allegiance to Pétain. *Miliciens* or Gestapo spies could not be handed over to the police with any degree of confidence that they would not escape. In these tragic circumstances, the Resistance did what it could – it set up its own system of makeshift courts. De Gaulle had done essentially the same thing when he oversaw the trial and execution of Pierre Pucheu in Algiers at the beginning of the year. It was a question of rough justice, or running the risk of no justice at all.

The dangers were evident enough – conviction on the basis of denunciations, with no supporting evidence, allowing for unscrupulous and mal-intentioned individuals to lethally pervert the process. Strictly speaking, this was nothing new. Throughout the Occupation, the Resistance had published the names of traitors – real or imagined – and had threatened them with death. Many local groups sent known collaborators paper coffins, describing their imminent fate. In some cases this was put into practice. The most spectacular example was the execution of Vichy's Minister of Propaganda, Philippe Henriot, who had crowed over the dead of the Glières maquis at the beginning of 1944. On 28 June a group of *résistants*, dressed as *miliciens*, marched into his ministry office in Vichy and shot him.[35]

However, there was a difference between what was acceptable – or even necessary – in times of war and Occupation, and what was appropriate when trying to replace the hated Vichy regime with something better. Many *résistants* were acutely aware of this, as SOE agent Francis Cammaerts recalled:

It was astonishing that the Liberation happened as it did. All you hear about is shaving women's heads, personal vendettas, and so on. But I had a lieutenant who came up to me and said, 'I've got 300 German prisoners. What do the international conventions say about how much food and exercise they are entitled to every day?' And those were Germans who had strung up Resisters and their families. There was something extraordinarily civilized about the Liberation.[36]

Writing at the end of August 1944, OSS agent Crane Brinton was equally positive about the situation, and put matters into a telling contemporary context:

> *Popular feeling toward the collaborators*: . . . What strikes me most is the
> evidence of all sorts of hatreds and antagonisms – the atmosphere is
> full of gossip and accusations. And yet nothing is done, certainly noth-
> ing violent in the good-old American lynching tradition. Certainly
> there have been isolated instances of violence . . . but even the vio-
> lence has been mostly haircutting.[37]

Five weeks later, having toured most of the north of the country,
Brinton seemed almost disappointed by what he found:

> I have seen no domestic violence at all; in fact, I haven't even seen
> a cropped collaboratrice. From Utah Beach to Paris the people,
> that great beast, has looked a very domesticated beast indeed . . .
> Obviously there were incidents in the Liberation, and obviously the
> FFI cut loose here and there. But the abiding impression of orderli-
> ness remains.[38]

The post-war period saw the *épuration* taken on to a higher level as there
were purges and prosecutions of those responsible for the worst crimes
of collaboration. Around 160,000 cases were opened against alleged
collaborators, of which nearly 120,000 eventually went to court. Of
these, nearly one quarter were found not guilty, while most of the
remaining 90,000 were either deprived of their civic rights (around
50,000) or were imprisoned (24,000). Among those sentenced to life
imprisonment was Gaveau, the traitor who had betrayed the Musée de
l'Homme group in 1941.[39] There were also death sentences, of which
800 were carried out. Another 800 executions apparently took place
under military justice.[40] Prominent among those sentenced to death
were the chief architects of collaboration and the vicious repression it
meted out: Laval and Darnand were executed in October 1945; Pétain
escaped the firing squad by virtue of de Gaulle's clemency and died in
prison in 1951.

Although many lower-ranking Vichy administrators were prosecuted
or at the very least sacked, some leading collaborators managed to slip
through the net. One of the most notorious examples was Maurice
Papon, who had been in charge of the police in Bordeaux, overseeing

the deportation of thousands of Jews. Papon wormed his way into the offices of the Commissaire de la République and carried on doing his job after the Liberation. He later went on to serve as Prefect of Paris, during which time the police massacred scores of protesting Algerians (1961) and charged a pro-Algerian independence demonstration at Charonne Métro, killing nine people (1962). Papon ended his career as Minister of the Budget under President Giscard d'Estaing.

In the months after the Liberation, the various tendencies in the Resistance drifted apart as the unity of purpose that had held them together evaporated. Frenay and d'Astier dreamed of founding a 'Resistance party' that would build on the comradeship and self-sacrifice they had experienced during the war. But their new party was soon sidelined by the Communist Party and by the Gaullists, each claiming the mantle of the Resistance, each rewriting history in their own image. The clearest example of the transformation of comradeship into outright political hatred was focused on Henri Frenay. In 1945 he was forced to resign as minister in charge of repatriating French POWs following a scurrilous Communist campaign that had the connivance of a Vichy POW leader who had gone over to the Resistance, François Mitterrand. Even de Gaulle was temporarily ushered from the political scene, when the voters rejected his proposal for a new constitution based on a strong presidency. In 1945 the British electorate turned their back on their war-time leader; in 1946 the French did the same.

And that was that. In 1945–6, as the first glimmers of the Cold War replaced the tension and excitement of clandestinity and Occupation, as hundreds of thousands of prisoners of war returned to their homes and the shattered survivors of the concentration camps attempted to make sense of life, the Resistance faded as a political force. In the decisive political events that shook France over the next few years, as Gaullists and Communists struggled to lead the country in conditions of political and economic crisis, the Resistance was nowhere to be seen.

\*

As it disappeared from the stage of history, the Resistance was transformed into a myth. Not in the sense of a fiction, but a myth in the sense of a story that gave meaning and coherence to life. Its existence provided the tens of millions of French men and women who were not *résistants* with a symbol of what they ought to have done, a way of indirectly taking credit for the struggle. Honour was preserved, and the French integrated another example of rebellion into their proud history. The anti-Nazi Resistance, as much as the anti-monarchical Revolution of 1789, came to define France's vision of itself.[41] In this respect the situation in France was unique. Not only was it the only Western European country to have a Resistance movement of any size, unlike the two other European examples of large scale resistance – Greece and Yugoslavia – there was no civil war to colour or confuse how the past was seen.[42]

With the passage of time, however, the details began to blur. A few years after the end of the war, there was a general amnesty for collaborationists, at which point the very existence of collaboration began to disappear from popular visions of the war. Even *résistants* participated in this process: in 1950, Rémy, the BCRA agent, claimed that ten years earlier France had needed both Pétain and de Gaulle, suggesting the two men were in some way complementary, and that Pétain was not a spineless collaborator.[43] The recognition that less than five per cent of the population had actively resisted the Nazis was soon replaced by the impression that everyone had resisted. Just as de Gaulle had hoped, Vichy was simply overlooked – a 'null and void' piece of history that could be forgotten in the name of national unity. In a way, Frenay and d'Astier got what they wanted – the Resistance became a permanent part of French society, but as a dead structural feature, not in the active, comradely form they impossibly wished to preserve. At the same time, leading Resistance publications like *Combat* or *Défense de la France* soon found survival difficult in a world in which they had actually to sell copies and make a profit. By the end of the 1940s both newspapers had been sold, and had lost much of their initial radicalism (in the case of *Défense de la France*, it had also lost its title, becoming *France-Soir*, which still exists as an evening tabloid). The Resistance had all but disappeared.

Emmanuel d'Astier had foreseen exactly this fate for the Resistance, in his song 'La Complainte des Partisans', written in 1943:

| | |
|---|---|
| Le vent souffle sur les tombes | The wind is blowing over the tombs |
| La liberté viendra | Freedom is coming |
| On nous oubliera | We will be forgotten |
| Nous rentrerons dans l'ombre | We will return to the shadows[44] |

As the years passed, many ex-*résistants* were horrified to discover that the new country they fought so hard to create was using the techniques of repression and torture that they imagined were the mark of the Nazis. It had begun at the same moment as the Nazis were finally defeated. On 8 May 1945, as war ended in Europe and there were wild celebrations all over the continent, demonstrations in support of Algerian independence took place in French North Africa. In the towns of Constantine and Guelma, French troops were ordered to fire on the crowd. Rioting erupted throughout the region, and the government launched a vicious attack on the population, using ground troops and air attacks, before finally ordering a cruiser to bombard the area. The number of Algerian dead was officially put at 1,500; a French enquiry later raised that figure to 15,000, while the independentists claimed that 45,000 people were killed.[45] Perhaps worse was to come nine years later, when the Algerian war of independence broke out and French soldiers carried out water-boarding, electrocutions and summary executions on their prisoners in a way that was no different from the Gestapo or their Milice henchmen. The moral high ground that had been gained by the sacrifice of the Resistance had been utterly lost.

Outraged, many *résistants* launched themselves into a campaign of opposition to the war, and in support of the Algerian people. As well as a courageous press campaign, spearheaded by Claude Bourdet, some militants set up an underground support network for the Algerian FLN (Front de Liberation Nationale), smuggling money to help the cause. The events of the Occupation were being replayed in French North Africa, with the French state once again on the wrong side.[46]

The Algerian war caused a profound political crisis in France, and in 1958 led to the return of de Gaulle, who immediately oversaw the creation of the kind of strong presidential regime he had dreamed of in 1946 but had been unable to obtain. De Gaulle's first task was to oversee the withdrawal from Algeria and to face down an armed struggle by the most reactionary forces within the French military, who were determined to stop what they considered to be a betrayal. Politics being a contradictory beast, those forces included former CNR leader Georges Bidault who set up a new 'CNR' to oppose de Gaulle.[47] Even *Combat* – still struggling on as a newspaper, and with the influence of Frenay and Bourdet long forgotten – was against the independence of Algeria.[48]

As the political views of those who had made up the Resistance spread through the whole spectrum of French politics, its nature became less clear and popular visions of the Resistance became increasingly distorted. The influence of the Communist Party (by far the largest single party in French politics until the end of the 1970s), the weight of de Gaulle's presidency (and of his war memoirs, published in the 1950s, which barely mentioned the Resistance), together with the ideological impact of the Cold War, all contributed to a polarization of views. For many people the Resistance soon became synonymous with the Communist Party and the FTP on the one hand and with the Free French on the other. Groups like Turma-Vengeance were soon forgotten, and eventually even Henri Frenay and Combat disappeared from the popular imagination. Although historians did their best to assemble oral histories of the Resistance, supported by an official Comité d'Histoire de la Deuxième Guerre Mondiale (Committee for the History of the Second World War), and eventually began to publish a series of learned books on the subject, the public was more influenced by the black-and-white mythology that was building up.[49] Commemorative postage stamps showing the faces of 'heroes of the Resistance' were issued, memorials were installed and local museums of resistance and deportation were created (although strikingly there was no national museum until the late 1980s). The rich detail of what the Resistance had been – and even who had been involved – gradually faded.

As part of this process, radical Resistance action was slowly transformed into a conservative symbol of the French state, through a series of official commemorations that presented a subtly selective view of the period. This culminated in the use of Jean Moulin to represent the whole of the Resistance. Forgotten in the post-war years, Moulin was metaphorically resurrected in December 1964, when his ashes were buried in a moving state ceremony at the Panthéon. André Malraux, who was Minister of Culture and had played a minor role in the final stages of the Resistance, made a speech at the Panthéon that has entered French history.[50] The oration turned into a shamanic invocation of the spirit of the Resistance as Malraux, in a voice trembling with emotion and cracked by decades of tobacco abuse, described the terrible sacrifice made by Moulin and 'the people of the shadows'.

In closing, Malraux called on French youth to be inspired by Moulin's devotion to his country, a call that was subsequently reinforced by the simple expedient of naming dozens of schools after him. From a purely functional point of view, Moulin was an ideal choice: a dead civil servant with no open political affiliations, he could be embraced by all as the unifier of the Resistance, even if his action had been the focus of ferocious struggles at the time. Moulin was unknown to the general public – indeed, in the immediate period after the war, even authoritative accounts of the Resistance put him very much in a subsidiary role behind Brossolette, who was generally seen as being the most significant of the many Resistance martyrs.[51] But Brossolette was both a socialist and a man whose impact on the Resistance had at times been divisive – even if this was also true of Moulin, his decisive achievement was the unification of the Resistance and the creation of the CNR.

After the publication of de Gaulle's war memoirs in the 1950s, which, to the extent they dealt with the Resistance, emphasized Moulin's work and barely mentioned Brossolette, Moulin began to take centre stage.[52] He symbolized the Resistance because he served de Gaulle and helped to unify warring tendencies – behind his elevation there was a subliminal message of order and social peace. This view was shared on both sides of the political spectrum – when the socialist François Mitterrand became President in 1981, his first public act was to lay a red rose on Moulin's tomb.[53] Today, Moulin has become the face of the Resistance, known to millions. The complexities of a human being fighting under the most difficult circumstances, a man who was loathed by many of those who worked with him, have disappeared. Instead, the image of a real man with contradictory and sometimes mysterious motives has been blurred into the icon of a kind of national saint.

As the Resistance was incorporated into the ideology of the French state, there was an inevitable tendency for a new generation to attack those symbols of power. This became particularly strong after May 1968, when young people rejected de Gaulle's paternalistic and authoritarian view of France and rebelled against him, hurtfully identifying his CRS riot police with the Nazi Occupation through the chant 'CRS-SS'.[54] De Gaulle resigned in 1969 and died in 1970, shortly before his eightieth birthday. His death, coupled with the sweeping changes in French society that occurred after May 1968, opened the road to a re-examination of the war period. In 1971, at a time when the Resistance was the subject of comical French films and popular views of the war were literally descending into farce, the film-maker Marcel Ophüls shocked audiences with his four-and-a-half-hour documentary *The Sorrow and the Pity*, which interviewed *résistants* and ordinary people about the Occupation and explored the reality of French collaboration. Although Ophüls' film clearly showed the courage and sacrifice of the Resistance, its main impact came through its acceptance that French people had made choices during the occupation, and that some had chosen collaboration.[55] Appearing at the same time as the first history of Vichy, written by US historian Robert Paxton, *The Sorrow and the Pity* helped re-open the wounds that had been plastered over twenty-five years earlier.

Throughout this period, the Communist Party and the Gaullists struggled over the rights to the Resistance franchise, as ageing *résistants* and party political historians argued over who had done what and when. Much of this history was based on eyewitness interpretations that should have been concordant but which often contradicted each other. This was partly due to the inevitable unreliability of memory, but also because the political issues underlying the view of each *résistant* inevitably coloured what and how they remembered.[56] These bitter squabbles faded as old *résistants* died and the Communists gradually lost their stranglehold on French intellectual and cultural life. One of the positive outcomes of these disputes was a substantial heritage in the form of a series of books and articles, including invaluable accounts of how various parts of the country were liberated. Strikingly, these were generally still written by the *résistants* themselves, and consisted of an uneasy combination of memoirs and historical self-justification. Finally, although there was initially no solid university tradition of academic study of the Resistance, that began to change in the 1970s.

The appearance of detailed and more nuanced accounts of the Resistance irritated some *résistants* but satisfied others. Pascal Copeau was one of those who welcomed the way in which historians stepped away from the heroic narratives that had characterized popular views of the Resistance in the 1950s and 1960s, revealing a reality that was richer and more intricate than many people had thought. But even Copeau was concerned that the political heart of the Resistance should not suffer from this re-examination:

> It would do no harm to the comrades who were sacrificed if history was to say who was responsible for various false strategies. But we should be careful of going on to destroy all myths. The nature and strength of the Resistance are mythical. But myths, after all, can be action. Through appropriate and well-chosen actions, terrorism seeks literally to bluff the enemy by raising the spectre of a threat that is far greater than that which would exist if the two forces were to meet in open battle. It would perhaps be better to leave some legends intact, and not run the risk of distorting a complex truth.[57]

In other words, while resisting was relatively straightforward (this was easy for Copeau to say), its consequences were complex and over the years had taken on important mythical qualities. These should be left unscathed, argued Copeau.

Copeau's pleas fell on deaf ears. The long period of soul-searching was expressed in a dark and cynical trend in French culture that openly rejected the Resistance myths. Louis Malle's 1973 film *Lacombe Lucien* dealt with the amoral choices of a young *milicien*, while in the 1980s a series of French thrillers used fiction to reveal the truth behind the image that some politicians had so carefully cultivated and which the courts still protected. For example, Didier Daeninckx's *Murder in Memoriam* (1984, translated in 1992) outlined Maurice Papon's involvement in the deportation of Jews during the war and in the massacre of Algerians in Paris in 1961, while Thierry Jonquet's *Du passé faisons table rase* (1982) recounted how an ordinary French worker who had cheerfully volunteered to work in a Messerschmitt aero factory in 1942 ended up as leader of the French Communist Party, his past an embarrassing secret. This was exactly what happened to Georges Marchais, leader of the Communist Party from 1972 to 1994 and a major figure in French politics of the period, who persistently pretended that he had been conscripted as part of STO in order to preserve his Party's Resistance myths.

The widespread assumption that nothing was as it seemed gathered strength in the 1990s when Frenay's allegation that Moulin was 'the Communist Party's man', first made in a letter published by Passy in 1950 and then again in a book by Frenay that appeared in 1977, resurfaced in a series of books that suggested the founder of the CNR had been a Soviet agent.[58] Moulin's new-found status as the sole known representative of the Resistance made him an even more attractive target for writers and for a public that seemed to have an endless appetite for books and magazine articles that claimed to have discovered new 'revelations' about the past, even when the evidence was tenuous or even non-existent. This corrosive tendency was given further impetus when, shortly before leaving office, President François Mitterrand revealed quite how close he had been to Pétain and the Vichy regime before he went over to the Resistance, showing the ambiguity of his own personal story and inadvertently highlighting the courage and clarity of those *résistants* who did not make the same mistakes.[59]

The fashion for debunking myths reached its height in 1997 when Raymond Aubrac was accused of working for Klaus Barbie, with the knowledge of his wife, Lucie – probably the most widely known living *résistant*. The Aubracs successfully sued the author of these allegations, but in an attempt to definitively clear their names, they organized a 'round-table discussion' with leading historians, which was published in the daily newspaper *Libération*.[60] The result was not what they had hoped for: the confrontation turned into a police-style interrogation and left the reader extremely uneasy – although the group of historians rejected the allegations, they were not satisfied by the Aubracs' inability to explain all the detail of events forty-five years earlier, nor did the academics understand why the Aubracs' stories had not been precisely identical every time they told them in the intervening decades.[61] What became known as 'the Aubrac affair' has in turn been studied in terms of what it revealed about French society, the idea of a 'court of history' and the malleability of memories.[62]

The 'case' against the Aubracs was largely based on the alleged testimony of Barbie, who in 1983 had finally been arrested in Bolivia, where he had been working for the CIA, and brought back to France for trial. He was eventually sentenced to life imprisonment in 1987 and died in prison four years later. The Barbie trial, which was filmed in its totality and is regularly used as an educational tool in French schools, was the most dramatic of a series of prosecutions that were seen as a way of finally exorcizing the ghosts of collaboration. In 1998, fourteen years after he had been convicted in the pages of Didier Daeninckx's novel, Maurice Papon was finally found guilty of overseeing the deportation of Jews from Bordeaux. (He was never tried for his role in the 1961 massacre of Algerians in Paris.) Four years earlier, René Bousquet was accused of involvement in the round-up of Jews in Paris and Marseilles (he was murdered by a mentally ill man before his trial began), while in 1994 Paul Touvier, a notorious leader of the Milice who worked with Barbie and had been amnestied by President Pompidou in 1972, was finally convicted for his crimes against the Resistance.[63]

There was some kind of official closure to the troubled period of collaboration when, in 1995, recently-elected President Jacques Chirac went to the site of the Vel' d'Hiv round-up and publicly apologized for the role of the Parisian police in the persecution of the Jews. This was a radical break with the Gaullist view of Vichy as 'null and void', as it accepted that the collaborationist state was part of the history of France. Chirac was able to make this gesture, which was widely applauded, precisely because he had not been part of the Resistance, and because the passionate debates it aroused had begun to fade.[64]

*

Despite these changes, the French remain culturally obsessed with the war. Barely a month goes by without French television broadcasting a new play or documentary dealing with the Occupation, which continues to be a favoured period in novels, cinema and comics. The Resistance and its evil twin, collaboration, are still very much alive in France. This is hardly surprising: the events of 1940 to 1944 raise some of the most important human characteristics – courage, self-sacrifice, betrayal and struggle. To explore these questions, the world-weary visions of the 1970s and 1980s that supplanted the heroic accounts of the post-war world have in turn been replaced by measured, human descriptions of how people of all kinds resisted – or not – in different ways. In a world in which we have lost our taste for uncomplicated heroes, these new representations of the Resistance speak more clearly to contemporary views. This version of the Resistance is not a Gaullist myth to be in awe of or to be sneered at, but a genuine piece of history that resonates down to the present day.

In recent years long-forgotten figures of the Resistance, like Frenay, Brossolette or Berty Albrecht, have been rediscovered, and their contributions acknowledged through the media and, in the case of Frenay, the naming of a Parisian square after him.[65] Through the indefatigable work of Lucie Aubrac, who continued to visit schools and give interviews until her death in 2008, new generations have been introduced to the human reality of the Resistance. Academic and popular historians have continued to produce re-examinations of what we thought we knew[66] and novel investigations of hitherto unexplored parts of the period, such as the Musée de l'Homme group, the Carte affair or the activities of the Bataillons de la Jeunesse.[67] As a key part of twentieth-century French history, the study of the Resistance is very much alive.

Despite the very French nature of the Resistance, it soon became a powerful symbol all around the world. In the 1950s and 1960s films, books and then TV in Britain and America told and retold the story, often with a local spin. British culture initially tended to emphasize the role of SOE agents and RAF pilots – for example, in the feature film *Carve Her Name with Pride* (1958) or the TV drama series *Moonstrike* (1963) and *Secret Army* (1977), before eventually parodying such programmes, in the shape of the ludicrous television comedy *'Allo 'Allo*. In the USA science fiction programmes such as *Star Trek* or films such as *Star Wars* projected the Resistance into outer space, portraying groups of brave rebels fighting against evil, thereby fusing the Resistance with the American national myth, the rebellion against the British.[68]

But the Resistance is too serious a moment in humanity's history to be left to belly-laughs or to a fantasy world of wookies and starships. Its lessons are for the here and now. Over sixty years later, the Resistance still retains its power to inspire. These were ordinary people who made extraordinary sacrifices, and many of them paid a terrible price. They fought for a variety of reasons, with different means. But the main point was that they did fight, they did not accept what appeared to be inevitable. And in so doing they discovered things about themselves.

In the 1950s, when the collaborationists were being amnestied and the whole meaning of the Resistance was being forgotten, Jean Cassou, founder of the Musée de l'Homme group and a Resistance leader in Toulouse, tried to explain what exactly the Resistance was. His words[69] cast a powerful light on the way in which the Resistance was experienced by those brave men and women:

> For each *résistant* the Resistance was a way of living, a style of life, a life that we invented. It lives in our memory as a unique period, different from all others, unsayable, like a dream. We see ourselves, naked and free, a strange and unknowable version of ourselves, one of those people that you can never find again. That version existed only because of the unique and terrible conditions, things that have since disappeared, become ghosts, or simply died. If each of us who went through that experience had to define it, we would give it a surprising name that we would not give to the ordinary aspects of our lives. We would say the word quietly, to ourselves. Some would say 'adventure'. I would call that moment of my life 'happiness'.

# Glossary

**2nd DB** – 2nd Division Blindée. Free French armoured division commanded by General Leclerc.

ALLIANCE – intelligence circuit led by Marie-Madeleine Fourcade and run by MI6.

**Armée Secrète (Secret Army)** – umbrella term for the armed groups of the main Resistance organizations (the MUR).

**BCRA (Bureau Central de Renseignements et d'Action)** – Free French intelligence service. Had several different titles.

**Ceux de la Libération** – small Resistance group in the northern zone.

**Ceux de la Résistance** – small Resistance group in the northern zone.

**CFLN (Comité Français de Libération Nationale)** – De Gaulle's organization, first in London, then in Algiers.

**CGE (Comité Général d'Études)** – Resistance think tank.

**CGT (Conféderation Générale du Travail)** – Trade union federation.

**Chantiers de la Jeunesse** – Vichy labour camps for youth.

**Circuit** – a group of intelligence or SOE agents.

**CND (Confrérie Notre-Dame)** – BCRA intelligence circuit set up by Rémy.

**CNR (Conseil National de la Résistance)** – Leadership of the Resistance, set up by Jean Moulin in May 1943.

**COMAC (Comité d'Action Militaire)** – Military leadership of the Resistance, set up by the CNR in 1944.

*Combat* – newspaper published by Henri Frenay's organization.

**Combat** – the most widely-used name for the Resistance organization set up by Henri Frenay, based on the name of the newspaper. The organization (like the newspaper) went through several name changes.

**Comité Allemagne Libre pour l'Ouest (CALPO)** – Group set up by German Communist exiles to work in Nazi Germany.

**Comité Parisien de Libération** – Parisian liberation committee, set up in spring 1944.

**Comités de la Libération** – local liberation committees, set up by the Resistance to act as local government during the Liberation.

**Comités Départementaux de la Libération** – departmental liberation committees, set up by the Free French to take over after the collapse of Vichy.

**Commissaire de la République** – representative of the Free French inside France. A kind of Resistance Prefect.

*Défense de la France* – mass-circulation Resistance newspaper.

**Deuxième Bureau** – French Intelligence.

**DM (Délégués Militaires)** – Liaison officers sent by BCRA to work with the Resistance in 1944.

**DRAGOON** – code name for Allied landings on French Mediterranean coast, August 1944. Also known as ANVIL.

**Escape line** – a group that helped Allied servicemen evade arrest in Occupied Europe and return to Britain.

**FFI (Forces Françaises de l'Intérieur)** – Umbrella title for all armed forces inside France, from 1944.

**FN (Front National)** – Broad organization set up by Communists in 1941–2 to group opposition to the Occupation.

**Forbidden Zone** – areas of Occupied France along Atlantic coast or in the far north of France that non-residents could visit only with a special pass.

**Franc-Tireur** – Lyons-based left-wing Resistance group and newspaper of the same name.

**FTP (Francs Tireurs et Partisans)** – Communist-led armed Resistance group.

**GMR (Gardes Mobiles de Réserve)** – Vichy reserve police force. Hated by the Resistance.

**Groupes Francs** – Resistance hit squads.

*Libération* – Title of separate newspapers published by Libération-Nord and by Libération-Sud.

**Libération-Nord** – Resistance group set up in northern zone by Christian Pineau.

**Libération-Sud** – Resistance group set up in southern zone by Emmanuel d'Astier de la Vigerie.

**Luftwaffe** – German air force.

**Maquis** – Resistance fighters in the hills.

**MI5** – British counter-intelligence service.

**MI6** – British intelligence service.

**MI9** – British organization for exfiltrating agents and members of the Allied armed forces from Occupied Europe.

**Milice** – ultra-violent and anti-Semitic armed group created by Vichy.

**Milices Patriotiques** – acted as police force after the Liberation. Set up on Communist initiative. Also called Gardes Patriotiques or Civiques.

**MLN (Mouvement de Libération Nationale)** – Frenay's Resistance group; published *Combat.*

**MOI (Main d'Oeuvre Immigrée)** – Communist-led armed Resistance group composed of immigrants and Jews.

**MUR (Mouvements Unis de la Résistance)** – Umbrella title for Resistance groups in southern zone after 1943.

**Musée de l'Homme** – early Resistance group, based in the Paris museum of the same name, led by Boris Vildé.

**NAP (Noyautage des Administrations Publiques)** – Resistance organization of public sector workers and of civil servants.

**Northern zone** – area of France to the north of the demarcation line. Synonymous with 'Occupied Zone'.

**OCM (Organisation Civile et Militaire)** – Right-wing Resistance organization based in northern zone.

**OSE (Oeuvre de Secours aux Enfants)** – Jewish children's charity.

**ORA (Organisation de Résistance de l'Armée)** – Resistance group based on Vichy army.

**OS (Organisation Spéciale)** – Communist Party armed group.

**OSS (Office of Strategic Services)** – US intelligence services; forerunner of the CIA.

OVERLORD – Code name for D-Day landings in Normandy, June 1944.

**OVRA** – Italian secret service.

**PCF (Parti Communiste Français)** – Communist Party.

**Prefect** – French state administrator of a département.

**Préfecture de Police** – police headquarters in Paris, opposite Notre-Dame cathedral.

*Réfractaires* – young men who refused to go on STO.

**SHAEF (Supreme Headquarters, Allied Expeditionary Force)** – General Eisenhower's headquarters, in charge of all matters relating to OVERLORD.

**Sicherheitsdienst (SD)** – SS intelligence service.

**SOE (Special Operations Executive)** – British military and intelligence organization set up in 1940, which used unorthodox methods. Its circuits in France were run by three sections: F (SOE only), RF (linked to the Resistance) and D/F (escape lines).

**Southern zone** – area of France to the south of the demarcation line. Synonymous with 'Non-Occupied Zone' or (more rarely) 'Free Zone'.

**STO (Servive du Travail Obligatoire)** – Obligatory labour conscription imposed by Vichy in 1943.

TORCH – Code name for Allied invasion of North Africa in autumn 1942.

**TR (Travaux Ruraux)** – Clandestine group in Vichy Intelligence devoted to hunting down Nazi spies in Vichy France. Led by Paul Paillole.

**TA (Travail Allemand)** – Communist Party Resistance group producing propaganda for German rank-and-file soldiers.

**Turma-Vengeance** – Resistance group in northern zone. Specialized in armed actions and intelligence work.

**UGIF (Union Générale des Israélites de France)** – Organization of French Jews set up by Vichy.

**USC (Unitarian Service Committee)** – US Protestant charity used as cover for various operations to support the Resistance.

**Valmy (détachement)** – Communist Party hit squad that punished Party 'traitors'. No connection with the newspaper of the same name.

*Valmy* **(newspaper)** – Parisian Resistance paper edited first by Paulin Bertrand ('Paul Simon'), then by Raymond Burgard. No connection with Communist Party group of the same name.

# What Happened to Them?

## BRIEF BIOGRAPHICAL INFORMATION ON THOSE WHO SURVIVED THE WAR

**Marcel Abraham** worked for UNESCO and the French education ministry. Died in 1955.

**Philip André** continued to be an active socialist politician. Died in 1970.

**Emmanuel d'Astier** de la Vigerie was a deputy until 1958, was close to the Communist Party. Wrote a number of docu-fiction books about the Resistance. Died in 1969.

**Lucie Aubrac** went back to teaching, later worked tirelessly to explain the events of the Occupation. For many French children she was the living face of the Resistance. Her memoirs were turned into a successful feature film (1997), *Lucie Aubrac*. Died in 2008.

**Raymond Aubrac** directed the urban renewal programme in France in 1950s, then worked for UNO in Rome.

**Claude Aveline** continued writing novels, detective stories and poetry until his death in 1991.

**René Balbaud** became a journalist specializing in Africa. He died in the 1990s.

**Jacques Baumel** was a lifelong member of the Gaullist movement; he was also a French mayor, deputy and senator. He published his memoirs in 1999 and died in 2006.

**Pierre de Bénouville** was a Gaullist Deputy for Paris. He died in 2001.

**Georges Bidault** was a right-wing politician, opposed to Algerian independence. He was in contact with ultra-right OAS terrorists, in exile 1962 to 1968. He died in 1983.

**Maxime Blocq-Mascart** became a company director, and opposed de Gaulle over Algerian independence. He died in 1965.

**Claude Hettier de Boislambert** was a deputy in the 1950s, then became ambassador to Senegal. He died in 1986.

**Emile Bollaert** returned from the camps and became high commissioner for Indo-China in 1947, then a company director. He died in 1978.

**Micheline Bood** became a writer and journalist.

**Claude Bouchinet-Serreulles** worked at UNO and the OECD, before becoming a company director. He died in 2000.

**Claude Bourdet** was a journalist who was deeply opposed to the use of torture in Algeria. He continued as a left-wing activist, and died in 1996.

**Howard L. Brooks** continued to do missionary work around the world.

**Gilbert Brustlein** returned from Britain after the war. Acted as rank-and-file member of the Communist Party before finally resigning in 1952.

**André Calvès** fought as a French soldier in Indo-China. Maintained his Trotskyist beliefs until his death in 1996.

**Jean Cassou** recovered from his wounds during the Liberation of Toulouse. Became conservator of the Musée National d'Art Moderne in Paris. Continued to write poetry. Died in 1986.

**Jacques Chaban-Delmas** was a loyal Gaullist, became mayor of Bordeaux and was Prime Minister of France from 1969 to 1972. He died in 2000.

**Gilberte Champion** survived the camps, and was still alive in 2008.

**Maurice Chevance** became a socialist deputy for French Guinea, and maintained commercial and political interest in Africa. Supported de Gaulle's return to power in 1958. Died in 1996.

**Pascal Copeau** had a brief political career, then turned to journalism in Africa and in Burgundy. Died in 1982.

**Daniel Cordier** had a long career as an art dealer, before deciding to write the biography of Jean Moulin, transforming himself into a historian.

**René Creston** continued his ethnological research, focusing on his native Brittany. Died in 1964.

**André Dewavrin ('Passy')** continued as French spymaster but was soon forced to resign because of a financial scandal. Became a businessman. Died in 1998.

**Louis Dolivet** became a Hollywood film producer; worked with Orson Welles and Jacques Tati. Died in 1989.

**Victor 'Vic' Dupont** returned to medicine. Was a witness at the Nuremberg trials. Died in 1976.

**Yves Farge** had a brief period as a deputy – he was close to the Communist Party – then became a journalist. Died in 1953 in a car accident in Georgia.

**Marie-Madeleine Fourcade** continued her intelligence activities in Nazi Germany. After the war became a Gaullist deputy. Died in 1989.

**Henri Frenay** became disillusioned with politics, but remained a convinced European; went into business. Died in 1988.

**Varian Fry** returned to academia. Died in 1967.

**André Girard ('Carte')** pursued a successful career in the United States until his death in 1968. Remained ferociously hostile to de Gaulle.

**Henri Giraud** was elected as a deputy in 1946. Died in 1949.

**Fernand Grenier** remained a leading member of the Communist Party and deputy. He was an unrepentant Stalinist right up until his death in 1992.

**Jean Guéhenno** became a famous French writer; elected to the Académie Française. Died in 1978.

**Georges Guingouin** became mayor of Limoges, and was thrown into jail on a trumped-up charge before being acquitted. Returned to teaching. Left the Communist Party in 1952. Died in 2005.

**Léo Hamon** was elected as a left-wing Gaullist deputy and then senator; also worked as a university professor. Died in 1993.

**Boris Holban** became a general in the Romanian army before returning to France in 1986.

**Agnès Humbert** was liberated from the camps by the Americans, she then participated in the Nazi hunts in Germany. Returned to France and died in 1963.

**Andrée de Jongh** went to work in leprosy camps in Africa until she became too frail. Died in 2007.

**Arthur Koestler** served in the British army then, after the war, turned back to writing and became a renowned author. Committed suicide in 1983.

**Maurice Kriegel-Valrimont** was a Communist leader until 1961, when he was expelled from the Party. Died in 2006.

**General Philippe Leclerc** was killed in an air crash in 1947.

**Sylvette Leleu** survived the camps, was still alive in the 1970s.

**Jean-Pierre Levy** became a civil servant. Died in 1996.

**Liliane Lévy-Osbert** survived the camps. Published her memoirs in 1995.

**Simone Martin-Chauffier** became a writer and translator. Died in 1975.

**Daniel Mayer** became Minister of Labour and then of Social Security (1946 to 1949). Continued to be an active socialist and was President of the Ligue des Droits de l'Homme. Died in 1996.

**François de Menthon** was a French prosecutor at the Nuremberg trials. He subsequently became a mayor and returned to university teaching. Died in 1984.

**Léon Morandat** was a left-wing Gaullist, who became a company director, and was briefly Secretary of State for Social Affairs in 1968. Died in 1972.

**Maroussia Naïtchenko** published her memoirs in 2003.

**Yvonne Oddon** was freed from Ravensbrück by the Red Cross before the end of the war. Subsequently worked for UNESCO around the world. Died in 1982.

**Alexandre Parodi** became a career diplomat. Died in 1979.

**Paul Paillole** became mayor of his Parisian suburb. Died in 2002.

**Bernard Pierquin** continued to work as a physician. Published his diary in 1983.

**Christian Pineau** was a deputy and a minister during the Fourth Republic. Profoundly hostile to the Gaullist Fifth Republic. Became a full-time writer in 1971. Died in 1995.

**Edgar Pisani** became a left-wing Gaullist, a deputy and a senator. Close to Jacques Chirac, he helped set up the Institut du Monde Arabe in Paris. Still alive in 2008.

**Adam Rayski** went to his native Poland to work as a publisher for the Polish Communist Party. Returned to France in 1957 and broke with the Communist Party. Died in 2008.

**Harry Rée** became a headmaster, then Professor of Educational Studies at York University. He died in 1991.

**Gilbert Renault ('Rémy')** supported calls for the rehabilitation of Pétain in the 1950s. Became a full-time writer. Died in 1984.

**Henri Romans-Petit** died in 1980.

**Henri Rol-Tanguy** became a soldier, but was suspected because of his Communist beliefs. Retired in 1962. He died in 2002.

**François Rouan** was a career soldier in the 1950s. Died in the 1990s.

**Edwige de Saint-Wexel** was still alive in the 1970s.

**Jean Texcier** became a journalist and socialist activist. He died in 1957.

**Germaine Tillion** was freed from Ravensbrück by the Red Cross before the end of the war. Studied the Nazi concentration camps and the experience of resistance and deportation. Denounced torture in Algeria. Died in 2008.

**Charles Tillon** left government in 1946. He was expelled from the Communist Party in 1952, then reinstated in 1957 and was expelled again in 1970 after opposing the invasion of Czechoslovakia. Died in 1993.

**Hugh Verity** continued to serve in the RAF until 1965. He died in 2001.

**André Weil-Curiel** returned to his law practice. Died in 1988.

**François Wetterwald** returned to medicine. Died in 1993.

**Pearl Witherington** returned to the UK and was awarded a civil MBE for her work with the SOE. Sent it back saying she deserved the military version. She died in 2008.

**'Tommy' Yeo-Thomas** escaped from Buchenwald, then after the war became Paris representative of the Federation of British Industries. Died in 1964.

# Acknowledgements

I have been waiting a long time to write this book. My first piece of extended writing (written when I was aged six and a half) was a play about the Resistance, set in Dijon. There was no family tradition involved – I'm not related to Richard Cobb, the historian of France, although in a bizarre coincidence he did have a son called Matthew, and my father was called Richard. I finally got my chance through the boldness of my then editor at Simon & Schuster, Andrew Gordon, who looked as if he'd been poked with a cattle prod when I mentioned the subject. As we developed the idea, he helped me keep my focus by saying he wanted 'visceral stories of human experience red in tooth and claw rather than a history of the socio-political foundations of the Fourth Republic'. I have done my best to follow his advice. Peter Tallack, my agent, provided invaluable help during the long process of planning the book, while my editor, Mike Jones, who took over from Andrew Gordon, was extremely supportive and enthusiastic from the moment we first met.

My thanks go to the staff at the John Rylands University Library of Manchester, the UK National Archives, the US National Archives and Record Administration, Chatham House (London), the Musée National de l'Ordre de la Libération, the Musée National de la Résistance et la Déportation and the Musées de la Résistance et de la Déportation in Toulouse and in Castellane. A number of people provided me with information, documents and support, for which I am extremely thankful: Fanny Balbaud, Julien Blanc, Marc Chantran, James Dorrian, Sebastien Laurent, Rod Kedward, Frédéric Ghesquier-Krajewski, Paul Mason, Juliette Pattinson and Victor Vacquier. Barbara Mellor graciously agreed to the use of quotations from her excellent translation of Agnès Humbert's memoir.

Professor Martin Alexander read Chapter 1 and saved me from many military and historical howlers; Professor Richard Vinen and Professor Rod Kedward both read the whole book and made a number of highly pertinent suggestions. I am extremely grateful to all three of them for their generosity and kindness. Christina Purcell's habitually precise comments helped me keep my focus, while my good friend Professor Jerry Coyne cast a layman's eye over the whole manuscript, kindly praising the good bits, rolling his eyes at unclear antecedents and rightly insisting I cut repeated references to glorious blue skies. Finally, my comrade Keith Hassell helped me bring out the underlying message, while Rory Scarfe at Simon & Schuster was incredibly patient as I continually tinkered with the manuscript and the proofs. As usual in such cases, I alone am responsible for the mistakes that remain.

The Society of Authors provided me with a generous grant to research the background to the book, for which I am extremely grateful. The most important support and understanding have come from my family – Tina, Lauren and Evie. All three of you have had to put up with far too much distraction and grumpiness. My love and thanks, and I promise I won't do it again. For a while, at least.

# Note on Translations and Terminology

Most of the translations are by myself. I have made two systematic changes to both quotations and descriptions. First, the Gaullist forces outside France went through several different name changes, but for the sake of simplicity I have used their first, widely known English title – the 'Free French' (see Chapter 2 for a discussion of the implications of this translation). Second, the French – then as now – generally refer to 'les Anglais' when they really mean 'les Britanniques'. Given the modern recognition of the importance of the other components of the United Kingdom, I have translated 'les Anglais' as 'the British'.

# Further Reading

There are no popular English books on the history of the Resistance that are in print, but David Schoenbrun's excellent *Soldiers of the Night* and John F. Sweets' more academic *The Politics of Resistance in France, 1940–1944* can both still be picked up from second-hand booksellers. The best accompaniment to the present book in terms of the overall context is Rod Kedward's *La Vie en Bleu: France and the French since 1900*.

There are a number of extremely well-written detailed studies of the period, each of which touches on the Resistance in a different way, all them highly recommended: *The French at War 1934–1944* by Nicholas Atkin, *SOE in France* by M. R. D. Foot, *Marianne in Chains* by Robert Gildea, *France: The Dark Years 1940–1944* by Julian Jackson, *Resistance in Vichy France* and *In Search of the Maquis* by Rod Kedward, *Occupation* by Ian Ousby and *The Unfree French* by Richard Vinen. Barbara Mellor's translation of Agnès Humbert's book *Résistance: Memoirs of Occupied France* is an invaluable and moving introduction to the early years of the Resistance and includes a number of contemporary documents, as well as an Afterword by French historian Julien Blanc.

For those who can read French, there are over 3000 books on the Resistance to choose from. Daniel Cordier's amazingly detailed four-volume study of Jean Moulin is incredibly rich, but the single best source is the *Dictionnaire Historique de la Résistance*, edited by François Marcot, Bruno Leroux and Christine Levisse-Touzé (2006), which summarizes the very best writing on the subject. I would have been lost without it.

# Bibliography

## ARCHIVES

BDIC Bibliothèque de documentation internationale contemporaine, Nanterre, France.
CH Chatham House, London.
NA National Archives, Kew, England.
NARA National Archives and Record Administration, USA.

## OTHER MEDIA

**CD:**
*11 novembre 1940: Témoignages & Archives historiques* (CD: Frémaux & Associés).
**CD-ROM:**
*La Résistance en Corse* (CD-ROM: AERI).
*La Résistance en Île-de-France* (CD-ROM: AERI).
*La Résistance en Lozère* (CD-ROM: AERI).
**DVD:**
*Eté 44: La Libération* (Patrick Rotman, 2004) (DVD: France Télévisions).
*Héros de la résistance: 3 films de Jorge Amat* (DVD: Doriane Films).
*La Bataille du rail* (René Clément, 1946) (DVD: Sony Music).
*La Résistance* (Christophe Nick, Felix Olivier & Patricia Bodet, 2008) (DVD: France Télévisions).
*Mai 40: Les 30 jours du désastre* (Jean-François Delassus & Yves Le Maner, 2004) (DVD: Éditions Montparnasse).
*The Sorrow and the Pity (Le Chagrin et la Pitié)* (Marcel Ophüls, 1969) (DVD: Arrow Films).

## PRINTED SOURCES

150 combattants et témoins (1975), *Maquis de Corrèze* (Paris: Editions sociales).
Ageron, Charles-Robert (1984), 'Les troubles du nord-constantinois en mai 1945: Une tentative insurrectionnelle?', *Vingtième Siècle. Revue d'histoire* 4:23–38.

Aglan, Alya (1994), *Mémoires résistants: Histoire du réseau Jade-Fitzroy 1940–1944* (Paris: Éditions du Cerf).

Aglan, Alya (2000), 'Christian Pineau et Jean Moulin' in Jean-Pierre Azema (ed.) *Jean Moulin face à l'histoire* (Paris: Flammarion) pp. 139–52.

Aglan, Alya (2006), *La Résistance sacrifiée – Histoire du mouvement 'Libération-Nord'* (Paris: Flammarion).

Aglan, Alya (2007), 'Comment meurent les réseaux' in Bernard Garnier, Jean-Luc Leleu & Jean Quellien (eds), *La Répression en France 1940–1945* (Seconde Guerre Mondiale: 7) (Caen: Centre de Recherche d'Histoire Quantitative) pp. 227–36.

Ajchenbaum, Yves-Marc (1994), *À la vie à la mort: Histoire du journal COMBAT 1941–1974* (Paris: Le Monde-Éditions).

Alexander, Martin S. (1990), 'The Fall of France, 1940', *Journal of Strategic Studies* 13:10–44.

Alexander, Martin S. (1997), '"No taste for the fight?": French combat performance in 1940 and the politics of the fall of France' in Paul Addison and Angus Calder (eds), *Time to Kill: The Soldier's Experience of War in the West 1939–1945* (London: Pimlico) pp. 161–76.

Alexander, Martin S. (2007), 'After Dunkirk: The French Army's performance against "Case Red", 25 May to 25 June 1940', *War in History* 14:219–64.

Amouroux, Henri (1964), *Le 18 juin 1940* (Paris: Fayard).

ANACR (2005), *1940–1945 La Résistance dans le 19e arrondissement de Paris* (Pantin: Le Temps des cerises).

Andrieu, Claire (2006), 'Le programme du CNR: programme de la Résistance et le projet d'une époque' in Bernard Garnier, Jean-Luc Leleu, Jean Quellien & Anne Simonin (eds), *Pourquoi resister? Résister pour quoi faire?* (Seconde Guerre mondiale: 6) (Caen: Centre de Recherche d'Histoire Quantitative) pp. 103–9.

Andrieu, Claire; Bourgeard, Christian; Douzou, Laurent; Frank, Robert; Guillon, Jean-Marie; Laborie, Pierre; Marcot, François; Mencherini, Pierre; Peschanski, Denis; Sainclivier, Jacqueline and Wolikow, Serge (1997), 'Déplorable leçon d'histoire', *Libération* 25 July 1997.

Anonymous (n.d.), *La grève des mineurs du Nord-Pas-de-Calais, 27 mai–9 juin 1941*, Collection 'Mémoire et Citoyenneté' No. 16 (Ministère de la Défense, Paris).

Anonymous (n.d. 1940?), *Why France Fell: The Lessons for Us* (London: Union of Democratic Control).

Anonymous (1959), 'Des rapports inédits de la Gestapo sur la Résistance communiste en France au début de 1941', *Recherches internationales à la lumière du marxisme* 9–10:69–90.

Anonymous (1978), *Fac-simile de La Vérité clandestine (1940–1944)* (Paris: EDI).

Atkin, Nicholas (2001), *The French at War 1934–1944* (London: Longman).

Aubrac, Lucie (1993), *Outwitting the Gestapo* (London: University of Nebraska Press).

Auglhon, Maurice & Barrat, Fernand (1975), 'Au dossier des "CRS à Marseille"' *Le Mouvement social* 92:75–91.

Avakoumitch, Ivan (1980), 'Le PCF vu par le commandement des troupes d'occupation allemandes (août 1940–mai 1941)', *Le Mouvement social* 113:91–9.

Aveline, Claude (1962), *Le Temps mort* (Paris: Mercure de France).

Azéma, Jean-Pierre (1990), 'La Milice', *Vingtième Siècle. Revue d'histoire* 28:83–105.

Azema, Jean-Pierre (1997), 'La mémoire, trop souvent passionnelle, doit s'effacer devant les documents. Affaire Aubrac: les faits sont tetus', *Libération* 28 August 1997.

Azéma, Jean-Pierre & Bédarida, François (1994), 'L'historisation de la Résistance', *Esprit* 198:19–35.

Balbaud, René (1941), *Cette drôle de guerre. Alsace-Lorraine – Belgique – Dunkerque. 26 août 1939–1er juin 1940. Telle que je l'ai faite –!* (Oxford: OUP).

Bankwitz, P. C. F. (1967), *Maxime Weygand and Civil-Military Relations in Modern France* (Cambridge, Mass: Harvard University Press).

Barasz, Johanna (2007), 'Un vichyste en résistance, la général de La Laurencie', *Vingtième Siècle. Revue d'histoire.* 94:167–81.

Barlone, D. (1943), *A French Officer's Diary (23 August 1939 to 1 October 1940)* (New York: Macmillan).

Baumel, Jacques (1999), *Resistér* (Paris: Albin Michel).

Baynac, Jacques (1998), *Les secrets de l'affaire Jean Moulin* (Paris: Seuil).

Baynac, Jacques (2007), *Présumé Jean Moulin (17 juin 1940–21 juin 1943): Esquisse d'une nouvelle histoire de la Résistance* (Paris: Grasset).

Beaubatie, Gilbert (1992), 'Le Parti Communiste Français en Corrèze dans les rapports de l'administration de Vichy (1940–1941)', *Annales du Midi* 104:323–34.

Bédarida, François & Azéma, Jean-Pierre (eds) (1983), *Jean Moulin et le Conseil National de la Résistance* (Paris: CNRS).

Beevor, Antony & Cooper, Artemis (2004), *Paris: After the Liberation 1944–1949* (London: Penguin).

Bell, Philip (2000), 'De Gaulle's broadcast of 18 June 1940: The British perspective' in Anne Corbett & Douglas Johnson (eds), *A Day in June: Britain and de Gaulle, 1940* (London: Franco-British Council) pp. 21–6.

Bellanger, Claude (1961), *Press Clandestine 1940–1944* (Paris: Colin).

Bellos, David (2008), 'France and the Jews' in Berr, Hélène (2008), *Journal* (London: MacLehose), pp. 277–91.

Belot, Robert (2000), 'Jean Moulin et Henri Frenay' in Jean-Pierre Azéma (ed.), *Jean Moulin face à l'histoire* (Paris: Flammarion) pp. 163–83.

Belot, Robert (2003), *Henri Frenay: De la Résistance à l'Europe* (Paris: Seuil).

Belot, Robert (2004), 'Le sort des juifs dans les discours et les pratiques du mouvement Combat', *Les Cahiers de la Shoah* 8:179–226.

Belot, Robert (2006a), *La Résistance sans de Gaulle: Politique et gaullisme de guerre* (Paris: Fayard).

Belot, Robert (ed.) (2006b), *Les Résistants* (Paris: Larousse).

Bensaïd, Daniel (1999), *Qui est le Juge? Pour en finir avec le tribunal de l'Histoire* (Paris: Fayard).

Bensaïd, Daniel (2000), 'D'un ton judiciaire adopté aujourd'hui en histoire', *Europe Solidaire Sans Frontières*, (http://www.europe-solidaire.org/spip.php?article1605) (accessed August 2008).

Berlière, Jean-Marc & Liaigre, Franck (2004), *Le Sang des communistes: Les Bataillons de la jeunesse dans la lutte armée – Automne 1941* (Paris: Fayard).

Berlière, Jean-Marc & Liaigre, Franck (2007), *Liquider les traîtres: La face cachée du PCF 1941–1943* (Paris: Laffont).

Berr, Hélène (2008), *Journal* (London: MacLehose).

Bertram, Barbara (1995), *French Resistance in Sussex* (Asbury: Barnworks).

Besse, Jean-Pierre (2007), 'PC: Le mythe des 75000 fusillés' in Bernard Garnier, Jean-Luc Leleu & Jean Quellien (eds), *La Répression en France 1940–1945* (Seconde Guerre Mondiale: 7) (Caen: Centre de Recherche d'Histoire Quantitative).

Besse, Jean-Pierre & Pennetier, Claude (2006), *Juin 40: La Négociation secrète* (Paris: L'Atelier).

Besse, Jean-Pierre & Pouty, Thomas (2006), *Les Fusillés: Répression et executions pendant l'Occupation (1940–1944)* (Paris: L'Atelier).

Bidault, Georges (1965), *D'une résistance à l'autre* (Paris: Presses du Siècle).

Blanc, Julien (2000), 'Le réseau du Musée de l'Homme', *Esprit* 261:89–103.

Blanc, Julien (2004), Introduction in Agnes Humbert (2004), *Notre guerre: Souvenirs de résistance* (Paris: Tallandier).

Bleicher, Hugo (1954), *Colonel Henri's Story* (London: Kimber).

Bloch, Gilbert (1987), 'Enigma before Ultra: Polish work and the French contribution', *Cryptologia* 11:142–55.

Bloch, Marc (1968), *Strange Defeat: A Statement of Evidence Written in 1940* (New York: Norton).

Blumenson, Martin (1978), *The Vildé Affair: Beginnings of the French Resistance* (London: Hale).

Bood, Micheline (1974), *Les Années doubles* (Paris: Robert Laffont).

Borden, Mary (1946), *Journey Down a Blind Alley* (London: Hutchinson).

Bouchinet-Serreulles, Claude (2000), *Nous étions faits pour être libres* (Paris: Grasset).

Bourdet, Claude (1975), *L'Aventure incertaine: De la Résistance à la Restauration* (Paris: Stock).

Bourderon, Roger (2004), *Rol-Tanguy* (Paris: Tallandier).

Brès, Eveline & Brès, Yvan (1987), *Un maquis d'antifascistes allemands en France (1942–1944)* (n.p.: Presses du Languedoc/Max Chaleil).

Brinton, Crane (1961a), 'Letters from liberated France', *French Historical Studies* 2:1–27.

Brinton, Crane (1961b), 'Letters from liberated France', *French Historical Studies* 2:133–56.

Brooks, Howard L. (1942), *Prisoners of Hope: Report on a Mission* (New York: Fischer).

Brossat, Alain (1994), *Libération, fête folle* (Paris: Autrement).

Brossolette, Gilberte (1976), *Il s'appelait Pierre Brossolette* (Paris: Albin Michel).

Broué, Pierre & Vacheron, Raymond (1997), *Meurtres au maquis* (Paris: Grasset).

Brunet, Jean-Paul (1986), *Jacques Doriot* (Paris: Balland).

Buton, Philippe (1993), *Les lendemains qui déchantent: Le Parti communiste français à la libération* (Paris: Presses de la Fondation nationale des sciences politiques).

Calmette, Arthur (1961), *L''O.C.M.' – Organisation civile et militaire. Histoire d'un mouvement de résistance de 1940 à 1946* (Paris: Presses Universitaires de France).

Calvès, André (1984), *Sans bottes ni médailles. Un trotskyste breton dans la guerre* (Montreuil: La Brèche).

Caron, Vicki (2006), 'Review: Adam Rayski. The Choice of the Jews under Vichy: Between Submission and Resistance', *The American Historical Review* 111:574–5.

Cassou, Jean (2001), *La Mémoire courte* (Paris: Mille et une nuits).

Chanal, M. (1982), 'La Milice française dans l'Isère (février 1943–août 1944)', *Revue d'Histoire de la deuxième guerre mondiale et des conflits contemporains* 127:1–42.

Chauvy, Gérard (1997), *Aubrac: Lyon 1943* (Paris: Albin Michel).

Chevance-Bertin, Général (1990), *Vingt mille heures d'angoisse 1940–1945* (Paris: Laffont).

Chevandier, Christian (2006), 'Le grief fait aux cheminots d'avoir, sous l'occupation, conduit les trains de la deportation', *Revue d'histoire des chemins de fer* 34:91–109.

Chevererau, Sebastien & Forlivesi, Luc (2005), 'Histoire et mémoire d'un massacre: Maillé, Indre & Loire', *Actes du Colloque La Repression en France a l'été 1994*, http://www.fondationresistance.org/documents/ee/Doc00004-008.pdf (accessed July 2008).

Chevrillon, Claude (1995), *Code Name Christiane Clouet* (College Station, Texas: Texas A&M Press).

Clinton, Alan (2001), *Jean Moulin, 1899–1943: The French Resistance and the Republic* (London: Palgrave).

Closon, Francis Louis (1974), *Le temps des passions: De Jean Moulin à la Liberation 1943–1944* (Paris: Presses de la Cité).

Cointet, Michèle (2005), *De Gaulle et Giraud: L'affrontement* (Paris: Perrin).

Cointet, Michèle (2006), *Marie-Madeleine Fourcade: Un chef de la Résistance* (Paris: Perrin).

Collin, Claude (1998), *Jeune Combat: Les jeunes Juifs de la MOI dans la Résistance* (Grenoble: Presses Universitaires de Grenoble).

Cookridge, E. H. (1966), *Inside SOE: The Story of Special Operations in Western Europe 1940–1945* (London: Barker).

Cordier, Daniel (1989a), *Jean Moulin, l'inconnu du Panthéon. 1: Une ambition pour la République, juin 1899–juin 1936* (Paris: Lattès).

Cordier, Daniel (1989b), *Jean Moulin, l'inconnu du Panthéon. 2: Le choix d'un destin, juin 1936–novembre 1940* (Paris: Lattès).

Cordier, Daniel (1993a), *Jean Moulin, l'inconnu du Panthéon. 3: De Gaulle, capitale de la Résistance* (Paris: Lattès).

Cordier, Daniel (1993b), 'La Résistance française et les Juifs', *Annales ESC* 3:621–7.

Cordier, Daniel (1995), 'Histoire et "Mémoires"' in Jean-Marie Guillon & Pierre Laborie (eds) *Mémoire et Histoire: la Résistance* (Toulouse: Privat) pp. 299–312.

Cordier, Daniel (1999), *Jean Moulin: La République des catacombes* (Paris: Gallimard).

Cornick, Martyn (2005), '"Fraternity among listeners." The BBC and French Resistance: Evidence from refugees', in Hanna Diamond & Simon Kitson (eds) *Vichy, Resistance, Liberation: New Perspectives on Wartime France* (Oxford: Berg) pp. 101–13.

Cornick, Martyn (1994), 'The BBC and the propaganda war against occupied France: The work of Emile Delavenay and the European Intelligence Department', *French History* 8:316–54.

Courtois, Stéphane (1980), *Le PCF dans la guerre. De Gaulle, la Résistance, Staline . . .* (Paris: Ramsay).

Courtois, Stéphane & Rayski, Adam (eds) (1987), *Qui savait quoi? L'extermination des Juifs, 1941–1945* (Paris: La Découverte).

Courtois, Stéphane; Peschanski, Denis & Rayski, Adam (1989), *Le Sang de l'étranger. Les immigrés de la MOI dans la Résistance* (Paris: Fayard).

Crémieux-Brilhac, Jean-Louis (1975), 'La Bataille des Glières et la "guerre psychologique"', *Revue d'Histoire de la deuxième guerre mondiale* 99:45–72.

Crémieux-Brilhac, Jean-Louis (1990), *Les Français de l'an 40. Tome 2, Ouvriers et soldats* (Paris: Gallimard).

Crémieux-Brilhac, Jean-Louis (1995), 'Les Glières', *Vingtième Siècle. Revue d'histoire* 45:54–66.

Crémieux-Brilhac, Jean-Louis (2001), *La France Libre: De l'appel du 18 juin à la libération* vols 1 & 2 (Paris: Gallimard).

Cruccu, Rinaldo (1976), 'Libération de la Corse' in Comité d'Histoire de la 2e Guerre Mondiale, *La Libération de la France: Actes du Colloque International tenu à Paris du 28 au 31 octobre 1974* (Paris: CNRS) pp. 163–74.

Cuvelliez, Jean-Louis (1995), 'Les débuts de la Résistance à Toulouse et dans la region' in Jean-Marie Guillon & Pierre Laborie (eds) *Memoire et Histoire: la Résistance* (Toulouse: Privat) pp. 121–36.

d'Aragon, Charles (1977), *La Résistance sans héroïsme* (Paris: Seuil).

d'Astier, Emmanuel (1958), *Seven Times Seven Days* (London: MacGibbon & Kee).

d'Astier, Emmanuel (1965), *De la Chute à la Libération de Paris* (Paris: Gallimard).

Dansette, Adrien (1946), *Histoire de la Libération de Paris* (Paris: Fayard).

de Beauvoir, Simone (1965), *The Prime of Life* (Harmondsworth: Penguin).

de Bénouville, Guillan (1945), *Le Sacrifice du matin* (Paris: Laffont).

de Dainville, Augustin (1976), 'L'ORA en 1944' in Comité d'Histoire de la 2e Guerre Mondiale, *La Libération de la France: Actes du Colloque International tenu à Paris du 28 au 31 octobre 1974* (Paris: CNRS) pp. 469–79.

de Gaulle, Charles (1962a), *Mémoires de guerre: L'Appel 1940–1942* (Paris: Plon).

de Gaulle, Charles (1962b), *Mémoires de guerre: L'Unité 1942–1944* (Paris: Plon).

de Gaulle, Charles (1962c), *Mémoires de guerre: Le Salut 1944–1946* (Paris: Plon).

de Montety, Étienne (2005), *Honoré d'Estienne d'Orves: Un héros français* (Paris: Perrin).

de Wailly, Henri (2002), 'Syrie 1941: La guerre censurée', *Histoire de Guerre* 24:49–61.

Debarge, Charles (2001), *Le Carnet de Charles Debarge* (Souchez: Gauheria).

Dejonghe, Étienne (1987), 'Chronique de la grève des mineurs du Nord/Pas-de-Calais (27 mai–6 juin 1941)', *Revue du Nord* 273:323–45.

Dejonghe, Étienne & Le Maner, Yves (2000), *Le Nord-Pas-de-Calais dans la main allemande* (Lille: La Voix du Nord).

Delpard, Raphaël (2005), *Les Convois de la honte* (Neuilly-sur-Seine: Lafon).

Diamond, Hanna & Gorrara, Claire (2001), 'The Aubrac controversy', *History Today* 41(3):26–7.

Domenach-Lallich, Denise (2005), *Une jeune fille libre. Journal (1939–1944)* (Paris: Les Arènes).

Dorrian, James (2006), *Saint-Nazaire: Operation Chariot – 1942: Battleground French Coast* (London: Leo Cooper).

Douzou, Laurent (1995), *La Désobéissance: Histoire du mouvement Libération-Sud* (Paris: Odile Jacob).

Douzou, Laurent (2000), 'Un an de réflexion? 1940–1941' in Pierre Azema (ed.), *Jean Moulin face à l'histoire* (Paris: Flammarion) pp. 81–92.

Douzou, Laurent (2005), *La Résistance française: une histoire périlleuse* (Paris: Seuil).

Dreyfus, Paul (1971), *Vercors: Citadelle de la liberté* (Geneva: Crémille).

Dubois, Edmond (1946), *Paris sans lumière: Témoignages* (Lausanne: Payot).

Ducellier, Jean-Pierre (2002), *La Guerre aérienne dans le Nord de la France: les raids de l'aviation alliée sur le Nord, l'Artois, la Picardie, le Pays de Caux, la région parisienne. Les secrets du bombardement de la prison d'Amiens, 18 février 1944, 'Jéricho'* (Abbeville: Paillart).

Ducellier, Jean-Pierre (2005), 'La manipulation d'Amiens: pourquoi bombarder une prison en 1944?', *Le Fana de l'Aviation* 432:18–27 (November 2005).

Dunan, René (1976), 'La magnifique et lamentable histoire de Dukson "Héros du XVIIe"' in Rémy (ed.), *La Résistance à Paris et dans la region parisienne Vol. 2* (Geneva: Famot) pp. 227–42.

Durand, Paul (1968), *La SNCF pendant la guerre* (Paris: PUF).

Durand, Pierre (1985), *Qui a tué Fabien?* (Paris: Messidor).

Durand, Pierre (1994), *Joseph et les hommes de Londres* (n.p.: Le Temps des Cerises).

Egremont, Max (1997), *Under Two Flags: The Life of Major General Sir Edward Spears* (London: Weidenfeld & Nicolson).

Erignac, Louis (1980), *La Révolte des Croates* (n.p.: Erignac).

Faivre, Mario (1975), *Nous avons tué Darlan* (Paris: La Table Ronde).

Favier, Pierre & Martin-Rolland, Michel (1990), *La Décennie Mitterrand. II. Les ruptures (1981–1984)* (Paris: Seuil).

Fishman, Jack (1982), *And the Walls Came Tumbling Down* (London: Souvenir).

Fishman, Sarah (1992), *We Will Wait: Wives of French Prisoners of War, 1940–1945* (London: Yale University Press).

Foot, M. R. D. (1978), *Resistance* (London: Granada).

Foot, M. R. D. (1996), 'Le SOE et le maquis' in François Marcot (ed.) *La Résistance et les Français: Lutte armée et maquis*, Annales littéraires de l'Université de France–Comté, vol. 617, série Historiques n° 13 (Paris: Belles Lettres) pp. 227–33.

Foot, M. R. D. (2004), *SOE in France: An Account of the Work of the British Special Operations Executive in France 1940–1944* (London: Cass).

Foot, M. R. D. (2005), 'The Dutch Affair', *Intelligence and National Security* 20:341–3.

Foot, M. R. D. (2008), *Memories of an SOE Historian* (Barnsley: Pen & Sword).

Foot, M. R. D. & Langley, J. M. (1979), *MI9* (London: Bodley Head).

Footitt, Hilary & Simmonds, John (1988), *France 1943–1945* (Leicester: Leicester University Press).

Fourcade, Marie-Madeleine (1972), *L'Arche de Noë* (Geneva: Crémille).

Fourcade, Marie-Madeleine (1973), *Noah's Ark* (London: Allen Unwin).

Fortrat, René (1945), 'René Gosse (1883–1943)', *Annales de l'Université de Grenoble* 21:7–15.

Fouché, Jean-Jacques & Beaubatie, Gilbert (2008), *Tulle: Nouveaux regards sur les pendaisons et les événements de juin 1944* (Saint-Paul: Souny).

Frenay, Henri (1976), *The Night Will End: Memoirs of a Revolutionary* (New York: McGraw-Hill).

Frenay, Henri (1977), *L'Enigme Jean Moulin* (Paris: Laffont).

Frey, Marc; Heidekinq, Jürgen & Mauch, Christof (1996), *American Intelligence and the German Resistance to Hitler: A Documentary History* (Boulder, Co: Westview).

Friang, Brigitte (1975), 'Les Glières' in Rémy (ed.) *La Résistance en Dauphiné et Savoie*, vol. 1 (Geneva: Famot) pp. 87–145.

Fridenson, Patrick & Robert, Jean-Louis (1992), 'Les ouvriers dans la France de la Seconde Guerre mondiale. Un bilan', *Le Mouvement social* 158:117–47.

Funk, Arthur L. (1974), *The Politics of TORCH: The Allied Landings and the Algiers Putsch of 1942* (Lawrence: University Press of Kansas).

Funk, Arthur L. (1981), 'Churchill, Eisenhower, and the French Resistance', *Military Affairs* 45:29–34.

Funk, Arthur L. (1992), *Hidden Ally: The French Resistance, Special Operations and the landings in Southern France, 1944* (London: Greenwood Press).

Gallissot, René (1971), 'Les communistes et les débuts de la Résistance', *Le Mouvement social* 74:130–43.

Gambiez, Général (1973), *Libération de la Corse* (Paris: Hachette).

Gambiez, Général (1976), 'La Libération de la Corse' in Comité d'Histoire de la 2e Guerre Mondiale *La Libération de la France: Actes du Colloque International tenu à Paris du 28 au 31 octobre 1974* (Paris: CNRS) pp. 137–62.

Gernoux, A. (ed.) (n.d. 1946?), *Pays nantais: La Guerre vue par les enfants* (n.p.).

Ghesquier-Krajewski, Corinne & Ghesquier-Krajewski, Frédéric (2002), 'La grève des mineurs de mai–juin 1941 dans la presse communiste régionale de la Libération à nos jours', *Bulletin MEMOR*.

Ghrenassia, Patrick (1987), 'Anatole Lewitzky: De l'ethnologie à la Résistance', *La Liberté de l'esprit* 18:237–53.

Gildea, Robert (2002), *Marianne in Chains: In Search of the German Occupation 1940–45* (London: Macmillan).

Gildea, Robert (2003), 'Resistance, reprisals and community in Occupied France', *Transactions of the Royal Historical Society* 13:163–85.

Granet, Marie (ed.) (1961), *Le Journal 'Défense de la France'* (Paris: PUF).

Granet, Marie (1964), *Ceux de la Résistance (1940–1944)* (Paris: Éditions de Minuit).

Granier, Jacques (1971), *Un général a disparu* (Paris: Presses de la Cité).

Grenier, Fernand (1959), *C'était ainsi . . . (souvenirs)* (Paris: Éditions sociales).

Grmek, Mirko D. & Lambrichs, Louise (1998), *Les Revoltés de Villefranche: Mutinerie d'un bataillon de Waffen-SS à Villefranche-de-Rouergue, septembre 1943* (Paris: Seuil).

Groussard, Georges A. (1964), *Service Secret 1940–1945* (Paris: La Table Ronde).

Guéhenno, Jean (2002), *Journal des années noires* (Paris: Gallimard).

Guillin, François-Yves (1995), *Le Général Delestraint: Premier chef de l'Armée secrète* (Paris: Plon).

Guillon, Jean-Marie & Laborie, Pierre (eds) (2005) *Mémoire et Histoire: la Résistance* (Toulouse: Privat).

Guingouin, Georges (1974), *Quatre ans de lutte sur le sol limousin* (Paris: Hachette).

Guiral, Pierre (1974), *Libération de Marseille* (Paris: Hachette).

Gunsburg, Jeffery A. (1984), 'Armée de l'air vs The Luftwaffe – 1940', *Defence Update International* 45:44–54.

Gunsburg, Jeffrey A. (1992), 'The Battle of the Belgian Plain, 12–14 May 1940: The first great tank battle', *The Journal of Military History* 56:207–44.

Hallie, Philip P. (1979), *Lest Innocent Blood be Shed: The Story of the Village of Le Chambon and How Goodness Happened There* (New York: Harper & Row).

Hastings, Max (1983), *Das Reich: Resistance and the march of the 2nd SS Panzer Division through France*, June 1944 (London: Pan).

Helm, Sarah (2006), *A Life in Secrets: The Story of Vera Atkins and the Lost Agents of SOE* (London: Abacus).

Heslop, Richard (1970), *Xavier: The Famous British Agent's Dramatic Account of his Work in the French Resistance* (London: Hart-Davis).

Holban, Boris (1989), *Testament* (Paris: Calmann-Lévy).

Horne, Alistair (1969), *To Lose a Battle: France 1940* (London: Macmillan).

Horne, Alistair (2000), 'Mers-el-Kebir, 1940' in Anne Corbett & Douglas Johnson (eds), *A Day in June: Britain and de Gaulle, 1940* (London: Franco-British Council) pp. 37–41.

Hostache, René (1958), *Le Conseil national de la Résistance: Les Institutions de la clandestinité* (Paris: PUF).

Hostache, René (1976), 'L'Organisation de la Résistance au printemps de 1944' in Comité d'Histoire de la 2e Guerre Mondiale, *La Libération de la France: Actes du Colloque International tenu à Paris du 28 au 31 octobre 1974* (Paris: CNRS) pp. 369–413.

Howard, Michael (1990), *British Intelligence in the Second World War. Volume Five: Strategic Deception* (London: HMSO).

Humbert, Agnès (2008), *Résistance* (London: Bloomsbury).

Jackson, Julian (2001), *France: The Dark Years 1940–1944* (Oxford: OUP).

Jackson, Julian (2003), *The Fall of France: The Nazi Invasion of 1940* (Oxford: OUP).

Jacquemin, François (1985), *Journal des Combattants* 1969, 7 Dec 1985, pp. 4–5.

Jansen, Sabine (2000), 'Jean Moulin et l'entourage de Pierre Cot' in Jean-Pierre Azéma (ed.), *Jean Moulin face à l'histoire* (Paris: Flammarion) pp. 39–54.

Jourdan, Louis; Helfgott, Julien & Golliet, Pierre (1946), *Glières, Haute-Savoie, 31 janvier–26 mars 1944, Première bataille de la Résistance* (Annecy: Association des rescapés des Glières).

Kaspi, André (2004), *La Libération de la France: juin 1944–janvier 1946* (Paris: Perrin).

Kedward, H. R. (1978), *Resistance in Vichy France* (Oxford: OUP).

Kedward, H. R. (1993), *In Search of the Maquis: Rural Resistance in Southern France 1942–1944* (Oxford: Clarendon).

Kedward, H. R. (2005), *La Vie en Bleu: France and the French Since 1900* (London: Allen Lane).

Keegan, John (1982), *Six Armies in Normandy* (London: Cape).

Kersaudy, François (1981), *Churchill and de Gaulle* (London: Collins).

Kersaudy, François (2004), *De Gaulle et Roosevelt: Le duel au sommet* (Paris: Perrin).

Kershaw, Ian (2007), *Fateful Choices: Ten Decisions that Changed the World 1940–1941* (London: Allen Lane).

Kirkland, Faris R. (1985), 'The French Air Force in 1940: Was it defeated by the Luftwaffe or by politics?', *Air University Review* 36:101–18.

Kitson, Simon (1995), 'The Police in the Liberation of Paris' in H. R. Kedward & Nancy Wood (eds), *The Liberation of France: Image and Event* (Oxford: Berg) pp. 43–56.

Kitson, Simon (2008), *The Hunt for Nazi Spies: Fighting Espionage in Vichy France* (London: University of Chicago Press).

Klarsfeld, Serge (1997a), 'À propos de Raymond Aubrac', *Le Monde* 25 July 1997.

Klarsfeld, Serge (1997b), 'Affaire Aubrac: Serge Klarseld répond à Jean-Pierre Azéma', *Libération* 1 September 1997.

Koestler, Arthur (1968), *Scum of the Earth* (London: Hutchinson).

Kramer, Rita (1996), *Flames in the Field: The Story of Four SOE Agents in Occupied France* (London: Penguin).

Kramer, Steven P. (1981), 'The political role of the Commissaires régionaux de la République', *The Journal of Modern History* 53(1) (supplement).

Krivopissko, Guy (ed.) (2006), *La Vie à en mourir: Lettres de fusillés (1941–1944)* (Paris: Tallandier).

Krivopissko, Guy & Porin, Alex (2004), *Les Fusillés de la Cascade du bois de Boulogne: 16 août 1944* (Paris: Mairie de Paris).

Labédan, Guy (1983), 'La Répression à la Libération dans la region de Toulouse', *Revue d'histoire de la Deuxième guerre mondiale* 131:105–12.

Laborie, Pierre (1980), *Résistants vichyssois et autres: L'évolution de l'opinion et des comportements dans le Lot de 1939 à 1944* (Paris: CNRS).

Lahiri, Shompa (2007), 'Clandestine mobilities and shifting embodiments: Noor-un-nisa Inayat Khan and the Special Operations Executive, 1940–44', *Gender & History* 19:305–23.

Langer, William L. (1947), *Our Vichy Gamble* (New York: Knopf).

Langlois, Suzanne (1997), 'Images that matter: The French Resistance in film, 1944–1946', *French History* 11:461–90.

La-Picirella, Joseph (1986), *Temoignages sur le Vercors* (Lyon: La-Picirella).

Lecoeur, Auguste (1971), *Croix de guerre pour une grève. Cent mille mineurs contre l'occupant, 27 mai–10 juin 1941* (Paris: Plon).

Lecourt, Serge (1999), 'Sur les traces de Jean Moulin à Lisbonne', *Espoir* 119:17–20.

Lefebvre, Michel (2001), '100 000 mineurs en grève contre l'occupant', *Le Monde* 10 June 2001.

Lescure, Yves (2007), 'L'Enquête de la Fondation pour la mémoire de la déportation', in Bernard Garnier, Jean-Luc Leleu & Jean Quellien (eds), *La Répression en France 1940–1945* (Seconde Guerre mondiale: 7) (Caen: Centre de Recherche d'Histoire Quantitative) pp. 159–62.

Lévy, Claude (1989), 'La résistance juive en France. De l'enjeu de mémoire à l'histoire critique', *Vingtième Siècle. Revue d'histoire* 22:117–28.

Levy, Jean-Pierre (1998), *Mémoires d'un franc-tireur: Itinéraire d'un résistant (1940–1944)* (Paris: Éditions Complexe).

Lévy-Osbert, Liliane (1992), *Jeunesse vers l'abîme* (Paris: EDI).

Livry-Level, Colonel & Rémy (1955), *The Gates Burst Open* (London: Arco).

Lorain, Pierre (1983), *Clandestine Operations: The Arms and Techniques of the Resistance, 1941–1944* (New York: Macmillan).

Lottman, Herbert (1992), *The Fall of Paris: June 1940* (London: Sinclair-Stevenson).

Luneau, Aurélie (2005), *Radio Londres (1940–1944): Les voix de la liberté* (Paris: Perrin).

Mackenzie, William J. M. (2000), *The Secret History of SOE: Special Operations Executive 1940–1945* (London: St Ermin's).

Macmillan, Harold (1984), *War Diaries: The Mediterranean 1943–1945* (London: Macmillan).

Madjarian, Grégoire (1980), *Conflits, pouvoirs et société à la Libération* (Paris: Union Générale d'Éditions).

Mandel, Ernest (1986), *The Meaning of the Second World War* (London: Verso).

Marcot, François (1996), 'Le service national maquis: Structures, pouvoirs et strategies' in François Marcot (ed.), *La Résistance et les Français: Lutte armée et maquis*, Annales littéraires de l'Université de France-Comté, vol. 617, série Historiques nº 13 (Paris: Belles Lettres) pp. 210–23.

Marcot, François (1999), 'La direction de Peugeot sous l'Occupation: pétainisme, reticence, opposition et résistance', *Le Mouvement social* 189:27–46.

Marcot, François; Leroux, Bruno & Levisse-Touze, Christine (eds) (2006), *Dictionnaire historique de la Résistance* (Paris: Laffont).

Marder, Arthur (1976), *Operation 'Menace': The Dakar Expedition and the Dudley North Affair* (London: OUP).

Marino, Andy (1999), *American Pimpernel: The Man Who Saved the Artists on Hitler's Death List* (London: Hutchinson).

Marks, Leo (1998), *Between Silk and Cyanide: A Codemaker's War 1941–1945* (New York: Touchstone).

Marnham, Patrick (2000), *The Death of Jean Moulin: Biography of a Ghost* (London: John Murray).

Marshall, Bruce & Yeo-Thomas, Forest Frederick Edward (1955), *The White Rabbit: Wing Commander F. F. E. Yeo-Thomas* (London: Pan).

Marshall, Robert (1988), *All the King's Men: The Truth Behind SOE's Greatest Wartime Disaster* (London: Collins).

Martin-Chauffier, Simone (1976), *A bientôt quand meme . . .* (Paris: Calman-Lévy).

May, Ernest R. (2000), *Strange Victory: Hitler's Conquest of France* (New York: Hill & Wang).

Meunier, Pierre (1993), *Jean Moulin, mon ami* (Précy-sous-Thil: L'Armançon).

Meyer, Ahlrich (2002), *L'occupation allemande en France* (Toulouse: Privat).

Michalon, Roger (1976), 'L'amalgame FFI – 1re armée et 2e DB' in Comité d'Histoire de la 2e Guerre Mondiale, *La Libération de la France: Actes du Colloque International tenu à Paris du 28 au 31 octobre 1974* (Paris: CNRS) pp. 592–665.

Michel, Henri (1962), *Les Courants de pensée de la Résistance* (Paris: Presses Universitaires de France).

Michel, Henri & Mirkine-Guetzévitch, Boris (eds) (1954), *Les Idées politiques et sociales de la Résistance (Documents clandestins – 1940–1944)* (Paris: Presses Universitaires de France).

Millar, George (2003), *Maquis: The French Resistance at War* (London: Cassell).

Minguet, Simonne (1997), *Mes années Caudron: Caudron-Renault, une usine auto-gerée à la Libération (1944–1948)* (Paris: Syllepse).

Minney, R. J. (2006), *Carve Her Name with Pride* (Barnsley: Pen & Sword).

Missika, Dominique (2005), *Berty Albrecht* (Paris: Perrin).

Moore, Bob (ed.) (2000), *Resistance in Western Europe* (Oxford: Berg).

Moore, Bob (2004), 'The rescue of Jews in Nazi-occupied Belgium, France and the Netherlands', *Australian Journal of Politics and History* 50:385–95.

Moulin, Laure (1982), *Jean Moulin* (Paris: Presses de la Cité).

Murphy, Brendan M. (1987), *Turncoat: The Strange Case of British Traitor Sergeant Harold Cole, 'The Worst Traitor of the War'* (London: Harcourt).

Naïtchenko, Maroussia (2003), *Une jeune fille en guerre: la lutte antifasciste d'une génération* (Paris: Imago).

Nal, Commandant (1975), 'Grenoble sous la botte' in Rémy (ed.), *La Résistance en Dauphiné et Savoie* (Geneva: Famot) pp. 67–86.

Narinksi, Mikhail (1996), 'L'URSS, le Komintern et la lutte armée en France' in François Marcot (ed.), *La Résistance et les Français: Lutte armée et maquis*, Annales littéraires de l'Université de France-Comté, vol. 617, série Historiques nº 13 (Paris: Belles Lettres) pp. 361–372.

Neave, Airey (1969), *Saturday at M.I.9.* (London: Hodder & Stoughton).

Némirovsky, Irène (2006), *Suite Française* (London: Chatto & Windus).

Neumaier, Christopher (2006), 'The escalation of German reprisal policy in Occupied France, 1941–42', *Journal of Contemporary History* 41:113–31.

Noguères, Henri & Degliame-Fouché, Marcel (1972), *Histoire de la Résistance en France. III, Et du nord au midi, novembre 1942–septembre 1943* (Paris: Laffont).

Noguères, Henri & Degliame-Fouché, Marcel (1976), *Histoire de la Résistance en France. IV, Formez vos bataillons!, octobre 1943–mai 1944* (Paris: Laffont).

Noguères, Henri & Degliame-Fouché, Marcel (1981), *Histoire de la Résistance en France. V, Au grand soleil de la Libération, 1er juin 1944–15 mai 1945* (Paris: Laffont).

Noguères, Henri, Degliame-Fouché, M. & Vigier, J.-L. (1967), *Histoire de la Résistance en France de 1940 à 1945. I, La première année, juin 1940–juin 1941* (Paris: Laffont).

Noguères, Henri, Degliame-Fouché, M. & Vigier, J.-L. (1969), *Histoire de la Résistance en France de 1940 à 1945. II, L'Armée de l'ombre, juillet 1941–octobre 1942* (Paris: Laffont).

Ousby, Ian (1997), *Occupation: The Ordeal of France 1940–1944* (London: Pimlico).

Ouzoulias, Albert (1975), *Les Fils de la nuit* (Paris: Grasset).

Overton Fuller, Jean (1952), *Madeleine: The Story of Noor Inayat Khan* (London: Gollancz).

Overton Fuller, Jean (1989), *Déricourt: The Chequered Spy* (Wilton: Russell).

Paillole, Paul (2003), *Fighting the Nazis: French Intelligence and Counter-Intelligence 1935–1945* (New York: Enigma).

Parent, Marcel (2006), *Georges Guingouin: Les écrits et les actes* (Pantin: Le Temps des Cerises).

Passy, Colonel (1947a), *Souvenirs: 2e Bureau Londres* (Paris: Solar).

Passy, Colonel (1947b), *Souvenirs: 1, Duke Street, Londres (Le B.C.R.A.)* (Paris: Solar).

Passy, Colonel (1951), *Missions secrètes en France (novembre 1942–juin 1943). Souvenirs du BCRA* (Paris: Plon).

Pattinson, Juliette (2007), *Behind Enemy Lines: Gender, Passing and the Special Operations Executive in the Second World War* (Manchester: Manchester University Press).

Pattinson, Juliette (2008), '"Turning a pretty girl into a killer": Women, violence and clandestine operations during the Second World War' in F. Alexander & K. Throsby (eds), *Gender and Interpersonal Violence: Language, Action and Representation* (London: Palgrave).

Paxton, Robert O. (2001), *Vichy France: Old Guard and New Order 1940–1944* (New York: Columbia University Press).

Péan, Pierre (1994), *Une jeunesse française: François Mitterrand 1934–1947* (Paris: Fayard).

Péan, Pierre (1998), *Vies et morts de Jean Moulin* (Paris: Fayard).

Péan, Pierre (1999), *La diabolique de Caluire* (Paris: Fayard).

Pearson, Michael (1978), *Tears of Glory: The Betrayal of Vercors 1944* (London: Macmillan).

Perkins, E. R. (ed.) (1962), *Foreign Relations of the United States: Diplomatic Papers 1942. Vol II: Europe* (Washington: US Government Printing Office).

Perrault, Gilles (1975), *La longue traque* (Paris: Fayard).

Perrin, Nigel (2008), *Spirit of Resistance: The Life of SOE Agent Harry Peulevé, DSO, MC* (Barnsley: Pen & Sword).

Peschanski, Denis (2002), *Des étrangers dans la Résistance* (Paris: L'Atelier).

Peyrefitte, Alain (1994), *C'était de Gaulle. 1: La France redevient la France* (Paris: Fayard).

Pierquin, Bernard (1983), *Journal d'un étudiant parisien sous l'Occupation (1939–1945)* (n.p.).

Piketty, Guillaume (1998), *Pierre Brossolette: Un héros de la Résistance* (Paris: Odile Jacob).

Piketty, Guillaume (2000), 'De l'oubli relatif à la commemoration nationale: Le parallèle Jean Moulin/Pierre Brossolette' in Jean-Pierre Azéma (ed.), *Jean Moulin face à l'histoire* (Paris: Flammarion) pp. 325–33.

Pineau, Christian (1960), *La Simple vérité 1940–1945* (Paris: Julliard).

Piquet-Wicks, Eric (1957), *Four in the Shadows: A True Story of Espionage in Occupied France* (London: Jarrolds).

Pluet-Despatin, Jacqueline (1980), *Les trotskistes et la guerre 1940–1944* (Paris: Anthropos).

Polino, Marie-Noëlle (2004), 'Léon Bronchart, ouvrier, soldat . . . et cheminot: un destin, une figure', *Revue d'histoire des chemins de fer*, hors série 7, 2e édition, pp. 160–72.

Poznanski, Renée (1995), 'Résistance juive, *résistants* juifs: retour à l'Histoire' in Jean-Marie Guillon & Pierre Laborie (eds), *Mémoire et Histoire: la Résistance* (Toulouse: Privat) pp. 227–45.

Poznanski, Renée (2001), 'The geopolitics of Jewish resistance in France' *Holocaust and Genocide Studies* 15:245–65.

Poznanski, Renée (2008), *Propagandes et persécutions: La Résistance et le 'problème juif'* (Paris: Fayard).

Prager, Rodolphe (1981), Preface in Prager, R. (ed.), *L'Internationale dans la guerre 1940–1946* (Montreuil: La Brèche).

Quellien, Julia (2003), *Les Réfractaires au travail obligatoire dans le Calvados* (Seconde Guerre Mondiale: 1) (Caen: Centre de Recherche d'Histoire Quantitative).

Rabino, Thomas (2008), *Le Réseau Carte: Histoire d'un réseau de la Résistance antialle- mand, antigaulliste, anticommuniste et anticollaborationniste* (Paris: Perrin).

Radtke-Delacor, Arne (2001), 'Produire pour le Reich: Les commandes alle- mandes à l'industrie française', *Vingtième Siècle. Revue d'histoire* 70:99–115.

Rainat, Max (2003), *Comme une grande fête* (Paris: Tirésias).

Rajsfus, Maurice (2004), *La libération inconnue: à chacun sa résistance* (Paris: Cherche midi).

Raskin, Richard (1991), '"Le Chant des Partisans": Functions of a wartime song', *Folklore* 102:62–76.

Ravine, Jacques (1973), *La Résistance organisée des Juifs en France 1940–1944* (Paris: Julliard).

Raymond, Philippe Ganier (1975), *L'Affiche rouge* (Paris: Fayard).

Rayski, Adam (1992), *Le Choix des Juifs sous Vichy: Entre soumission et résistance* (Paris: La Découverte).

Rayski, Adam (2005), *The Choice of the Jews under Vichy: Between Submission and Resistance* (Notre Dame, Ind.: University of Notre Dame Press).

Reid, Donald (2006), 'French singularity, the Resistance and the Vichy Syndrome: Lucie Aubrac to the rescue', *European History Quarterly* 36:200–20.

Rémy (1948), *Memoirs of a Secret Agent of France. 1: June 1940– June 1942. The Silent Company* (New York: Whittlesey House).

Rémy (1966), *Mémoires d'un agent secret de la France libre. III: juin 1942–septembre 1943* (Paris: Presses Pocket).

Reynolds, David (1990), '1940: Fulcrum of the twentieth century?', *International Affairs* 66:325–50.

Rohwer, Jurgen (1999), 'Signal intelligence and World War II: The unfolding story', *The Journal of Military History* 63:939–51.

Romans-Petit, Henri (1974), *Les maquis de l'Ain* (Paris: Hachette).

Rossel-Kirschen, André (2002), *Le Procès de la Maison de la Chimie (7 au 14 avril 1942)* (Paris: L'Harmattan).

Roussel, Eric (2002), *De Gaulle 1: 1890–1945* (Paris: Perrin).

Rousso, Henri (1992), 'L'épuration en France, une histoire inachevée', *Vingtième Siècle. Revue d'histoire* 33:78–105.

Rousso, Henri (2000), 'La mémoire d'un héros emblématique' in Jean-Pierre Azéma (ed.) *Jean Moulin face à l'histoire* (Paris: Flammarion) pp. 299–309.

Rouxel, Roger (1999), *Les Mystères de la source K* (Bordeaux: Les Dossiers d'Aquitaine).

Rude, Fernand (1974), *Libération de Lyon et de sa region* (Paris: Hachette).

Ruffin, Raymond (1980), *Ces chefs de maquis qui gênaient* (Paris: Presses de la Cité).

Ruscio, Alain (2007), 'Les communistes et les massacres du Constantinois (mai–juin 1945)', *Vingtième Siècle. Revue d'histoire* 94:217–29.

Saint-Exupéry, Antoine de (1942), *Flight to Arras* (London: Heinemann).

Sansico, Virginie (2007), 'Les cours martiales de Vichy en 1944: Un cas extrême de justice d'exception' in Bernard Garnier, Jean-Luc Leleu & Jean Quellien (eds) *La Répression en France 1940–1945* (Seconde Guerre Mondiale: 7) (Caen: Centre de Recherche d'Histoire Quantitative) pp. 277–88.

Sawyer, John E. (1947), 'The reestablishment of the Republic in France: The de Gaulle era, 1944–1945', *Political Science Quarterly* 62:354–67.

Scamaroni, Marie-Claire (1999), *Fred Scamaroni: Mort pour la France* (Paris: France Empire).

Schmidt, Mária (2004), 'Noel Field – The American Communist at the center of Stalin's East European purge: From the Hungarian archives', *American Communist History* 3:215–45.

Schoenbrun, David (1981), *Soldiers of the Night: The Story of the French Resistance* (London: Hale).

Schreiber, Marion (2002), *Rebelles silencieux: L'attaque du 20ᵉ convoi pour Auschwitz* (Brussels: Racine).

Schreiber, Marion (2004), *The Twentieth Train: The True Story of the Ambush of the Death Train to Auschwitz* (London: Atlantic).

Schroeder, Liliane (2000), *Journal d'occupation. Paris 1940–1944. Chronique au jour le jour d'une époque oubliée* (Paris: F-X de Guibert).

Seaman, Mark (1997), *Bravest of the Brave: The True Story of Wing Commander 'Tommy' Yeo-Thomas – SOE Secret Agent – Code Name 'The White Rabbit'* (London: O'Mara).

Sebag-Montefiore, Hugh (2006), *Dunkirk: Fight to the last man* (London: Viking).

Sentis, Georges (1982), 'Les communistes du 1er bataillon de FTPF de l'Aveyron et l'amalgame à la 1ère Armée française (septembre 1944–mai 1945)' *Cahiers d'histoire de l'institut de recherches marxistes* 10:31–51.

Serbat, Guy (2001), *Le PCF et la lutte armée 1943–1944: Témoignage* (Paris: L'Harmattan).

Serge, Victor (1978), *Mémoires d'un révolutionnaire* (Paris: Seuil).

Shennan, Andrew (2000), *The Fall of France, 1940* (Harlow: Pearson).

Shlaim, Avi (1974), 'Prelude to downfall: the British offer of Union to France, June 1940', *Journal of Contemporary History* 9:27–63.

Silvani, Paul (2001), *. . . Et la Corse fut libérée* (Ajaccio: Albiana).

Silvestri, Gibo (1978), Review of Blumenson, *The American Historical Review* 83:739–40.

Simon, Paul (1942) *Un seul ennemi: l'envahisseur* (n.p.: Hachette).

Sowrey, Frederick (1989), 'The Royal Air Force and clandestine operations in North-West Europe', *Proceedings of the Royal Air Force Historical Society* 5:7–45.

Spears, Edward L. (1954), *Assignment to Catastrophe. Volume II. The Fall of France June 1940* (London: Heinemann).

Srodes, James (1999), *Allen Dulles: Master of Spies* (Washington: Regnery).

Suleiman, Susan Rubin (2004), 'History, heroism and narrative desire: The "Aubrac affair" and national memory of the French Resistance', *South Central Review* 21:54–81.

Suleiman, Susan Rubin (2006), *Crises of Memory and the Second World War* (London: Harvard University Press).

Sweets, John F. (1976), *The Politics of Resistance in France, 1940–1944. A history of the Mouvements unis de la Résistance* (DeKalb, IL: Northern Illinois University Press).

Taubmann, Michel (2004), *L'affaire Guingouin: La véritable histoire du premier maquisard de France* (n.p.: Lucien Souny).

Taylor, Lynne (2000), *Between Resistance and Collaboration: Popular Protest in Northern France 1940–45* (London: Macmillan).

Teissier du Cros, Janet (1962), *Divided Loyalties: A Scotswoman in Occupied France* (London: Hamish Hamilton).

Terrisse, René (1993), *Bordeaux 1940–1944* (Paris: Perrin).

Terrisse, René (1996), *Grandclément. Traître ou bouc émissaire?* (Bordeaux: Aubéron).

Texcier, Jean (1945), *Écrit dans la nuit* (Paris: La Nouvelle edition).

Thomas, Martin (1996), 'The discarded leader: General Henri Giraud and the foundation of the French Committee of National Liberation', *French History* 10:86–111.

Tillion, Germaine (2000), 'Première Résistance en zone occupé: Du côté du réseau "Musée de l'Homme-Hauet-Vildé"', *Esprit* 261:106–24.

Tillon, Charles (1972), *Les FTP* (Genève: Crémille).

Tillon, Charles (1977), *On chantait rouge* (Paris: Laffont).

Torre, Evelyn (1999), 'Résistance et société en Corse' in Jean-Marie Guillon & Robert Mencherini (eds) *La Résistance et les Européens du sud* (Paris: L'Harmattan) pp. 237–46.

Trempé, Rolande (1983), 'Aux origines des comités mixtes à la production: Les comités d'entreprise dans la région toulousaine', *Revue d'histoire de la deuxième guerre mondiale* 131:41–64.

Tuquoi, Jean-Pierre (1987), *Emmanuel d'Astier: La plume et l'épée* (Paris: Arléa).

Vader, John (1977), *The Prosper Double-Cross* (Goonengerry: Sunrise).

Veillon, Dominique (1995), *Vivre et survivre en France 1939–1947* (Paris: Payot).

Veillon, Dominique & Alary, Eric (2000), 'Caluire: Un objet d'histoire entre mythe et polemique', in Jean-Pierre Azéma (ed.) *Jean Moulin face à l'histoire* (Paris: Flammarion) pp. 184–94.

Vergnon, Gilles (2002), *Le Vercors: Histoire et mémoire d'un maquis* (Paris: L'Atelier).

Verity, Hugh (2000), *We Landed by Moonlight: The Secret RAF Landings in France, 1940–1944* (Manchester: Crécy).

Verrier, Anthony (1991), *Assassination in Algiers* (London: Macmillan).

Veyret, Patrick (2003), 'Le Vercors et les Alliés (1943–1944)', *Histoire et Guerre* 41:24–41.

Vigreux, Marcel (1996), 'Sociologie de maquis de Bourgogne' in François Marcot (ed.), *La Résistance et les Français: Lutte armée et maquis*, Annales littéraires de l'Université de France-Comté, vol. 617, série Historiques n°. 13 (Paris: Belles Lettres) pp. 303–14.

Vildé, Boris (1997), *Journal et lettres de prison 1941–1942* (Paris: Allia).

Vinen, Richard (2006), *The Unfree French: Life under the Occupation* (London: Allen Lane).

Virgili, Fabrice (2000), *La France 'virile': Des femmes tondues à la Libération* (Paris: Payot).

Vistel, Alban (1970), *La nuit sans ombre* (Paris: Fayard).

Walters, Jo (2006), 'Remarks concerning a research note on *The Dutch Affair*', *Intelligence and National Security* 21:459–66.

Webster, Paul & Webster, Marcella (2004), *Voyages sur la ligne de demarcation: Héroisme et trahisons* (Paris: Le Cherche midi).

Weil-Curiel, André (1945), *Le Temps de la honte. I: Le jour se lève à Londres* (Paris: Myrte).

Weil-Curiel, André (1946), *Le Temps de la honte. II: Eclipse en France* (Paris: Myrte).

Weil-Curiel, André (1947), *Le Temps de la honte. III: Un voyage en enfer* (Paris: Myrte).

Weitz, Margaret Collins (1995), *Sisters in the Resistance: How Women Fought to Free France 1940–1945* (London: Wiley).

Wetterwald, François (1946), *Vengeance: Histoire d'un corps franc* (Paris: Mouvement Vengeance).

Wieviorka, Olivier (1996), 'Défense de la France et la lutte armée: evolution ou conversion?' in François Marcot (ed.), *La Résistance et les Français: Lutte armée et maquis*, Annales littéraires de l'Université de France-Comté, vol. 617, série Historiques n°.13 (Paris: Belles Lettres) pp. 97–106.

Wieviorka, Olivier (2007), *Histoire du débarquement en Normandie: Des origins à la libération de Paris 1941–1944* (Paris: Seuil).

Wolton, Thierry (1993), *Le Grand recrutement* (Paris: Grasset).

Wood, Nancy (2003), *Germaine Tillion, une femme-mémoire: D'une Algérie à l'autre* (Paris: Autrement).

Zamir, Meir (2005), 'An intimate alliance: The joint struggle of General Edward Spears and Riad al-Sulh to oust France from Lebanon, 1942–1944', *Middle Eastern Studies* 41:811–32.

Zamir, Meir (2007), 'De Gaulle and the question of Syria and Lebanon during the Second World War: Part I', *Middle Eastern Studies* 43:675–708.

Zapruder, Alexandra (ed.) (2004), *Salvaged Pages: Young Writers' Diaries of the Holocaust* (Yale: Yale University Press).

# *Notes*

## CHAPTER 1

1 There are many accounts of this period. Apart from references to specific incidents, in the short, general description given here I particularly relied upon Alexander (1990, 1997), Jackson (2003), Kershaw (2007), Lottmann (1992), Shennan (2000) and Spears (1954). For an alternative analysis, focusing on the successes and failures of Allied and German Intelligence, see May (2000).

2 Balbaud (1941), p. 8.

3 Balbaud (1941), p. 22.

4 All the memoirs covering this period have a similar tone, highlighting the contrast between the idyllic late-spring weather and what was to come. For example: 'The sky was cloudless and innocent, the air sweet, the untroubled earth went quietly about the business of nourishing all tender green young things, and we went quietly about ours, oblivious of the calamity that was bearing down upon France.' Borden (1946), p. 32.

5 There were 3,270 German combat aircraft deployed on 10 May, as against 1,610 Allied machines. Kirkland (1985), p. 102.

6 Balbaud (1941), pp 48–9. German rank-and-file soldiers also understood the impact of the dive-bomber attacks. A few days before, on the other side of the Nazi lines, Sergeant Prümers of the 1st Panzer Regiment had watched in appalled fascination as wave after wave of Stukas attacked French positions at Sedan: 'Simultaneously, like some bird of prey, they fall upon their victim and then release their load of bombs on the target. We can see the bombs very clearly. It becomes a regular rain of bombs that whistle down on Sedan and the bunker positions. Each time the explosion is overwhelming, the noise deafening. Everything becomes blended together; along with the howling sirens of the Stukas in their dives, the bombs whistle and crack and burst. A huge blow of annihilation strikes the enemy, and still more squadrons arrive, rise to a great height, and then come down on the same target. We stand and watch what is happening as if hypnotized; down below all hell is let loose!' Horne (1969), p. 247.

7 This was not so unusual – the command post of the Supreme Commander of Land Forces, General Gamelin, had no radio communication. Alexander (1990).

8 Gunsburg (1984); Gunsburg (1992), p. 225.

9 Gunsburg (1992), pp. 234–5.

10 Saint-Exupéry (1942), p. 48. The English translation has 'grains of dust'. This is a literal translation of the original 'graines de poussière', where 'graines' should be translated as 'specks'.

11 Saint-Exupéry (1942), p. 3.

12 Koestler (1968), p. 180.

13 There are many accounts of Dunkirk. I have used Sebag-Montefiore (2006).

14 In 1942 the historian Marc Bloch – an Anglophile who served as a rank-and-file soldier in 1940 – described the British soldier as 'by nature, a looter and a lecher: that is to say, he is guilty of two vices which the French peasant finds it hard to forgive when both are satisfied to the detriment of his farmyard and his daughters'. Bloch (1968), p. 70.

15 Barlone (1943), p. 60.

16 Cited in Jackson (2003), p. 206. The PPS in question was the future Prime Minister Alec Douglas-Home.

17 'Now it starts', *Time*, 20 May 1940.

18 Bankwitz (1967). According to Borden (1946), p. 47, the experience of coming under fire for the first time shook Weygand to the core. This was reported to her by her husband, Edward Spears. In his memoirs published eight years later, Spears makes no reference to this story in his account of their conversation. Spears (1954), p. 96.

19 Humbert (2008), p. 3.

20 Saint-Exupéry (1942), p. 72.

21 Spears (1954), p. 76.

22 Bloch (1968), p. 49.

23 On 26 June the population of Paris had collapsed to about thirty-five per cent of its pre-war figure. Around seventy-five per cent of the population of the sixteenth arrondissement fled, as against only fifty-four per cent of the poor, predominantly Jewish fourth arrondissement. Lottmann (1992), pp. 293–4.

24 Dubois (1946), p. 62. This period is well described in Irène Némirovsky's novel *Suite Française*, written at the time but published only in the twenty-first century. Némirovsky (2006).

25 Spears (1954), p. 151.

26 Spears (1954), p. 138.

27 Spears (1954), p. 178.

28 Spears (1954), p. 148.

29 Cited in Jackson (2003), p. 99. Weygand later sneered that when the British had to fight the Nazis, they would have their neck wrung like a chicken. Churchill's famous riposte was: 'Some neck. Some chicken.'

30 Spears (1954), p. 156.

31 The initial point of this clause was to ensure that, in case of victory, both sides would agree on how they carved up Germany. It took on a very different meaning in the light of an approaching Nazi victory.

32 Spears (1954), p. 206.

33  For details of the probable origins of the story, see Lottmann (1992), p. 328. The key point is that Weygand wanted to believe it.

34  Dubois (1946), p. 60. The cows were apparently from the Ferme d'Auteuil, a Parisian park.

35  Lottmann (1992), pp. 304–8.

36  Lottmann (1992), p. 319.

37  Bloch (1987), Rohwer (1999).

38  'Paris falls to the Germans', *Manchester Guardian*, 15 June 1940.

39  Lottmann (1992), p. 356.

40  Shlaim (1974), p. 38.

41  Shlaim (1974), p. 53.

42  Spears and de Gaulle have given two very different accounts of this journey, illustrating the difficulty of reconstructing history solely on the basis of memoirs. According to Spears, de Gaulle said to him that he feared he would be arrested under the orders of the defeatists who had gained the ascendancy, and asked to be taken to London. Spears then explains, in gripping detail, how, in order not to arouse suspicion, they travelled separately to the aerodrome, under the pretext of de Gaulle saying farewell to Spears. Having been delayed for five nerve-racking minutes while some string was found to attach de Gaulle's trunk full of papers, Spears hauled de Gaulle on board as the plane began to taxi, and the pair flew to London. This dramatic and apparently believable story contrasts with de Gaulle's account: 'Our departure took place without romanticism and without difficulty.' De Gaulle (1962a), p. 80. On the basis of the assurances he received from de Gaulle and his aide-de-camp, Geoffrey de Courcel, who was also present, the French journalist and historian Henri Amouroux dismissed Spears' account as worthy of *The Three Musketeers*. Amouroux (1964), p. 328.

43  Amouroux (1964), p. 332.

44  Koestler (1968), p. 206. The writer and teacher Jean Guéhenno was only slightly kinder in his diary entry for 17 June: 'There, it's over. An old man who no longer even has the voice of a man, but speaks like an old woman, told us at half past twelve that last night he had pleaded for peace.' Guéhenno (2002), p. 15.

45  Passy (1947a), p. 21.

46  There were cynical attempts to put a positive spin on the collapse. In his diary for 19 June, Koestler wrote with his customary sharpness: 'Listened during breakfast to repetition of new Foreign Minister Baudouin's broadcast of yesterday night: "It is because we are sure of the French people's spirit of independence . . . that we have asked on what conditions the carnage of our sons might be stopped." Strange how melodious a self-contradictory sentence can be made to sound in French. "Because we love independence, we accept Nazi domination."' Koestler (1968), p. 199.

47  Frenay (1976), p. 4.

48  Levy (1998), p. 35.

49  Barlone (1943), p. 78.

50  Koestler (1968), p. 199.

51 Koestler (1968), p. 276.

52 For explorations of the nature of Vichy, see Paxton (2001) and Jackson (2001) pp. 142–212. For a discussion of the distribution of right-wing political forces on either side of the demarcation line, see Kedward (1978) pp. 82–90. For the reality of life under the Occupation, see Vinen (2006) and Gildea (2002).

53 Saint-Exupéry (1942), p. 94.

54 Alexander (1997), p. 173.

55 Figures taken from Alexander (1997). For a close examination of the French army's performance after Dunkirk, see Alexander (2007).

56 Kirkland (1985).

57 Reynolds (1990).

58 Moulin's scarf-wearing pre-dated his suicide attempt. The iconic photo of Moulin, wearing a hat, overcoat and scarf, dates from before the war. There are many accounts of Moulin's life in French, some of them contentious and polemical. The best by far is that by Daniel Cordier (1989a, b, 1993a, 1999). In English, the most recent accounts are Marnham (2000) and Clinton (2001).

59 Alexander (1990).

60 Kershaw (2007), p. 63. See also n. 29 pp. 496–7.

61 During the 1936 strike wave, factories were occupied, and the bosses feared that revolution was around the corner. In fact the French Communist Party (PCF) was entirely under the thumb of Stalin, who wanted to maintain France as a friendly ally, faced with the threat of Nazi Germany, and the Communist leaders loyally argued that the strikes should end. Paid holidays and a shorter working week were immediately two of the real reforms introduced following the strike wave, but over the next three years business leaders and the right-wing parties gradually clawed these back.

62 Anonymous (n.d. 1940?), p. 13. The source is given as 'A British General, who is also a Conservative MP, and speaks excellent French, returned from Bordeaux.' This is clearly Spears.

63 Anonymous (n.d. 1940?), pp. 12–3.

64 Serge (1978), p. 381. An example of the reactionary mindset to be found at the summit of the armed forces was given by Maurice Gamelin, the commander-in-chief who had been in charge during the collapse of May 1940. In a report written while the battle still raged, Gamelin argued that the military leaders bore no responsibility for the impending defeat. He claimed it was all the fault of the French soldier, who 'did not believe in the war. His curiosity did not extend beyond the horizon of his factory, office or field. Disposed to criticize ceaselessly all those having the least authority, encouraged in the name of civilization to enjoy a soft daily life, today's serviceman did not receive the moral and patriotic education during the years between the wars which would have prepared him for the drama in which the nation's destiny will be played out.' Cited in Alexander (1997), p. 161. Alexander rightly describes this position as 'notorious, self-serving . . . grotesque'.

65 Crémieux-Brilhac (1990), p. 237. The Party was utterly discredited – swastikas were daubed on portraits of Party leader Maurice Thorez, militants

were spat at in the street. The PCF was viewed with even greater suspicion by the government and the state forces: not only were Communists loyal to Moscow rather than Paris, but they were now potentially the tools of the Nazis.

66 Crémieux-Brilhac (1990), p. 238.
67 Lottmann (1992), pp. 214–5.
68 Koestler (1968), p. 214.
69 http://www.winstonchurchill.org/i4a/pages/index.cfm?pageid=418 (accessed November 2008).
70 These events are described in Bell (2000).
71 The exact time of the broadcast is the subject of a surprising amount of debate, made more complicated by the fact that there are no clear records at the BBC. Contemporary accounts are clouded by the fact that the Germans had put the Occupied Zone on Berlin time (GMT-2), but it is not clear whether this was universally applied. For a summary of the conflicting evidence, which at least shows how difficult it can be to provide precise information even about such a minor event, see Luneau (2005), pp. 29–36. She thinks it most likely that de Gaulle's broadcast was at 22h00 London time.
72 De Gaulle's speech has been widely reproduced. Marcot et al. (2006), p. 1027.
73 Humbert (2008), p. 7.
74 Shennan (2000), p. 18.

## CHAPTER 2

1 Mandel (1986), p. 49.
2 Simon (1942), p. 23.
3 d'Aragon (1977), p. 18.
4 Cuvelliez (1995), p. 123.
5 Blumenson (1978), p. 70; Besse & Pouty (2006), p. 139.
6 Pineau (1960), p. 78.
7 Texcier (1945), pp. 8–20. For how the pamphlet was printed, see p. vii.
8 Humbert (2008), p. 14.
9 Blumenson (1978), p. 88.
10 To avoid Allied bombers using transmitters as navigation beacons, Radio Vichy and Radio Paris both stopped their long-range transmissions at 7.15 p.m. This left the field open for the BBC. Luneau (2005), p. 45.
11 Luneau (2005), pp. 78–82. This edition includes a CD of archive extracts of the Free French broadcasts on the BBC.
12 Cornick (2005).
13 When the Nazis eventually invaded the Free Zone, in November 1942, they made straight for the remaining ships of the French fleet moored at Toulon. See Chapter 5.
14 Kersaudy (1981), p. 85.
15 Horne (2000).
16 Martin-Chauffier (1976), p. 68.

17 Martin-Chauffier (1976), pp. 68–9.

18 Details from Radtke-Delacor (2001).

19 Diary entry for 19 October 1940. Schroeder (2000), p. 55. Liliane Schroeder's maiden name was Jameson.

20 Martin-Chauffier (1976), p. 71; Schroeder (2000), p. 77.

21 Guéhenno (2002), p. 89.

22 Diary entry for 10 January 1941. Schroeder (2000), p. 64.

23 Diary entry for 17 January 1941. Schroeder (2000), p. 66.

24 Vinen (2006), pp. 227 and 245.

25 BBC broadcast of November 1940, track 24, *11 novembre 1940: Témoignages & Archives historiques* (CD: Frémaux & Associés).

26 Luneau (2005), p. 85.

27 Bood (1974), p. 42. Subsequent quotes below are from pp. 45–6.

28 Not everyone got the joke, however – sixteen-year-old Communist militant Maroussia Naïtchenko was completely perplexed by the fishing rods. Naïtchenko (2003), p. 189.

29 Jean Guéhenno, diary entry for 15 November: 'On 11 November, around 5.30 p.m., I went to the Champs-Elysées. I saw the French police, under German orders, remove the flowers that passers-by had placed at the foot of the statue of Clemenceau. I saw the German soldiers bayonet-charge the school students on the pavements, I saw officers throw them to the ground. I heard machine-gun fire three times.' Guéhenno (2002), p. 66.

30 Schoenbrun (1981), p. 92.

31 Bood (1974), p. 45.

32 Schoenbrun (1981), p. 94.

33 A Parisian square and a Métro station now bear his name.

34 Bood (1974), p. 46.

35 See, for example, Kersaudy (1981), p. 81. Despite this whiff of messianism (which Churchill could also share), de Gaulle was lucid about his initial resources – 'At my side, not the shadow of a force, or of an organization. In France, no resonance and no fame. Abroad, neither credit nor justification' he later wrote in his memoirs (de Gaulle, 1962a, p. 82). Churchill was equally lucid and equally bold. On 27 June he met de Gaulle in Downing Street and said: 'You are alone – well! I shall recognize you alone.' Kersaudy (1981), p. 83.

36 Rémy (1948), p. 24.

37 Passy (1947a), p. 33.

38 Weil-Curiel published three volumes of memoirs relating to this period. However, they are generally taken to be of uncertain accuracy. Later, when in Gestapo custody, Weil-Curiel unwisely accepted a proposal to write anodyne reports on Vichy France for them. Although he did not betray anybody, his account reveals a systematic and strong streak of self-justification. Weil-Curiel (1945, 1946, 1947). See note 61 below.

39 Weil-Curiel (1946), p. 197.

40 Aveline (1962), p. 160.

41 Blanc (2004), p. 23.

42 Diary entry for 6 August 1940. Humbert (2008), p. 11.

43 There is only one published account of this period of the Resistance in any language (Blumenson, 1978). However, this work has no references, and although the author was able to interview many of the survivors in the 1970s, the wealth of verbatim detail ultimately undermines the book's credibility. As a reviewer put it: 'The effect of such passages, and there are many of them, is to detract from the verisimilitude of Blumenson's account, not add to it.' Silvestri (1978). French academic Julien Blanc has recently turned his attention to this period and has completed a PhD thesis on the subject.

44 Wood (2003). Hauet was supported by a group based in Versailles which included another retired colonel – Maurice Dutheil de la Rochère, a veterinary surgeon and a forty-eight-year-old Dominican monk. The veterinary surgeon was Julien Lafaye, who died at Sonnenbourg prison camp on 15 May 1944. The monk was Father Joseph Guihaire, who was beheaded in Brandenbourg camp on 5 December 1942. La Rochère was a reactionary and proud of it. He was a Catholic monarchist who had an office in an Education Ministry building, from where he could safely coordinate the activity of a wide range of individuals – firemen, a local bookseller, a cobbler, provincial shopkeepers and civil servants. From September 1940 this group produced a small journal entitled *La Vérité française* ('The French Truth'), the first regular Resistance periodical – thirty-two issues were produced before the Nazis smashed the organization in November 1941.

45 Ghrenassia (1987).

46 Humbert (2008) p. 18.

47 Martin-Chauffier (1976), p. 104.

48 Humbert (2008), p. 18. The Toulouse philosopher Georges Friedmann concurred, praising Vildé as 'the very image of the young communists I knew in the USSR'. Humbert (2008), p. 31.

49 *Résistance* 1, December 1940. Facsimile and transcription at http://www.vilde.fr/pages-f/resistance-f/resistance-1.htm (accessed 25 March 2008). See also Barbara Mellor's translation of the whole article in Humbert (2008), pp. 309–10.

50 Humbert (2008), p. 24. The fire was alight in case the police or the Gestapo should arrive – the idea was that the articles could be thrown into the flames. As additional cover, there was also a portrait of Pétain on the mantelpiece. After the editorial meeting was over, the Martin-Chauffier family would huddle around the dying embers. The family's Siamese cat purred. 'It was our weekly celebration of comfort and spirit,' wrote Simone Martin-Chauffier, in her diary (Martin-Chauffier, 1976, p. 80).

51 Humbert (2008), p. 29.

52 Blanc (2000).

53 Martin-Chauffier (1976), p. 78.

54 Humbert (2008), p. 20.

55 Tillion (2000).

56 La Rochère, Tillion and Hauet were all in contact with Captain d'Autrevaux, who was the main Paris agent of Vichy Intelligence (Blanc, 2000). Sections

of the Vichy military apparatus were keeping their options open in case the military tide began to turn against the Germans, and they passed information on to their colleagues in both US and UK Intelligence. Furthermore, Vildé himself had two possible connections with MI6, one direct, the other indirect. Georges Ithier may have been an MI6 agent, while two women from the US embassy, Penelope Royall and Josie Meyer, made regular visits and apparently acted as liaison with US Intelligence agents at the embassy. These suggestions are made by Blumenson (1978) and Blanc (2000), and may well be true, but there is no evidence.

57 See Dorrian (2006). Plans of the Saint-Nazaire pens were also obtained by the French ALLIANCE intelligence circuit, which worked for MI6 (Fourcade, 1973, p. 71).

58 Gernoux (n.d. 1946?), p. 15.

59 Humbert (2008), p. 28.

60 Humbert (2008), p. 28.

61 Weil-Curiel was unable to leave France and was eventually persuaded by Gaveau to return to Paris. He was arrested on the way. See note 38 above.

62 The group had no name at the time. 'Musée de l'Homme' was the title given to the group after the war by Germaine Tillion, when she was filling out an official form that would entitle the members and their descendants to various pension rights. As the official 'liquidateur' of the group, she had to come up with a name in a matter of minutes (Tillion, 2000).

63 When Germaine Tillion learned that Gaveau was the traitor, she hatched a plot, in conjunction with MI6, to kidnap him. This came to nothing. Wood (2003), p. 98 n. 113.

64 Tillion (2000), p. 121.

65 Humbert (2008), p. 93.

66 Sénéchal was found guilty of espionage but was acquitted of a charge of intelligence with the enemy. The reason for this apparent discrepancy was that the sole evidence of contact with the enemy was a letter he was carrying, which he had written, and which was addressed to de Gaulle. This letter was dictated to him by Gaveau. Roskothen considered it would have been immoral to condemn Sénéchal for something that a Gestapo agent had set him up to do. He was still executed. Wood (2003), p. 97.

67 Wood (2003), p. 101.

68 Vildé (1997), pp. 87–9.

69 Aveline (1962), pp. 161–3.


CHAPTER 3

1 Douzou (1995), pp. 36–7.

2 A copy of Frenay's manifesto has been found in a Toulouse archive. Cuvelliez (1995). For a slightly different version, see Cordier (1989a), pp. 25–8. In his memoirs, Frenay described the content of his manifesto quite honestly (Frenay, 1976, p. 14).

3 This number is still growing, as archives reveal hitherto unknown publications. This figure is taken from Aglan (2006). For an early survey of the underground press in France, see Bellanger (1961).

4 Frenay (1976), p. 20.

5 The title was a reference to the claim that there had been a Nazi 'fifth column' inside France prior to June 1940, conspiring for the defeat of France.

6 Schoenbrun (1981), p. 152.

7 Aglan (2006), p. 123.

8 Named after a decisive 1792 battle in which the forces of Revolutionary France defeated the Prussian army.

9 Simon (1942), p. 54. For an English-language account, see *La Lettre de la France Libre* 15 February 1942, pp. 18–19. A PDF of this publication is available: http://www.perfumefromprovence.com/associationsocfull.pdf (accessed August 2008).

10 See photo in Simon (1942), opposite p. 64.

11 Aglan (2006), p. 89.

12 Quoted in Langer (1947), p. 141. These illusions provoked a stinging criticism from General Spears, who wrote a memorandum in his usual sharp terms: 'Our painstaking attempts to propitiate the Vichy government might, conceivably, make a dispassionate observer conjure up the picture of a well-meaning person bent on feeding a lettuce to a rabbit while it is being chased around its cage by a stoat. A waste of lettuce, at best, since, if the rabbit were grateful, which would be unlikely, it will remain at the mercy of the stoat, bent on its ultimate destruction. Vichy is completely at the mercy of the Germans. Who can doubt it? Our pandering can no more alter the fact than can its own efforts at conciliation.' Kersaudy (1981), p. 127.

13 See Groussard (1964). He was eventually released, and in 1942 made his way to Switzerland, where he worked for MI6.

14 Vinen (2006), p. 135.

15 See Kitson (2008). There is a self-serving account of this period by the creator of the TR, Colonel Pierre Paillole (Paillole, 2003).

16 Aglan (2006), p. 90.

17 Bellanger (1961), pp. 32–7. *Pantagruel* was probably the first underground newspaper, appearing in October 1940 in Paris. It was produced and entirely written by Raymond Deiss, a music publisher. The odd title came from the name of a giant in Rabelais' eponymous poem 'Pantagruel'. Deiss produced sixteen issues before he was arrested in October 1941. He was beheaded by the Nazis in Cologne on 24 August 1943.

18 Pineau (1960), p. 95.

19 Pineau (1960), p. 99.

20 Pineau (1960), p. 93.

21 Pineau (1960), p. 100.

22 From the earliest days, ordinary people had expressed their opposition to the Occupation in an unorganized and often incoherent way. Those with a more political outlook tended to act in a typically political fashion, although not necessarily particularly effectively. So, for example, on 17 June 1940 –

even before de Gaulle had made his famous broadcast from London – Edmond Michelet, a Christian-Democrat in Brive, south of Limoges, handed out a leaflet consisting merely of six quotations from the French writer and philosopher Charles Péguy, who was killed at the beginning of the First World War, and which simply called for the fighting to continue. For discussions of women's involvement in all kinds of Resistance, see Weitz (1995); for the particular experience of the wives of POWs, see Fishman (1992).

23 Bood (1974), pp. 92–3.

24 Anonymous (1959), p. 88.

25 In Bordeaux, for example. See Terrisse (1993), p. 176.

26 Simon (1942), p. 58.

27 In the US science-fiction TV series *V* (1985), in which humans fight against an alien occupation in an unsubtle parallel with the Nazi Occupation, Resistance fighters scrawled V everywhere. When the programme was broadcast, the UK was in the midst of the year-long Great Miners' Strike. The miners, seeing a further parallel in the occupation of their pit villages by the police, in turn sprayed V on the sides of pit buildings.

28 As early as June 1940 the Nazis had a giant V on a flag in Paris, apparently to celebrate their victory over France, even though the German word for 'victory' is 'Seig'. Ousby (1997), p. 221.

29 Guéhenno (2002), p. 177. Simon (1942), p. 80, suggests that the Nazis introduced a weekly travel card in the Métro in order to prevent tickets being used by the Resistance. What later became known as the 'Carte Orange' continued to function in Paris until recently, when it was replaced by electronic passes.

30 Over 200,000 jobs were lost in the aviation industry after June 1940; the Renault car factories sacked a third of their workforce. In the key industrial area around Lille and Calais – the Nord-Pas-de-Calais, which was annexed by the Nazis and put under control of their Brussels HQ – unemployment soared from 18,000 in April 1940 to 248,000 by August. Details from Courtois (1980) and from Fridenson & Robert (1992).

31 This section is based on Anonymous (n.d.), Lecoeur (1971), Courtois (1980), Dejonghe (1987), Dejonghe & Le Maner (2000), Taylor (2000) and Lefebvre (2001).

32 Ever since the Nazis increased the working week by thirty minutes on 1 January 1941, the coalfield had seen a series of isolated protests over working time, lack of food or against victimization, involving strikes and sit-down protests at the bottom of the pit. Each time, a mixture of minor concessions and coercion – including arrests, deportation and occupation of the pitheads by German troops – put an end to the movements.

33 Taylor (2000), p. 75.

34 Dejonghe (1987), pp. 335–6. A group of Polish miners living in the region explained the situation in a leaflet: 'The appalling conditions imposed on the miners and their families have led to the magnificent movement. Some thought that the miners would behave like slaves, that they would bow their heads without saying a word. They were very much mistaken. It could not be

otherwise – the slave regime imposed on the miners, together with terribly reduced rations, has been made worse by the fact that pay has fallen far behind the cost of living . . . that's why all workers support this strike.' Ghesquier-Krajewski & Ghesquier-Krajewski (2002), p. 8 n. 39.

35 Ouzoulias (1975), pp. 87–9.

36 Security staff working for the Lens Mining Company spied on a typical women's demonstration on 3 June: 'Around fifty women with a hundred children marched from the Rue Saint-Pierre and the Avenue de la Fosse to a meeting at the pit, stopping at the pit gates; Paroy, a young lad aged around ten years old, marched with his mother, carrying a placard which we could not read. The movement was mainly led by the wives of the workers who live at 64 Rue de Flandre and 6 Rue de Picardie. Also involved were Simone Vasseur, an accountant at pit 12, Madames Coutiez, Ohermant, Abas, Scubic, Davalt and the daughters of Paul Adolphe. The demonstration began at 12h50, the Germans arrived and dispersed the protesters.' Lecoeur (1971), pp. 81–2.

37 Dejonghe (1987), p. 334.

38 Some families are still hurting, nearly seventy years later. In January 2005 the son of one of the deported miners, Gaston Damette, put an appeal on the Internet asking for anyone who had information about the end of his father's life. Damette senior died in Dachau on 21 June 1944.

39 For example, the Société des Mines de Lens received 428,287.50 francs in compensation for the 57,101 tons of coal it lost during the strike. Lecoeur (1971), p. 99.

40 Dejonghe (1987), p. 341.

41 Dejonghe (1987), p. 341.

42 In contrast, the number of tanks used in the attack was only slightly more than that employed to crush the French army, while fewer aircraft were involved compared with 1940.

43 Bood (1974), p. 108.

44 On 22 June seventeen-year-old Maroussia Naïtchenko and her comrades from the Jeunesses Communistes (Communist Youth) in the eleventh arrondissement of Paris were on a camping weekend on the banks of the Seine, in the countryside near Paris. One of the campers heard about the invasion on a cats' whisker radio, and the news flashed around the camp in an instant. Maroussia recalled: 'Some comrades went into the town to buy a newspaper. They brought it back and read it on the riverbank. I took a photo of them. Maurice Fiferman (whom we called Fifi), Maurice Feld and myself decided to swim across the Seine, while Titi got hold of a rowing boat to accompany us . . . We returned, accompanied by Smulz ['Titi'] Tizselman. I took a photo of him, in his borrowed rowing boat. There he is, so young, his hair tightly curled . . .' (Naitchenko, 2003, p. 217). The photo of Titi – slightly blurred – shows a thin, pale young man of seventeen, wearing large black bathing trunks and pulling hard on an oar as he struggles against the current. He is looking down and behind slightly, as though trying to see what is coming. Photo in Berlière & Liaigre (2004).

45 Naïtchenko (2003), pp. 168 and 180.

46 Had she and her comrades known of the anti-Semitic and equivocal terms that were used in the secret negotiations with the Occupiers (these have recently come to light – Besse & Pennetier, 2006) they would have been even more appalled. The negotiators reminded the Nazis that the Communist Party had supported the Stalin–Hitler pact and had not been beaten by what they called the 'Jewish dictatorship' of Interior Minister Mandel – indeed, they argued that the Communist Party's intransigence had hastened the Nazi victory. Finally, the Party leaders promised the Nazis to do nothing for them, but nothing against them. Despite the Nazi refusal to play ball and legalize the paper, the Communist Party leadership more or less kept to this promise until June 1941 (Besse & Pennetier, 2006, pp. 10–13).

47 Courtois (1980), p. 152. For analyses of the PCF's early attitude to the Occupation, see Gallissot (1971), Avakoumitch (1980), Courtois (1980) and Beaubatie (1992).

48 Courtois (1980), p. 189.

49 Instead, the PCF claimed, 'the National Independence Front, in order to fulfil its mission of liberation, must have as its fundamental force the working class of France with the Communist Party at its head'. In 1941 the Party was still determined to go it alone. Courtois (1980), p. 191.

50 Courtois (1980), p. 220.

51 Lévy-Osbert (1992), p. 37.

52 Lévy-Osbert (1992), p. 39.

53 Lévy-Osbert (1992), p. 46.

54 In the end, there were demonstrations at both places. See Guéhenno (2002), p. 177.

55 Lévy-Osbert (1992), p. 48.

56 This underlines the fact that the Nazis' savage reprisal policy was instituted *before* the wave of attempted sabotage and assassinations. Neumaier (2006).

57 Berlière & Liaigre (2004), p. 106.

58 Berlière & Liaigre (2004), p. 107.

59 For an excellent account of the Bataillons, the reasons why some historians doubted the existence of a group by that name, and details of how their history was subsequently distorted by the Communist Party, see Berlière & Liaigre (2004). This section owes much to their detailed archival study and compassionate analysis.

60 Moser's fine uniform may have led Fabien to believe he was shooting a high-ranking officer. In fact Moser was merely in charge of the navy's clothing depot at Montrouge. Berlière & Liaigre (2004), p. 324, n. 397.

61 The pistol had belonged to the Marquise d'Andurain, the mother of a Jeunesse Communiste member. An incredibly wealthy aristocrat, she was a cocaine addict who dealt opium from her smart Longchamp mansion, was allegedly involved in British, German and French spy networks, told her son she had killed three people, and ended her life in the Bay of Tangiers, murdered. Berlière & Liaigre (2004), pp. 98 and 325, n. 405, n. 406 and n. 415–18. For more information see her son's website http://dandurain.org (accessed January 2009).

62 See 'Terrorism cuts both ways', *Time*, 8 September 1941. Tony Bloncourt and Roger Hanlet shot at the German officer in the Bastille Métro station. Berlière & Liaigre (2004), p. 118.

63 Brustlein's 1989 account, quoted in Berlière & Liaigre (2004), pp. 130–1.

64 A German teacher in Nantes who knew Hotz well claimed in his diary that the dead man 'was in no sense a Hitlerian' (Gildea, 2003, p. 165). However, Hotz encouraged his subordinates to impose a 'strict control' of the Jewish population in order to ensure they were not exercising a profession that was forbidden under the new anti-Semitic laws (Berlière & Liaigre, 2004, p. 333, n. 560). Further, it seems unlikely that Hotz could have reached such a distinguished position without being 'Hitlerian' in at least some sense. For a general account of how the French responded to the Occupation, see Gildea (2002).

65 On 22 September Jean Guéhenno wrote in his diary: 'Twelve hostages were shot the day before yesterday, in reprisal following an attack against a German army officer. And Stülpnagel warns us that he will do much better the next time. At the other end of Europe, Leningrad, Kiev and Odessa are besieged, and every day thousands of men die. This thought virtually never leaves me.' Guéhenno (2002), p. 188.

66 Berlière & Liaigre (2004), p. 62.

67 Terrisse (1993), pp. 83–4.

68 Guéhenno (2002), p. 200.

69 Berlière & Liaigre (2004), p. 134.

70 There are conflicting views on why forty-eight hostages were killed, not fifty. Neumaier (2006) argues convincingly that the Germans simply made a mistake, and named two hostages who were not in fact in custody at the time.

71 Krivopissko (2006), pp. 80–1. In October 2007 Moquet's letter became a subject of national debate. First, the letter was tastelessly read to the French rugby team in the dressing room shortly before their opening match in the 2007 Rugby World Cup, apparently to motivate them. Embarrassingly, they lost. Then, on 22 October 2007, President Sarkozy ordered the letter to be read out in all French high schools. Many teachers were outraged by what they saw as an attempt to manipulate the history of the Resistance and to interfere in the education system (*Le Monde*, 23 October 2007).

72 Guéhenno (2002), p. 201.

73 Guéhenno (2002), p. 201.

74 Debarge (2001), p. 38. This is the third version of Debarge's notebooks to be published, but the only one that is reliable. It contains a concordance of the differences between the three editions, and a depressing account of how the PCF manipulated the text for its own ends in the post-war period.

75 In his notebook, Debarge repeatedly claims that a derailment he carried out in September 1941 at Quiéry-la-Motte led to the death of fifty Nazi soldiers.

76 Dejonghe & Le Maner (2000), p. 298.

77 Conrad Miret-Muste said to Brustlein: 'On behalf of the Party leadership, I say to you: "Well done, lads! Now we should go for von Stülpnagel."' Berlière & Liaigre (2004), p. 141. One of the participants, Tony Bloncourt, eventually began to wonder how he could be certain that the leadership had in fact

wanted them to carry out these actions (Berlière & Liaigre, 2004, p. 220). This, however, was understandable paranoia caused by their isolation. They were indeed carrying out the orders of the Party and, ultimately, of Stalin. For these young people there could be no higher calling.

78 Berlière & Liaigre (2004), p. 88.

79 Reproduced in Noguères et al. (1969), p. 156. They point out that in the version of this text that was subsequently published by de Gaulle in his memoirs, the phrase 'not to kill Germans openly' replaced the blunter 'not to kill Germans', which was how it was originally pronounced on the BBC.

80 'While the derailment of a munitions train that leads to the arrest of a devoted militant is a pin-prick for Hitler, it's a serious loss for the working class, which lacks leaders . . . The masses hate the regime. But they do not yet believe in the possibilities of struggle, because Hitler continues to win victories, even if they are costly . . . It would be a profound error to sacrifice the working-class vanguard – that is, tomorrow's Revolution – for the mediocre results of the current sabotage campaign.' *La Vérité* 20, 15 September 1941, p. 1. Reproduced in Anonymous (1978), p. 59.

81 Lévy-Osbert (1992), p. 52.

82 Guéhenno (2002), p. 202.

83 Naïtchenko (2003), pp. 246–7.

84 Courtois (1980), p. 239.

85 Berlière & Liaigre (2004), p. 325, n. 422.

86 For analyses of the Nazi reprisal policy, see Besse & Pouty (2006) and Neumaier (2006).

87 One of the most notorious of these was the trial that took place in the Maison de la Chimie – see Rossel-Kirschen (2002). Courtois (1980, pp. 201–2, n. 24) suggests that Péri could have been saved but that the PCF leadership around Jacques Duclos preferred to gain a martyr and rid themselves of a troublesome independent thinker. Given the brutal cynicism of the Stalinist leadership, this is quite possible.

88 Rémy (1948), p. 328.

89 Calculation from Berlière & Liaigre (2004), p. 246.

90 Naïtchenko (2003), pp. 254–5.

91 Berlière & Liaigre (2004), p. 255.

92 Pineau (1960), p. 94.

93 de Montety (2005), p. 275.

94 de Montety (2005), p. 278.


## CHAPTER 4

1 See list of all RAF flights to France in Verity (2000), pp. 191–210.

2 Noguères et al. (1969), p. 141. The boys also met de Gaulle, but because of the row over his Brazzaville comments, this was not publicized. A slightly different version of the boys' account can be found at http://www.france-libre.net/temoignages_documents/1_6_1_8_Manche_en_canoe.htm (accessed August 2008). A photo of

their visit to 10 Downing Street, mistitled as 'French scouts who are going to join the FFL Naval School', can be found in Noguères et al. (1967) between pp. 368 and 369.

3 Much of what follows about Moulin is based on the work of Daniel Cordier (Cordier 1989a, 1989b, 1993a, 1999). During the final months of Moulin's life, Cordier was his secretary; in the 1980s Cordier ceased being an art dealer and became Moulin's biographer in an attempt to counter Frenay's 1977 allegation that Moulin had been a Soviet agent. The four massive volumes of Cordier's (unfinished) project (over 4,000 pages) are a masterly account of Moulin's life and work.

4 Baynac (2007), p. 71. Cot moved to the USA after de Gaulle decided not to give him a post in the Free French apparatus, while Dolivet moved in January 1941, shortly after meeting Moulin in Marseilles. Cot is thought to have been the source of the $3,000 that Moulin received from the USA at the beginning of 1941, but there is no clear evidence for this (Baynac, 2007, p. 129). Cot eventually rallied to de Gaulle, and in 1943 was sent to negotiate with the USSR. After the war Dolivet went to Hollywood, became a close friend of Orson Welles and produced Welles' 1955 film *Mr Arkadin*. Péan (1998), followed by Marnham (2000), insinuates that Cot and Dolivet were linked to Soviet Intelligence and may have directly or indirectly involved Moulin. There is no evidence for this (see note 9 below). For a sober discussion of Moulin's relation to the entourage of Pierre Cot, see Jansen (2000).

5 Moulin met Pierre Meunier and Robert Chambeiron several times in Paris between November 1940 and April 1941 and discussed collecting material for his report. Meunier (1993).

6 Some of Moulin's contacts over this period were with people connected with foreign Intelligence services, including Harry Robinson, the Paris chief of Soviet Intelligence, and Toussaint Raffini, a member of an MI6 intelligence circuit. These facts have excited a great deal of speculation, but there is no evidence that Moulin knew of the clandestine activities of these people. Moulin claimed he helped produce and give out Resistance material in Marseilles and Montpellier. Cordier (1999), p. 68. This may not have been the case – see Douzou (2000), p. 91.

7 Howard L. Brooks, 'Confidential report on France', sent to International Free World Association (n.d. autumn 1941?). Partially reproduced in Baynac (1998), pp. 419–26. For the full report, see US National Archives RG OSS E 92, Box 99, Folder 17. Dolivet wanted the proposed 'service' to run through Geneva, apparently with the aid of the British. But because of MI6's decision to veto all collaboration with Dolivet, none of Brooks' telegrams to the USA, sent via the British in Geneva, were ever transmitted (Péan, 1998, pp. 323 and 342–3; see also pp. 2–3 of Brooks' report – Baynac, 1998, pp. 421–2). On his return to the US, Brooks gave an account of his mission to a British agent in New York (Baynac, 2007, p. 184). He also discussed with OSS agent John Hughes in May 1942, and made a good impression on OSS spy chief Allen Dulles, who called him 'a solid citizen' (Memorandum from Allen

Dulles to Hugh R. Wilson, 16 May 1942, US National Archives RG OSS E 92, Box 99, Folder 17). Baynac (1998) p. 94, cites an FBI report which states that Brooks' mission had the support of the US Office of Strategic Services (OSS) – the forerunner of the CIA. This report dates from 1967, and merely quotes another source, from 1947. There is no contemporary proof of the involvement of OSS, or any other US agency, in the Brooks mission. Note that OSS was created only in June 1942, while its predecessor, the Office of the Coordinator of Information, was not set up until June 1941, by which time Brooks was already in France – see Srodes (1999). The British were suspicious of Brooks, as they were of other Americans in France at the time (Baynac, 2007, p. 83).

8  Péan (1998), pp. 307–16.
9  Péan (1998), pp. 317–20 and 324–34. On 2 June 1941 the man who was most enthusiastic about using Dolivet, the Labour Minister of Economic Warfare, Hugh Dalton, apparently accepted that 'The final decision [about working with Dolivet] will be taken by MI5' (Péan, 1998, p. 332). Péan's book has virtually no references to the copious archive material he cites, and the reader is therefore obliged to take his sources, translations and editing on trust. Dolivet had been a supporter of the Comintern, the international organization of Communist Parties. Cot was a Stalinist fellow-traveller, while the director of the USC in France was Noel Field, who had been recruited by Soviet Intelligence in 1935. Péan (1998) insinuates that the Brooks mission was a Stalinist plot, while Baynac (2007) claims that it was designed 'to put the Resistance under the financial control of the USA' (Baynac, 2007, p. 183). The truth is much simpler. Dolivet and Cot wanted to support the Resistance and to encourage US intervention in the war. They were prepared to work with any number of clandestine services – Dolivet's approaches to the British prove as much – but in 1941 none was prepared to help the Brooks mission. There is no evidence that at this time Moscow had anything to do with Field, or the USC, or Cot or Dolivet. Dolivet was in close contact with British Intelligence (see above) and was viewed with deep suspicion by Harry Robinson, the chief Soviet agent in Paris (Baynac, 2007, p. 88). Nor is there any proof that any US or British agency was involved in setting up or supporting the Brooks mission (indeed, the British apparently sabotaged Brooks' communications). Field became a Communist in the 1920s and an NKVD (Soviet Intelligence) agent in 1935 when he worked for the League of Nations in Switzerland. In 1937, during the Stalinist purges, his NKVD handlers, Reiss and Krivitsky, broke with Moscow. Krivitsky defected to the West, while Reiss became a Trotskyist, publicly denouncing Stalinism, before being murdered by his ex-comrades. Field's last contact with the NKVD was in 1938, when he participated in the plot to assassinate Reiss. Field subsequently joined the USC, where he gave preferential treatment to Communist refugees. According to a study made after the opening of the East European archives, Field 'did not do this at the direction of Soviet Intelligence, which had not re-established contact with him after his 1938 Moscow visit'. Schmidt (2004), pp. 234–5.

10 See Brooks (1942). For Fry's amazing story, see Marino (1999).

11 In his memoirs, written in the 1970s, Frenay claims he had previously met Brooks in 1940 (Frenay, 1976, p. 88). There is no evidence that Brooks travelled to France before May 1941; it appears that Frenay's memory failed him.

12 Brooks (1942), p. 105.

13 Brooks (1942), p. 106. Frenay was suspicious of Moulin because he was not linked to any movement, and he might therefore be either a Communist – in which case Frenay thought he would be untrustworthy – or a 'de Gaullist' – in which case he would be watched by the police. Despite Frenay's doubts, the meeting eventually took place in Marseilles in August 1941, shortly before Brooks returned to the USA. A depressing amount of energy and bile has been dispensed by French historians on the subject of the exact date of this meeting – for which there is no decisive proof, Frenay himself giving contradictory dates. Behind the squabbling lurks the spectre of Moulin's supposed links with Soviet Intelligence. If Moulin was a Stalinist agent, goes the argument, he would have shown a clear commitment to go to London only after Hitler's attack on the Soviet Union in June 1941. Therefore, continues the argument, those like Daniel Cordier who claim that Moulin was not a Stalinist agent have insisted that the meeting took place before June 1941. Whatever may have been Cordier's motivations, a number of authors, such as Belot (2003) and myself, do not consider that Moulin was a Soviet agent and are quite happy to accept that the meeting with Frenay took place in August. Cordier now apparently accepts this. Baynac (2007), pp. 142–4, contains a triumphant and somewhat tendentious account of the dispute.

14 Frenay (1976), p. 90.

15 For photos of Moulin's two residences in Lisbon, see Lecourt (1999).

16 The history of SOE has been written many times. The most important summaries are by Mackenzie (2000) and Foot (2004). For an overview of SOE's history and activity, see the memoirs of its main historian, M. R. D. Foot (Foot, 2008). For an insight into how people were recruited to SOE without even knowing what they were working for, and the perils that awaited them, see Nigel Perrin's biography of SOE agent Harry Peulevé (Perrin, 2008). SOE knew Moulin was going to Lisbon – they had heard of his plans back in April, through Louis Dolivet (Péan, 1998, p. 317–20). Throughout the summer Dolivet pestered Lisbon about Moulin's supposedly imminent arrival, much to the irritation of the embassy. When Dolivet finally heard that Moulin had arrived in Lisbon, he cabled SOE in London, urging his old friend to come to New York (NA HS 7/220, p. 1612). London duly transmitted the message to Moulin, who merely reiterated his determination to go to London and sound out the Free French (Péan, 1998, pp. 320 and 365–6; Baynac, 2007, p. 211). According to a message from SOE Lisbon to London, Moulin claimed he had not seen Dolivet for two years (Baynac, 2007, p. 212). If this was an accurate transcription of Moulin's response, he either told a deliberate lie or was confused: the two men had met in Marseilles ten months earlier, at the end of 1940.

17 Baynac (2007), p. 225. By this time Moulin had already been in London for over a month.

18 That evening Moulin wrote a letter to Pierre Cot: 'I am happy to be able finally to write to you from a free country, and to send you my fondest regards . . . For some time, you've known that I have decided not to go to America, thinking that I could better help our poor country by following another road and being closer to our British friends. On the other hand, I heard, from various sources, that you were more useful in the USA, and that you are still working hard for the Allied cause. To each their destiny . . . In France, despite the spectre of Communism, so carefully conjured up by Berlin, Paris and Vichy, we are bearing up, and morale in the Occupied Zone is fantastic. We will have a great victory.' Cordier (1999), p. 80.

19 Cordier (1999), p. 80.

20 Piquet-Wicks (1957), p. 41.

21 There are no records of the meeting. Emmanuel d'Astier's description of his first meeting with de Gaulle is striking: 'He's even taller than one expects. His movements are slow and heavy like his nose. His small head and waxen face are carried on a body of indeterminate structure. His most habitual gesture is to raise his forearms while keeping his elbows to his side. At these moments, his inert, very white, rather feminine hands, their palms turned downwards and attached to his arms by too-slender wrists, seem to be raising a whole world of abstract burdens.' D'Astier (1958), p. 72.

22 The US considered that the Free French Intelligence (BCRA) was 'an agency of the Gestapo'. Cordier (1999), p. 135. For an examination of the various 'affairs' that were used to justify this view, in particular the death of a prisoner in BCRA's jail in its Duke Street headquarters in London, see Belot (2006a), pp. 532–47.

23 Brossolette (1976), p. 144. This letter to Pierre Cot has never been found, and may never have existed; this quote is based on the memory of Pierre Brossolette's wife, Gilberte, recalling a conversation with Pierre Cot. The passage in her memoirs reads: 'Discussing the role that the head of state might play, once peace came, seemed premature to him [Pierre Brossolette]. He would decide later. He said that to me. He also said it to close friends like Daniel Mayer and Pierre Cot. The latter said to me one day: "There were many of us who thought that way. Jean Moulin himself, my old *chef de cabinet*, my friend, wrote to me in his letters: *For the moment, we must be with de Gaulle. Afterwards, we'll see.*"'

24 'Interview with M. Moulins' (sic), document dated 4.11.41. NA FO 898/198, p. 3.

25 All references are to the SOE English translation of Moulin's document, 'Report on the activities, plans and requirements of the groups formed in France with a view to the eventual liberation of the country', which was used at the time. Foot (2004), pp. 437–46. There has been some debate by French historians over the implications of the terms used by Moulin to describe his relations with the three Resistance groups (only one of which he had any contact with). The SOE translation says that he had been 'entrusted' with

writing the report by the Resistance, and concludes that he was 'a mere messenger, briefed by the movements LLL to transmit an SOS to London' (Foot, 2004, p. 445). The SOE summary of Moulin's situation, before he arrived in the UK, says that 'he had been commissioned by "Libération", "Libération Nationale" and "Liberté" to place their case before the British and de Gaulle authorities' (NA HS 7/220, p. 1612, document dated 26–30.9.41). Some historians have argued that Moulin was 'bluffing' by pretending to have been 'mandated' by the groups, when in fact he was not. These arguments revolve around different French translations of the English translation by SOE. The French original does not seem to have been found. This fact, the relevance of which does not seem to have been recognized by French historians, is indicated by Belot (2000), p. 397, n. 51. The two contemporary English translations – 'entrusted' and 'commissioned . . . to place their case' – do not seem too far off the real situation.

26 De Gaulle's reputation in London began to decline in September 1940 when a joint Free French and British attempt to seize the West African French naval base at Dakar failed dismally, partly because neither the local population nor the garrison were impressed by the presence of de Gaulle in the fleet offshore. The fact that the British allowed six Vichy cruisers to sail through the Strait of Gibraltar to Dakar did not help. Afterwards, de Gaulle was deeply depressed; the mission was a disaster and he had handed Vichy a propaganda coup – his forces had fired against Vichy French troops. See Marder (1976) and Kersaudy (1981). After the Syrian campaign in 1941, a secret protocol was agreed behind de Gaulle's back, under which 30,000 Vichy troops, together with their arms and nearly 3 tons of gold, were repatriated to Vichy France. Crémieux-Brilhac (2001); Kersaudy (1981); de Wailly (2002) provides a peculiarly pro-Vichy account. De Gaulle's accusation about the British attitude towards France was made in Brazzaville in August 1941. On the plane back, de Gaulle further criticized the British, in a conversation which was reported back to London by René Balbaud, who had joined the Free French after escaping from Dunkirk (see Chapter 1). Mackenzie (2000), p. 262, n. 4. Balbaud was by now an SOE agent who was working as a radio broadcaster in Africa (NA HS 9/79/3).

27 When de Gaulle returned to the UK and requested a meeting with the Prime Minister, Churchill replied icily: 'Until I am in possession of any explanation you may do me the honour to offer, I am unable to judge whether any interview between us would serve a suitable purpose' (Kersaudy, 1981, p. 153). Nearly two weeks later, the two leaders finally met. They had a blazing row, banishing the translator so they could go at each other directly. However, Churchill eventually got an apology and pressed home his advantage, suggesting that de Gaulle should create a collective leadership of the Free French movement. This proposal, which was intended to weaken de Gaulle's influence, coincided with a plot to oust de Gaulle, led by the head of the Free French navy, Admiral Muselier, and by the physicist and journalist Dr André Labarthe. Muselier was largely motivated by jealousy, while Labarthe (who had been a colleague of Moulin's and later admitted to

having been a Soviet agent since 1935) distrusted de Gaulle's right-wing tendencies and wanted to give the Free French a more 'social' orientation. The outcome of a week of feverish politicking and British mediation was indeed a Comité National Français (French National Committee), but all the power lay in de Gaulle's hands. Muselier was neutralized, and Labarthe was banished from the inner circles of Free French power. Churchill was not amused: 'This is very unpleasant. Our intention was to compel de Gaulle to accept a suitable council. All we have done is to compel Muselier and Co. to submit themselves to de Gaulle.' Cited in Kersaudy (1981), p. 167.

28  Foot (2004), p. 444.
29  Baynac (2007), p. 261.
30  Foot (2004), p. 446.
31  Péan (1989); Cordier (1989b), pp. 50–1.
32  Moulin, together with the head of the Free French secret service, Passy, had travelled to Manchester in late October, where they underwent the parachute training course at Ringway aerodrome (now Manchester International Airport). They landed in the nearby park of Broughton Hall (now Tatton Park). There is a memorial in the park to all those who trained at the site during the war, many of whom never returned from their missions.
33  Passy (1947a), p. 236.
34  For accounts of the affair, and the subsequent fate of Admiral Muselier, who tried to mutiny against de Gaulle in March 1942, see Kersaudy (1981) and Kersaudy (2004).
35  Mandel (1986), p. 66.
36  US National Archives RG OSS E 92, Box 99, Folder 17.
37  This was the opinion of Pascal Copeau, d'Astier's right-hand man, in June 1943. Cordier (1999), p. 165.
38  This scene is described in de Bénouville's novel *Le Sacrifice du Matin* (1945), p. 231.
39  Cordier (1999), p. 142. Cordier says there is only one copy of this document, in the SOE archives in the National Archives at Kew, but gives no reference.
40  Noguères et al. (1969), p. 306.
41  Frenay (1976), p. 123.
42  Cordier (1999), pp. 144–6.
43  Claude Bourdet later wrote: '. . . on a local level it was not always easy to find enough able leaders for each service, and we also discovered that those who were supposedly put in reserve in the AS [Secret Army], waiting for a hypothetical day, ran the risk of being rusty on the day we needed them, of going soft.' Bourdet (1975), p. 116.
44  Frenay (1976), p. 124.
45  Belot (2006a), p. 170.
46  Cornick (1994).
47  Foot (2004), p. 102.
48  Aubrac (1993), pp. 20–1. Aubrac was bluffing; she simply chose a message that was broadcast at lunchtime and told the Prosecutor it would be broadcast in the evening.

49 Rémy (1948), p. 246.

50 Rémy (1948), pp. 239–41.

51 Bertram (1995), p. 46.

52 Brossolette (1976), p. 118.

53 Brossolette (1976), p. 120.

54 Rémy (1948), p. 238.

55 Brossolette (1976), p. 121.

56 Piketty (1998), p. 165.

57 Calmette (1961). Despite this link with the Vichy military, the OCM was deeply hostile to the Pétain regime. In January 1941 an internal position document set out the OCM's perspective, which was clearly impregnated with the classic views of the French far right, and led them to rally to de Gaulle: 'There is neither esteem for the Vichy government nor any hope for it . . . The failure of the Vichy government is blatantly obvious . . . It is not for the mass of the population to decide what the new order should be. It is for leaders to shake public opinion out of its confused thinking.' Calmette (1961), p. 25.

58 Calmette (1961), Perrault (1975).

59 For the Free French in London, and in particular for Passy's BCRA, the growth of the CND was incredibly important. The British were above all interested in German troop movements in the Occupied Zone; through the CND Passy could now not only show the BCRA's worth to the British, he could also trade its intelligence in exchange for material favours.

60 Pineau (1960), p. 130.

61 On his return to Paris, Pineau was brought back to earth with a terrifying bump: the Gestapo had raided his apartment and had arrested René Parodi, a leading member of Libération-Nord. A few days later, Parodi was found hanged in his cell.

62 Passy (1947b), p. 61. See also Chapter 3, n. 87.

63 It was broadcast by the BBC on 7 March 1942. Crémieux-Brilhac (2001), p. 438.

64 Pineau (1960), p. 145.

65 Verity (2000), p. 35.

66 Although Rémy (1948) describes the plane getting stuck (p. 287), Pineau's account makes no reference to this (Pineau, 1960, p. 147). Verity (2000), p. 192, confirms Rémy's account and gives the precise duration of the incident: seventeen minutes (this is presumably based on the pilot's records). The landing field is indicated by a stone marker, by the side of the N147 heading north-west out of Loudun in the Vienne département. The site was never used again.

67 Barbara Bertram, who welcomed Resistance visitors to her Sussex manor house (see note 71 below), woke on 1 May to find a freshly cut bunch of Lily-of-the-valley on her breakfast table, brought over from France in the night and presented, in the French tradition, for May Day (Bertram, 1995, p. 23).

68 In 1988 Hugh Verity recalled the problems faced by Lysander pilots: 'Very few pickups failed because of enemy action or errors in pilot navigation.

With only a voice back-bearing over the Channel, a map, a compass, a clock and blind flying instruments, how was it done? Well, there were six things one had to do, and four of them before taking off. The first was to plan a route avoiding *Flak*, with a good landmark at the end of each leg. Second, cut half-million maps to cover fifty miles on each side of the planned track, and fold it like a concertina . . . Having prepared the map, the third thing to do was to study it for an hour or two before take-off, memorizing the shapes and the compass bearings of major landmarks. Fourthly, one had to calculate the gen card in the light of forecast wind, and then, fifthly, . . . you had to fly the planned headings and speeds very accurately until the error in the forecast wind showed up because you had drifted off your planned track. Then you had to do a bit of mental geometry in the light of the different wind, and adjust your heading and, of course, the sixth thing, very obviously, mapreading when weather permitted . . . for this, water was the best landmark, coast, rivers or lakes, and, after that, forests and railways, and the last leg, which could only be a couple of minutes long, really, had to be from a really certain visual fix, a particular village or stream, or railway crossing or something like that which you could be certain you were identifying and from there do an accurate timed run of two or three minutes when, lo and behold, you would see the agreed Morse letter flashing up from the dark ground and that was really quite a thrill.' Sowrey (1989), pp. 26–7.

69 Verity (2000), p. 192. Pineau does not seem to have noticed that it was the same pilot, whom he calls 'Henry' (Pineau, 1960, pp. 234–46).

70 NA HS 9/932. His full name was William Guy Lockhart. He joined SOE on 12 January 1943 but was 'posted away for service reasons to A.I.2.c.' on 1 May 1943. Lockhart's SOE file shows that in December 1941 he and his wife, Ruby Lockhart, had one child. According to Rémy, in 1942 Lockhart's baby son had recently died, and he carried a pair of small white shoes as a mascot (Rémy, 1948, p. 284).

71 The story of the house and of the Bertrams' work is given in Barbara Bertram's charming memoir, *French Resistance in Sussex* (Bertram, 1995).

72 All details are from Pineau (1960), p. 150.

73 Pineau (1960), p. 153.

74 Passy was particularly impressed by Pineau – 'Full of dynamism and courage, he could easily absorb an incredible amount of detail' (Passy, 1947b, p. 64).

75 Pineau (1960), p. 157.

76 Pineau (1960), p. 157.

77 Pineau (1960), p. 158.

78 Pineau (1960), pp. 158–9.

79 Bourdet (1975), p. 98.

80 Pineau (1960), p. 185. For an examination of how de Gaulle treated the Resistance in his public declarations during the course of the war (in general he ignored it ), see Rajsfus (2004), pp. 257–67.

81 Pineau (1960), p. 222.

## CHAPTER 5

1 Chevance-Bertin (1990), p. 75.

2 Frenay (1976), pp. 131–2.

3 Frenay (1976), p. 149.

4 Frenay (1976), pp. 149–51.

5 Kitson (2008), pp. 135–6. For Paillole's account, see Paillole (2003), pp. 243–4.

6 Frenay's semi-verbatim account of the meeting, written soon afterwards, is reproduced in Belot (2003), pp. 259–62.

7 Brunet (1986), p. 236.

8 Frenay (1976), p. 141. This is not included in the apparently truncated, semi-verbatim account drawn up by Frenay the same day (Belot, 2003, pp. 264–6).

9 Frenay later recalled: 'What a bizarre situation! What luxury! And what fine fare in this elegant restaurant. Mme. Rollin was a very refined woman and not indifferent to political questions; in fact, she was bursting with political observations. She was a Russian, one of those whose accent never lets you forget it. Perhaps because of her origin she was sympathetic to the Allies. She tended to minimize all German victories, always implying that they were transitory, insubstantial. As I listened to her I began to wonder whether it was I or she who was representing the Resistance.' Frenay (1976), p. 142. A few weeks later, Rollin was pursuing another lead and questioned Marie-Madeleine Fourcade, head of the ALLIANCE intelligence circuit, who worked for MI6. (At this stage her name was Marie-Madeleine Méric; after the war, she married again and changed her name to Fourcade, by which she is now generally known.) A similar discussion took place, with the result that some ALLIANCE spies were released from jail, and Rollin provided Fourcade with official ID in a false name. It was on the way to this meeting that Fourcade came up with the famous animal code names for the hundreds of ALLIANCE agents (Eagle, Fawn, Firefly, etc. – Fourcade herself was Hedgehog). This choice led the Nazis to call her circuit 'Noah's Ark'. Fourcade (1973), pp. 109–14. The English translation truncates a number of minor details found in the original (Fourcade, 1972, vol. 1, pp. 182–5).

10 The best account of these discussions (including an accurate dating), and of the positions of Frenay and Combat, is in Belot (2003), pp. 267–73. Thirty-seven of the forty-five Combat prisoners were finally condemned to sentences of less than a year. This was academic, however, as most of them had already gone underground and they were tried in their absence.

11 For details, see Belot (2003), pp. 273–6.

12 Piketty (1998), p. 171.

13 Douzou (1995), p. 103.

14 D'Astier and Frenay met in Lyons, together with Moulin. There was a furious exchange, as d'Astier accused Combat of 'serious errors' and 'grave compromises' (Frenay, 1976, p. 146). Moulin did his best to restrain d'Astier's self-interested (and perhaps somewhat artificial) indignation, and at the end of March he called a meeting of the leaders of both groups to discuss

the situation. To make the situation less confrontational, Moulin also invited a representative of the new Lyons newspaper, *Le Franc-Tireur*. Moulin seems to have worked diplomatic wonders, as the outcome was 'complete agreement' and, after a delay of several months, the publication of a common statement which not only brought formal closure to the affair, but also concluded by reinforcing the link between the Resistance and de Gaulle: 'We affirm that we are carrying out a united action, aimed at the same goal, motivated by the same ideal, and that we recognize General de Gaulle as the leader and symbol of the French resistance' (*Libération* 25 August 1942). The appearance of this statement was preceded by an important shift in the attitude of Frenay and of Combat, both of which finally abandoned their previous ambiguity towards Pétain and Vichy, and publicly embraced the cause of the Free French (Belot, 2003, p. 279).

15 Cordier (1999), pp. 172–3.

16 Moulin wrote to de Gaulle giving his overall verdict on Frenay: 'F [Frenay] has been a member of the Resistance from the very beginning, he has created a very important organization and is full of courage and dynamism; his good faith in this affair cannot be questioned . . . However, it is deeply regrettable that his more or less open hopes in the possibility that the Marshal would make a sharp change of tack – hopes which he entertained until relatively recently – led him to maintain his contacts with some Vichy leaders.' Cordier (1999), p. 173 and Péan (1998), p. 409. From the beginning of 1942 Frenay showed his loyalty to the Gaullist project. A year earlier he received a substantial sum of money from General Viscount Benoit-Léon Fornel de la Laurencie, who was hostile to collaboration but considered de Gaulle to be a traitor – he had been a member of the military tribunal that had sentenced de Gaulle to death in autumn 1940 (Barasz, 2007). In November 1941 Frenay met la Laurencie in the presence of two Americans, 'Mr Smith' and 'Mr Scott'. Smith was in fact Colonel Legge, the US military attaché in Berne. Frenay (1976) subsequently claimed that 'Scott' was US spymaster Allen Dulles. However, Dulles was still in the US at this time (Belot, 2003, p. 284, n. 2). Barasz (2007) has made the most intensive investigation of these events, but has been unable to discover the real name of 'Scott'. Legge was probably the source of the money la Laurencie gave to Frenay, although not as part of an official policy. A month later Frenay and d'Astier met la Laurencie and emphasized that the General had to reach an agreement with the Free French. When Frenay asked what he would do when de Gaulle returned to France, la Laurencie breezily dismissed the problem: 'Of course, I'll grant him amnesty,' he said. Frenay (1976), pp. 106–7. Barasz (2007) wonders whether this comment was ever actually made (although la Laurencie apparently made a similar remark to Christian Pineau – Pineau, 1960, p. 99). Moulin reported to London that he had seen off both la Laurencie and the 'Americans'. A joint statement from Combat and Libération declared that de Gaulle, not la Laurencie, was their leader and a copy was pointedly sent to President Roosevelt. *Combat* even denounced la Laurencie in its pages, instructing its members to have nothing further to do with him. This impressed Moulin,

who in August 1942 wrote to de Gaulle: 'I emphasize his loyalty in the la Laurencie affair. He went even further than the wishes of the other movements and of myself, by criticizing la Laurencie by name in his newspaper, which was not strictly necessary.' Cordier (1999), p. 164. La Laurencie himself was arrested by the Vichy police, imprisoned, and played no further part in the Resistance.

17 Frenay (1976), p. 155.

18 Frenay (1976), p. 164.

19 Baynac (2007), p. 335.

20 Roussel (2002), p. 409.

21 Summary of Moulin's telegram in War Diary for May 1942. NA HS 7/232, p. 3797.

22 NA HS 7/232, pp. 3796–7. There were various repercussions after the May Day demonstrations. In Annecy local fascist bully boys, frustrated at seeing the population protesting against Vichy, decided to humiliate François de Menthon, the Combat leader who lived in the town. On 2 May they dumped him in the fountain in front of the town hall. Damp but unbowed, de Menthon cycled home, after making an official complaint to the police. More important, Lyons continued to be the focus of Resistance activity. On 18 May the Berlin Philharmonic was due to play in the Salle Rameau, the prestigious Lyons concert hall. That evening, about 1,000 demonstrators – including Morandat – protested outside, singing the 'Marseillaise' and shouting 'Down with the Huns, death to Hitler, free our prisoners!' Even the coded summary description sent to London did not hide the excitement of the night. NA HS 7/232, p. 3796. Frenay (1976), p. 155 gives the date as 18 March. I have assumed that the contemporary records are accurate.

23 Guéhenno (2002), pp. 250–1.

24 Courtois (1980), pp. 263–4.

25 Cordier (1999), p. 272.

26 Durand (1994).

27 Cordier (1999), p. 273.

28 Foot (2004), p. 205.

29 Belot (2003), p. 252.

30 Cordier (1999), pp. 277–9.

31 The exchange rate – a difficult thing to calculate accurately across time – is taken from Baumel (1999), p. 107.

32 See messages quoted in Cordier (1999), p. 277. The PCF may also have received arms from Free French agent Raymond Laverdet, who was part of an SOE/BCRA operation called DASTARD – Berlière & Liaigre (2007), p. 156.

33 Berlière & Liaigre (2007), p. 425, n. 220, and photo on p. 157.

34 Berlière & Liaigre (2007) is entirely devoted to the activities of the détachement Valmy.

35 Berlière & Liaigre (2007), p. 156.

36 Cordier (1999), p. 281.

37 Berlière & Liaigre (2004), p. 173.

38 Berlière & Liaigre (2004), p. 242.

39 Described in Grelot's last letter, written on the day of his execution. Krivopissko (2006), p. 164.

40 Letter reproduced on the website devoted to the martyrs of the Lycée Buffon:
http://pagesperso-orange.fr/memoire78/pages/bu.html (accessed August 2008). See also the French Defence Ministry pamphlet *Les cinq étudiants du Lycée Buffon* (Collection Memoire et Citoyenneté no 31, n.d., n.p.). The family archives of the Benoît family, including many letters from Pierre, have been put online by his niece:
http://pagesperso-orange.fr/AnnetteBenoit/Benoit.htm (accessed August 2008).

41 Most of what we know about Turma-Vengeance comes from François Wetterwald's post-war memoir (Wetterwald, 1946). While many of the other Resistance movements and intelligence circuits have been studied intensively by French historians, there has been no work on this group. Wetterwald claims that by mid-1943 the group had over 10,000 members (Wetterwald, 1946, p. 46). The overall balance sheet would tend to support this: there were 30,000 officially attested members, of whom 584 died (389 did not return from deportation, 96 were executed, while 78 were killed during the fighting after D-Day). The Turma-Vengeance archives have been deposited in the BDIC in Nanterre, outside Paris, where they remain, unexploited (BDIC – F Delta res 844, Fonds *Turma-Vengeance*). These archives contain 17,873 documents grouped in 704 files; the inventory alone runs to 250 pages (http://www.bdic.fr/pdf/turma.pdf – accessed August 2008). Many of those documents are 'demandes d'attestation d'états de service' – post-war requests from members to have their work for the group officially vouched for. Much of the published material relating to the group has been placed online by Marc Chantran: the group, however, awaits its biographer. http://chantran.vengeance.free.fr (accessed August 2008).

42 All the information on Keller is taken from Rouxel (1999). A Parisian street and a nearby public swimming pool are named after Keller; the swimming pool entrance hall contains a small display about Keller, who is a symbol of the Resistance work undertaken by PTT workers.

43 D'Astier's view was not shared by most of the members of Libération. His close comrade François Copeau later explained that he felt no particular loyalty to Libération, and that the reason why he had joined d'Astier's group was largely a matter of chance: 'I could just have easily stumbled upon Combat,' he recalled (Noguères et al., 1969, p. 548).

44 Cordier (1999), p. 191.

45 D'Astier told Basin he had to get to London urgently to meet de Gaulle. Basin demurred, saying it was not so straightforward, and that d'Astier would have to be mandated by all the Resistance groups. Two weeks later, d'Astier met Basin again and told him that there had been a meeting, and everyone had agreed he should go. This was a complete lie, and Basin did not have the wit to check it out.

46 Douzou (1995), p. 107.

47 Passy (1947b), p. 81.

48 The impact of d'Astier's trip to the USA is hard to discern. Tuquoi (1987), p. 133, claims that d'Astier's US press conference received very favourable coverage in *Time-Life* magazine, including a cover photo. This is all wrong. Apart from the fact that *Time-Life* is an anachronism (the two magazines were separate at the time), there was no coverage at all of d'Astier's visit in *Time*, nor was his photo used on the cover of *Life*. Passy (1947b), pp. 83–6, has a caustically negative view of the effect of d'Astier's visit. For d'Astier's novelized version of his exploits, see d'Astier (1958).

49 Foot (2004), pp. 184–7, and Bourdet (1975), pp. 74–9. For a less jaundiced view, see the recent sympathetic history of the Carte circuit by Thomas Rabino (Rabino, 2008). However, much of the novel information in Rabino's account is based on Girard's unpublished memoirs, which should be read with a pinch of salt.

50 Rabino (2008), p. 121.

51 Mackenzie (2000), p. 267. This book, written immediately after the war, was classified as top secret for over half a century. Even in its finally published version, several sections are marked 'Paragraph deleted on the grounds of national security'. M. R. D. Foot provides an excellent introduction describing the fate of Mackenzie's manuscript.

52 Mackenzie (2000), p. 567.

53 Cordier (1999), p. 317.

54 Cordier (1999), p. 318.

55 NA HS 7/232, p. 3798.

56 Bourdet (1975), p. 118.

57 Cordier (1999), p. 179.

58 Bourdet (1975), p. 124.

59 Tillon (1977) pp. 356 and 359.

60 At its height, *Combat* was produced by fourteen different printers around the country, and had a print-run of 400,000. In the northern zone, *Défense de la France* was similarly influential. Both journals continued into the post-war world; *Combat* closed in 1974; *Défense de la France* became *France-Soir*, which still exists.

61 Cordier (1999), p. 176.

62 This was highlighted by General Gubbins of SOE, who in October 1941, after discussing with Moulin, had dismissed Frenay's movement with a curt 'the organization does not possess a clear programme for the future' (Belot 2006a, p. 154).

63 For an overall view of the demarcation line, yesterday and today, see Webster & Webster (2004).

64 Pineau (1960), p. 134.

65 Pineau (1960), p. 136.

66 Rémy (1948), pp. 101–2.

67 Piquet-Wicks (1957), pp. 142 and 144.

68 Piquet-Wicks (1957), pp. 162–8; Terrisse (1993), p. 225.

69 Baumel (1999), pp. 13–8 and 169–70. Much of Baumel's book is equally powerful.

70 Guéhenno (2002), p. 244.

71 Schroeder (2000), pp. 130–1.

72 Schroeder (2000), p. 134.

73 Veillon (1995), p. 220.

74 For a recent detailed and extensive account of how the Resistance saw the Jewish question, and how this changed over time, see Poznanski (2008).

75 Vinen (2006), pp. 142–3.

76 Veillon (1995), p. 244; Vinen (2006), p. 142.

77 Berr (2008), p. 100. Details of solidarity expressed by French people from Schroeder (2000), p. 141; Veillon (1995), pp. 239–40.

78 Vinen (2006), pp. 143–4.

79 Meyer (2002), p. 156, quotes the report from the Nazi commander.

80 Chevrillon (1995), pp. 60–1. Claude Chevrillon was Renée's elder cousin. She went on to play a vital role as a Resistance radio operator in the Paris region (see Chapter 6).

81 *Défense de la France* 20 (30 July 1942). In Granet (1961), p. 102.

82 Cordier (1999), p. 196.

83 Cordier (1993b), p. 626. For a detailed discussion of the relation between Combat and the Jews see Belot (2004). For a detailed examination of how the Resistance dealt with the 'Jewish question', see Poznanski (2008).

84 Courtois & Rayski (1987), p. 147.

85 http://www.ibiblio.org/pha/policy/1942/420702a.html (accessed August 2008).

86 Kersaudy (1981), p. 187. The Afrika Korps were on their way to besiege the British 8th Army in Tobruk. For over ten days Rommel tried to take the French positions at Bir Hakeim. This delay in the German advance on Tobruk allowed key British forces to retreat and regroup in Egypt before Tobruk finally surrendered. Abandoning their positions under the cover of thick fog, the French retreated safely with relatively minor losses. As well as laying the basis for the British defeat of Rommel in the first battle of El Alamein a month later, Bir Hakeim restored the reputation of French soldiers following the catastrophe of the fall of France. Churchill's speech was made in the House of Commons debate following the fall of Tobruk.

87 Churchill explained that the Americans were still under the illusion that Vichy would come over to the Allied cause and reassured de Gaulle that the British had no designs on the French Empire. As a result, the Free French did not dissolve (indeed, it was during one of these discussions that Churchill apparently suggested they adopt the title 'Fighting French') and they did not decamp to Moscow. For descriptions of the Madagascar affair, and of events in the French colony of New Caledonia in South East Asia, where the Americans simply took over without reference to de Gaulle, see Kersaudy (1981), pp. 185–92, and Crémieux-Brilhac (2001), pp. 393–401 and 405–8.

88 See NA HS 7/246, pp. 3–5, for summaries of Moulin's messages describing the demonstrations.

89 *Le Franc-Tireur* 8 (June 1942).

## CHAPTER 6

1 For the full details of Giraud's escape and journey to France, see Cointet (2005) and Granier (1971).

2 Letters that were not joined up within handwritten words were the key to the code. See one of Mme. Giraud's letters in Granier (1971) opposite p. 241.

3 Fourcade (1973), p. 125.

4 Bourdet (1975), pp. 141–2.

5 Pierquin (1983), p. 78.

6 See, for example, Perkins (1962), pp. 297 and 334 et seq. The Allies had first tried to involve General Weygand, but he turned them down flat, unable to imagine breaking with discipline.

7 For full details of TORCH and its background, which are only touched on here, see Funk (1974) and Verrier (1991).

8 Fourcade (1973), p. 154.

9 Perkins (1962), p. 415.

10 Fourcade (1973), p. 165. By an odd coincidence, they were broadcasting from a villa owned by a man called Giraud when the Nazis homed in on their radio transmission. On another whim, General Giraud insisted that the (British) submarine have a US crew (Fourcade, 1973, p. 156). The arrests of the ALLIANCE members were of such importance that MI6 tried to save what they could of the circuit by getting the BBC to broadcast an immediate warning to the remaining members making reference to the animal code names used by the circuit: 'Beware! In the south of France, the animals are ill with the plague' (Fourcade, 1973, p. 171).

11 Although Darlan's presence in Algiers appears to have been a coincidence, the US began contacts with him in mid-October. Perkins (1962), pp. 398–401 and 404 et seq. Eisenhower, Supreme Allied Commander of Operation TORCH, was saddled with the negotiations with Giraud: 'It isn't this operation that's wearing me down – it's the petty intrigue and the necessity of dealing with little, selfish, conceited worms that call themselves men . . . Giraud, in his first conference with me, even made a point of his rank. Can you beat it? Yet he's supposed to be the high-minded man that is to rally all North Africa behind him and save France.' Thomas (1996), p. 95. Jean Monnet, an economist working for the British in Washington, later wrote of Giraud: 'If his ingrained sense of hierarchy had not made it unbearable for him, a five-star general, to take orders from a two-star general only recently promoted [de Gaulle], he would willingly have confined himself to a military command. But the honour of his caste was too much for him: in the end he lost everything because he wanted to concede nothing.' Thomas (1996), p. 111.

12 Domenach-Lallich (2005), pp. 103–4.

13 See the entry on 'Camouflage du Matériel' (the title given to this programme) in Marcot et al. (2006), p. 169.

14 Frenay (1976), p. 226.

15 Some of the arms may have made their way into the hands of the Resistance. An SOE note from July 1943 describes the handing over of '135 tonnes of arms', which was organized at two meetings held in Lyons on 8 February (NA KV 6/24).

16 Crémieux-Brilhac (2001), pp. 579–81.

17 This is Philip's verbatim account from 1947, based on his notes taken at the time. A version from the US point of view was written by Sumner Welles, Under-Secretary of State, who observed the encounter. Although less florid, it has a similar tone. In particular, Roosevelt is recorded as saying 'any decision as to which French people will administer liberated territory will be decided by the American government alone'. For full details, and archival sources, see Crémieux-Brilhac (2001), pp. 579–81.

18 Cordier (1999), p. 202.

19 Foot (2004), p. 198.

20 Thomas (1996), pp. 96–7.

21 For an account by one of de la Chapelle's co-conspirators, see Faivre (1975). Two days later, de la Chapelle was executed with indecent haste, encouraging speculation that the assassination was a put-up job by the Allies. There is, however, no evidence for this understandable view.

22 Passy (1947b), p. 371.

23 Verrier (1991), p. 247.

24 Cointet (2005), p. 292. In the same speech (written by Jean Monnet) Giraud sang the praises of the Resistance – 'the *franc-tireurs*, the saboteurs, the hostages, the deported, the heroic multitude who have fallen for the cause of liberty' (Cointet, 2005, p. 292). George Bernard Shaw was impressed by the speech, but not by Giraud, who he immediately realized had not actually written it: 'No soldier since Caesar, Cromwell or Wellington has been able to realize such an exploit.' Cointet (2005), p. 293.

25 The struggle between de Gaulle and the Allies, with Giraud acting as the hapless fall-guy, is a fascinating and complex political story, but sadly it is outside the scope of this book. The wartime diaries of Harold Macmillan, who was appointed British Resident-Minister to North Africa, give an acerbic and often amusing first-hand account of the events (Macmillan, 1984). Kersaudy (1981, 2004), Thomas (1996) and Crémieux-Brilhac (2001) all provide good summaries of the struggle. The most detailed account is Cointet (2005), but the most rounded political analysis can be found in Belot (2006a). Cordier (1999) describes the Resistance's influence over this struggle in the first half of 1943. Giraud's downfall, partly a consequence of his own political naivety and incompetence, led Macmillan to comment in 1944: 'I would suppose that never in the whole history of politics has any man frittered away so large a capital in so short a time' (Thomas, 1996, p. 86). Giraud would, however, play an important part in the liberation of Corsica (see Chapter 7).

26 Paul Paillole, head of the clandestine Travaux Ruraux run by Vichy counter-intelligence, fled over the border to Spain, made his way to London and later turned up in North Africa, running counter-intelligence first for Giraud, then for de Gaulle. But Paillole was a rare example.

27 Teissier du Cros (1962), pp. 217–8.

28 On the same operation Pineau's one-time RAF pilot, Guy Lockhart, managed to escape back to London.

29 See Pineau (1960), pp. 261–71, for the full story.

30 Fourcade (1973), p. 189.

31 Frenay (1976), pp. 194–6.

32 Levy (1998), p. 78. Levy's first description of the events gave the name of the landing field as EPINARD (Noguères et al., 1969, p. 589). There is no record of any such place (Verity, 2000). In his posthumous memoirs, Levy called the field MARGUERITE; this appears to be correct (Verity, 2000, p. 193).

33 Noguères et al. (1969), pp. 589–90.

34 Cordier (1999), p. 200.

35 For a biography of Delestraint, see Guillin (1995).

36 A summary of this document was published by Passy (1947b), pp. 272–3, according to which the Secret Army was allowed to carry out industrial sabotage, including the 'neutralization' of factories working for the Germans. The version used here is from Cordier (1999), pp. 200–1, and is based on the original archival source.

37 Passy (1947b), p. 248. A slightly different version is given by Frenay in his memoirs written twenty-five years later (Frenay, 1976, p. 218). The heart of the matter is identical, however.

38 Rémy (1966), pp. 198–215.

39 Cordier (1999), p. 284.

40 Cordier (1999), p. 284.

41 All quotes from Cordier (1999), p. 284.

42 See Cordier (1999), pp. 273–83, for an account of how Moulin's contacts helped lay the basis for Rémy's work.

43 Bourdet (1975), p. 217.

44 Pierre Brossolette 'La France devant les Français combattants'; speech to the Royal Institute of International Affairs, Chatham House, 17 November 1942. CH 8/876.

45 Cordier (1999), p. 400.

46 The Socialist Daniel Mayer pointed out the fundamental weakness of Brossolette's ideas in a letter to his comrade: 'The national leaders of the Resistance imagine that the political parties are dead and will never return. They imagine – wrongly – that they are the single party of tomorrow (a kind of left fascism, or in any case, a Resistance fascism)'. Moulin undoubtedly shared Mayer's opinion. Cordier (1999), p. 244.

47 Baynac (2007), pp. 559–60.

48 Verity (2000), p. 64.

49 Verity (2000), p. 65.

50 Verity (2000), p. 195.

51 It was initially called the Conseil de la Résistance, but it is now generally known by the name that was eventually adopted, the Conseil National de la Résistance, or CNR.

52 Wieviorka (1996).

53 Brossolette succeeded in involving Ceux de la Libération and Ceux de la Résistance, and he became particularly close to the OCM, which he saw as providing the basis of the military leadership in the northern zone. For a sympathetic summary of the BRUMAIRE mission, see Piketty (1998), pp. 267–72. Claude Bourdet provided a vigorous defence of the importance of the northern zone Coordinating Committee in his intervention at a meeting to mark the fortieth anniversary of the CNR (Bédarida & Azéma, 1983, p. 43).

54 This was a reflection of his long-held view that the groups in the Occupied Zone were in some way more serious and more representative than those in the Non-Occupied Zone. As Brossolette had put it in London in November 1942: 'the occupied zone has not spoken for two and a half years, and this is unfortunate because there is a difference of degree between the Occupied Zone and the Free Zone; the real resistance is that of the Occupied Zone, which was launched first. The real heart of France is beating in the Occupied Zone and the recovery and reconstruction of France will naturally come from the Occupied Zone.' Pierre Brossolette, 'La France devant les Français combattants'; speech to the Royal Institute of International Affairs, Chatham House, 17 November 1942. CH 8/876, p. 2.

55 Cordier (1999), p. 373. This tone was repeated in a letter from Philip, which Moulin brought back from London and immediately transmitted to Brossolette.

56 Brossolette also invited the Front National to the Coordinating Committee. He accepted Moulin's refusal to discuss with the FN in the southern zone, where it represented nothing, but in the north, he argued, things were very different. From this point of view, the existence of the northern zone Coordinating Committee was essential in welding the FTP to the main Resistance organizations. See Bourdet's comments in Bédarida & Azéma (1983), p. 43.

57 The three men had briefly met the day before, in the Bois de Boulogne.

58 This is based on Passy (1951), pp. 180–1, and Meunier (1993), p. 92.

59 Passy (1951), p. 181. Péan (1998), p. 467, provides an uncorroborated third-hand account – allegedly based on a verbal description from Meunier to Sabine Jansen and Maurice Voutey, given perhaps half a century after the event – according to which Moulin was so furious that at one point in the row he bared his backside to Brossolette, shouting: 'That's what I think of you!' The vulgarity of such an action would explain the shock expressed in Passy's memoirs ('there was a violent and painful incident which I would like to be able to completely forget, because the protagonists . . . were without doubt among the greatest heroes of this war and two of the most faithful and loyal collaborators of General de Gaulle' – Passy, 1951, p. 180). But there is no other indication that such an event took place. Furthermore, the violence of the argument as described by Passy might well have been sufficient to

elicit his appalled reaction. Finally, in his own memoirs, co-written by Voutey and published in 1993, Meunier gives no hint of any such incident (Meunier, 1993, p. 92).

60 Frenay's report is reproduced in Noguères & Degliame-Fouché (1972), pp. 376–9. His 8 April 1943 letter to Moulin in which he complained that London was trying to 'bureaucratize' the Resistance is on pp. 279–84.

61 Cordier (1999), p. 408.

62 The full text of Moulin's report to de Gaulle of 7 May 1943 is given in Closon (1974), pp. 80–96. This quote is from p. 94. Closon was an active participant in these events: he was sent back from France to London by Moulin with this report, with explicit instructions not to let Passy see it, but instead to hand it straight to André Philip. Passy discovered that Closon had the document, and insisted that he hand it over. Closon refused, and there was a stand-off which finished with Passy accepting the situation, but saying 'You will never go to France again.' Closon replied: 'We shall see.' Exactly four months after leaving, Closon was back in France. (Closon, 1974, pp. 80 and 121).

63 See Bourdet's intervention in Bédarida & Azéma (1983), p. 42.

64 As Liliane Jameson wrote in her diary on 25 March: 'A beautiful day today. Ever since this morning the sky is a brilliant blue, pure, luminous and deep. The wide-open windows let a warm breeze come in and heat the inside of the house, still freezing from winter. In the courtyard the cats sleep on the lawn, birds hop about and perch on the slender young tree with its naively youthful leaves; children squeal, run after each other, happy to enjoy their enthusiasm for life. What a pleasure to no longer be smothered in heavy clothes. Everything would be so fantastic if . . . This "if" is a continual reminder, a shadow in our sleep, which turns even the slightest joy into sadness, which hovers, invisible and vast, unchallengeable and tyrannical . . . The situation is both more impossible and more acceptable when the weather is fine and nature seems joyful. That is, a beautiful sky cheers you up, but makes it even worse that we cannot fully enjoy it, without any worries. And you listen to the latest communiqué, the latest speech, grabbing on to some vague illusion, and wait.' Schroeder (2000), p. 180. Hélène Berr's wartime diary is similarly punctuated with moments of great pleasure. For example, on 26 July 1942, three days after describing the horrors of the Drancy camp where her father was being held for not wearing the yellow star correctly, she wrote: 'Life is extraordinary. This is not an aphorism. This evening I feel exalted. It's as if I am living in the atmosphere of a novel, I can't explain it. It's like having wings . . . We spent a marvellous afternoon in the library listening to records, with the windows open on to an infinitely tranquil yet buzzing sun-drenched garden . . . I am enchanted. There is enchantment in my life at present. I am grateful for it with all my heart.' (Berr, 2008, pp. 109–10.) Elsewhere in her diary Hélène writes: 'But in my inner world, all seems dark and I see only anguish ahead; I have always in my mind the thought that a trial awaits me. It feels as if a huge black corridor separates me from the moment when I come out into the light again' (Berr, 2008, p. 176).

65 A discussion of the CNR in June 1983, organized by the Institut d'Histoire du Temps Présent, included contributions from many of the participants (Bédarida & Azéma, 1983). This was one of the few occasions in which *résistants* presented their different points of view, face to face. The conflict of memories and their relation to documentary evidence make fascinating reading.

66 Peyrefitte (1994), pp. 143–4.

67 See Cordier's article in Bédarida & Azéma (1983), p. 128.

68 Although Gaullist mythology tends to emphasize the importance of the CNR in cementing de Gaulle's domination over Giraud, some historians consider it played little if any role (e.g. Jackson, 2001, p. 458). Others, such as Thomas (1996), do not even mention the CNR, which presumably amounts to the same thing. Macmillan was well aware of the foundation of the CNR – it made a splash in the press and he was contacted by London about it (Baynac, 2007, p. 688). But he made no reference to the event in his diary, which suggests it was not at the forefront of his mind during his negotiations with Giraud and the Free French (Macmillan, 1984). Even Crémieux-Brilhac (2001) is less emphatic about the role of the CNR than earlier historians. However, there was a clear correlation between the announcement of the CNR and Giraud's decision to take a step towards de Gaulle. Furthermore, the growing role of the Resistance and the existence of the CNR were both a decisive factor in shaping UK and US public opinion, and in tempering the staunch anti-Gaullism of Churchill and Roosevelt at this point.

69 Crémieux-Brilhac (2001), p. 705.

70 On 12 June Churchill was secretly briefing the British press against de Gaulle: 'He has undoubted Fascist and dictatorial tendencies. At one time he presents himself as the sole barrier against Communism; at another, as enjoying Communist support.' Kersaudy (1981), p. 286. Five days later Roosevelt concurred in a letter to the British Prime Minister: 'we must divorce ourselves from de Gaulle because . . . he has proven to be unreliable, uncooperative, and disloyal to both our governments . . . The war is so urgent and our military operations so serious and fraught with danger that we cannot have them menaced any longer by de Gaulle.' Kersaudy (1981), p. 288.

71 All details from Quellien (2003), pp. 13–9.

72 There were protests in Lyons, organized jointly by the Resistance movements, the underground trade union Mouvement Ouvrier Français, the Front National and the Communist Party. At the Ouillins railway depot a hundred railway workers were arrested after refusing to be conscripted. After a series of demonstrations and the organization of a strike committee, the imprisoned workers were released. These protests continued into 1943, spreading all over the country. At the beginning of January in Montluçon, a small town in the middle of France, around 6,000 people – many of them workers from the local Sagem engineering plant – gathered at the station and surged on to the platform to stop a trainload of conscripted workers from leaving for Germany. Although the police managed to get the train out

of the station, despite a hail of stones thrown by the demonstrators, railway workers then blocked its passage and it had to return to the station. The Wehrmacht were called in and the train eventually left, but not before many of the workers had escaped. Most of the escapees were arrested the next day and sent off to Germany. Quellien (2003), pp. 35–6.

73 Kedward (1993), p. 19.

74 Kedward (1993), p. 40. This was also the view of the young Daniel Cordier, who telegrammed Moulin in London on 4 March, warning him that 'INTENSIVE DEPORTATION OF YOUNG MEN AND WORKERS TO GERMANY . . . THREATENS DESTRUCTION OF MOVEMENTS IN NOZ AND OZ AND OF SECRET ARMY' (Cordier, 1999, p. 322).

75 Cordier (1999), p. 322.

76 The exact details of this first group remain unclear. Kedward (1993), pp. 26–30, provides a balanced account based on what documentary evidence exists. Baynac (2007), pp. 568–71, implies that the Haute-Savoie 'maquis' was very short-lived and was exaggerated by the Swiss press.

77 French historians and *résistants* have squabbled over this episode. Passy (1951), p. 72, claimed that six British planes were sent and were met over the drop spot by anti-aircraft fire that downed three of them. He implies (with no evidence) that this might have been due to imprudence by Pascal Copeau (whom Passy detested). This version has been repeated in many subsequent works. Baynac (2007) uses evidence from both the Swiss press and, more convincingly, the British archives to suggest that no planes were shot down, and indeed that bad weather prevented the planes from dropping their supplies. That was certainly what Churchill wrote in a draft letter to de Gaulle on 18 March 1943 (Baynac, 2007, p. 571).

78 Kedward (1993), p. 30.

79 Kersaudy (1981), p. 243.

80 In truth, Moulin's main 'victim' was the Communist Party – not only did he cut off all funding to the FTP in April (they had previously been funded by Rémy, then Passy), he also refused to fund the Front National. Although this caused a row in London when Grenier complained, there was no change in Moulin's policy. Cordier (1999), pp. 335–6, provides a personal account of this crisis. Intensely embarrassed, he had to explain the situation to Joseph. Moulin's clear discrimination against the Communists is difficult to explain if, as some have argued, he was a Stalinist agent.

81 Cordier (1999), p. 357.

82 Frenay's letter read: 'if we arrived at such an extreme situation, which I do not wish for, but which I must envisage, we would retain the main forces of Planchon [the Resistance] in particular those involved in immediate action and the SA [Secret Army].' Cordier (1999), p. 359.

83 Delestraint made incredibly detailed logistical demands to London: 15,000 kilogrammes of vaseline in 20-gramme tins, 17,514 torches and batteries, 119,096 bandages, 142,614 rucksacks, etc. (Baynac, 2007, p. 563). Baynac astutely points out that this career officer forgot one of the most important items of a soldier's kit, especially in the mountains: boots.

84 Cordier (1999), p. 342.

85 Belot (2003), p. 331.

86 Cordier (1999), p. 343.

87 Frenay (1976), p. 190. For a lyrical description of Renouvin, see d'Aragon (1977), pp. 86–8.

88 De Bénouville (1945), pp. 336–8, contains scattered details of the attempt by Renouvin's second-in-command, 'Bastos', to free him. The exact fate of Bastos and the other members of the commando sent northwards is not known, but they are all presumed to have been killed.

89 Noguères & Degliame-Fouché (1972), p. 322. See also SOE note 'France. Free French arrests' (28 July 1943), NA KV 6/24.

90 Chevrillon (1995), p. 103.

91 A detailed account of the arrests can be found in Baynac (2007), pp. 585–91.

92 Moulin (1982), p. 349.

93 Aubrac (1993), p. 80.

94 Closon (1974), pp. 95–6.

95 Guillin (1995), pp. 227–49.

96 Missika (2005), p. 278.

97 Cordier (1999), p. 445.

98 For more on Moog, see Noguères & Degliame-Fouché (1972), pp. 419–20. Moog disappeared at the end of the war, his crimes unpunished.

99 It seems probable that Hardy's lover, Lydie Bastien, who was linked to the Gestapo, was involved. Péan (1999), pp. 7–18.

100 As the prisoners were taken away, Hardy managed to escape, although he was shot in the leg. Lucie Aubrac, convinced by his miraculous evasion that Hardy had betrayed the meeting to Barbie, sent him a poisoned pot of jam in hospital. Hardy, suspicious, did not eat it.

101 Pineau (1960), pp. 122–4. Cordier (1999), p. 471, is scornful, stating that although this story had been told for half a century, he attached little credit to it. This makes no sense, and Cordier gives the reader no reason not to believe Pineau's account – it is hard to see what Pineau would gain by lying. A piece of strong corroborative evidence has been provided by Alya Aglan, who discovered in Pineau's clandestine diary, written in semi-code, the following entry for 24 June: 'DESCENTE ESCALIER – 958 G – CONFIT. NOIX – RASAGE MALADE' ('Went down staircase – 958 G – jam[?], nuts – shaved sick person'). Aglan argues convincingly that 'malade' is an odd choice of term, which can be explained if the succession of the letters M and L was a code – perhaps subconscious – for 'Moulin' (Aglan, 2000).

102 For a pithy summary, see Veillon & Alary (2000).


CHAPTER 7


1 Guingouin (1974). Guingouin's book of memoirs contains reproductions of official accounts of his exploits from both the police and the gendarmerie, underpinning the truth of his descriptions.

2 For a rich discussion of the relations between the rural population and the maquis, see Kedward (1993).

3 Paradoxically, despite the long-term Gestapo presence in the capital, the MUR leaders felt more secure there than in Lyons – many of them were originally from Paris, and the fact that they were not known there in their Resistance roles made it far safer. Bourdet (1975), pp. 239–40.

4 The problems caused by the historical leaders of the Resistance had long been recognized. In May, as tensions between Frenay and Moulin came close to breaking point, leading members of Libération plotted to get Frenay out of France. At the end of May François Copeau wrote to Emmanuel d'Astier: 'In his rather outrageous manner, with which you are only too familiar, Raymond [Aubrac] went so far as to say that right now the greatest service we could render to the Resistance would be the elimination by any means necessary of a certain number of people, beginning with Gervais [Frenay] himself. That's why we agreed, following your telegram calling Gervais to London, to ask to make sure that the absence of the leader of Combat should last as long as possible, and preferably be permanent.' Letter from Copeau to d'Astier, June 1943, Cordier (1999), p. 423. Many years later Copeau claimed that Moulin was also involved in these discussions – given the problems with Frenay, it would hardly have been surprising: 'To tell the truth, Max [Moulin] and I plotted quite a bit about eliminating the historical leaders, so that they could leave the second wave of leaders the possibility of working without carrying the weight of all the earlier conflicts.' Belot (2003), p. 424. In French the verb 'éliminer' is as ambiguous as 'eliminate' in English: it can mean 'remove' or 'kill'. However, there is no evidence that the latter interpretation was meant here.

5 The overall number of *maquisards* was estimated on 1–2 September 1943, when regional commanders of the maquis met in Lyons. See Marcot (1996), p. 218. The age and composition of the maquis is taken from Vigreux (1996), pp. 307–8.

6 This is the title of a chapter in Tillon (1972), p. 88.

7 Vistel (1970), p. 615.

8 Ruffin (1980), p. 37.

9 Guingouin (1974), pp. 74–82. A police map of the operation, drawn up by the gendarmes, is given on pp. 80–1. On his return to the maquis camp, Guingouin was stopped by a gendarme, whom he shot dead. The Wattelez plant has long since been closed, but the community is still dealing with industrial pollution from the site.

10 Taubmann (2004), pp. 80 and 82.

11 Kedward (1993), pp. 81.

12 Taubmann (2004), p. 82.

13 Guingouin (1974), p. 83. Fermigier's family still lives in Bujaleuf. Martine Fermigier has a shoe and clothes shop in Eymoutiers.

14 Kedward (1993), p. 41.

15 Foot (1996), p. 229.

16 Foot (2004), pp. 421–3.

17 In fact 938 tons – 693 tons from the RAF (6,096 containers and 619 packages) and 73 tons from the USAAF (619 containers and 228 packages), with a further 172 tons arriving from the Mediterranean. This was far less than the amount sent to Tito's guerrillas in Yugoslavia. Foot (2004), pp. 421–6, and Lorain (1983), pp. 110–1.

18 The Ratier plant is still there, and still producing military aircraft propellers. Its main client is now the European-owned company Airbus.

19 Noguères & Degliame-Fouché (1976), pp. 331–3, and Laborie (1980), p. 299. The main source used by Noguères was Cookridge (1966), pp. 330–1. 'Cookridge' was the pseudonym of Edward Spiro (1908–1979). Cookridge's book on SOE contains no explicit references – at the time, SOE files were all closed, so Spiro consulted copies of the relevant documents in US and French archives. Foot (2004) provides an account that is similar to that of 'Cookridge' (Foot, 2004, pp. 333–4).

20 In May 1944 Yves Ouvrieu was caught in a Nazi ambush. He killed two Gestapo members and a French traitor before being killed himself (Cookridge, 1966, p. 331, n. 1).

21 http://www.bbc.co.uk/history/programmes/timewatch/feigl_diary_03.shtml (accessed August 2008).

22 In 1946 Feigl emigrated to the United States, where he still lives. Substantial extracts from Peter's diary were published in Zapruder (2004). Peter's diary – written in French and German – is held at the United States Holocaust Memorial Museum (USHMM). Much of this paragraph (and this note) is based on the information on the USHMM website. There were two volumes to the diary; the first – dedicated to his parents – was lost when Peter left Le Chambon-sur-Lignon. Amazingly, it was discovered in a flea market at the end of the 1940s and eventually published in France in 1970 by a historian of Jews in the Resistance, David Diamant. It was finally returned to Feigl in 1987. An hour-long video testimony by Peter Feigl can be seen at http://www.youtube.com/watch?v=8DayKPRAaho (accessed January 2009).

23 See Philip P. Hallie's moving account of Le Chambon and of Trocmé's work (Hallie, 1979, p. 103).

24 Hallie (1979), p. 171.

25 See plate section.

26 Teissier du Cros (1962), p. 288.

27 Heslop (1970), p. 151.

28 Romans-Petit (1974), p. 27.

29 Romans-Petit (1974), pp. 30–1.

30 Foot (2004), p. 315.

31 The high quality of *Bir-Hakeim* led to unfounded suspicions from other sections of the Resistance that it was produced and funded in Switzerland. Further problems arose when it began to publish blacklists of supposed collaborators, some of whom were completely innocent. As a result, the CNR made clear that it took no responsibility for the material in *Bir-Hakeim*, while *Franc-Tireur* criticized its 'stupid and provocative campaigns' and *Front*

*National* went so far as to describe it as 'an organ of the enemy'. Bellanger (1961), pp. 150–1. The film, together with a dramatic reconstruction (irritatingly filmed in high summer), can be seen in the film *La Lutte armée*, as part of the DVD *La Résistance* (2008).

32 Pictures of the demonstration and of the spoof issue of *Le Nouvelliste* can be found in Romans-Petit (1974) between pp. 96 and 97.

33 Guingouin (1974), pp. 107–9, and Kedward (1993), p. 97.

34 Taubman (2004), p. 80.

35 Guingouin (1974), p. 109.

36 Kedward (1993), p. 97.

37 Guingouin (1974), p. 100.

38 Guingouin (1974), p. 157.

39 Marcot (1996), p. 221.

40 Parent (2006), p. 71.

41 Guingouin (1974), p. 140.

42 Guingouin (1974), p. 72.

43 Serbat (2001), p. 38. A slightly different version of these words is given by Taubmann (2004), p. 92. Although Taubmann gives no reference, the context indicates it is based on an interview by Serbat (Taubmann, 2004, p. 94 n. 1). Taubmann (2004), p. 94, states that Faure was a member of the PCF's clandestine 'service des cadres'. However, his name does not appear in the recent extensive history of this shadowy group (Berlière & Liaigre, 2007). According to Taubmann (2004), p. 94, Guingouin was convinced that the order came from PCF leader Léon Mauvais, who was on the fringes of the service des cadres (Berlière & Liaigre, 2007, pp. 409–10, n. 109). See Chapter 10 for further conflicts between Guingouin and the PCF, over the liberation of Limoges. After the war the PCF leadership continued to persecute Guingouin, playing an important role in framing him in a trial during the 1950s, which saw him unjustly imprisoned. See Taubmann (2004) for a full account of the post-war 'Guingouin affair'. The PCF generously 'rehabilitated' him in 1998, but even in 2005, his obituary in the PCF daily *L'Humanité* carefully avoided any mention of the attempts to kill him during the war, or of the PCF's role in the 'judicial machination that sent him to prison, into a coma and into a psychiatric hospital' (*L'Humanité*, 31 October 2005).

44 Berlière & Liaigre (2007). See especially pp. 39–49.

45 Since the Moscow show trials of the 1930s, Trotskyists were considered fair game by the Stalinists – Trotsky was murdered by a Stalinist assassin in August 1940, as were several leading Trotskyists in France and Switzerland, including Trotsky's son. Two other notorious victims, both killed by the KGB in 1938, were Rudolf Klement, assassinated outside Paris, and Ignace Reiss, the KGB agent who went over to Trotskyism, whose assassination involved Noel Field (see Chapter 4, note 9). The differences between the Stalinists and Trotskyists related to how each group saw the socialist future, and above all how to get there. For the Stalinists, the USSR would be the motor of all future change, and protecting its interests – or, rather, the interests of the

bureaucrats who controlled it – was paramount. On the other hand, the Trotskyists held to Marx's view that 'the emancipation of the working class will be the act of the working class itself', and thought that Stalin's dictatorship had to be overthrown.

46 See Vichy document of 24 June 1942, reproduced in Broué & Vacheron (1997), pp. 21–2. Broué & Vacheron make a reasonable insinuation, but do not prove (p. 24), that the raid was linked to the activities of KGB agent Noel Field (see Chapter 4, note 9), who took a close interest in the lists of refugees helped by the CAS, and in particular their political affiliations. Passy reports that in 1941 he sent an agent to contact the Trotskyists in Marseilles, perhaps in the CAS (Passy, 1947a, p. 156).

47 Chapelle claimed to have been in contact with the Secret Intelligence Service (SIS). Although this may have been the case, Chapelle was probably in contact with SOE (Broué & Vacheron, 1997, p. 117).

48 Broué & Vacheron (1997), p. 151; see note 43 above.

49 This occurred through the publication of *Meurtres au maquis* (Broué & Vacheron, 1997). The breakout was well known, but the subsequent events were not. In November 1943 Demazière described the escape in glowing terms in the Trotskyists' underground newspaper, *La Vérité* (no 54, 20 November 1943 – reproduced in Anonymous, 1978). Because Demazière was unaware of what had happened about a month earlier, there was no mention of the assassination of his four comrades. The article closed at the point they arrived at the Wodli maquis camp, and described their friendship with the PCF militants: 'The feeling of solidarity which unites us in the same combat was stronger than the scheming and odious calculations of some bureaucrats: shoulder to shoulder with the comrades of the PC, our life as partisans began.' After the war, the Trotskyists realized what had happened to Tresso and the three others. In 1973 Demazière indicated to Henri Noguères that his four comrades had been assassinated, and this appeared in volume 4 of Noguères' monumental *Histoire de la Résistance en France* (Noguères & Degliame-Fouché, 1976, p. 29).

50 Broué & Vacheron (1997) provide a detailed account, including many interviews with *maquisards*, which forms the basis of the preceding paragraphs. Pages 145–66 contain the description of the execution. On 7 May 1996 then-PCF leader Robert Hue responded to a letter from Demazière, supported by fifty signatories, including Germaine Tillion of the Musée de l'Homme group (reproduced in Broué & Vacheron, 1997, pp. 253–4). *L'Humanité*, 24 March 1997, contains a review of Broué & Vacheron's book, which includes quotes from Hue's letter.

51 Estimates of the total number of *résistants* (not just Communists) who were executed during the Occupation vary from 9,800 to 30,000. For a discussion of these figures, and how the PCF's claim took root in the post-war years, see Besse (2007).

52 For an overall discussion of the MOI, see Courtois et al. (1989).

53 Holban (1989). Holban's real name was Boris Bruhman. After the war he

returned to Romania, where he had been brought up, and became a general in the Romanian army before falling victim to a Stalinist purge. He emigrated to France in 1984 and was given the Légion d'Honneur. He died in 2004.

54 Holban (1989), pp. 146 and 157.

55 Holban (1989), p. 161.

56 Despite subsequent legends, it appears that no one was injured in the operation. Holban (1989), pp. 163–8, gives a sober account of what actually happened. The fact that Schaumburg was not killed in the attack was revealed in an article in *Le Monde* (27 February 1965).

57 Raymond (1975), p. 230; Holban (1989), pp. 168–71.

58 The reasons for this change of leadership remain unclear. The most balanced (and completely inconclusive) account of the reasons that may have been involved can be found in Bourderon (2004), pp. 228–33.

59 One of the police reports on these tailing operations is reproduced in Peschanski (2002), p. 96.

60 Holban (1989), pp. 205–6.

61 Holban (1989), p. 205.

62 See entry on L'Affiche rouge in Marcot et al. (2006), p. 996.

63 Krivopissko (2006), p. 250.

64 In 1941, aged only twenty-six, Scamaroni had set up a short-lived Corsican intelligence network, COPERNIC. Before the war, Scamaroni had been on the way to becoming a prefect, like Jean Moulin – the two men had met in Marseilles in March 1941 (Piquet-Wicks, 1957, p. 101). Piquet-Wicks was an SOE officer who knew Scamaroni. His account of Scamaroni's work is very imaginative, but is backed up by (unreferenced) quotes from messages sent by Scamaroni back to London. M. R. D. Foot sums up Piquet-Wicks' book thus: 'Essentially true; colours touched up a little.' (Foot, 2004, p. 409). There is a recent biography by one of Scamaroni's relatives (Scamaroni, 1999).

65 Gambiez (1976), p. 147.

66 Gambiez (1973), p. 119. Gambiez cites (but gives no sources for) an Italian counter-intelligence report on Scamaroni's suicide with a piece of wire. Silvani (2001), p. 61, cites (but gives no sources for) a report by a Professor Ceccaldi, of the Italian forensic service, who suggests that Scamaroni inserted the wire under the skin of his neck, pushed it behind an artery and then pulled, severing the blood vessel. Piquet-Wicks (1957), p. 141, claims Scamaroni took a cyanide pill, but provides no evidence. Despite his betrayal, Hellier was executed by the Italians in July (Piquet-Wicks, 1957, p. 141).

67 Cruccu (1976), p. 165, claims that the Italian army put no strain on food supplies, and made not a single requisition of food.

68 For a discussion of how the Resistance grew in Corsica, see Torre (1999).

69 Gambiez (1973), p. 152. For more details on Nicoli, see Silvani (2001), pp. 67–78.

70 Silvani (2001), p. 65.

71 Gambiez (1973), p. 154. Cruccu (1976), p. 171, points out that there is no trace of any such communication in the Italian army archives.

72 Silvani (2001), p. 147.

73 Gambiez (1973), p. 154.

74 Gambiez (1973), p. 254. For extracts from von Senger und Etterlin's memoirs, see Silvani (2001) pp. 199–203.

75 These figures are from Gambiez (1976), p. 159, which contains the simplest account of the fighting. The number of civilians killed is less clear. On 3 October, when the civilian population were hiding in the hills, Bastia was shattered by a series of explosions as the Germans destroyed their remaining fuel supplies and all the equipment they could not take as the last soldiers left. The streets of the city were littered with the burning detritus of a military evacuation. The next day, as the French Moroccan troops gingerly entered the ruined port, the USAAF, unaware that the Germans had all embarked, launched a massive bombing raid, two days too late. Silvani (2001), pp. 163–8.

76 Buton (1993), p. 28.

77 Buton (1993), p. 28.

78 Cointet (2005) describes the struggle between the two men.


CHAPTER 8

1 Howard (1990), p. 74.

2 Operation MINCEMEAT was a macabre and cunning part of this deception: a dead man, dressed as a British marine officer, was put into the Mediterranean together with fake documents, suggesting that the Allies were planning to invade Greece (this story was filmed as *The Man Who Never Was*).

3 Foot (2004), p. 422.

4 The circuit was technically entitled PHYSICIAN, but it is rarely called by that in modern accounts. 'Prosper' was Suttill's code name.

5 Foot (2004), p. 274. Marshall (1988) claims that London manipulated the PROSPER circuit as part of operation COCKADE's attempt to deceive the Germans. Marshall (supported by one-time SOE F-section head, Maurice Buckmaster; p. 163) claims that Suttill met Churchill during his visit to London in May 1943 and that the Prime Minister told Suttill of the supposedly imminent invasion of the Cotentin peninsula (pp. 160–4). Other versions of the story have Churchill telling Suttill that the invasion would *not* take place but that he had to sacrifice himself and his circuit for the sake of COCKADE. Unfortunately for the conspiracy theories, Suttill and Churchill never met in 1943. Suttill was indeed in London in May: he left France on 14 May by Lysander (Verity, 2000, p. 196), and parachuted back into France on 20 May (Helm, 2006, p. 28). But throughout that time, Churchill was in the USA: on 12 May Churchill and Roosevelt began the Trident conference in the White House; on 19 May Churchill gave an address to the US Congress; he then flew to Algiers (via Newfoundland and Gibraltar), where he arrived on 27 May (Macmillan, 1984, p. 94).

6 Foot (2004) argues that the events in Caluire were of far greater importance,

because 'these losses disrupted the whole system for articulating a national uprising of the French people, and were of far graver consequence for the allied cause' (p. 308).

7 Déricourt does not appear to have played a role in the collapse of PROSPER. The most likely explanation of the PROSPER tragedy lies in its sprawling nature, with its dozens of sub-circuits and hundreds of members, and the lax security shown by its members. In this respect it is striking that virtually the only parts of PROSPER to survive were those linked to the Communist Party, which had long experience of clandestine work and strict security procedures. Foot (2004), p. 283.

8 Déricourt's treachery was never unmasked by the British, although it could have been. In spring 1943 a wave of arrests hit recently parachuted agents; Suttill became suspicious about Déricourt, but London dismissed his concerns. Déricourt continued to work in France, systematically betraying his comrades, until February 1944. Déricourt later claimed that he was run by a German agent inside SOE and/or MI6 (Overton Fuller, 1989). There is no concrete evidence for this, and, according to the Abwehr agent 'Colonel Henri' (Sergeant Hugo Bleicher), Déricourt 'was a completely unscrupulous man without any code of ethics, without that curious rule of conduct that all other agents had irrespective of their loyalties. Gilbert [Déricourt's Nazi code name] was completely self-centred. Only his own advancement mattered to him. He was prepared to do anything for that, including treason. The soldiers had a word for his sort – *charakterschwein* – a swine at heart' (Bleicher, 1954, p. 122). There is no reason to believe that after the war Déricourt suddenly started telling the truth, nor is it easy to see why 'Colonel Henri' would have lied.

9 Suttill was executed at Sachsenhausen concentration camp in September 1944, while Norman was killed at Mauthausen in the same month. Using the PROSPER radio codes, the Nazis played a 'radio game', supplying the British with false information. When the Nazis forced Norman to send a message to his London handlers, he followed SOE tradecraft and omitted his 'true check' – a code that indicated he was safe and was broadcasting freely. SOE head Maurice Buckmaster was handed Norman's signal, and immediately sent a reply in which he scolded Norman because he had 'forgotten' to insert his true check, and accused him of committing 'a serious breach of security which must *not*, repeat must *not* be allowed to happen again!' (Marks, 1998, p. 326). The Nazis were able to string Buckmaster along for several weeks before it finally became clear that Norman had been captured. Foot (2004), pp. 292 and 296–7, gives a number of similar examples of London ignoring desperate warnings by agents that they were operating under duress. Noor Inayat Khan, descendant of an Indian sultan and an SOE agent, was PROSPER's radio operator. She was arrested on 13 October, and the Nazis also used her codes in a radio game. Noor was imprisoned with fellow SOE agent John Starr, and Léon Faye of ALLIANCE (Fourcade, 1973, p. 279). After a failed escape attempt – the three managed to get on to the roof of Gestapo headquarters but were discovered – the Nazis demanded

that they give their word of honour not to try and escape again. Starr accepted while Noor and Faye refused and were immediately deported to Germany. Noor was eventually sent to Dachau, where, early in the morning of 13 September 1944, she was executed together with three other SOE women agents. Faye was killed in January 1945, along with 800 other prisoners, mown down as the Nazis fled from the advancing Soviet forces (Fourcade, 1973, p. 367). On Noor, see Overton Fuller (1952), Kramer (1996), Foot (2004), Helm (2006) and Lahiri (2007). On the general question of women's role in clandestine operations, see Pattinson (2007, 2008).

10 See, for example, Vader (1977) or Marshall (1988).

11 There is no evidence that COCKADE and its associated operations involved any intervention in France at all, while the man in charge of the deception section, Colonel Bevan, felt that SOE was too insecure a structure to be taken seriously and used in such a ploy. Howard (1990), pp. 71–83; Foot (2005). Although Bevan's opinion specifically refers to the use of SOE agents in the Netherlands, this would have also been the case for France. For the contrary view, see Walters (2006). Marshall (1988) argued that Déricourt was also an agent of an unofficial sub-section of MI6 (Maurice Dansey's 'Z' group). It has also been claimed that the collapse of PROSPER was the work of Burgess, Maclean and the other Soviet spies within British Intelligence (Vader, 1977). There is no concrete evidence for any of these theories. Kramer (1996) contains a balanced summary of the various arguments (pp. 237–98). For the general context in SOE, see Helm (2006).

12 This was carried out by the Vengeance group – see Chapter 9. Wetterwald (1946), p. 153.

13 Laborie (1980), pp. 299 and 302, n. 42.

14 Noguères & Degliame-Fouché (1976), p. 411. For a slight correction to Hamon's account, with regard to the participation of Rol-Tanguy in an earlier attempt to set fire to the files, see Bourderon (2004), p. 239.

15 Noguères & Degliame-Fouché (1976), p. 411. Hamon was a member of Ceux de la Résistance who had been involved in the Musée de l'Homme group (Humbert, 2008, pp. 44–5). For another version of this operation, and the overall context of the work of CDLR, see Granet (1964), pp. 142–4.

16 Marcot (1999); Foot (2004), p. 256. The Nazis soon realized something was up, and Sochaux managers were arrested or sacked, while Jean-Pierre Peugeot was threatened (he was apparently saved through the intervention of Ferdinand Porsche, director of the eponymous car company, in an act of ruling-class solidarity).

17 NA HS/9/355/2. Letter from MARIE 11.3.44.

18 NA HS/9/355/2. Letter from MARIE 5.4.44, 'Brought back by Lysander 9/10th April 44'. 'Villiers' was the pseudonym of the socialist Daniel Mayer, but it seems unlikely he was Witherington's Villiers – Mayer was based in Paris, and was a member of the CNR and was presumably not involved in sabotage in Clermont-Ferrand. After the war, Witherington was better known as Pearl Cornioley – she became engaged to her future husband, who was also in the Resistance, during her time in France. She died in February 2008.

19 Durand (1968), pp. 580–1.

20 There is a moving memorial to the dead at Ascq. After the war, the commanding officer of the SS division, Hauck, was tried in France and was sentenced to life imprisonment.

21 For most of the period since the war, this lack of action was not discussed – a major history of the role of French railway workers in the Resistance, published in 1968, contained barely a mention of the role of the French railways in the Nazi deportation programme (Durand, 1968). For a polemical questioning of the record of the Resistance in this respect, see Rajsfus (2004), p. 280.

22 Courtois & Rayski (1987), p. 37. Poznanski (2008) surveys the whole output of the Resistance with regard to the Jewish question and argues that the relative weight given to these issues was more a reflection of a political choice – conscious or unconscious – rather than the result of ignorance or disbelief.

23 Courtois & Rayski (1987), p. 154.

24 Chevandier (2006), p. 97. Similar descriptions can be found in the memories of Belgian Jews held in the Malines transit camp, before leaving for Auschwitz (Schreiber, 2000, p. 214).

25 Courtois & Rayski (1987), pp. 13–4. The insidious way in which the Nazis' anti-Semitic policies gradually took over the whole of the lives of French Jews, eventually taking so many of them to destruction, is movingly shown in Hélène Berr's diary (Berr, 2008), and in the afterword by the translator, David Bellos (Bellos, 2008). Hélène eventually died in Bergen-Belsen five days before the camp was liberated by British troops. Her diary, which closes in February 1944 with the words 'Horror! Horror! Horror!', shows she never realised that the Nazis were intent on exterminating the whole Jewish population of Europe.

26 Courtois & Rayski (1987), p. 154.

27 Courtois & Rayski (1987), pp. 179–80.

28 The membership figures for the Union de la Jeunesse Juive (Union of Jewish Youth) hovered around the 500 mark (Collin, 1998, pp. 73–83). The breadth of Resistance activity by Jews is described in Poznanski (1995).

29 Lescure (2007), p. 162.

30 Cited in Delpard (2005), p. 186. Bronchart's book of memoirs *Ouvrier et Soldat* (1969), from which this quote is taken, is incredibly difficult to obtain; only two library copies are known to exist (Polino, 2004).

31 All details from Polino (2004).

32 Incredible as it may seem, treatment of the Gypsies was even worse – they had no access to toilets, and were let out of their cells for one hour a day, during which they were beaten. Information about Mechelen is taken from Laurence Schram, Historian and Archivist at the Musée Juif de la Déportant et de la Résistance de Malines, article at http://www.massviolence.org (search for 'Mechelen' – accessed August 2008).

33 Schreiber (2002), p. 197. All the material on the Mechelen convoy is based on Marion Schreiber's book on the action of Livchitz and his comrades, which originally appeared in German in 2000. There is also an English translation (Schreiber, 2004).

34 Schreiber (2002), p. 221.

35 Schreiber (2002), p. 248.

36 Schreiber (2002), p. 252.

37 See, for example, Lévy (1989); Rayski (1992); Poznanski (2001).

38 Adam Rayski has collected some bitter memories from people who were teenagers in the UGIF homes, where they were in fact held captive. In 1988 this reality was recognized by the French government, when it accorded the children who had been kept in UGIF-run homes the title of 'political internees'. Rayski (1992), p. 208–9. This section is based on Rayski's work. There is an English translation (Rayski, 2005). For a critical review of Rayski's approach, see Caron (2006).

39 Poznanski (2001).

40 The Maison d'Izieu is now a Memorial Museum.

41 Rayski (1992), pp. 215–6.

42 For a general discussion of the rescue of Jews by gentiles, see Moore (2004).

43 Rayski (1992) p. 218.

44 Brès & Brès (1987), p. 109. In the southern zone, two similar publications were produced: *Unser Vaterland* ('Our Fatherland') and *Soldat am Mittelmeer* ('Soldier on the Mediterranean').

45 In summer 1942 Radio Moscow reported that deserters carrying these passes and copies of *Soldat im Westen* had gone over to the Soviets. Very little has been written on Resistance work towards German soldiers. The information in these paragraphs is taken from an interview given by London in the 1960s (Noguères et al., 1969, pp. 570–2), and from Bellanger (1961), p. 219. In his interview, London calls the TA 'Travail anti-Allemand'; this is contradicted by other sources, e.g. the entry on *Travail allemand* in Marcot et al. (2006), pp. 214–5.

46 Frey et al. (1996), pp. 354–9. See also *Le Monde* 2, 6–7 June 2004, pp. 38–41.

47 Prager (1981). Shortly after D-Day, Monat was arrested by the Gestapo, shot and left for dead in the Bois de Vincennes. He survived and managed to get to the Rothschild Hospital, where his life was saved. But before he could be taken to safety, the Gestapo came for him again and he disappeared.

48 It appears that only one copy of this leaflet still survives, in a rather parlous state. See Anonymous (1978), pp. 197–8 and 210. Pages 181–210 contain reproductions and translations of *Arbeiter und Soldat*. The leaflet is also described as *Arbeiter im Westen* (Calvès, 1984, p. 73) and, in a document written by Calvès, apparently in 1944, as *Der Arbeiter*. (André Calvès, 1944?, 'La trahison de Conrad LEPLOW octobre 1943'. Manuscript in Fonds Calvès, BDIC, Nanterre, France). Also available at: http://michel.calves.free.fr/autres r%E9dactions/La trahison de Conrad LEPLOW octobre 1943.htm (accessed August 2008).

49 Calvès (1984), p. 72.

50 Calvès (1984), pp. 71–7; Pluet-Despatin (1980), pp. 67–8. Calvès escaped capture and made his way to Paris, where he helped Monat produce *Arbeiter und Soldat*. For more on Calvès, see Chapter 10.

51 Erignac (1980); Grmek & Lambrichs (1998).

52 Brès & Brès (1987), p. 126.

53 This latter exploit later earned Lucie a place in a 1946 issue of the US publication *True Comics* (number 49), in a story entitled 'Lucie to the rescue'. As the subtitle of *True Comics* had it – 'TRUTH is stranger and a thousand times more thrilling than FICTION'. The opening page of the story can be seen at: http://archive.lib.msu.edu/AFS/dmc/comicart/public/all/true-comics49/AOH040.gif (accessed August 2008).

54 This account is based on Aubrac (1993), Raymond Aubrac's near-contemporary accounts, reproduced in Chauvy (1997), pp. 320–47, Klarsfeld (1997a,b) and Azéma (1997). Understandably, the accounts given by Lucie and Raymond Aubrac varied slightly over half a century, in terms of the detail of pseudonyms, precise dates, or what Barbie knew when. Chauvy (1997) used these variations, together with the 'testimony' of Klaus Barbie to insinuate that Raymond Aubrac worked for Barbie and that Lucie knew this. Chauvy also used the claim by a minor *résistant* that he had been told that British Intelligence launched the prison convoy attack to free him, and that Aubrac's escape was a fortuitous by-product. There was no reason to believe any of this, apart from the inherently untrustworthy claims of an unrepentant Barbie, and the disquiet felt by those readers who considered that the minor differences in the accounts provided by the Aubracs must show they were hiding something. For more on this, see Chapter 11.

55 Bouchinet-Serreulles (2000), p. 344. See also Verity (2000), p. 205, and Aubrac (1993), pp. 224–6. Lucie Aubrac does not mention Claude Bouchinet-Serreulles at all in her account.

56 This was its later name. At the time it was known as Operation RENOVATE.

57 Noguères & Degliame-Fouché (1976), p. 364.

58 The historian of SOE, M. R. D. Foot, described Operation JERICHO as 'mysterious' (Foot & Langley, 1979, p. 85). Livry-Level & Rémy (1955) and Fishman (1982) provide detailed accounts of the operation (including implausibly precise contemporary conversations), but neither contains any detailed references to their sources. However, Rémy was in BCRA headquarters in London when the operation was planned, while Fishman spoke to many of the survivors, including MI6 operatives. Fishman concludes that the main aim of the operation was to free the MI6 prisoners. Both books state that the pilots were told that 100 *résistants* were due to be executed, and that the aim of the operation was to free these men. Ducellier (2002, 2005) claims there is no proof of any impending executions, that the National Archives at Kew contain no indication that the purpose of the raid was to free prisoners, and he concludes that the raid was part of the FORTITUDE deception operation, focusing Nazi attention on the Pas-de-Calais as the Allies' chosen invasion site. The lack of any archival support for the 'liberation' claim is not necessarily surprising as there are no MI6 documents available – the only documents relating to the operation are those from the RAF (NA AIR 37/15). Furthermore, the presence on the operation of an unladen Mosquito solely for the purpose of filming the result of the raid fits ill with the suggestion that the whole thing was a ploy to fool the Nazis. At

the end of 1944 a brief British propaganda newsreel film of the operation ('The Jail Breakers') was released, using the footage from the raid. A low-resolution version of this film can be obtained, free, from www.britishpathe.com (Film ID = 34095) (accessed August 2008).

59 MI9 was officially created on 23 December 1939, and was initially housed in room 4242 of the Metropole Hotel in Northumberland Avenue, London (Foot & Langley, 1979, p. 34).

60 The O'Leary line was betrayed by British con-man and petty thief, Harold Cole. Cole was eventually killed in confused circumstances in Paris in autumn 1945. Neave (1969), pp. 310–11. For Cole's life, see Murphy (1987).

61 Foot & Langley (1979); obituary of Andrée de Jongh, *Independent*, 6 December 2007, p. 49.

62 Aglan (1994) shows the problems with writing the history of these circuits in the absence of archival evidence. Her book contains moving and sometimes contradictory oral testimony, but even so long after the events, some interviewees did not want their accounts to be published. The following section on JADE-FITZROY is based entirely on Aglan's book.

63 For example, when explaining that she had taken over the circuit following the arrest of Loustaunau-Lacau, she used the masculine grammatical form in her message to show she was supported by her comrades – 'ENTOURÉ FIDÈLES LIEUTENANTS', instead of 'ENTOURÉE' (Cointet, 2006, p. 110).

64 Fourcade (1973), pp. 80–3.

65 Fourcade (1973), p. 203. Among its many successes, ALLIANCE obtained intelligence about the V2 rockets being built at Peenemunde, including the size and range of the weapons, and also provided details of the kind of security papers that would be needed to get into the testing grounds. (There is a reproduction of the report on the V2 weapons, dated July 1943, in Fourcade, 1973, plate 13.) The British recognized the importance of the circuit and gave it a great deal of logistical support – for much of the war, ALLIANCE had more radio sets than the rest of the Resistance put together. The price paid by all the various intelligence circuits was incredibly high – for the Germans, these *résistants* were simply spies, and they were given even more brutal and summary treatment than was normally the case. ALLIANCE involved up to 3,000 people, 431 of whom were executed or died in deportation. Hundreds more were arrested. Sometimes these losses were the result of betrayal. The first MI6 agent who was sent to work with the circuit, 'Bla' (Arthur Bradley Davies), turned out to be a fascist who had infiltrated British Intelligence in the 1930s and worked as a Gestapo double agent within ALLIANCE for over a year (Cointet, 2006, p. 171). When he was eventually unmasked, Fourcade helped interrogate him and then sentenced him to death with the approval of MI6. She was not present when he was executed (Fourcade, 1973, pp. 151–3). After the war, Bla's German handler, Robert Alesch, claimed that Davies had not been killed, but instead had been given money to leave France and had settled in Tunisia (Cointet, 2006, p. 176). Léon Faye, who was supposed to have carried out the execution, died in deportation (see note 9 above). It seems unlikely the truth will ever be known.

66 See the many references to Hentic in Verity (2000).

67 Aglan (1994), p. 133.

68 Aglan (1994), p. 137. For a description of the terrible repression against the intelligence circuits, see Aglan (2007).


## CHAPTER 9

1 Pierquin (1983), p. 107.

2 There have been attempts to re-examine these two cases. For Farjon, see Perrault (1975); for Grandclément, see Terrisse (1996).

3 In June 1943, shortly before he was captured by the Nazis, Jean Moulin informed London that Joseph Darnand (not yet leader of the Milice) was prepared to join the Free French – 'LEAVE IT TO YOU TO DECIDE ON THIS SENSATIONAL PROPOSITION,' cabled Moulin (Cordier, 1999, pp. 275 and 908, n. 30). For London this was 'morally unacceptable'. Cordier (1999), p. 908 n. 30. Darnand was prepared to think the unthinkable and go over to the Free French because he was 'disgusted' with Vichy and with its total subservience to the Nazis (Darnand was a fascist, but he was not a Germanophile). However, Darnand was put off by London's precondition that he would have to explain himself on the BBC and then would become a rank-and-file soldier in the Free French army. Increasing Resistance activity, the growth of the maquis and the evident threat of an Allied invasion constituted a real menace; as Darnand put it to fellow members of the Milice in November 1943: 'We are proud that we will fight by the side of the Germans. It is a question of life or death. You will be hanged with me, we will all hang if we do not know how to fight.' Azéma (1990), p. 92.

4 Azéma (1990), p. 95.

5 This mistaken choice was dramatized in Louis Malle's 1974 film *Lacombe Lucien*, in which the young man of the title joins the Milice, but only after trying to join the maquis. There were plenty of real Lucien Lacombes, some of whom later realized their mistake and changed sides after D-Day. For contemporary descriptions of why people joined the Milice, see Chanal (1982).

6 For a discussion of the military courts, see Sansico (2007).

7 Krivopissko (2006), pp. 196–7.

8 Piketty (1998), p. 303.

9 For the history and impact of 'Le Chant des Partisans', in particular the song's role after the war, see Raskin (1991). Various versions of the song are available online; iTunes classifies the lyrics, by Joseph Kessel and Maurice Drouon, as 'explicit'. French rappers Ruffneck Smala and the Toulouse rock group Zebda have both performed the song in recent years, showing its continuing power and resonance.

10 Nal (1975), p. 83.

11 For details of the Milice in Grenoble and the surrounding region, including first-hand accounts of why people joined, see Chanal (1982). The fury of the Milice may have been partly due to the fact that Grenoble was the scene of

many operations by Liberté, a group of Jewish partisans that regularly claimed responsibility for attacks on factories and power supplies (Ravine, 1973, pp. 252–63).

12 The anti-fascist soldier was called Kospiski; he escaped and joined the maquis, but was eventually killed during fighting in August 1944.

13 Noguères & Degliame-Fouché (1976), pp. 116–7; Vistel (1970), pp. 352–6; Nal (1975); Fortrat (1945); Frenay (1976), p. 329.

14 *Défense de la France* 44 (15 March 1944) in Granet (1961), p. 247.

15 The local paper reported: '35 young people recently took part in training sessions for cadres of the charity "Effort et Joie". Their aim was to spread the practice of camping and life in the open air . . . For over a week these young-sters carried out intensive physical training. Eventually, our young sportsmen put on their rucksacks and returned to the capital, determined to return to their task the next fine day.' Wetterwald (1946), p. 120.

16 Jacquemin (1985). Jacquemin's description is available at: http://chantran.vengeance.free.fr/Doc/Jacquemin%2014.pdf (accessed August 2008).

17 Baynac (2007) has argued that, shortly before Moulin died, he was in nego-tiations with the Americans and wanted to 'go over' to the US. The evidence that Baynac has assembled is thin at best and tendentious at worst, and the meaning he puts on it is not generally accepted.

18 In reality the Central Committee was not able to impose its authority over either the Armée Secrète or the maquis, and what little influence it had slowly oozed away over the following nine months. There are several accounts of this complex organizational struggle at the highest level of the Parisian Resistance. See, for example, Hostache (1958), pp. 216–9 and 389–404; Hostache (1976), the interventions that followed, and Hostache's reply (pp. 415–32); Crémieux-Brilhac (2001), pp. 1103–37.

19 Piketty (1998), pp. 318–9.

20 Bollaert had been proposed by Brossolette, who had been passed over by de Gaulle when there were discussions about who should succeed Moulin at the head of the CNR. Before the war, Emile Bollaert had been a Prefect, in 1942 de Gaule appointed him the future Prefect of Paris. Brossolette may have felt he could influence Bollaert by acting as a kind of mentor to him (Piketty, 1998, p. 311).

21 See Marshall & Yeo-Thomas (1955) and Seaman (1997).

22 Bourdet (1975), p. 233.

23 Seaman (1997), pp. 98 and 99.

24 Seaman (1997), p. 99.

25 Over half a century later, Serreulles pointed out that there was no further consequence of the raid on the Rue de la Pompe, suggesting that none of the nine talked (Bouchinet-Serreulles, 2000, p. 336).

26 Seaman (1997), pp. 104–8.

27 Piketty (1998), p. 328. For Cordier's restrained riposte to these criticisms – written after both Brossolette and Yeo-Thomas were long dead and the whole question was of purely historical interest – see Cordier (1999),

pp. 513–9. On the other hand, when it comes to criticizing Brossolette's actions, Cordier is anything but neutral (e.g. pp. 520–5).

28　Seaman (1997), p. 110.

29　Seaman (1997), p. 112.

30　Cordier (1999), p. 528.

31　In mid-1943 Francis Closon was dispatched to help set up the Comités de la Libération, embryos of the future Gaullist state. Six months later he wrote bitterly to London and Algiers, complaining that he had received not one single instruction (Closon, 1973, pp. 157–8). He later wrote of his impression that 'At the foot of the towering peak de Gaulle, Algiers apparently lived in fog'. Closon (1973), p. 160.

32　See Cordier (1999), pp. 528–32. Cordier points out that de Gaulle gave Passy the 'choice' of whether to recall Bingen or not. This was effectively a test of Passy's loyalty – was he more devoted to his scheming with Brossolette or to de Gaulle's leadership?

33　One of the passengers was Émile Cossoneau, a Communist deputy. PCF leader Marty claimed from Moscow that Cossoneau had been 'assassinated' by the BCRA (Crémieux-Brilhac, 2001, p. 946); for details of the accident and of the burial site of the pilot, Flying Officer Bathgate, and of 'Moreau' (Cossoneau), see Verity (2000), pp. 144–5 and 204.

34　Seaman (1997), p. 117. The memories of the pilot and of Yeo-Thomas with regard to this event are not identical, but both indicate that London was determined he should leave.

35　Bouchinet-Serreulles (2000), pp. 345–6; Verity (2000), p. 205.

36　Cordier (1999), p. 538.

37　Cordier skips over Brossolette and Bollaert's active attempts to free themselves, simply stating: 'Finally, incarcerated in Rennes prison, they remained for a month and settled into the routine of prison life while, outside, their friends were busy trying to get them out.' Cordier (1999), p. 538.

38　During his interrogation, Bollaert was apparently told by the Nazis that an uncoded document referring to their arrest had been seized at the Spanish frontier (Piketty, 1998, p. 337). Serreulles repeatedly denied that any such document was sent by him or anyone else (Piketty, 1998, p. 337); indeed, it seems extremely unlikely that he was responsible, given that he was in London from the beginning of March (Bouchinet-Serreulles, 2000, p. 346). After the war, the story was believed by many in the Resistance, including Brossolette's wife, who described it as 'a stunning example of stupidity that was either murderous or unthinking, perhaps the most revolting in the whole history of the circuits' (Brossolette, 1976, p. 248). However, Piketty (1998) carried out an extensive search for such a document and found no trace whatsoever, concluding: 'Given our current knowledge, the identification of Paul Boutet remains inexplicable' (Piketty, 1998, p. 338).

39　Seaman (1997), p. 140.

40　Seaman (1997), pp. 137–46.

41　Seaman (1997), p. 89.

42　Noguères & Degliame-Fouché (1976), p. 447.

43 Frenay (1976), p. 329.

44 Cordier (1999), p. 585.

45 This late conversion came about after a meeting between Pierre Brossolette and General Revers. Piketty (1998), pp. 319–20. This was also the swansong of the Resistance movements, as their Central Committee ceded power to COMAC, and then dissolved itself. Before the ORA was finally accepted into the Resistance, it had to prove its loyalty. As well as making a declaration in which they repudiated Vichy and promised not to be involved in politics, they also had to pool their weapons with the Resistance and promise to support the national insurrection. After a humiliating appearance before the Bureau of the CNR, ORA leader General Revers (who two years earlier had been Admiral Darland's right-hand man) was made a non-voting member of COMAC. See de Dainville (1976).

46 Narinksi (1996).

47 Crémieux-Brilhac (2001), p. 946.

48 De Gaulle, with his acute political sense, was probably well aware of this geopolitical truth (Crémieux-Brilhac, 2001, p. 1122).

49 Cordier (1999), p. 598. De Gaulle spoke as the chairman of yet another structure, the Comité d'Action en France (COMIDAC – Committee for Action in France), set up in Algiers in September 1943. COMIDAC was supposed to oversee the creation of the future Gaullist state in France, but it had done little beyond find a place on one of the many organizational diagrams ('organigrammes') the Free French loved so much.

50 Cordier (1999), p. 604.

51 Granet (1964), pp. 156–66.

52 Cordier (1999), p. 495.

53 Crémieux-Brilhac (2001), p. 1124.

54 Cordier (1999), pp. 569–71.

55 Bouchinet-Serreulles (2000), p. 356.

56 Seaman (1997), p. 112. During his train journey back to Paris, Yeo-Thomas had one of those fortuitous encounters that would strain credulity if it appeared in the pages of a thriller. In the dining car he found himself seated next to a young German officer – Klaus Barbie of the Lyons SS. Yeo-Thomas had no idea of Barbie's role in the murder of Jean Moulin, but he had heard enough about the Nazi to be extremely wary, and managed to keep the conversation to routine chit-chat about the scandals of the black market. Seaman (1997), p. 113. This contradicts the suggestion that Barbie was in Italy during this period (Klarsfeld, 1997a).

57 The Resistance leader in charge of the maquis summarized the situation, underlying the lack of weapons and ammunition: 'In those départements that are the best equipped, we can say that in the maquis barely one man in ten is armed, while in the Secret Army it is one in a hundred. The best-supplied weapons have around 10 or 20 rounds each, and the only region that has obtained some weapons (because it has received parachute drops from the British for months) has a few heavy machine guns with 300 rounds each.' The verbatim minutes of this meeting – seventy pages long – have

survived, but have still not been published or properly exploited by historians. Extracts can be found in Noguères & Degliame-Fouché (1976), pp. 54–61, and are briefly discussed in Marcot (1996).

58 Noguères & Degliame-Fouché (1976), p. 60.

59 Funk (1981), p. 30.

60 The minutes of the War Cabinet meeting of 27 January 1944 are partially reproduced in d'Astier (1965), pp. 305–7; see also Seaman (1997), p. 126. This position was cemented on 1 February, when Yeo-Thomas was invited to meet Churchill to give his first-hand opinion on the situation of the Resistance; he spoke passionately about the need for more weapons, strengthening Churchill's commitment.

61 General d'Astier's conception of the Resistance was very different from that of his brother, and he claimed to Eisenhower that it was 'composed largely of former members of the French army, under the direction of trained officers'. Funk (1981), p. 31.

62 Above all, Eisenhower, like Churchill, did not want anything like the 'national insurrection' that the Resistance had long promised would coincide with national liberation. See Funk (1981).

63 Richard Heslop ('Xavier') of SOE and his BCRA colleague, Jean-Pierre Rosenthal ('Cantinier').

64 Crémieux-Brilhac (1975), p. 55. For general accounts of the Glières events, see Jourdan, Helfgott & Golliet (1946); Tillon (1972), pp. 148–53; Friang (1975); Crémieux-Brilhac (1975, 1995); Kedward (1993), pp. 132–41.

65 Paxton (2001), pp. 322–4.

66 Noguères & Degliame-Fouché (1976), p. 22. For the de Gaulle quote, see Marcot et al. (2006), entry on Pucheu, p. 845. At the same time as Schumann issued his warning, the Resistance stepped up its offensive, assassinating Lespinasse, the chief prosecutor of Toulouse, and bombing the house of Fernand de Brinon, Vichy Secretary of State.

67 Crémieux-Brilhac (1975), p. 55.

68 Crémieux-Brilhac (1975), p. 56. This article contains many transcripts of messages from the BBC as well as archival material from the BCRA.

69 Tillon (1972), p. 148.

70 Crémieux-Brilhac (1975), p. 58.

71 Crémieux-Brilhac (1995), pp. 60–1.

72 Crémieux-Brilhac (1975), p. 61.

73 After one of these encounters, Tom Morel was killed by the commandant of the GMR, who had been captured by the maquis. Accounts differ as to exactly how this occurred: the Vichy man had either hidden his gun or had asked to retain it for the sake of honour, and had been given this privilege as a mark of respect for his rank.

74 Kedward (1993), p. 139.

75 Heslop (1970), p. 213. For a particularly critical account of the role of the BCRA in encouraging the static maquis, as a way of controlling their activity, see Rajsfus (2004), pp. 98–101.

76 Crémieux-Brilhac (1995), p. 66.

77 For a collection of such documents, see Michel & Mirkine-Guetzévitch (1954). For a political analysis, see Michel (1962).

78 For a discussion of the Action Programme, focusing on why the CNR was the only Resistance organization in Europe to produce such a document, see Andrieu (2006).

79 The Action Programme of the CNR has been widely and repeatedly reproduced over the last sixty-five years. See, for example, Marcot et al. (2006), pp. 1063–6.

80 At the Tehran conference, Roosevelt suggested to Churchill and Stalin that no one over the age of forty should be allowed to participate in a future French government, as all those above that age were fatally tainted with collaboration. Kersaudy (2004), p. 352.

81 Kersaudy (2004), pp. 352–3.

82 The declaration of independence had the mischievous encouragement of British Major-General Spears (Egremont, 1997, pp. 250–60; Zamir, 2005). De Gaulle's man in Beirut, Helleu, responded to the declaration by arresting the President, the Prime Minister and key ministers of the newly elected government, dissolving parliament and suspending the constitution. He then used violence to suppress the inevitable protests. The Free French claimed (apparently with some justification) that Helleu 'stops being lucid at some times of the day'. For the Lebanese affair, see Crémieux-Brilhac (2001), pp. 983–92; Kersaudy (2004), pp. 346–53; and Zamir (2007). Extracts from the minutes of the Tehran meeting are given in Kersaudy (2004), pp. 352–3. Macmillan (1984), pp. 290–301 gives his uncomplimentary contemporary views about the role of Spears, who, he felt, was 'out for trouble and personal glory' (p. 295).

## CHAPTER 10

1 Fourcade (1973), pp. 308–9.

2 Pierquin (1983), p. 125.

3 Pierquin (1983), p. 125. For a brilliant portrayal of the Resistance on the railways, see René Clément's film *La Bataille du rail* (1946) which won the Palme d'Or at the 1946 Cannes Film Festival.

4 The classic account of this period is George Millar's memoir, *Maquis*, first published in 1945 (Millar, 2003).

5 There are many books on the Allied campaign, which is not the focus of this chapter. For the background material on military matters, I have relied on Keegan (1982), Funk (1992) and Wieviorka (2007).

6 Vergnon (2002), p. 86. There are other examples of virtually identical formulations – Vergnon (2002), p. 113, n. 19.

7 Koestler (1968), p. 276.

8 For detailed accounts of the arguments, see Kersaudy (1981), pp. 337–54 and Crémieux-Brilhac (2001), pp. 1220–31.

9 All examples in this paragraph taken from Kedward (1993), pp. 199 and 186.

More detail on the Fontjun maquis (without sources) can be found at: http://cessenon.centerblog.net/471936-L-affaire-de-Fontjun   (accessed August 2008).

10 Guingouin (1974) reproduces the FTP order on pp. 178–9.

11 Guingouin (1974), p. 175; Taubmann (2004), p. 97; Fouché & Beaubatie (2008), pp. 40–1. Hastings (1983), p. 128, reproduces a claim from a Communist Party publication according to which, on the evening of 7 April, the Tulle FTP appealed to Guingouin for help but were turned down flat. There is no mention of this alleged appeal in Fouché & Beaubatie (2008) and it does not appear in the edition I have consulted (150 combattants et témoins, 1975), even though this is the edition cited by Hastings (1983). Fouché & Beaubatie (2008), pp. 235–43, examine the changes between the five editions of this work (*Maquis de Corrèze*) and raise doubts about its usefulness as an historical account. It should be remembered that from this time right up to his death, the PCF leadership was extremely hostile to Guingouin (see Chapter 7).

12 Kedward (1993), p. 172. Hastings (1983) gives the figure of 139 German dead (p. 139). Figures for the number of German prisoners taken, and the reason for their execution, vary. For a detailed examination of the various versions, see Fouché & Beaubatie (2008), p. 96.

13 Fouché & Beaubatie (2008), pp. 112–8.

14 Guingouin (1974), p. 181.

15 Fouché & Beaubatie (2008), p. 112–3.

16 Elie Dupuy, in command of an FTP batallion, later recalled: 'At around 9 p.m., Jean Baldous, on sentry duty at the town hall, heard a low and powerful noise coming from the town . . . Together with a few men, he went on a scouting expedition. After a few minutes they encountered the German tanks, which immediately opened fire with their machine guns: our men leaped into nearby gardens and hid themselves from both sight and the firing line of the armoured vehicles. Miraculously, no one was hurt.' 150 combattants et témoins (1975), p. 378.

17 Fouché & Beaubatie (2008), p. 97.

18 'Rapport du lieutenant Kléber (J.-J. Chapou), 8 juin 1944' reproduced in Fouché & Beaubatie (2008), p. 100.

19 150 combattants et témoins (1975), p. 379.

20 There were claims that some of the Nazi dead showed signs of torture and mutilation, but there is no direct evidence of this. Hastings (1983), pp. 138–9. The way in which this story appeared and was then propagated by the Nazis and by their apologists after the war is described in Fouché & Beaubatie (2008), pp. 143–8.

21 Fouché & Beaubatie (2008), p. 174, examines all the possible reasons – time, miscounting by officers, unrest among rank-and-file German soldiers. Hastings (1983), p. 145, considers that rope was the reason. There are a number of alleged images of the hangings, either photos or a drawing, supposedly by German officers, none of which can be authenticated; for a detailed account of the problems associated with the provenance of these images, see Fouché & Beaubatie (2008), pp. 243–8.

22 Noguères & Degliame-Fouché (1981), pp. 124–5.

23 Schoenbrun (1981), p. 378.

24 For a sober account of the events, with many references to contemporary German documents, see Meyer (2002), pp. 185–212. After the war, the main perpetrators were put on trial: it turned out that many of the rank-and-file soldiers involved were French men, conscripts from Alsace, which had been annexed by the Nazis in 1940. This caused huge tensions in the country, and in 1953, shortly after the sentences were announced, the French parliament amnestied the French citizens involved. Noguères & Degliame-Fouché (1981), p. 134. There was another victim of the Das Reich that day. About fifty kilometres south-east of Oradour, near Salon-la-Tour, a German patrol stumbled on a black Citroën car, which stopped suddenly as a man and a young woman leaped out, carrying machine guns. In the firefight that followed, the woman was captured. She was twenty-three-year-old SOE agent Violette Szabo, who only four days earlier had parachuted into the Limousin on her second mission to France. She was deported to Ravensbrück and was executed in January 1945. Minney (2006) (originally published in 1956) describes her life; see also the feature film of the same name, *Carve Her Name with Pride* (1958).

25 Crémieux-Brilhac (2001), p. 1255.

26 For a more detailed account, see Kedward (1993), pp. 166–9.

27 There are many accounts of the events that followed. I have used Dreyfus (1971), Rude (1974), La-Picirella (1986), Vergnon (2002) and Veyret (2003). Pearson (1978) sadly has no detailed references to back up an otherwise excellent English account.

28 Although most of these new recruits were untrained and inexperienced, there was a small group of around fifty troops from Senegal, who had been freed from a Lyons barracks by a Resistance raid, and two sets of gendarmes, from the towns of Nyons and Saint-Marcellin, who came over to the maquis lock, stock and barrel.

29 As an official declaration plastered on the walls of the towns and villages of the plateau put it: 'On 3 July 1944 the French Republic was officially restored in the Vercors ... Our region is in a state of siege. The National Committee of Liberation requests that the population do the impossible, as it will itself do, and put all available means at the disposal of the military commanders, who have the weighty task of protecting us from an increasingly barbarous enemy. Inhabitants of the Vercors, the great Republic has been reborn in your land. You should be proud. We are sure that you will know how to defend it. We hope that for the Vercors, the 14 July will be yet another occasion to show your republican convictions and your attachment to the great fatherland. Long live the French Republic. Long live France. Long live General de Gaulle.' Vergnon (2002), p. 96.

30 Vergnon (2002), p. 103.

31 Vergnon (2002), p. 97.

32 Foot (2004), p. 345.

33 Details from Veyret (2003), p. 39.

34 Vergnon (2002), p. 109.

35 Foot (2004), p. 346.

36 When news of the catastrophe eventually reached Algiers, there was a major governmental crisis, as one of the Communist Party's ministers, Fernand Grenier, released Chavant's message and then accused the Free French of betraying the Vercors fighters and of 'political opportunism' in not sending Free French planes. Furious, de Gaulle gave Grenier a choice – resign or withdraw his comments. Grenier ate his words. For a summary of the dispute, see Rajsfus (2004), pp. 103–6. Grenier's own account can be found in Grenier (1959), pp. 200–11. Amazingly, in 1947, Rémy, by now a leading figure in de Gaulle's political party, the Rassemblement pour la France, accused Grenier of being responsible for the lack of air support for the Vercors. See Grenier (1959), pp. 212–4.

37 On 4 and 5 June there were huge rows between de Gaulle, Churchill and Eisenhower over the Allies' plans to distribute their own paper money, and the detail of Eisenhower's planned radio broadcast to France after the operation had begun. At one point Churchill threatened to have de Gaulle put on a plane back to Algiers – it was during one of these rows that Churchill allegedly made a statement which accurately summarized not only his personal politics, but also summed up the whole orientation of the British in the subsequent sixty years: 'in the case of a disagreement between the United States and France, Britain would side with the United States' (Kersaudy, 1981, p. 343). In the end, Washington and London did not budge an inch, and de Gaulle broadcast in the evening of D-Day, long after Eisenhower, who did not even mention de Gaulle or the Free French, and gave orders to the French population. In turn, de Gaulle avoided all mention of the American troops and made it clear that the French should obey only the 'French government' (that is, the Free French). De Gaulle spoke so well that Churchill sat listening to the broadcast with tears rolling down his cheeks. See Kersaudy (1981), pp. 337–59, and Crémieux-Brilhac (2001), pp. 1220–31.

38 Brinton (1961a), p. 12. Brinton was not your average OSS operative – he was a professor of history at Harvard, who specialized in French history.

39 In one of his OSS reports, Crane Brinton perceptively highlighted this point and went on to make a criticism of Allied attitudes: 'I think many of us in London and Washington underestimated the effective unity toward precisely this end – the assumption of control in liberated France – attained by the French Committee of National Liberation (FCNL) and the Resistance . . . This assumption of power by the Provisional Government has been made possible . . . by the willingness of the French population in the hitherto liberated regions to have it do so.' Brinton (1961a), pp. 12–3.

40 Paxton (2001), p. 327.

41 Footitt & Simmonds (1988), pp. 79–82. Full recognition of the Provisional Government would not occur for several months.

42 First code-named ANVIL, then DRAGOON, the Mediterranean landings initially involved 150,000 troops, including substantial numbers of Free French soldiers, most of them from the empire, under the command of General de Lattre. (The story of some of these soldiers is told in the French 2006 feature film *Days of Glory*, originally entitled *Indigènes*.) The Allies easily

overcame German resistance in the south, which effectively evaporated as the Nazi high command ordered that all forces gradually withdraw from France, with the exception of key port garrisons, such as Marseilles and Saint-Nazaire, which were ordered to fight to the death. A combination of German withdrawal and Resistance action meant that Allied progress north was far more rapid than expected. For example, a reconnaissance column under the command of General Butler reached Grenoble in seven days, when they were expected to take three months, because the Resistance had cleared the way. Kedward (1993), p. 216.

43 Thanks to the breaking of the German ULTRA code, Allied commanders in both Normandy and Provence were well aware of this order and its implications, and were able to take advantage. Keegan (1981), pp. 255–9; Funk (1992), pp. 110–4.

44 This point is well made by Jackson (2001), p. 549. The chapter covering August 1944 in one French history of the Resistance covers nearly 300 pages (Noguères & Degliame-Fouché, 1981). Local historians throughout France have provided an astonishingly rich picture of what occurred, virtually none of which can be presented here. For one local example that is referred to below, and which is close to the author's heart (see note 99 below), see the description of the Resistance in the nineteenth arrondissement of Paris and its role in the Liberation (ANACR, 2005).

45 Buton (1993) pp. 104–5. On the basis of detailed historical records, Buton puts forward a typology of liberation: those cities that saw a fully fledged insurrection (Paris, Lille, Marseilles, Limoges and Thiers – these included all of the main French conurbations with the exception of Lyons), 28 cities that saw partial insurrections (including Annecy, Nancy, Le Havre, Nice, Toulon, Toulouse, Castellane and Brest), and the remaining 179 which saw no insurrection at all. See map on p. xi above.

46 The clearest account in English of the Paris insurrection is Footitt & Simmonds (1988), pp. 104–51. For a brief description of the events and of what happened in the years that followed, see Beevor & Cooper (2004).

47 Verity (2000), p. 208. Fourcade's departure had been delayed by the D-Day operations. Her pilot was Flight-Lieutenant Affleck, who had such problems with Lucie Aubrac's flight to London earlier in the year.

48 Fourcade (1973), p. 327. See note 53 below.

49 Fourcade (1973), p. 336.

50 Cointet (2006), pp. 272–4.

51 Rajsfus (2004), p. 213, citing von Choltitz's memoirs.

52 Rajsfus (2004), p. 217.

53 The previous commander, General Boineburg, had been recalled to Berlin, suspected of being involved in the 20 July plot to assassinate Hitler.

54 All information in this paragraph from Krivopisko & Porin (2004).

55 There are many accounts of these events. For example, Dansette (1946), pp. 97–120. For a particularly acerbic analysis, see Rajsfus (2004), pp. 184–92.

56 Dansette (1946), p. 155. Jackson (2001), p. 566, points out that part of the reason the strike was so effective was that many workers were already on leave.

57 For a balanced account of the role of the police, see Kitson (1995). Rajsfus (2004), pp. 127–43, provides a more polemical view.

58 On 9 August Jean Guéhenno wrote in his diary that a kilo of butter cost 1,000 francs, while a kilo of peas was 45 francs. The real problem, however, was finding these precious commodities. Guéhenno (2002), p. 428.

59 For a description of Eisenhower's reasoning, see Kaspi (2004), pp. 120–2.

60 Schoenbrun (1981), p. 422.

61 Historians and participants (including de Gaulle himself) have often ridiculed the tendency for maquis leaders to give themselves unjustified military titles. This was not limited to the Resistance, however. 'General' Chaban-Delmas had been given his title by General Koenig a few months earlier. He was not a soldier but a high-ranking civil service economist. On 25 August the ultimatum addressed to General von Choltitz was signed by 'General' Billotte of the Free French army. Billotte was only a colonel, but gave himself a higher rank to impress the German commander (Dansette, 1946, p. 370).

62 Jackson (2001), p. 561. The unstated pendant to this message was surely the declaration of the Sun King, Louis XIV, 'L'état, c'est moi'.

63 Bourderon (2004), pp. 384–5.

64 De Beauvoir (1965), pp. 592–3. De Beauvoir's companion, Jean-Paul Sartre, was eventually involved in writing for *Combat* but played no important role in the Resistance.

65 Dansette (1946), pp. 133–4.

66 This was the subject of an exchange between Rol-Tanguy and Léo Hamon at a meeting of COMAC. Dansette (1946), p. 164. See also Wieviorka (2007), p. 406.

67 Dansette (1946), pp. 212–4.

68 The role of the ceasefire has been an unhealed sore in the history of the Resistance, not so much for what it accomplished (it had very little effect on the outcome of events) as for what it might have done. For a sober summary, see Jackson (2001), pp. 563–7; for a polemical version of the arguments against the ceasefire, see Rajsfus (2004), pp. 224–43.

69 Dansette (1946), p. 263–4.

70 Kaspi (2004), pp. 114.

71 This astonishing film can be seen on the CD-ROM/DVD *La Résistance en Île-de-France* (AERI, 2005). A small version, with English subtitles, is available free at http://www.archive.org/details/LaLiberationdeParis1944 (accessed August 2008). For a discussion of the representation of the Resistance in film after the war, which played an important role in fixing the popular vision of the war years, see Langlois (1997).

72 Dansette (1946), p. 283.

73 Dansette (1946), p. 282.

74 Dansette (1946), p. 271.

75 Calvès (1984), p. 102.

76 Calvès (1984), p. 102.

77 Madeleine Riffaud's eyewitness account in Jorge Amat's film *Avoir vingt ans en août 1944* (2004); see also ANACR (2005), pp. 289–92.

78 Bourderon (2004), p. 382.

79 Kaspi (2004), pp. 122–6, summarizes the reasons behind Eisenhower's change of mind. The appeal from the insurgents was less important than the news that the German garrison was extremely weak, and the existence of what Eisenhower saw as the threat of a Communist insurrection.

80 Wieviorka (2007), pp. 364–6, cites the original documents from the US National Archives and Record Administration.

81 It appears that the colonial troops were not actually removed from the 2nd DB. Wieviorka (personal communication). A newspaper account of Wieviorka's book, however, states that there were no colonial troops ('Liberation: The hidden truth', *Independent*, 31 January 2007). Contemporary descriptions of the arrival of Captain Dronne's 2nd DB column suggest that Moroccan Spahis were involved (Dansette, 1946, p. 354). Contemporary film shows soldiers wearing the red *calot* of the Spahis, but their ethnic origin is not clear (e.g. *Été 44: La Libération*, Patrick Rotman, 2004).

82 Bourderon (2004), p. 444.

83 Dansette (1946), p. 350.

84 Dansette (1946), p. 353.

85 Bourderon (2004), p. 450.

86 Dansette (1946), p. 362.

87 Von Choltitz was not consulted about this change, which later caused some excitement among the more legally minded. See Dansette (1946), pp. 386–8; for Rol-Tanguy's opinion, see Bourderon (2004), pp. 452–6.

88 De Gaulle described his disapproval in his memoirs (de Gaulle, 1962b, p. 341). Bourderon (2004), p. 455, questions whether this is actually true, citing the rushes of an amateur film of the encounter between de Gaulle and Leclerc. These can be seen in the film *Été 44: La Libération* (Patrick Rotman, 2004); a French lip-reader would resolve the issue.

89 Jackson (2001), p. 565.

90 It is generally said that he went on to a balcony. Contemporary film clearly shows him standing precariously on a window sill (*Été 1944: La Libération*, Patrick Rotman, 2004).

91 De Gaulle (1962b), p. 344. This was in keeping with the ordinance adopted by de Gaulle's Comité Français de la Libération Nationale at the beginning of the month, which declared all legislation adopted since 16 June 1940 to be null and void. Jackson (2001), p. 602.

92 Brossat (1994), p. 135.

93 Rajsfus (2004), p. 251. If this story is not true, it ought to be.

94 De Gaulle (1962b), p. 347.

95 Dukson – sometimes written Duckson – came to a sad end. He became involved in a black-market operation to sell German stores; arrested by the FFI, he was shot in the leg while trying to escape and died on the operating table. Dunan (1976).

96 Daniel Mayer's eyewitness account. Noguères & Degliame-Fouché (1981), p. 565.

97 There are no definitive figures. Dansette (1946), p. 434, gives the figures quoted in the text; Jackson (2001), p. 567, gives different figures for the French (901 FFI and 582 civilian dead; 2,000 wounded); Wieviorka (2007), p. 408 states the dead were 1,000 FFI, 600 civilians and 71 from the 2nd DB. None of these authors gives a source.

98 The following day, the Luftwaffe bombed the nineteenth arrondissement, in reprisal for the insurrection, killing 110 people and wounding 700. ANACR (2005), p. 285.

99 Interview with Madeleine Riffaud, *Guardian*, 21 August 2004. Riffaud appears in a contemporary picture of the FTP Saint-Just FTP brigade, which features on the front cover of Calvès' book of memoirs. She is also the subject of Jorge Amat's moving film *Avoir vingt ans en août 1944* (2004). There is a brief fictionalized account for young people, describing the work of the Saint-Just brigade, including the death of Michel Tagrine, written in 1946 by Riffaud's comrade, Max Rainat, when he was only seventeen. Rainat (2003). There is now a Parisian 'street' – in fact, a staircase – named after Michel Tagrine, in the nineteenth arrondissement. My family and I used to live at the bottom of it.

## CHAPTER 11

1 Chevererau & Forlivesi (2005). In 2005 the Prosecutor General of Dormund, Herr Maass, began an enquiry into who was responsible for the massacre, and why. In July 2008 a German team of investigators visited Maillé as part of their enquiries.

2 See Noguères & Degliame-Fouché (1981), pp. 647–51, for the details of this episode, which was explicitly disowned by the Free French and General Koenig. Similar threats were made – but not carried out – by Rol-Tanguy during the Liberation of Paris, when he threatened to execute ten German soldiers, ten SS and ten German women auxiliaries if the German commander of Colombes, near Paris, carried out his plan to execute ten French hostages (Dansette, 1946, p. 359).

3 For summaries of the events and the dispute, see Rude (1974), pp. 87–126, and Noguères & Degliame-Fouché (1981), pp. 651–70. Alban Vistel was the overall FFI commander, while his two subordinates, Bayard of the Armée Secrète and Darciel of the FTP, were the main protagonists; Vistel generally supported Bayard. The row rumbled on for decades; see Vistel (1970), pp. 546–71.

4 Funk (1992), pp. 243–8.

5 Funk (1992), p. 252.

6 Brossat (1994), pp. 159–60.

7 In Marseilles the German commander absurdly ordered the whole French population to evacuate as the Allied armies approached; in riposte, the Resistance blew up railway and road bridges and then, on 18 August, launched a general strike followed by an insurrection. But months of savage

repression had severely weakened the Resistance – with fewer than 1,000 insurgents, many of them without weapons, they were in danger of being wiped out. French troops had made unexpectedly rapid progress past Toulon, so to save the insurrection on 23 August they stormed their way into the centre of Marseilles. Shortly afterwards the Commissaire de la République, Raymond Aubrac, took control of the partially liberated city. After more fierce fighting, Marseilles was officially liberated on 28 August, heavily scarred by the explosions of German and Allied shells. A hundred FFI fighters and a hundred civilians died freeing their city. Guiral (1974), p. 107. Two days later there was a celebratory parade, at which Free French General de Lattre presided over an 'unforgettable and poignant procession of all the makers of this second victory – the *tirailleurs*, the Moroccan Tabors, troopers, Zouaves and gunners – followed by the motley, fevered, bewildering mass of the FFI, between the two lines of a numberless crowd, frenzied, shouting with joy and enthusiasm, whom the guardians of order could not hold back'. Funk (1992), p. 215.

8 Cassou's injuries caused a power struggle at the top of the Resistance, as Free French loyalist Bertaux took over as commissaire. This led to a long dispute that lasted nearly fifty years over exactly what happened in Toulouse and why.

9 Trempé (1983), p. 45.

10 Trempé (1983).

11 Trempé (1983), p. 51. Even the Catholic Church got caught up in the heady atmosphere – on 3 September Cardinal Salièges declared at a victory Mass in the city that 'the proletariat must disappear', and went on to outline a series of socialist measures that would encourage that to happen.

12 Part of the problem was the rapid explosion in the size of the Resistance. For example, in the Morvan region near Dijon, the maquis grew from 18 members on D-Day to 48 at the end of June, 151 a month later and 576 at the end of August (Kaspi, 2004, p. 137). In Paris, in the five days of the insurrection, the FTP Saint-Just brigade swelled from 30 members to 800 (Calvès, 1984, p. 104). These recent recruits were potentially less disciplined than those who had been fighting for longer.

13 Buton (1993), p. 111.

14 Madjarian (1980), p. 113–4. The first group of FFI fighters to abandon their Resistance role and join the army was a column of about 1,000 men led by the young Communist who took the fatal step in the Party's turn to armed struggle back in 1942 – Pierre Georges, now known as 'Colonel Fabien'. The Fabien column – including André Calvès and young Max Rainat from the Saint-Just FTP brigade – joined Patton's army and fought its way north during the Alsace campaign. In December Fabien was killed while he was demonstrating how to use a mine. The Communist Party claimed the mine had been sabotaged and hinted that right-wing forces were at work, but there was no decisive evidence. Shortly afterwards, the column was integrated into the regular French army. Durand (1985), pp. 251–66; Calvès (1984), pp. 113–4.

15 The French Communist historian Albert Soboul, whose speciality was the French Revolution, wrote a series of articles on the parallels between 1944 and 1793 in an FFI regional newspaper. Buton (1993), p. 134. At the end of August Gaullist CNR member Deb-Bridel explained the importance of the policy in the pages of *Libération*: 'by the side [of the regular army], the soldiers without uniforms who make up the whole of the FFI constitute a huge reserve of soldiers who have proved themselves with mediocre weaponry . . . This popular army, similar to that of the volunteers of 1793 . . . must not be weakened in its cohesion . . . Carrying out the *amalgame* is one of the concrete tasks of the government.' Madjarian (1980), p. 109.

16 Calvès (1984), p. 113–4. For two contrasting views on the success of the *amalgame*, from either side of the political spectrum, see Sentis (1982) and Michalon (1976).

17 Rajsfus (2004), p. 254. Farge could be extremely undiplomatic; when de Gaulle asked him what he thought of the crowd in Lyons, Farge replied that there were 'about as many people as for Pétain's last visit'. Rajsfus (2004), p. 255.

18 Noguères & Degliame-Fouché (1981), p. 776.

19 A local Communist leader declared the committees would 'ensure the correct functioning of the factories and increased production. If people speak about the "soviets" of Toulouse, it is a lie. These people are patriots, all patriots, who have made this agreement to win the war.' Trempé (1983), p. 59.

20 De Gaulle (1962c), p. 22; for FFI leader Serge Ravanel's detailed account of the day, see Noguères & Degliame-Fouché (1981), pp. 777–80.

21 De Gaulle (1962c), p. 20.

22 Foot (2004), p. 369.

23 Foot (2004), p. 369; de Gaulle (1962c), p. 21. Kedward (1993), pp. 272–3, contains an interview with Starr's radio operator, Yvonne Corneau, which includes details of their activity but not any further clue as to why de Gaulle was so infuriated.

24 Brinton (1961b), p. 140.

25 Brinton (1961b), p. 141.

26 Minguet (1997), pp. 32–6. The views of those involved in these movements were expressed in an interview with workers from the Juno aviation company in Argentueil, near Paris, in December 1944:
'Q: How did you come to take over the factory?
A: On 17 August, after the German managers left, we took over, together with FFI members who worked in the factory, in order to stop any pillage or destruction.
Q: How did you appoint your managers and supervisors?
A: Each shift elected its leaders. Line managers, supervisors, shop supervisors, and a provisional director were then ratified by an assembly of the whole workforce. Our management was officially recognized on 14 November. A delegate from the ministry surveys the activity of the factory. He is very happy with the workers' management.

Q: How are you paid?

A: We have built a first set of twelve motors without being paid. The work currently been done in the factory is supported by unemployment benefits.

Q: What is the financial situation of the factory?

A: We don't have a penny. We receive no financial help. We want to give France the embryo of an air force. Everything we do or build is done for free.

Q: Do you hope to be nationalized?

A: Yes. And we hope that this will spread to all industries of national importance.' (Madjarian, 1980, p. 172–3.)

27 The final step was taken at the beginning of 1945, when the PCF made clear their commitment to rebuilding the capitalist economy – 'Produce, produce and again produce!' they told workers (Buton, 1993, p. 196), denouncing strikes as 'the weapon of big business' ( Madjarian, 1980, p. 336).

28 These were soon renamed Gardes Patriotiques or Gardes Civiques because of potential confusion with the Vichy Milice.

29 Between September and December, delegates from the Comités de Libération (CdLs) met in a series of conferences, in which they appeared to be a potential threat to centralized government power. As a resolution adopted at their first meeting put it: 'The CdL has the duty to carry out all the plans of supply and transport, to publicly denounce and arrest all those who seek to delay these measures. The prefect is at its side to execute the decisions of the CdL and to inform it of the measures taken by the Provisional Government of the Republic. Although its legal authority flows from the government, the government should not forget that the real power has been given to it by the people in arms, and that it is therefore in the service of the people, represented by the CdL.' Buton (1993), p. 141. For more on relations between the CdLs and local government, see Madjarian (1980), pp. 75–164 and Kramer (1981).

30 The only Resistance-inspired force that was acceptable was the Forces Républicaines de Sécurité, created by Raymond Aubrac in Marseilles and subsequently transformed into the CRS riot police. Auglhon & Barrat (1975).

31 A clear contemporary summary of the political aspects of the resolution of dual power can be found in Sawyer (1947). Sawyer was a US academic who 'observed' French affairs in Algiers and France from October 1943 to November 1945. He was in fact an OSS agent.

32 Buton (1993), p. 195. In September 1944 OSS agent Crane Brinton interpreted these events in what is probably one of the few references to Trotsky's *History of the Russian Revolution* to be found in the files of US Intelligence: 'it is clear that Trotsky's classic analysis of the "dual power" applies very well here . . . what is happening here is a process in part revolutionary, the taking over of power by "new" men long carefully organized for just this aim' (Brinton, 1961a, p. 18). 'Dual power' refers to the suggestion that many revolutions share a common feature – a temporary, unstable period when contending forces may each have partial control of the key structures in society (army, economy and state apparatus). Brinton did not think that France was on the brink of a proletarian revolution – he was

certain that the Communist Party was following Moscow's line and merely sought to gain influence without openly challenging de Gaulle's authority (Brinton, 1961b, p. 138). But the changeover between Vichy and the new authorities, and the disputes over the armed strength of the Resistance, suggested to him that the country was in a situation of 'dual power'. Writing to Moscow on 15 September, Soviet diplomat Kozyre agreed: 'In the liberated regions of the country and in Paris there is dual power. This is particularly the case in the provinces, where, alongside the regional commissars named by de Gaulle, there are local commissars appointed by the comités de liberation. As a result, real power is in the hands of the organs of the Resistance' (Buton, 1993, p. 142). However, the elements of dual power that did exist in France at the time were extremely embryonic, and the two sides involved in the conflicts over the armed forces and the economy did not clearly represent the interests of two different classes. But there was a potential for them to do so, as the events of autumn demonstrated. Thorez's declaration marked the end of this period. For other interpretations of events in France in the light of 'dual power', see Sawyer (1947), Madjarian (1980) and Kramer (1981).

33 There are many studies of the *tondues*. See, for example, Virgili (2000). For an excellent discussion of the social and cultural implications of this practice, and how it has been studied in recent years, see Vinen (2006), pp. 346–56. The second part of Marcel Ophüls' documentary film *The Sorrow and the Pity* (1969) contains an interview with a woman from Clermont–Ferrand who was denounced during the *épuration*. The interview reveals the confusion of the time, leaving the viewer with an uncomfortable impression of ambiguity.

34 Rousso (1992). For one of many discussions of how these national figures have been arrived at, see Kaspi (2004), pp. 189–98. An examination of myth and reality in a particular locality can be found in Labédan (1983).

35 In retaliation, the Milice murdered Georges Mandel, who had been Minister of the Interior in 1939–40 and was opposed to Vichy.

36 Kedward (1993), p. 279.

37 Brinton (1961a), p. 8.

38 Brinton (1961b), pp. 136–7.

39 Blumenson (1978), p. 266.

40 All figures from Rousso (1992).

41 The fact that in the last two decades of the twentieth century the far-right politician Jean-Marie Le Pen repeatedly surged to the front of political debate reveals the gulf that often exists between national myths and national realities. It also shows that Vichy was not simply an aberration, but was part of a long tradition of anti-Semitism on the French right, which stretched back to the Dreyfus affair and forward to today.

42 For discussions of why France was unique, and comparisons with other countries, see Foot (1978) and Moore (2000).

43 See the entry on Rémy (Gilbert Renault) in Marcot et al. (2006), pp. 512–3.

44 D'Astier's song was made popular in the 1970s in an English version by

Leonard Cohen, entitled 'The Partisan'. Cohen changed the final line to a more romantic and positive outlook than d'Astier's bleak and accurate vision:

Oh, the wind, the wind is blowing,
Through the graves the wind is blowing,
Freedom soon will come;
Then we'll come from the shadows.

45 The French ambassador to Algeria has recently accepted that the events constitued a 'massacre' – *Le Monde*, 28 April 2008. For a discussion of the origin of the massacres and the problem of ever knowing the number of victims, see Ageron (1984). Charles Tillon was the Communist Party Minister for Air at the time, yet he claimed he knew nothing of the deployment of French aircraft in the massacre. For a discussion of the Communist Party's sometimes ambivalent attitude to the events, see Ruscio (2007).

46 See Kedward (2005), pp. 327–48 for a summary of the Algerian War and the attitude of *résistants* to it.

47 Bidault (1965), pp. 273–7.

48 Ajchenbaum (1994), p. 347.

49 For excellent accounts of the way in which the history of the Resistance was written, see Azéma & Bédarida (1994) and Douzou (2005).

50 Claude Bourdet of Combat recalled Malraux's attitude when the two men met at the end of 1941. Bourdet came asking for help, but Malraux gave him the brush-off: 'Come and see me again when you have money and weapons,' he said. The great writer does not seem to have thought it was his role to help in getting either. Bourdet (1975), p. 73.

51 Azéma & Bédarida (1994), p. 31, n. 8.

52 Rousso (2000). For a discussion of the contrast between the views of the two men, see Piketty (2000).

53 Mitterrand also laid roses on the tombs of the socialist Jean Jaurès, assassinated in 1914, and the nineteenth-century French anti-slavery campaigner Victor Schoelcher (Favier & Martin-Rolland, 1990, p. 68). Given Mitterrand's subsequent revelations about his pro-Pétain past (Péan, 1994), his gesture with regard to Moulin can be interpreted as a cynical manoeuvre, an attempt to assuage his guilt, a genuine homage or a mixture of all three, depending on your view of Mitterrand.

54 This chant can still be heard on French demonstrations as the riot police close in.

55 For a balanced discussion of the impact of the film, see Douzou (2005).

56 See Daniel Cordier's discussion of how his own memory played tricks on him, even on details he thought were quite clear. Cordier (1995).

57 Rude (1974), p. 9. (Preface by Pascal Copeau.)

58 See Frenay's letter to Passy in Passy (1951), pp. 389–415. The section dealing with Moulin's alleged loyalty to the Communist Party can be found on pp. 413–4. See also Frenay (1977). The main works published in the 1990s were Wolton (1993) and Péan (1998).

59 Péan (1994).

60 The book was by journalist Gérard Chauvy (1997).

61 The historians wanted to know why Raymond Aubrac could not explain why he had not been transferred to Paris with the other Caluire detainees. As Klarsfeld (1997a) pointed out, this was profoundly unjust. There was no reason why Aubrac should know the explanation – he was the prisoner, not the jailer.

62 Some of the historians who were involved in the 'round table' subsequently expressed their unease at the proceedings in a collective letter published in *Libération* (Andrieu et al., 1997). Discussions of the 'Aubrac affair' can be found in Diamond & Gorrara (2001), Suleiman (2004, 2006), Douzou (2005) and Reid (2006). Bensaïd (1999, 2000) criticizes the notion of history as a court, and the danger of historians setting themselves up as judges. The complex relation between memory and history was the subject of one of a series of important academic meetings that took place in the 1990s around the Resistance, each of which produced a valuable collection of articles. For the work on memory, see the papers from the 1995 colloquium held in Toulouse, collected in Guillon & Laborie (1995). For a highly romanticized account of the liberation of Raymond Aubrac, you could do worse than watch Claude Berri's entertaining film, *Lucie Aubrac,* a success at the box office if not in the minds of historians. The fact that the film, too, came out in 1997 may not have been entirely unconnected with Chauvy's desire to publish, or with the importance given to the subsequent 'affair' by the French media.

63 Papon was sentenced to life imprisonment 1998 but was released four years later on grounds of ill health; he died aged ninety-six in 2006. Bousquet was banned from office after the war but was eventually amnestied in 1958. He became close to François Mitterrand, but when Bousquet's wartime role was revealed, their friendship ceased. Touvier was sentenced to death after the war but escaped and was hidden by right-wing priests until he was eventually found in 1983. Despite having been pardoned in 1971, Touvier was convicted of crimes against humanity in 1994 and died in prison in 1996.

64 See Kedward (2005), pp. 625–30 for an overview of this period.

65 The 'square' in question is a rather sad construction which is part of the Gare de Lyon. There is no street named after Jean Moulin in Paris, although Google Maps claims there are twenty-seven in France as a whole, as compared with nine named after Henri Frenay.

66 See, for example, the work of Robert Belot, who has produced a detailed biography of Frenay (2003), a stimulating analysis of the anti-Gaullist tradition in the Resistance (2006a) and a richly illustrated popular account of the Resistance (2006b).

67 See Julien Blanc's forthcoming work on the Musée de l'Homme network, Thomas Rabino's study of Carte (2008), and the ground-breaking investigations of the Communist Party's armed struggle by Berlière & Liaigre (2004, 2007).

68 The *Star Trek: Voyager* programme was based on the premise that there was a rebel faction called the maquis.

69 Cassou (2001), p. 39.

# Index